PARTIES AND POLITICS
IN NORTHERN NIGERIA

Parties and Politics in Northern Nigeria

by

B. J. DUDLEY

FRANK CASS & Co. Ltd.

1968

First published in 1968 by
FRANK CASS AND COMPANY LIMITED
67 Great Russell Street, London WC1
Copyright © 1968 B. J. Dudley
SBN 7146 1658 3

Printed in Great Britain
by Billing & Sons Limited, Guildford and London

Contents

Tables

DIAGRAMS AND MAPS

Preface

In retrospect it now seems clear that the federal elections of December 1964 and the constitutional crisis which followed mark the apogée of the civilian government headed by Sir Abubakar Tafawa Balewa. The 'broadbased' government which emerged from the crisis represented, at best, a shaky compromise. The virulence of the opposition (UPGA, the AG/NCNC southern alliance) to the elections in the West in October 1965, in which ballot papers were available to the government party (NNDP) members before the polling, and in which regulations governing the counting of votes and the announcing of results were openly flouted, showed that the compromise was not really accepted by the South. And when the federal government supplied security forces to prop up the government of the West, a government which not only lacked popular support but which had become an object of derision, it eroded whatever vestiges of legitimacy it had possessed.

The decisive jolt came when in the early hours of January 15, 1966, a group of young army officers, mainly Ibo, led some soldiers in a coup which ended in the death of the Federal Prime Minister of Nigeria, Sir Abubakar. The regional Premiers of the North and the West were also killed, as were a number of high-ranking Hausa and Yoruba officers. After some confusion, the government of the federation was taken over by Major-General Aguiyi-Ironsi, the head of the armed forces.[1] Thus began Nigeria's slow decline into civil chaos and now, the possibility of political disintegration.

With the widespread allegations of corruption by the political leadership of the civilian government and the prevailing general incompetence, most Nigerians felt a welcome relief when the January 15th coup took place. In the North, which suffered most from the changes, the electorate was not unhappy at the elimination of the Premier, the Sardauna of Sokoto, though they felt very differently about the deaths of 'their' Prime Minister and top northern army officers. But the people were prepared to accept even this in the spirit of the new compromise, and Major-General Ironsi, head of the military government, began his rule with some degree of popularity with Northern soldiers. But within six months the new régime had turned sour, and particularly with Northerners. Where did it go wrong?

First, to the radical elements in the North, it did not appear that there had been any significant changes in the North. General Ironsi, realising the losses the North had suffered, in an attempt to conciliate the region, allowed members of the old political class to return to their respective Native Authorities. Unlike in the West where investigations into their past activities were initiated, the ex-politicians of the North were left free to enjoy the fruits of office.

The radical elements are to be found amongst the 'new intelligentsia' of the North, the civil servants, university students and school teachers. And these now felt their interests threatened by the measures being taken by the Military Government. The decree on unification, decree No. 34, issued on May 24, which abolished the regions, was seen as the first step to depriving them, the intelligentsia, of the privileges which the old federal system guaranteed them. The attempt to unify the different administrative systems in the country was taken as a confirmation of this. In the federal public service, Northerners constituted slightly more than one per cent of the total number of civil servants, whereas in the Northern public service, Southerners were excluded. Thus Northern university students, particularly those at the Ahmadu Bello University, saw their chances of an automatic entry into the administrative class of the Northern civil service dwindling away. In a unified bureaucracy, they would have faced competition for the available posts from the numerically greater southern graduates. The way was therefore left open for the erstwhile politicians to play on the fears of the intelligentsia and for these two groups, in combination, to exploit the dissatisfaction of the urban unemployed. The result was the May 29th, 1966, outbreaks in Zaria, Kaduna, Kano, Jos and Katsina in which hundreds of Ibos (many of whom, it was reported, had openly provoked Northerners through careless statements) were attacked and killed. This was to be a prelude to the July 29th outburst.

Meanwhile, the politicians had also succeeded in converting Northern NCO's and other ranks to their way of thinking. They, in collaboration with some members of the political élite and a few of the intelligentsia from the Western region, had managed to instil in a section of the Northern soldiery a fear of domination by the Ibos. They pointed to the fact that Major-General Ironsi was an Ibo; his close advisers were in the main also Ibos; the overwhelming majority of those promoted in the post-January 15th period were Ibos (although it was alleged, the Supreme Military Council had agreed on a moratorium on all promotions in the army for a period of one year); that no Ibo was killed in the January 15th coup; and that some leaders of that coup were found to have consorted with politicians from the East soon after the coup. Ironsi's announcement of his proposal to rotate the Military Governors and appoint military prefects was taken as a 'proof' of the plan for an Ibo hegemony in the country. What was being insinuated was that the Northern soldiers who had participated in the coup had been misled delibe- rately and used in a coup which had been planned by officers aided and abetted by Ibo politicians.

Amongst the Ibos on the other hand, there was resentment at the conciliatory attitude of General Ironsi to the North. Many felt that the pace of change was not rapid enough. But even so, some of the Ibo academics, worried by the May disturbances in the North and the hostility of the Yoruba intelligentsia towards them, had suggested that the East reconsider its continued association with the rest of the country.

By late July, there was hostility and mutual suspicion on all sides. Ibo soldiers were alleged to be planning to complete the affair of January 15th. The Northerners were also suspected of getting ready for a counter-coup. The question was who would move first. The Northerners did—on July 29 and the second killing of Ibos began.

The intervention of some top federal civil servants and a few others in negotiating a 'cease fire' saved the day and Nigeria. Lt. Colonel Yakubu Gowon became the Supreme Military Commander and the Head of the federal Military government after the kidnapping and disappearance of Ironsi and the Military Governor of the West, Lt. Colonel Adekunle Fajuyi. Though their fate still remains unknown, it is widely believed that they were both killed by their kidnappers.

In August, a small group of representatives from the four regions, summoned by Gowon, met in Lagos. They suggested that military personnel should be repatriated to their regions of origin. A larger body was to be summoned to decide the constitutional future of the country, which in the meantime had returned to being federal, the decree No. 34 having been abrogated. This group met in Lagos on September 12. In his address to the opening session, Lt. Colonel Gowon suggested that the delegates were free to advocate any form of association for the country, other than a unitary system of government or a break-up of the federation.

The memoranda submitted by the delegations showed complete disagreement in the detailed arrangements suggested by the regions.[2] In general, the Western region advocated a scheme for a 'Com-

monwealth of Nigeria'; the North, a 'Common Services Organization' based on the East African experience. The East's position was
scarcely different from that of the West or the North. All three
suggested that each region should have a right unilaterally to secede.
Only the Mid-West agreed to a continuation of the federation. At
first, in the negotiations and bargaining which followed, agreement
was reached that the country should continue as a federation, with a
head of State, head of government and a federal cabinet and that
some twenty-one of the forty-five items on the exclusive federal list
in the Constitution should be retained by the federal authority.
There was no agreement on keeping a common currency or banking
system. Elaborate safeguards regarding the armed forces and the
police were suggested. The armed forces were to be organized on the
basis of regional units composed of the indigenes of each region.
Federal control was to be provided through a Defence Council.
There was to be no head of the armed forces, but a Chief of Staff,
whose office was to be held in rotation by the regional commanders
for fixed periods not exceeding twelve months. A not dissimilar
provision was made in respect of the police. The conference adjourned on September 30 to reconvene on October 24.

The turning point at the conference had been on September 20,
when the delegates reassembled after the adjournment of September
16th. Over that crucial week-end, it was reported that a group of
Northern soldiers had met the delegates of the North and demanded
a reversal in the North's position. The delegates were to demand an
"effective central government" while at the same time agreeing to
the creation of more states in the country. It was known that the
soldiers from the 'Middle-Belt' of the North wanted a 'Middle-Belt
State'.

The reversal of the stand of the North from a position which would
have amounted to a break up of the federation to one demanding an
"effective central government" was both in the interests of the
North, which needed the framework of the federation, and of the
federation itself.

But the reversal was to lead to tragic consequences. In a last-ditch
effort to preserve the North as an inviolate unity in order to protect
their positions, the 'old guard' of the North conspired to incite the
people and dissident soldiers into attacking the Ibos in the North.
It was a last desperate attempt to nullify whatever the conference had
achieved. The killings which began in Jos rapidly spread throughout
most of the North, culminating in the massacre of Ibos in Kano by
the mutinous troops on October 1. Though no figures are yet
available (it is doubtful if any will be) some estimates put the number

of those killed at 10,000, apart from those wounded, maimed or blinded.

The immediate result of this massacre was the exodus of Ibos from the North. By the end of October about 600,000 had been repatriated. But the exodus did not stop with the North. Ibos also fled from the West, Mid-West and Lagos. In the East, after a regrettable lapse in the self-restraint which the people had maintained so well, a lapse which led to the killing of some Northerners in Port-Harcourt and Onitsha, the Military Governor was forced to order all non-Easterners (other than Mid-Western Ibos and Ijaws) from the region. For all practical purposes, it could be said that the East has seceded from the federation.

What becomes of the federation after all this is far from certain. The threat of disintegration cannot be dismissed. Yet, it is possible that the logic of half a century of close association may prevail and thus hold the country together as a single political and economic unit.

As regards the North, the events since January 15 have brought about numerous changes which would require separate treatment if they are to be adequately described. This book, which began as a doctoral thesis submitted at the University of London, is a prolegomenon to such a study as well as providing a background to the events described above. As such, I have felt it desirable to leave a few things, for instance, the description of the political system of the North; reference to persons, e.g. to Sir Ahmadu Bello, late Premier of the North, unchanged.[3] One further reason for so doing is that this preserves, in some measure, the vividness of the period discussed.

But this is not all. One of the things this discussion of parties and politics in Northern Nigeria sets out to do, albeit implicitly, is to question some of the assumptions of much of the academic writing on the politics of the 'new states' such as Almond and Coleman's *The Politics of Developing Countries* (Princeton, 1960); Lucien Pye's *Politics, Personality and Nation Building* (Yale, 1962) and the series on 'Studies in Political Development' sponsored by the Committee on Comparative Politics of the Social Science Research Council. As the titles of these studies show, they are all concerned with 'political development' (whatever this means) or nation building (both concepts not infrequently being equated one to the other). One assumption common to all of these is the notion that 'political development' or nation building is episodic with differentiated stages succeeding one another in a linear order. Compare for instance, Pye's three 'stages of socialization' or Apter's three models of 'modernizing' systems. It is not difficult to see that these 'theories' are a restatement, in modern dress, of the eighteen-century ideas of progress. This is not the place to enter into arguments about the idea of progress, but what this study shows, I hope, is that assumptions of linearity common to these theories besides being over-simple, if not naïve, is false.

It is not often possible to acknowledge the help of all to whom one is indebted. Invariably, a few are singled out for mention for one reason or the other. In this case they are: Alhajis Ahman Pategi, Nuhu Bamali, Abdul Razaq, Othman Ladan Baki, Sani Gezrawa, Salihu Mohammed, Ibrahim Imam, Aminu Kano, Yesufu Dantsoho, Raji Abdallah, Mohammadu Ja'afra, Mallams Sani Darma, Gambo Sawaba, Tanko Yakasai, Yahaya Abdullahi, Garba Abuja, Messrs. Patrick Dokotri, Vincent Orjime, Joseph Abaagu and Bitrus Rwang Pam. To Alhaji Salihi Abdullahi, I owe a special debt of gratitude.

The staff of the NEPU headquarters in Kano were a great help. With the chaotic state in which the files of the party were kept, it remains a surprise that they were able to find most of my requests. A Tiv friend, Mr. B. Nwiyo, helped in obtaining for me unpublished materials from UMBC files in Jos, Makurdi and Gboko, while Mallan Garba Abuja (NPC clerical assistant 1950–56, administrative secretary 1956–60) was invaluable with NPC headquarters files. Mallan Abuja resigned from the NPC in 1960 and in his position as administrative secretary had with him a mass of the party's files dating from the inception of the party to the time he left. Most of the NPC documents cited here come from these files.

I have profited immensely, in preparing the manuscript for publication, from the comments and criticisms of Professor K. E. Robinson, Mr. Thomas Hodgkin, Mr. Denis Austin, Mr. Ken Post and my colleague at the University of Ibadan, Dr. James O'Connell. Professor Robinson, as my supervisor, read through the whole of the manuscript and made invaluable suggestions for improving the style besides saving me from making obvious errors. Wherever possible I have attempted to meet and accommodate much of the penetrating criticisms made by Mr. Hodgkin and I am grateful to him for his suggestions. My gratitude also goes to Mr. J. O. Dipeolu, Deputy Librarian of the University of Ife, for the preparation of the Index. None of these people bear any responsibility for any errors and misrepresentations which may be in this book.

Dept. of Political Science,   BILLY J. DUDLEY
University of Ibadan,
Ibadan, Nigeria.
12th Dec. 1966

NOTES

1. See *Government Statement on the Current Nigerian Situation*, Federal Ministry of Information, Lagos, 1966.

2. See 'The Ad Hoc Conference on the Nigerian Constitution', *Nigerian Crisis*, 1966, vol. 4, Government. Printer, Enugu, 1966.

3. Some of the changes made by the Military Government which took over the government of the federation on January 16, 1966, are the following: Decree No. 1 of January 17, 1966, suspended Parliament, the offices of President and Prime Minister of the federation, regional Governors, Premiers and their Executives and the regional Legislatures. Decree No. 34 of May 24, 1966, dissolved 81 existing political parties, prohibited the formation of new ones and banned 20 Tribal Unions (Nigeria Yearbook 1967, pp. 47–48 gives a list of these organizations). References to Ministers, Legislatures and the like in the text should therefore be read with these changes, which are still in force, in mind. The section of Decree No. 34 which abolished federalism as a system of government was abrogated by Col. Gowon when he took over control of the government after the disturbances of July 29, 1966.

Introduction

The pattern of Nigerian politics was perhaps radically altered, when at the 1958 Constitutional Conference in London, the decision was taken to base representation in the Federal Parliament on a population basis, rather than on the previous (pre-1958) system which was one of equality of representation between the North and the South. With this change, which gave Northern Nigeria a representation greater than the combined total of the East and West Regions, the balance of power tended to shift to the North. With 'regionally'[1] based political parties, and a tendency for these parties to control the regions in which they are based, the possibility of a one-party system emerging in Nigeria was suggested in 1962.[2] The possible domination of Nigerian politics which this implies suggests that to understand the politics of the country, one must understand the politics of Northern Nigeria.[3] But one can hardly expect to comprehend present-day Northern Nigeria without an understanding of its background and this, only the historian can provide.

In his own cryptic way, Soren Kierkegaard was, in effect, stating the same principle when he wrote that "Life is to be understood backwards but lived forwards".[4] The present is but a reflection of the past and is itself to be reflected in the future. This, however, raises the problem of how far into the past one has to go before one can begin to understand the present.

The problem is particularly difficult in the case of a place like Northern Nigeria where for a large part of the area there is hardly any documentary material available, from which a history can be written, even for such recent time as as the nineteenth century. Its history thus tends to be a compound of facts and myths. Initially, therefore, it will be useful to make the distinction suggested by Malinowski: between what he calls "objective history", that is documented or written history, and the "mythological charter" of customs, cultural usages and myths of origin.[5]

B

I. THE MAKING OF NORTHERN NIGERIA

Varying accounts exist of the origins of the peoples who now inhabit the northern half of Northern Nigeria. The evidence adduced in support of the various accounts is inconclusive and to continue the debate would be pointless and irrelevant. Taking Malinowski's distinction, what may safely be said, is that such accounts pertain to the "mythological charter" of the peoples. In fact, similar accounts exist for almost all the peoples of present-day Northern Nigeria. The Kanuri peoples of Bornu, for instance, who formed part of the original Kanem Empire, trace their origins to a certain 'Sef', who gave his name to the dynasty—the Sefawa. The Hausa 'States' to the west of Bornu trace their origins to a certain 'Bayajayyida', who founded the 'state' of Daura from which grew the original seven Hausa 'States'—the Hausa Bokwoi, and from there the other seven 'illegitimate' Hausa 'States'—the Banza Bokwoi. Similarly, the peoples of Nupe trace their origins to a certain 'Edegi' or Tsoede who supposedly came from Idah. The Tivs reckon their lineage system to Tiv—the original Adam, while the Jukuns—the Kwororofas—trace their beginnings to somewhere in the Middle East.[6]

It is important to note, however, that whilst one can talk of the Kanuris, the Tivs, the Igalas, Nupes and so on, as definite ethnic groups, the word 'Hausa' does not connote a similar grouping but a 'language group', or as Fage wrote: "there are no Hausa people; there are only people who speak the Hausa language and practise the Hausa way of life".[7]

Whatever speculation there might be about the early history of the peoples of Northern Nigeria, the objective history for at least the northern half can be traced with some degree of certainty. The influence of Islam was first noted in Bornu in 1097 when its first Muslim King Hume made the pilgrimage in that year; and it is known that by 1250 there were sufficient Kanemi students in Cairo to justify the founding of a *riwaq* (or club).[8] The establishment of Bornu as a state can be dated from the reign of Ali Ibn Dunama (1476–1503). It was he who brought the dynastic wars between the various clan heads to an end, establishing the rudimentary outlines of an administrative system centred around his capital of Ngazragamu. Also, under him, the influence of Bornu was extended westwards, with the effect that most of the Hausa States, including Kano, were paying tribute to Bornu in the sixteenth century.[9] Bornu reached the height of its political influence during the reign of Idris Ibn Ali-Idris Aloma in the early seventeenth century. As Sultan

Bello put it: "Fortune having assisted them, their government flourished for some time and their dominion extended to the very extremity of this tract of the earth . . . the country of the Hausa, with those parts of the province of Bauchi which belong to it, were in their possession."[10] And Greenberg has suggested that most of the cultural features of Mediterranean origin found in Hausaland can be traced to this Kanuri influence.[11]

It was Aloma who brought about the political unification of Bornu, and rationalized the political system by introducing a number of needed reforms, including the separation of the judiciary from the executive and the political heads, the substitution of Sharia for the customary laws and the institution of the Islamic or qadi courts.[12] By the time of the reign of Mai Aloma, as Trimmingham has noted, we see "the change in the conception of chieftaincy from that of a Sheikh, a *primus inter pares*, of a nomadic tribe to a Sudanese despot exercising rule over his own people and holding the allegiance of a varying range of semi-independent peoples".[13] Towards the end of the seventeenth century, however, Bornu lost some of its predominance and by the eighteenth century it was but a mere shadow of its former self. Not till the nineteenth century was Bornu again revived.

By the eleventh century the seven Hausa States—the Hausa Bokwoi—Daura, Kano Zaria, Gobir, Katsina, Rano and Biram, were already established. The Kano Chronicle gives a list of the successive rulers of Kano from the tenth century to the coming of the Fulanis. Islam, according to the Chronicle, was introduced into Kano during the reign of Yaji (1349–85), but only gained ground in the fifteenth century during the period of reign of Muhammed Runfa (1463–99).[14] In Katsina, where the first succession of dynasties was founded in the twelfth century by Kumayo, Islam made its appearance in the period around 1320–53 during the reign of Korau, and by the seventeenth and eighteenth centuries it had become the most widely known of the Hausa States. Towards the end of the eighteenth century it was superseded by Kano to which it had been a tributary in the fifteenth century according to Leo Africanus.[15] In the plateau district south-east of Katsina, the towns of Bauchi and Gombe had developed from amongst the heterogenous communities of the district by the seventeenth century. Katumbe, the king of Kano raided these areas between 1623 and 1648.[16] Of the Banza Bokwoi States, Zamfara, Kebbi, Nupe, Gwari, Yauri, and Yoruba were founded sometime in the fifteenth century. With an ethnic composition differing from the other Hausa States, it was from its capital, Dutsi, that a soldier of fortune went in the sixteenth century to found the State of Kebbi.[17] In Zaria, the first succession of dynasties was noted in 1370.[18]

There was hardly any historical unity between the Hausa States, only a history of mutually antagonistic town-states. This mutual antagonism in part explains why most of these states became tributary to the Jukun Empire in the late sixteenth and early seventeenth century. Sultan Bello in his 'Infrakul Maisuri' referred to this Empire as "one of the seven greatest Kingdoms of the Sudan, the territory of which included all the lower and part of the middle portion of Hausaland". An attack by the Jukuns on Katsina was unsuccessful, but they occupied Kano in 1671 only shortly thereafter to lose it to Bornu. Jukun power which was formidable in the sixteenth and seventeenth centuries gradually declined and by the nineteenth century their power had so declined that they were successfully overrun by the Fulani in 1815.[19]

Of the variety of peoples who inhabit the southern half of Northern Nigeria, very little is known before the Fulani Jihad of the early nineteenth century. This excludes, however, what is now known as Ilorin province which was already an outpost of the old Oyo Empire.

In the main, much of the pre-nineteenth century history of the North can be seen as a series of unsuccessful attempts at founding larger political units by the various peoples of the area. These attempts include that of Queen Amina (c. 1421–38) of Zaria who in the fifteenth century extended her dominion to include much of the areas now covered by Kano, Daura and Bauchi down to the northern banks of the rivers Niger and Benue. This was succeeded by the Kebbi empire of Kanta Kotal (c. 1512–45) over much of Hausaland in the early sixteenth century; itself to be followed by the hegemony of Bornu in the late sixteenth century. Then there was the Kwororofa attempt to dominate Bornu and Hausaland in the seventeenth and early eighteenth centuries. In the eighteenth century, Kwororofa pre-eminence gave way to that of Gobir. This succession of régimes was a major factor of political instability which the Fulani under Uthman dan Fodio was to exploit in starting the Jihad.

Islamic revivalism has often been cited as one of the factors which brought about the Fulani Jihad and though Islam was introduced comparatively early into Northern Nigeria, it should not be thought that it was widely accepted.

J. F. Schon, for instance, observed of Kano that "there are no pagans seen in it, but only Mussulmen; but in the country, in small towns and not far from it, many pagans are met with".[20] Some consequences of its introduction may, however, be noted. In the first place, Greenberg has suggested that the absence of a clan organization among the Hausas, unlike most of the other peoples of Northern Nigeria, may have been due to Islamic influences.[21] Secondly, as many of the 'chiefs', at least nominally, embraced Islam long before the rest of the people, this tended to disturb the precarious balance which held between the chief and the people, the former no longer showing interest in "the traditional religious ceremonies which weld the community into a single congregation".[22] Thirdly, it has been suggested that as a result of the proselytizing zeal associated with Islam, it tended to bring into the traditional organization of society a new 'class' distinction—that between Mohammedans and non-Mohammedans or pagans, the two differing not only in terms of religious observances but also in their general way of life. For those who have accepted it, Islam presents a new *weltanschauung* different from that traditionally held, and very much in opposition to it. Lastly, the establishment of Islam, it has been suggested, entails modifications in the political organization of society as it leads "to a dissociation in the State between administrative and political functions".[23]

Whatever may have been the influence of Islam on the traditional political and social organization of Northern Nigeria, its present-day influence can hardly be exaggerated, the decisive change being the Fulani Jihad. In itself, the Jihad is one of the most significant events in the modern history of Northern Nigeria and therefore deserves some greater attention.

II. THE FULANI CONQUEST OF NORTHERN NIGERIA

The eighteenth century witnessed the emergence of Gobir and Zamfara as two powerful Hausa states. Zamfara had conquered Kano in 1700 and by the middle of the eighteenth century was in the process of establishing itself in a position of supremacy in Hausaland. At the same time, Gobir, because of pressure on its northern borders by desert tribes, was looking for expansion into the fertile lands of Zamfara to the south. By 1764 the Gobirawa had sufficiently infiltrated Zamfara for Babari, the King of Gobir, to attack and sack Birnin Zamfara. By the end of the eighteenth century, Gobir had become the dominant state in Hausaland.

The expansion of Gobir brought the Gobirawa ruling class into conflict with the Fulanis, the chief proselytes of the Moslem religion in Hausaland, who criticized the religious laxity and 'illegal' taxation in Gobir. The focus of this conflict centred around an elderly Fulani scholar of the Toronkawa clan, Uthman dan Fodio. Uthman began his career as an itinerant preacher in Kebbi in 1774–75 where he gathered around him a group of disciples most of whom were to become leaders of the Jihad. Uthman's real agitation, however, began in 1786 when he began a religious campaign in Zamfara and neighbouring states, at the same time keeping up a correspondence with Fulani clerics throughout Hausaland. His propagandist activities brought him against Nafata, king of Gobir, who saw in Uthman a threat to his position at the centre of the pagan rites of kingship. Nafata, to combat the propaganda of Uthman then decreed that only those born Muslims should practise Islam; recent converts were to return to their traditional religion. He also forbade the wearing of turbans. Nafata died in 1802 and was succeeded by his son, Yunfa (a former pupil of Uthman's) who took up the opposition of his father as he realised that Uthman's teachings were subversive to his régime.

Hostilities broke out when Uthman released some Moslems whom he had noticed in a group of prisoners being led into slavery. In the face of this open provocation, Yunfa then marched on Degel where Uthman lived and the latter fled to Gudu. From the date of his flight (Feb. 21, 1804), the *hijra* (reminiscent of the Prophet Mohammed's flight), Uthman regarded himself as one chosen by Allah to execute his divine Will. From Gudu he called on all devout Muslims to support his cause and proceeded to proclaim a Jihad or Holy War, a war which was to lead to the eventual subjugation of most of Northern Nigeria to Fulani rule. Aided by the people of Zamfara, his first success was against Yunfa whom he defeated in the battle at Kwotto Lake in 1804. His victorious army then proclaimed him Amir al-muminin (Hausa, Sarkin Musulmi), a title formerly held by Askia Mohammed of Songhai and now by the Sultans of Sokoto, the descendants of Uthman.[24]

Sultan Bello, in his *Infaku'L Maisuri*, has suggested that the principal cause of the Jihad was his father's desire to purify the religion of Islam which had been debased and mixed with pagan practices by the Hausas.[25] Hodgkin, placing the Jihad in the context of similar Fulani revolutions in the West and Central Sudan has by implication, tended to lend force to this argument. On the other hand, Burdon commented that: "In its beginnings, the struggle was purely racial, the attempted extermination by an alien-race of the inhabitants of the land", adding, contrary to the interpretation of Bello, that: "It was not a sudden unprovoked religious war for the conversion of the country".[26] It is hardly to be expected, however, that the Jihad would have succeeded as it did, without either the support or the indifference of the Hausa commoners—the Talakawa —a point which led Olderogge, giving a 'Marxist' interpretation, to

THE FULANI EMPIRE
IN THE 19th CENTURY.

THE FULANI EMPIRE IN THE NINETEENTH CENTURY

suggest that the Jihad represented a revolt of the commoners against the old Hausa dynasties, a revolt, that is, against the oppression of the ruling class of Hausa chieftains.[27] Obviously no one single explanation will suffice. Any attempt to explain the Jihad will therefore have to take into consideration the various religious, social, economic and political factors involved. Ultimately, the aim of the Jihad was the foundation of a Muslim theocracy in Northern Nigeria.

Before Shehu Uthman left Degel, he sent letters to some of his former pupils and lieutenants: Adama at Adamawa (who gave his name to that Province), Yakubu in the Bauchi region and Buba Yero who was around the lower reaches of the Gongola river and subsequently in Gombe. Uthman's march became the signal of insurrection which was taken up by these men and many others throughout Northern Nigeria. Between 1804 and 1843, Yakubu, aided by his lieutenant Madaki Hassan reduced the Jukun communities of Akyelura, Dampar and Wase to Fulani rule. Yakubu established himself at Bauchi and installed Hassan in Wase. East of Bauchi, Yero, who received his 'flag' from Uthman at the same time as Yakubu, marched on Gombe which he conquered. A younger brother of Yero, Hamarua, took Muri. Conflict between Yero and Hamarua over who should rule Muri led to the latter's execution. The dispute was settled when Hamarua's son, Haman, appealed to the Sheikh who confirmed him as ruler of Muri.

Farther north, the original Hausa states which had combined to oppose the Fulani incursion were attacked. Katsina, in 1807, fell to a 'flag-bearer' of Uthman, M. Umaru Dallaji. Zaria, whose Habe ruler, Makau, fled before the attacking force of M. Musa, was conquered in 1804. Makau moved southwards and subsequently founded the Habe (or Hausa) state of Abuja. Kano was taken over by Sulemanu in 1807, the same year that the ancient Habe state of Daura was overrun by Isiaku, the Fulani herdsman of the ruler of that state. By 1810, four of the seven Hausa States—Zaria, Katsina, Kano and Daura—had been taken by the Fulani, and Sokoto from which the Fulani Empire was to be governed had been established. Uthman had retired to a life of teaching and contemplation, leaving the work of extending the Empire to his son, Muhammed Bello and his (Uthman's) brother, M. Abdullahi.

Other Fulani conquests followed. In 1810 Katagun fell to M. Zaki (who then took the title of Sarkin Bornu) and Kazaure to Ibn Kazaure Dan Tunku, head of the Fulani Yerimawa clan. Hadeija, north-east of Kano and on the borders of Bornu submitted to the local Fulani leader, M. Umaru with hardly any opposition.

Misau was conquered by Yakubu, Emir of Bauchi, who gave it to Haman Manga in 1827 in recognition of Manga's father's services to him and Manga was later recognized by Sokoto as Emir of Misau. Jamaari fell to Haman Wabi in 1824. When he was killed by keri-keri pagans[28] in 1825, his brother, Sambolei, was recognized by Mohammed Bello as Emir.

Farther south, the lieutenants of M. Musa were engaged in extending the boundaries of the Emirate. An attempt by Abdu Zango, the conqueror of Keffi, to gain recognition from the Sheikh for himself was repressed by M. Musa who compelled Zango to accept his suzerainty. But Zango's second son, Imoru Makama, succeeded in carving out the Emirate of Nassarawa for himself. Kebbi, which was taken by M. Usuman, was like Keffi, forced to become a vassal state of Zaria. The Hausa ruler of Kebbi, Mohammadu Fodi (1803–26) who fled before the attack of Usuman, subsequently founded Argungu and his brother, Karari, became the first Kebbi king of Argungu.

Lapai was occupied by the Fulani before the Jihad but the first recognized Emir was Daudu Maza who was given a flag by Abdullahi, Emir of Gwandu in 1830. Kontagora was established under Fulani rule by Ngwamatse, who with his two sons Modibo and Ibrahim quelled the peoples of that area. Ngwamatse would have extended his influence to Yauri in the north but for that division being recognized as a fief of the Emir of Gwandu. Maliki, who got a flag from Uthman through a follower of his M. Wari, established himself at Lafiaji in 1806 but no permanent settlement took place until 1810. Maliki later was to attack Bida which had come under Fulani rule through the activities of M. Dendo. When Maliki attacked Bida, Dendo, his sons, and three others, moved out and went to Rabah. It was from here that Usuman Zaki later set out to retake Bida, the Nupe capital in 1835. Zaki relinquished the throne in 1841 only again permanently to establish himself in 1850. The Emirate of Agaie was in 1822 established by one of the three followers who accompanied Dendo to Rabah.

With the upheavals in the Hausa states, Afonja, the Alafin of Oyo's representative at Ilorin, decided to use the opportunity to become independent of Oyo. Towards this end he invited M. Alimi, who came with his Fulani followers. A subsequent attempt by Afonja to cut himself loose from his Fulani allies led to his death, with Alimi becoming the first Fulani Emir of Ilorin in 1832.

With the fall of Katsina, the Fulani extended their attacks to the North East. Concerted action by Yakubu of Bauchi, his lieutenant Gwani Muktar, Buba Yero and Ibrahim Zaki led to the fall of the

Bornu capital, Ngazargamo, in 1808, the Bornu ruler Mai Ahmed, fleeing to the Kanemi Sheikh El Aminu for military help. Aided by Sheikh El Aminu, the Fulani under Muktar were driven from Ngazargamo. Aminu was to relieve Bornu a second time in 1811–12, to end further Fulani encroachment on Bornu, and to wield the only effective power in Bornu until he retired in favour of his son, Umar in 1835. Umar's execution of his brother Abdurahman in 1854 removed the one challenge to his rule which continued till his death in 1880.

By the middle of the nineteenth century, Fulani rule had been established over much of Northern Nigeria, excluding some of the mountainous districts in what is now the Plateau province, the Tiv areas in Benue province and of course Bornu. With the establishment of the Fulani, Northern Nigeria settled down to a period of comparative peace till the coming of the British in the latter part of the nineteenth century. The only major disturbance was in Bornu. Here Rabeh, a flag bearer of the Egyptian slave trader, Zubair Pasha, taking command of the remnant forces of Sulaiman (son of Zubair and later killed in 1878 by Gessi Pasha), attacked Bornu in 1891, defeating Shehu Hashim's forces at Ngala. With his capital established at Dikwa in 1894, Rabeh divided Bornu into districts under chiefs resident at Dikwa. His régime continued until 1900 when he was killed by the French, who then installed Umar Sanda as Shehu of Dikwa. Later, in 1904, the British were to restore the old Bornu dynasty under Abubakar Garbai, and three years later built the present capital of Bornu, Maiduguri, or Yerwa as the Kanuris call it.

In 1816, Uthman dan Fodio died and his son, Muhammed Bello took over command. The Fulani empire was 'split' into three. Adamawa came under the successors of M. Adama while of the remaining empire, the eastern sector came under Bello, and the western, under Bello's uncle, Abdullahi Emir of Gwandu. Of this split between Sokoto and Gwandu, however, Mr. Arnett has pointed out: "It does not appear that there was any intention of permanently dividing the Empire, but merely one of decentralizing its administration. It happened, however, that Abdullahi was in Gwandu at the time of Shehu's death and before he returned to Sokoto, Bello was elected Sarkin Musulumi."[29] Abdullahi at first refused to recognize the claims of Bello but after the latter had helped him to quell the revolt of Abdul Salame at Kalemba, he gave in and accepted Bello as the overlord of all the Muslims west of Bornu. Zaria, Bauchi, Kano, Katsina, Bida and many other small Emirates thus becames tributary to Sokoto, while Yauri, Lapai, Kontagora and others came under Gwandu. By the time the British came to Northern Nigeria, however, this dual control was already weakening, though "the extent to which the Fulani empire survived through the nineteenth century as an effective political unit"[30] has often been underestimated by western commentators.[31] The bonds that held the Caliphate together were in the main the ties derived from the Jihad; the religion of Islam and finally inter-marriages between Sokoto and the Emirs of the different Emirates.[32]

With the Fulani came the centralization of political power in the person of the Emir. Their rule was based on a system of fief holding and clientage, the authority of the Emir being maintained through an administrative machine, a complex system of taxation and the institution and extension of Islamic law and courts. It was this system which was later adopted by the British, suitably modified and which was to form the basis of what later was to be known as 'Indirect Rule'. Basically, however, the Fulani political system was merely a modification of the original Habe form of political organization.[33]

Though the system was feudal in nature, hierarchically organized with an almost extreme centralization of political power, the Emirs, even within their own domains, were never complete autocrats. The comments by two acute observers may serve to illustrate this. Barth, who visited Kano in the middle of the nineteenth century, noted that: "The authority of the Government (i.e. Emir) is not absolute, even without considering the appeal which lies to his liege lord in Sokoto or Wurno." And of Bornu, Barth wrote: "With regard to the government in general, I think, in this province—where publicity is given very soon to every incident, it is not oppressive—though—there is no doubt a great deal of injustice inflicted in small matters."[34] C. L. Temple, once Lt. Governor of Northern Nigeria also pointed out: "Before our occupation of these territories, the great Emirs and Chiefs, though nominally autocrats, were nevertheless subject, and also very susceptible to public opinion . . . they generally ruled their own people with moderation and justice."[35]

Much of this was change with the establishment of British rule in Northern Nigeria, a point which Temple noted and which is forcibly expressed in a letter by the Emir of Kano to Mr. E. D. Morel: "As regards secular matters and affairs of this world, we can do everything however great a change it might be—since our people are accustomed to law and to obey the orders of their rulers."[36] It is the changes which took place under British administration which will next be examined.

III. BRITISH OCCUPATION AND ADMINISTRATION

The motive forces or interests which led to the British occupation of large tracts of Africa have been debated and discussed by various writers.[37] The process of occupation has often been, first through the incursions of trading concerns, followed by the missionaries, and finally intervention by the Government. Northern Nigeria was no exception. The first decisive step here was the formation, through the coming together of a number of small trading concerns along the Niger, of the United Africa Company under Sir George Goldie in 1878.[38] Three years later the name of the company was converted to the National African Company, which succeeded in entering into trading agreements with the multifarious peoples of the middle Niger and Benue. Competition from France and Germany led the company to seek recognition from the Sultan of Sokoto in 1885, and a year later, the Company was granted a royal Charter as the Royal Niger Company. Between 1893 and 1898, the Company entered into agreements with Germany and France which recognized its exclusive trading rights along the Niger-Benue basin. In 1897 trouble from the Emir of Bida, ruler of the Nupes, led to the conquest of Bida, and a successor favourable to the British was appointed to replace the deposed Emir of Bida. To forestall further competition from the French—active in the north east around Bornu and towards the west around Borgu, by an Order in Council,[39] 'The Protectorate of Northern Nigeria' was declared in 1899 and the territories of the Royal Niger Company were transferred to the Colonial Office. On January 1, 1900, the British flag was formally unfurled over Northern Nigeria, with Sir (later Lord) F. D. Lugard as the first Chief Commissioner. Local disturbances in Kontagora in 1901 led to its capture that year, the Emir fleeing northwards and harassing the outlying districts of Zaria. An appeal from the Emir of Zaria to Lugard gave the later the opportunity to establish British rule in Zaria in 1902, the same year that Bauchi was occupied. The rejection of friendly overtures from Lugard by the Sultan of Sokoto, made conflict between the two seem inevitable, but the first target was Kano, which fell to the British early in 1903, Later in the year, Sokoto was also brought under British rule. Thus by 1904 practically the whole of the Northern Nigeria was under British control. This, however, was not fully completed until the end of the first decade, by which time all Northern Nigeria was under British rule.[40] In all the emirates conquered by the British, the ruling Fulani aristocracy was reinstated, except in Daura, where the old Habe dynasty, driven out by the

Fulani and centred around Zango, was restored under M. Musa who then became the Sarkin Daura.[41] And in all the emirates, Argungu, which was never conquered by the Fulani, Daura, and Abuja, to which the Habe ruler of Zaria migrated, are the only three with non-Fulani ruling families. The restoration of the Fulani aristocracy was a policy of Lugard's, which he stated in his Annual Report of 1900.[42]

The immediate intention of the Government was laid down by Lugard in an address to the Sultan, Waziri and elders of Sokoto after the fall of that town in March 1903. The appointment of the Sultan and Emirs was to be by the Chief Commissioner, who was to be guided by "the usual laws of succession and wishes of the people and Chiefs.... The Emirs who are appointed will rule over the people as of old time and take such taxes as are approved by the High Commissioner, the Alkalis and Emirs will hold the law Courts as of old.... Government will in no way interfere with the Mohammedan religion. . . ." [43] In short very little was to be changed. The consequences of this policy will be discussed later, but the idea of the Emirs ruling over the people as of old, guided by British advisers, the basis of 'Indirect Rule', as this came to be known, needs to be expanded in some detail.

In one respect at least, the term 'Indirect Rule' as applied to the North is misleading, if only because it creates the impression that the principle was applied to the North as a whole. In practice, a distinction was recognized between the Fulani-dominant areas in which there was some form of a centralized authority and the rest of Northern Nigeria, mainly the areas around the mountainous fortresses of Bauchi, Plateau and Adamawa provinces and the forest areas in the Niger–Benue basin where there was no corresponding authority similar to the Emirs. Indirect Rule applied only in the Fulani Emirates while 'Direct Rule' was practised in the other parts of the Protectorate. This statement, however, has to be qualified slightly, for the British, where possible, attempted to group together some of the non-Emirate 'pagan' peoples under a chief, as for instance, with the Kagoro,[44] a procedure which often met not merely with partial successes, but with direct opposition in the early period of British administration. Where such a 'chief' was 'found', Indirect Rule was equally applied.

Indirect Rule as a principle of administration was by no means an original idea of Lugard's and in fact, it is arguable, as some of his statements in his '*Annual Reports*' and in his '*Political Memoranda*' show, that he had no precise conception of what it implied. For instance, the statement in his 'Report' of 1904: "The system of Rule was essentially one, and one only, in which each of us, as subjects of

His Majesty bore our respective parts and carried out that portion of the work which might be assigned to us."[45] Statements of such a nature could be multiplied from the writings and many pronouncements of Lugard, and the ambivalent attitude of some of his successors to the administrative implications of Indirect Rule can be directly traced to the often conflicting interpretations they placed on these statements.

The practical application of the policy, however, was by a series of Proclamations and ordinances such as the Native Courts Proclamation 1900, Native Revenue Proclamation 1904, Land Revenue Proclamation 1904 and the Native Authority Proclamation 1907, to cite but a few. The implications of these ordinances and proclamations will be more easily discussed under three headings: the chiefs, taxation and the courts.

The first obvious move was the delimitation of the area of authority of the respective Emirs and the constitution of these into provinces. Over each emirate, the Emir became the Sole Native Authority, and though Councils were organized to help advise the Emir, he was not bound to accept or to act on such advice, a policy which tended to turn the Emirs into the autocrats they later became. The delimitation of emirates also had a consequence which is best shown by taking the case of Kano. Kano previously included Katsina, Kazaure, Daura, Hadeija, Gummel and Katagum. Of these, in present terminology, only Kano itself, Katsina, Hadeija and Katagum had Emirs with the status of a 'First Class' chief. But by reconstituting provinces and delimiting the areas under the several district Headships, places like Kazaure, Daura and Gummel became full-fledged emirates, the Emirs of which then secured the same 'constitutional' status as the Emir of Kano. The area of the emirate now became the Native Authority area. The Native Authority was made responsible for the administration of justice and the collection of taxes, the two functions they first acquired. Later, other functions were added as the system developed, while Lugard made it a rule that all employees of the Native Administration should be natives of the area and subject to the control of the local Native Authority, in other words, the Emir.[46] District Heads, the former fief-holders, were then encouraged to reside in their respective districts, while the various 'middle-men' who existed in the 'traditional system' had their offices either abolished, or new jobs found for them.[47]

Taxation was one of the main linch-pins which upheld the traditional system and buttressed the authority of the Emir. Lugard, in pursuit of his policy, was next faced with reforming the old system in an attempt to reduce it into a more manageable structure. The methods of taxation in the emirates were based on a series of taxes: the *Zakat*, alms paid by Muslims which was fixed in relation to the property owned by the payer; the *Kurdin Sarauta*, that is, accession duty, a tax paid by 'office-holders' on appointment by the Emir; the *Kharaj*, tax paid on land; *Gandu*, capitation tax paid to the Emir by conquered tribes; *Jangali*, tax paid on livestock, and other 'taxes' (or rather 'gifts') paid to the Emir on his accession, harvest periods and during the times of Muslim festivals.[48] Of these several forms of tax, the Government decided to retain the Jangali, Kharaj and the Kurdin Sarauta, the last to enhance 'the status of the Emir' over office-holders.[49] Jangali and the Kharaj might be paid by the same person, but usually the former was levied only on the pastoral tribes. Taxes were assessed on the taxable wealth for each area and the collection made by district and village heads, 25% of the assessed tax being paid to the Government.[50] These new fiscal measures, which involved a good deal of decentralization, enhanced the status of the Emirs by ensuring them a steady and fixed income. In 1911 a decisive step was taken with the creation of native authority treasuries—the *Beit-el-mal*.

The Native Court Proclamation of 1900 'legalized' the Native Courts. The next step forward was the authorization to Residents of Provinces to set up Courts by warrant either as Alkali Courts or as Provincial Courts. While the former, which were graded into A, B, C, and D, with a descending right of authority, dealt principally with 'Natives', the latter administered 'British law' in cases involving non-natives. Emirs were given the right to appoint the personnel of the Native Courts, with the approval of the Resident and or the High Commissioner, a right which the Emirs had never before possessed. With the creation of Judicial Councils or Emirs Courts in 1906, the Emirs were in fact given judicial powers which were co-extensive with the Alkali Courts, both having concurrent jurisdiction.

The over-all control of this structure, in each of the provinces, was with the Resident, who was a political officer rather than an administrator. Under the Residents were the District Officers. Shortage of British personnel, in the early period of the occupation of Northern Nigeria, has often been used to suggest that Indirect Rule was a product of expediency rather than principle. If it was an expedient procedure at the time it was instituted, it later came to be regarded as a sacrosanct principle which was best left as it was. Lugard's injunction to his Residents that in advising Emirs, they were to "clothe (their) principles in the garb of evolution not revolution"[51] was taken literally to mean that they (the Residents) were to do nothing about bringing the system in line with changing times. In

1916 the whole system was stabilized with hardly any change before 1933, when the Native Authority Ordinance came into effect and the Ordinance has remained the basis of all subsequent legislation on the subject.

The most significant product of Indirect Rule, was the enhancement of the status of the various Emirs. With little check from the British Residents, an established and secure income, divorced from most responsibility, either to the people or to the 'expatriate' officials, given wide political power and authority over the judiciary through their control of appointments, the Emirs became more and more autocratic in their attitude towards the mass of the people.

The gulf which now separated the Chiefs from the people is illustrated by taking only two examples. The first, the proposal to create special schools for the sons of Emirs; the second, the suggestion for the creation of District and Emirate Economic Boards. Both came up for discussion in the Conference of Chiefs of the Northern Provinces in 1938. When it was asked if the Emirs would like the school for their sons to be made 'open', the general feeling of the Chiefs was expressed by the following two Emirs. The Emir of Kano considered that "association with children of common people would be inclined to inculcate the outlook of the peasant", while the Emir of Kontagora thought that " the character of the chiefs' children was adversely influenced by association with the children of ordinary people".[52]

The plan to create District and Emirate Economic Boards had two aims in view; firstly to provide a forum for the Emir to meet the village and district heads to discuss problems of the general welfare of the people; secondly, to discuss programmes whereby the level of agricultural productivity could be raised. This time the Shehu of Bornu expressed the sentiments of the chiefs when he said that one meeting between District Heads and the Emir each year was sufficient.[53] The Emir of Kano agreed. There was practically no reason why the Emir should meet the village head once the latter had been appointed by the Emir.

The autocratic system which developed under 'Indirect Rule' has been attested to by several competent observers and we can hardly do better than to note a few of their observations. It has already been pointed out that though Emirs' Councils were created to advise the Emir, he was in fact not bound to accept such advice. The Emir, by law, was the Sole Authority. Not only was the authority of the Emir unchecked by his Council: paradoxically, the decision of the Government that District Heads and fief-holders should reside in their respective districts meant the cessation of the Council which was composed of the District Heads. And in the absence of these, the Emir quickly became an absolute ruler, the District Head in turn becoming absolute in his own domain. The judgment of F. W. de St. Croix on this issue was that:

> "The Emirs' power over the whole province greatly increased and in each district, the Chief became, and still is an absolute ruler in his own domain".[54]

At about the same period that this was being written, an American Negro visitor to Northern Nigeria, noted that: "No dictator ever had greater power than those black agents of British Colonial Rule."[55] If the writer may be accused of an 'anti-colonialist' prejudice, or exaggeration, it is well to note the observation by Miss Perham, whom few could possibly accuse of such bias, or exaggeration. "It has been said that there has been a great advance in Northern Nigeria in the last thirty years. It is, however, well to understand its nature. The form has been the concentration of responsibility in the Emir, whose autocracy, exercised through his Council, his District and Village Heads, has been preserved and even increased by a tradition which debars officers from any direct action."[56] The degree of nepotism practised by the Emirs and effectiveness of control by the Residents, was pointed out also by a one-time Resident and acting Lieutenant-Governor of the Northern Region, Sir Richmond Palmer, who noted that the majority of the personnel of the Native Authority, both at headquarters and in the districts, were dismissed in favour of the Emir's friends without the Resident's knowledge. Even "the support promised by the Government for the native authority was quite often ignored" by the Emir.[57] The extreme 'personalism' in native administration, the centralization and revolution of governmental activity around the Emir has been described by no less a person than the Sultan of Sokoto.[58] 'Indirect Rule' and the new status of the Emir under it considerably influenced future development in the North, as will be shown later on, which is one reason why such attention has been given to it in this analysis of the system.

IV. THE NORTHERN REGION AND NIGERIA

For the first decade and a half after the formation of the protectorate of Northern Nigeria, the region was administered as a separate political entity. Economic difficulties, however, led to the amalgamation of the Region with the protectorate of S. Nigeria into a single

C

political unit in 1914. Lugard, the former High Commissioner of the Northern region, became the Governor-General of the newly constituted Nigeria, a title personal to him. The boundry between the two units, the North and the South, remained with the exception of minor rectification practically unaltered. A Lieutenant-Governor responsible to the Governor-General was appointed and placed directly in charge of the affairs of the Northern provinces, and though there existed a 'Legislative Council' in Lagos, this had only an advisory capacity, and even then, its activities were restricted solely to the South.

In 1916 a new body, the 'Nigerian Council', was created. Unlike the old Legislative Council, the Nigerian Council's activities were extended to include the North, though this was more in theory than in practice. Except for the Lieutenant-Governor and a few of the Northern Residents, the North was hardly represented in the Nigerian Council. In 1922 a new 'Constitution' was introduced which constitutionally brought a return to the pre-1916 state of affairs. The 1922 Legislative Council was precluded "from discussing Bills of any description pertaining to the North without the express consent of the Governor"[59] though the two regions were to be regarded as a single political unit for fiscal and budgetary purposes. Also, all legislation relating to custom and excise duties, and the criminal law was made applicable to the North, which remained, constitutionally, a separate territory from the rest of Nigeria for the next quarter of a century. Included in the framework of a single Nigeria in 1914, the North was made politically separate a decade later, thus removing it from those influences which shaped the political attitudes of the 'southern politicians'.

So real was the separation, and so well-shielded was the North from the rest of Nigeria, that when a person such as Sir Ahmadu Bello, Premier of the North, visited Lagos for the first time in his life in 1939, it was with a lack of comprehension, suspicion and dissatisfaction, if not outright hostility, that he viewed southern politics and politicians.[60] How far the subsequent suspicion and dislike of the South by the North can be attributed to these first impressions of the Sardauna and his associates will remain an interesting topic of research for the psychologist interpreting the pattern of Nigerian politics.

If 'Indirect Rule' was a product of circumstances, the decision politically to separate the two Protectorates of Nigeria was consciously taken. This was in furtherance of the policy of preserving "the very special identity"[61] of the North, so different from that of the South. The line of development, however, proved somewhat different from that envisaged by Lugard who had said that in the North there were not "two sets of rulers working either separately or in co-operation".[62] Part of his intention was the gradual assimilation of the emirates into the framework of modern, direct administration, but this had been so little realized that British administrators were now wondering if the policy of 'Indirect Rule' had not been pushed too far. Two reasons may be given in explanation of the increased powers of the Emirs and the tendency towards the development of semi-autonomous 'native states' or Emirates.

In the first place, it was felt that in order to train the Emirs and their Native Authorities to understand the complexity of modern administration and therefore better to fit them to undertake the new duties which would devolve on them, they should be allowed the utmost freedom from the 'evils' of bureaucratization and red-tape inseparable from centralization. From this developed the attitude of some of the Residents of regarding the Native Authorities and the Emirs as their 'special charge' to be protected as much as possible from the unregulated influences of departmental officials. Besides, as Miss Perham put it: "The good Resident did not wish the Emir, however imposing in public, to be privately an automaton, forced to carry out all commands. His sense of chivalry recoiled from using his undoubted power to oblige a chief to perform acts that offended his social and religious prejudices."[63]

The second factor was the British Government's attitude to Islam, an attitude which contrasts with the French, and (in the context of Islam) reflects the differing policies of the French and the British in their respective African colonies. France believed that the twin policies of assimilation and centralization of power, policies written into the sections of the 1946 Constitution of the 4th Republic dealing with the Overseas Territories, could only be achieved by strangling the political aspirations of Islam, the rival movement which enjoins on its adherents its own social and political unity. This is illustrated by the instructions issued by the Ministry of Overseas France to the High Commissioner in French West Africa in September 1950: ". . . Our Islamic policy shall aim at preserving friendly but watchful relations with traditional Islam in view of imminent dangers to the French cause arising from the spread in West and Central Africa of Islamic forms which are inspired by political programmes and anti-French ideas. . . .[64]

In contrast to this policy, British administrators were more of the opinion that subversive Islamic movements, such as might exist, were more likely to wither or be smothered by local Moslem opinion if a non-interventionist policy were pursued. Lugard, in his speech to the Sultan of Sokoto in 1903, had already promised non-intervention in matters of religion. But in Islam, the dividing line between the political and the religious is extremely tenuous and not easily discernible. The wisdom of non-intervention was felt to be rewarded by the loyalty of the Emirs in the 'Satiru Revolt' of 1905. From that period the British became not unaware of Islamic political propaganda in Northern Nigeria. In 1923, Palmer, for instance, intercepted messages from M. Sai'd Hayatu[65] to one Dankara Jauro Maza in Gombe to the effect that he (Hayatu) was arranging for the delivery of 2000 rifles from French Territory. Two years earlier, twenty-two separate disturbances had been noted in the Gombe area, while in 1922 there had been an attempt to depose the Sultan of Sokoto in favour of Sarkin Gobir Isa who belonged to the Muhammed Bello branch of the Sokoto family and who was related to Hayatu.[66] 'Mahdist' influences were also detected in the disturbances in Katsina in 1927, and as late as 1952 a confidential administrative report on Islamic political movements cautiously noted that "If . . . Sir Abderahman-el-Mahdi secures political dominance in the Sudan, and the ties between Northern Nigeria and that country are strengthened, as appears probable, the influence of the Mahdiyya may rise again".[67]

The feeling that Mahdism was a threat to British rule encouraged the idea that British interests would be best served with a minimum intervention in Emirate affairs and that as much as possible, the natives were to be made to feel that policy was determined not by the British but by the Emir. Policy was therefore geared towards extending the authority of the Emir, and any innovation discouraged. But a policy of maintaining the *status quo* in Northern Nigeria was hardly consistent with a rapidly changing Nigeria. The dilemma, if a dilemma it was, was put effectively by Sir Donald Cameron in 1933. Referring to the habit amongst British officials of regarding the Emirates as a feudal monarchy, he pointed out: "It would be a direct contradiction in terms for me to say . . . that it is the avowed intention of the Government that the natives should not 'stay put' and at the same time that I accept the view last stated that a feudal monarchy . . . is all we are seeking. . . . The policy accepted for some considerable time that the Moslem administration should be sheltered as far as possible from contact with the world—the century-old doctrine of political untouchability . . . could not be expected to stand up against the natural forces of a western civilization that was gradually but quite perceptibly creeping further and further north in Nigeria; a curtain being drawn between the Native administration in the North and the outer world. . . . But we have advanced now to the stage that the curtain is being gradually withdrawn and, I hope, will be fully withdrawn within a comparatively brief period."[68]

An immediate step towards lifting the 'curtain' was the passing of the Native Authority Ordinance of 1933 which introduced a re-classification of the Native Authorities, a modification of policy with regard to the non-Moslem areas of the North, and a redefinition of the class of persons subject to the rules of the Native Authority. A decade after the passing of the Ordinance, 'Outer Councils' were constituted to advise the Emirs and to bring them in closer touch with the affairs of the Emirate. The idea, which was implicit in the action of Lugard in summoning a meeting of the Chiefs in 1916, was accepted and extended and from 1931 such meetings (which were annual) became a regular feature.

The second World War interrupted the process of change already begun, but it also made further change imperative. In the Gold Coast and Southern Nigeria, there were demands for constitutional change which could hardly be denied or postponed much longer. In Northern Nigeria, a meeting between the Governor, Sir Bernard Bourdillon, and the Chiefs in 1942 helped in convincing them of the necessity for changes if the North was not to be left behind in a changing Nigeria. In 1943 the Conference of West African Governors recognized the need for constitutional changes and proposals were made towards this end. Sir Arthur Richards, who succeeded Sir Bernard in 1943, became the chief architect of the new constitution.

On the 1st January 1947, the constitution, subsequently known as the 'Richards Constitution', came into effect after having been debated for only one day in a Legislative Assembly in which the North was not represented. The new constitution reversed the 1924 position, and once again the North was brought into contact with the rest of Nigeria.

In informal discussions on the Constitutional proposals, the attitude of the North was probably shown by the statement of the editor of the only newspaper published there: "The people of the North are ready to accept any form of government, provided that it is not such as will upset the present system on which the government was built up. This established system of government in the North, with each district under its own Emir or Chief, had been in existence before the Europeans came to this country."[69] The Constitution left virtually intact the "present system on which the government was built". It provided for the creation of a Northern House of Assembly composed of 'official' and 'unofficial' members, the latter with a majority of one, being nominated from and by the native authorities. The Assembly had no legislative powers. Its functions were deliberative and advisory. It sent desired legislation to the central legislative Council which embraced the three regions into which Nigeria was now divided and in which the North had nine representatives.[70] Only the Legislative Council had the power to make laws.

Dissatisfaction with the new Constitution, and particularly with certain enactments—the "four obnoxious Bills"[71]—led to a country-wide tour by the National Council of Nigeria and the Cameroons (now National Council of Nigerian Citizens, a southern political organization) in an attempt to raise funds for a delegation to the Colonial Secretary to ask to have the constitution abrogated. From April 23 to June 5, 1946 (and later between November 13 and 19, 1946), the delegation covered most of Northern Nigeria where the reception given them was either indifferent or hostile.[72] Only in a few towns were the delegates well received, for instance, in Bauchi, where they were met by the Emir. In September, 1946, the artisans, mainly of Southern origin, of the Sokoto Native Authority went on strike over a demand for increased wages.[73] In Kano and Maiduguri there were similar demands. The Emir of Kano, on a visit to Lagos, was shouted at and abused while at the house of a leader of the 'Egbe Omo Oduduwa'.[74] These events were naturally associated by northerners with the NCNC tour of the North, while statements critical of the North, made by the delegates, angered Northern leaders who resented the Southern claim to the leadership of the country. In a letter to the *Nigerian Daily Times*, the second member for the North in the Legislative Council, Mallam (now Alhaji, Sir) Abubakar Tafawa Balewa pointed out that: "Let the South know that we will never co-operate with that gang of agitators who are not even sure of what they are doing."[75] Earlier, he had threatened that if the South did not desist from its attacks on the North, the North would be forced to continue its "interrupted conquest to the Sea", that is, to the South.[76]

The Constitution, which was intended by its author to bring the peoples of Nigeria into closer unity and to foster the spirit of co-operation between them, had instead revealed the wide gap which separated the North from the South, a gap already recognized by British administrators and which they did very little to bridge (if they did not actually help to widen it by their policies in the North). By 1948 it was acknowledged that the pace of political advance in Nigeria had made the 'Richards Constitution' outdated. If the people had little say in the making of the 1946 constitution, the new Governor, Sir John MacPherson, was determined that the next constitution was to have the widest possible publicity. This entailed discussions at various levels from the village to the province, thence to the Region, and finally the 'general conference' of representatives of the three regions. These 'conferences', however, revealed the diversity of opinion in the North and gave the first sign that there was already a body of opinion which was no longer quiescent in the face of such rapid changes.

At the Zaria Provincial Conference, for instance, a member objected to chiefs being allowed to go to the Legislative Council as representatives of the North. When his objection was rejected, the Conference accepted the suggestion that 'Chiefs' should be regarded as 'official' members, in other words, as representatives of the Government and not the people. Unlike the Kano Provincial Conference which agreed that provinces bordering on the South should be allowed to go to the South should the people so wish, the Zaria Conference voted (33–4) against changes in regional boundaries.[77] The Kaduna Conference wanted, as did Zaria, regional autonomy for the North. Like Kano, it was prepared to have places like Ilorin province transferred to the South, but demanded that representation in the Northern Assembly should be from the various provinces, with direct elections if possible, and not from the Emirs' Councils. At the Regional Conference a delegate from Maiduguri, M. Ibrahim Imam, opposed (though with little effect) the idea of including chiefs on the Committee to draft the 'Resolutions' on the review of the Constitution. What is interesting here is the difference in opinion about boundary changes and the place of the chiefs in the political system.

More significant than these local differences in opinion was the division between the North and the South which emerged at the 'general conference' in Lagos. The issue in dispute was the representations to be given to the respective regions. While the South demanded a greater representation in the Legislative Council in conformity with the ratio which obtained in the old Assembly (nineteen from the South and nine from the North), the North wanted representation on a population basis, which would shift the balance in its favour. The dispute brought to light a significant fact about the North, one of which the people in the South were totally unaware, which was the considerable unanimity of opinion to be found when the interests of the North were thought to be at stake. On a call for 'Money to Help the North' from the Sultan of Sokoto, a considerable amount was very quickly collected, with the aim of sending a delegation to the Colonial Secretary to press the issue of representation if the South did not modify its intransigent attitude.[78] However, a compromise was reached when it was agreed that the two areas—the North and the 'South'—should be given equal representation. As under the new system the regions were to be given greater powers, the second question over which there was disagreement between the North and the South, was the basis on which revenue was to be allocated as between the regions. It was eventually agreed that this should be left to a special commission.[79] Related to the issue of the legislative powers to be assigned to the regions was the question whether there were to be African Ministers in the new system. While the South demanded African Ministers, the North demurred, feeling it had not the men with the requisite experience to assume ministerial responsibility. An agreement was reached when it was decided to allow this to be settled regionally by the assemblies, while the North agreed that at the centre there should be African Ministers in the House of Representatives chosen equally from the three regions.

The proposals agreed to at the General Conference were embodied in the MacPherson Constitution, which came into effect in 1951. Under it, the three regions were given some degree of autonomy in the control of their internal affairs. But the regions were, in the last analysis, made subject to the central Assembly, now to be known as the House of Representatives. Under the constitution, elections, which were indirect, were held for the first time in the Northern Region, thus giving rise to the emergence of political parties in the North. But once the Constitution became operative, difficulties inherent in it became noticeable and made its working problematic.[80] Within a year of its introduction, the MacPherson constitution was suspended. The final break-up came over the question of independence for the country. A motion tabled by a private Action Group member of the House demanding independence for Nigeria in 1956 was amended by the North to read, in effect, as soon as practicable. Feeling that they were as yet not fully prepared to undertake the burdens of independence, with a civil service still largely dominated by non-Northerners, educationally backward as compared with the two regions in the South and with a level of capital formation[81] behind both the East and West regions, the North did not want to commit itself to any definite date. As there was no possibility of a compromise, the Action Group and some of the NCNC ministers in the Council of Ministers 'walked out' and the House adjourned *sine die.*

The 'Kano Riots' of May 1953, which were the sequel to the events in the House, significant in themselves, help to show how bitterly the Northerners felt the treatment they received from the Southerners after the House adjourned.[82] In a speech to the Kano Native Authority workers, M. Inuwa Wada, then the Native Authority Information Officer, put the matter simply: "Having abused us in the South, these very Southerners have decided to come over to the North to abuse us, but we have determined to retaliate the treatment given us in the South. We have therefore organized about 1,000 men ready in the city to meet force with force; those men will parade all Kano tomorrow, singing and shouting that the delegates are not wanted at Kano and that no lecture or meeting will be delivered by them. We shall get permit for this purpose."[83] The 'delegates' referred to were members of an Action Group delegation, led by Chief Samuel Akintola, to publicize in the North the Action Group's stand on the question of Independence. Disturbances at the first meeting of the delegation, said to have been started by the 'Jam'iyyar Mahaukata' (society of mad-men), a group wearing red head-bands, led quickly to open rioting which went on for three days and resulted in the death of thirty-six people, with 241 wounded and damage to property estimated at £10,418.

The dissolution of the legislatures of the country was followed by Conferences in London (July–August 1953) and Lagos (January 1954) to decide on the future political development of the country. An eight-point programme was submitted by the North as a basis of negotiation, the most important item being greater autonomy and increased legislative powers for the regions. The decisions issuing from the Conferences led to the promulgation of a new Constitution for Nigeria. Unlike the 1951 Constitution, under the new dispensation, specific powers were allocated to the Federal government, which shared jurisdiction with the regions over the new class of power—the concurrent power. All powers not restricted to the Federal Government or included in the concurrent list were reserved to the regions—a division which in many respects was patterned on the constitutions of Australia, and the United States. Also, unlike the system in 1951, elections to the Federal and Regional Houses were now to be separate, while the public service and the judiciary were regionalized. In short, the new dispensation marked the introduction of a much more 'federal' system of government into Nigeria and made the prospect of power in the regions a reality. As a consequence of the decisions of the 1953–54 conferences, both the Eastern and Western regions became internally self-governing in August 1957.

In March 1957 a motion for the Independence of Nigeria in that year was tabled in the House of Representatives. An amendment to change the date to 1959 was accepted, while Alhaji Abubakar Tafawa Balewa, as leader of government business and deputy President of the Northern Peoples' Congress, the North's governing political party signified the acceptance of that date by the North.

The reality of independence in the East and West, and the prospect of a self-governing Nigeria in the near future brought into the open minority dissatisfaction which had been latent since 1951. In the North, with a population of 16·8 million according to the 1952 Census figures, the Hausa–Fulani numbered 8·5 million, or over 50% of the total population. Of the four largest groups identified, the Hausas formed 32·6%, the Fulanis 18%, the Kanuris 7·8%, and the Tivs 4·6% of the total population. Taking the Hausa–Fulani–Kanuri alone, they formed 58·4% of the population. Over 200 other ethnic groups identified in the 1931 Census formed only 30% of the total. Religious differences complicated the ethnic diversity, the Moslems constituting roughly 70% or 11·6m., Christians of all denominations 4% or 0·5m. and 'animists and others' 26% or 4·6m. of the total population.[84] The religious differences, however, were made more complex by the difference in the distribution of the three categories as between the various provinces. Comparable situations were to be found in the Eastern and Western Regions. The demand for separate states by the 'minorities' was based not only on religious and ethnic differences. Related to these were allegations of economic discrimination and political oppression. In 1957 it was eventually decided that minority demands should be referred to a special Commission, which reported in 1958 and recomended against the creation of new states.[85] As will be shown later, the issue is as yet unsettled even for the North, and it has influenced and shaped the pattern of political relations considerably. However, with the prospect of Independence in view, the consensus of opinion was for leaving minority problems to be settled after self-government.

In March 1959 the North became a self-governing unit within the federation, two years after the two regions in the South. The federation itself became an independent state within the Commonwealth in October 1960, with a new Constitution which departed only slightly from that of 1954. As a result of agreements reached at the 1958 Constitutional Conference, representation in the Parliament to be elected in 1959 and which was to lead Nigeria into self-government was to be based on a population basis, which gave the North 174 seats, as against 138 for the East and Western regions combined. Two main reasons can be suggested to explain the South's acceptance of this change. The first was the expectation of the southern based political parties that they would win substantial numbers of seats in the North in that region's first direct elections. The second was the proposal to establish a second chamber in which all the regions would be given equal representation. This, it was thought, would provide some checks against a lower house in which the North might be heavily represented. In the event the NPC, the governing party, won 134 seats, which gave it a majority over any other party in the country. As a result Sir Abubakar was invited to become the Prime Minister and to form a government which he did in a coalition with the N.C.N.C.

From being the backward partner in 1951, the North, within a decade, has emerged into a controlling position in the federation.

V. THE POLITICAL STRUCTURE OF THE NORTH[86]

The long association between Nigeria and Britain has meant in practice that in the transition from colonial status to independence, the pattern of government has been built on the main outlines of the 'Westminster model'.[87] In the federation, the constitutional structure of the 'regions' is similar, and each a replica of the central government. In the North, at the top of the hierarchy is the Governor in whom is vested the executive power of the region. The Governor, however, in the exercise of his powers acts on the advice of his Ministers, who constitute the second layer in the hierarchy. The Council of Ministers is made up of the Premier and his Ministers, who are appointed by the Governor on the advice of the Premier himself appointed by the Governor acting on his own initiative. Unlike the other governments of the federation, the constitution of the Northern region provides for the Premier to be appointed from either of the two houses which together form the legislature of the North—the House of Assembly, which is directly elected, and the House of Chiefs,[88] composed of all first-class chiefs sitting as of right and some 'second' and 'third class' chiefs nominated by the government. Again, unlike the other governments of the federation where the second chamber has a 'right of delay' limited to a period of six months, in the North, conflicts between both Houses are resolvable by a joint committee of both Houses drawn from equal numbers nominated by each House. The chairman of the committee is the President of the House of Chiefs who has a 'casting vote'.

The next layer in the structure is the administrative machine—the regional secretariat, made up of the various ministries. Representing the administration in the provinces and forming the last rung of the governmental ladder are the 'Provincial' authorities: these constitute the liaison, in the provinces, between the regional government and the Native Authorities. The Provincial Commissioners Act of 1962 was the first consistent attempt to define the relationship between the Provincial Authorities and the Native Authorities.[89]

Sandwiched within this structure, and with varying degrees of 'independence', are the various quasi-governmental organs such as the Public Service Commission, the Judicial Service Commission, the Regional Electoral Commission, the Regional Marketing Board and the Northern Region Development Corporation. Most of these developed with the regionalization of government in 1954.

The Native Authority, or local government structure, is a bewildering system difficult to describe in a brief space.[90] From the hesitating steps taken with 'Indirect Rule', the North has made considerable progress in trying to reform and modernize its local government system. A major step towards reform was the highly critical speech by Abubakar Tafawa Balewa in the Northern House of Assembly in 1950, during which he pointed out: "In our present traditional system of administration, no consideration is given to the demands of the people or their welfare. In the Chiefs Ordinance no provision is made for the people. None of the Chiefs knows his exact powers and worst of all, neither chiefs nor their employees are aware of their obligations."[91] Attempts made to survey the system led to the passing of the Native Authority law of 1954 which, with subsequent amendments, still forms the basic legislation. Reforms in the East and the West added impetus to the drive for modernization. Basically, there are two types of Native Authorities, the Native Authority proper and the subordinate Native Authority, the latter to be found mainly in the non-Moslem areas of the North. The extent of the reform made is shown in the following table.

TABLE 1

Types of Native Authorities in Northern Nigeria

	Subordinate Native Authority			Native Authority		
	1950	1958	1962	1950	1958	1962
Chief-in-Council[92]	—	19	20	4	43	39
Chief-and-Council	22	27	23	14	9	11
Council	80	28	6	9	12	18
Group of Persons	—	2	—	—	—	—
Sole Chief	14	—	—	86	—	—
Caretaker/or Dis. Officer	—	—	—	1	—	2
TOTAL	116	76	49	114	64	70

The process has thus been one of both a reduction, through amalgamation, in the number of Councils and of a 'democratization' of the Councils. Part of the latter process was the introduction of elected representatives into the various councils, and the following shows summarily, the degree to which this has been carried.

	1962
Traditional and nominated members only	5
Traditional, nominated and elected minority	7
Traditional, nominated and elected majority	36
Caretaker or Sole Native Authority	2

The North, so far, has not pushed the principle of elected Native Authority Councils as far as either the East or the Western regions, the limiting factors being, as the Minister for Local Government pointed out, "the degree of political awareness and sophistication of the Native Authority area: the political temperament of the people; their traditional idea of authority and its meaning and the necessity to ensure that there are sufficient experienced people to carry out the duties of a native authority."[93] The last point raises some interesting contrasts, however, with the regional governments of the South. The first point is that unlike the other regions, the North allows certain classes of Native Authority employees to contest elections to Native Authority Councils "but must resign from the service (of the authority) on winning the election, except if they are District, village and hamlet heads".[94] Secondly, Native Authorities in the North exercise wider powers and carry out more functions than their counterparts in the South, though some of these are gradually being taken over by the regional government. Thus, for example, only the Kano Native Authority still runs a native authority hospital. The regional Government has taken over all other such hospitals. Thirdly, the North makes a more conscious effort to train its Councillors for the jobs they are to do.[95]

If the Native Authority system is still peculiar to the North, the structure of its legal system is radically different from that in the other parts of the federation. This difference is due principally to the predominance of Islam. The North operates two roughly parallel systems, the one based on Shari'a law, applied in the Alkali Courts, and the other based on the system of laws handed down by the British. From the Native Authority Courts, which are graded in terms of their powers from A to D, appeals lie to either the Regional High Court (which applies 'received law') or the Shari'a Court of Appeal which applies Shari'a law. On all matters pertaining to criminal law, now governed by the new Penal Code, the Shari'a

Court of Appeal is the final court. In cases of conflict of law between 'received law' and the Shari'a, reference is made to the Court of Resolution for a decision on the principles that are to apply. In civil matters and other questions not covered by the Penal Code, appeals can be made from the Regional High Court to the Federal Supreme Court.

It is necessary for a full understanding of the background to give a brief description of the economic position of the North at this point. The North is making some progress, economically, though the region is still backward as against the other regions. Ignoring the Colonial Development and Welfare programme of 1945, the first

THE COURTS OF THE NORTH

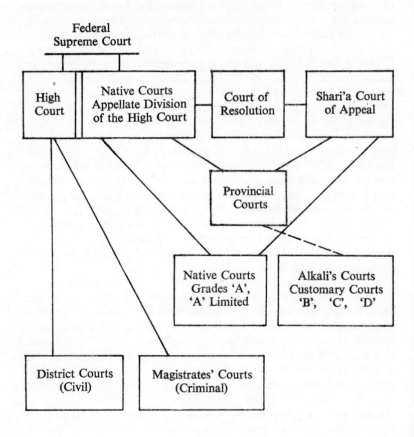

Maximum Punishments in Criminal Cases

Type of Court	Powers	Type of Court	Powers
High Court	Unlimited punishment.	Native Court Grade 'A'	Unlimited punishment.
Chief Magistrate	Imprisonment for 5 years or a fine of £500 or both.	Native Court Grade 'A' Limited	Unlimited power imprison and fine but the court has no power to impose death sentence.
Magistrate 1	Imprisonment for 2 years or a fine of £200 or both.	Native Court Grade 'B'	Imprisonment for 3 years or a fine of £150 or both.
Magistrate 2	Imprisonment for 1 year or a fine of £100 or both.	Native Court Grade 'C'	Imprisonment for $1\frac{1}{2}$ years or a fine of £30 or both.
Magistrate 3	Imprisonment for 3 months or a fine of £25 or both.	Native Court Grade 'C'	Imprisonment for 9 months or a fine of £15 or both.

development plan for the North was drawn for the period 1955–60, involving a capital expenditure of some £27m., while overall expenditure stood at £83·5m. This programme was extended for another two years, with an additional estimated capital expenditure of £19m. The latter part of the plan was unfulfilled and has been carried into the new 1962–68 Six-Year Development Plan for the North, which is part of that for Nigeria as a whole. And for the new programme, a total of £98·8m. is scheduled for direct capital expenditure, while total expenditure is expected to be of the order of some £293·8m. Part of this is to be raised internally, while expected external aid to help fulfil the plan is put at £44·5m. The fulfilment of the plan thus depends, in part, on the expectation of foreign aid being realized.

Much of the new capital programme is in the extension of agricultural production, on which the region depends for most of its revenue. But a sizeable proportion of the capital programme is in the processing of agricultural products and the development of industries. Of the £98·8., £71·25m. is to be spent on new investment thus: iron and steel (£29m.), oil refinery (£12m.), textiles (£10·4m.), cement (£5m.), paper and oil-seed crushing (£3m. each), fibre sacks and tarring (£2·4m. and £1·0m. respectively). With the new capital expenditure, it is expected that by 1968, the terminal year of the plan-period, the North will be processing 20% of its cotton crop (as against the present 7%); groundnuts 42% (present 25%), hides, 65% (4%), and skins 50% (as against 11%).

The recurrent expenditure estimated in the programme, approximately two-thirds of total expenditure, is to be spent in the extension of existing basic services—health, communications, transport, power and education The large proportion allocated to these services will do much to raise the low level of services existing in the North. The success of the plan depends, in part, on how rapidly the educational system expands. By 1970 it is expected that some 800,000 or 28% of the children of school age, will be in primary schools. This contrasts unfavourably with the other two regions, where universal primary education has already been achieved. The contrast is no less sharp when it is realised that only 10% of those who eventually leave the primary schools, can be found places in the secondary schools.[96] Deplorable as this might seem, one favourable point about it is that it might be possible to gear the educational output to the needs of the economy, thus lessening the problem of unemployment, amongst, especially, primary and secondary school leavers, a problem which already confronts the other two regions.[97]

Only a brief account of the governmental structure of the North has been given here. What part the political parties play in this structure, what relations, if any, hold between the various parties, will be the subject of subsequent chapters. However, before this is done, an attempt to describe and analyse the 'traditional' system of social and political organization will be made. This helps not only to further our understanding of present-day politics, it also puts in proper perspective, the process of political change taking place in the North.

NOTES

1. This statement has to be slightly modified. The NCNC, for instance, is fairly well represented in Western Nigeria, and the Action Group's claim to support in Northern Nigeria, however, has to be taken with caution. Its ally, the UMBC has so far rejected all demands by the Action Group for a complete merging of the two. In all local elections in the Tiv area, the UMBC invariably stood on its own platform.

2. J. P. Mackintosh, 'Electoral Trends and The Tendency towards a One Party System in Nigeria', *Journal of Commonwealth Political Studies*, vol. I, no. 3, November 1962.

3. Sir Ahmadu Bello, *My Life*, Cambridge, 1962. Sir Ahmadu, the Premier of Northern Nigeria in his autobiography has already contended that what the North's stand will be in a Nigeria where the South has a representation greater than the North's, is impossible to predict. He hoped, however, that such a situation would never arise.

4. Soren Kierkegaard, *The Journals of Soren Kierkegaard*, edited and translated by A. Dru, London, 1960, p. 23.

5. B. Malinowski, Culture—in *Encyclopedia of the Social Sciences*, (London 1931) vol. 4, p. 640.

6. For a select bibliography on the various accounts of such history see: E. W. Bovill, *Caravans of the Old Sahara*, Oxford University Press for I.A.I., 1933; R. H. Palmer, 'The Bornu Girgam,' *Journal of the Royal African Society*, October, 1912; S. Hogben, *The Mohammedan Emirates of Nigeria*, Oxford University Press, 1930; H. R. Palmer, 'The Kano Chronicle,' *Journal of the Royal Anthropological Society*, vol. 38, 1908; E. J. Arnett, 'A Hausa Chronicle,' *Journal of the Royal African Society*, vol. 9, pp. 191–267; A. Shultze, *The Sultanate of Bornu*, translated by P. A. Benton, 1913, reprinted by Frank Cass, 1967; J. A. Burdon, *Northern Nigeria, Historical Notes on Certain Emirates and Tribes*, London, Waterlow & Sons, 1909; Sultan Mohammed Bello, *Infraq. al-Maisuri*, translated by E. J. Arnett as 'The Rise of the Sokoto Fulani', n.d.; O. Temple, *Notes on the Tribes, Provinces, Emirates and States of the Northern Provinces of Northern Nigeria*, 1919, reprinted by Frank Cass, 1966; H. R. Palmer, *Sudanese Memoirs*, 3 vols., 1928, reprinted by Frank Cass, 1967, esp. vol. 3; R. H. Palmer, *The Bornu Sahara and Sudan*, John Murray, 1936; S. F. Nadel, *A Black Byzantium*, Oxford University Press, 1942; S. F. Nadel, Nupe State and Community,' *Africa*, vol. 8, 1935; C. K. Meek, *The Northern Tribes of Nigeria*, 2 vols., London University Press, 1925; C. K. Meek, *Tribal Studies in Northern Nigeria*, 2 vols. esp. vol. I, Routledge and Kegan Paul, 1931, and *A Sudanese Kingdom*, Routledge and Kegan Paul, 1931; *Akiga's Story*, translated by R. M. East, I.I.A.L. & C., Oxford, 1939; Laura and Paul Bohannan, *The Tiv People*, London Crown Agents, 1940; M. Clifford, 'A Nigerian Chiefdom,' *Journal of the Royal Anthropological Institute*, vol. 66; and the Ethnographic Survey of Africa series: Forde, Brown and Armstrong, *Peoples of the Niger-Benue Confluence*, 1955; H. Gunn, *The Pagan Peoples of the Central Area of Northern Nigeria*, 1956; H. Gunn and F. P. Connant, *Peoples of the Middle-Niger Region of Northern Nigeria*, 1960; F. L. Shaw, *A Tropical Dependency*, 1905, reprinted by Frank Cass, 1965.

7. J. D. Fage, *An Introduction to the History of West Africa*, Cambridge, 1955, p. 34; and contra C. W. J. Orr, 'The Hausa Race', *Journal of the Royal African Society*, 1908, pp. 278–83.

8. J. S. Trimingham, *A History of Islam in West Africa*, Oxford University Press, 1962, pp. 107–08; H. R. Palmer, *Gazetteer of Bornu Province*, Lagos, 1929; H. R. Palmer, 'The Central Sahara and Sudan in the 12th Century A.D.,' *Journal of the Royal African Society*, vol. 26, no. 103, April 1927.

9. H. R. Palmer, *A Bornu Girgam*, op. cit.; *Kano Chronicle*, op. cit., pp. 58, 98; H. R. Palmer, *Sudanese Memoirs*, vol. 3, p. 112; C. K. Meek, *A Sudanese Kingdom*, p. 123, fn. 2, pointed out that Ngarzagamo, which he calls Ngasrgomo or Ngarsgami was not the earliest capital of Bornu though it was "a former capital".

10. Sultan Bello, *Infraq' al Maisuri*, translated by E. J. Arnett as *The Rise of the Sokoto Fulani*.

11. J. H. Greenberg, 'Linguistic Evidence for the Influence of the Kanuri on the Hausa' *Journal of African History*, vol. I, no. 2, 1960, pp. 205–12.

D

12. See *History of the First Twelve Years of the Region of Mai Idris Alooma of Bornu*, by his Iman Ahmed Ibu Fartua, translated by H. R. Palmer, Lagos, Government Printer, 1926.

13. Trimingham. op. cit., p. 124 ff.

14. E. J. Arnett dates the introduction of Islam into the Hausa States at about 1456. See 'A Hausa Chronicle', *Journal of the Royal African Society*, vol. 9, pp. 161–67; also W. F. Gowers, *Gazetteer of Kano Province*, London, Waterlow & Sons, 1921.

15. F. de F. Daniel, *A History of Katsina*, Colonial Office accession no. 18177, n.d.; H. R. Palmer, 'History of Katsina', *Journal of the Royal African Society*, vol. 26, no. 103, April 1927.

16. C. K. Meek, *Northern Tribes of Nigeria*, London University Press, 1925, vol. I, p. 93.

17. E. J. Arnett, *Gazetteer of Sokoto Province*, London, Waterlow & Sons, 1920; K. Krieger, *Geschichte von Zamfara*, Berlin, 1959; also M. Crowder, *The Story of Nigeria*, London, 1962.

18. E. J. Arnett, *Gazetteer of Zaria Province*, London, Waterlow & Sons, 1920.

19. On the Jukuns see C. K. Meek, *A Sudanese Kingdom*, Routledge and Kegan Paul, 1931; C. J. Wilson-Haffenden, *The Red-Men of Nigeria*, 1930, reprinted by Frank Cass, 1967, p. 148 et seq. Meek pointed out that politically the Jukun Empire was "a loose confederacy composed of a number of semi-independent chiefdoms, the heads of which recognised the supremacy of the king of Kororofa and later of Wukari", op. cit., p. 342.

20. J. F. Schon, *Mangana Hausa*, London, 1885, p. 182 quoted by J. Greenberg, *The Influence of Islam on a Sudanese Religion*, monograph of the American Ethnological Society, no. 10, New York, 1946, p. 9.

21. J. Greenberg, op. cit., p. 13; also his, Islam and clan organization among the Hausa, *S. W. Journal of Anthropology*, vol. 3, 1947, p. 208 and 211.

22. Nadel, *A Black Byzantium*, Oxford University Press, 1942, reprinted 1946, p. 67; J. S. Trimingham, *Islam in West Africa*, Oxford University Press, 1959, p. 140, however, points out that: "In Nigeria, chiefs who have joined Islam during the last 100 years naturally keep up the old rites. The Chief of Biu, controlling the Pabir and Bura, who belongs to the category of divine kings, carries out all the rites his position entails."

23. J. S. Trimingham, op. cit., p. 144.

24. Short biographies of Uthman-dan Fodio will be found in F. de F. Daniel 'Shehu dan Fodio', *Journal of the African Society*, vol. 25, no. 99, 1926; T. L. Hodgkin, 'Usman dan Fodio', *Nigeria*, Special Independence Issue, October, 1960; Bello, *Infaku' L Maisuri*, pp. 20–24. A selection from the teachings and speeches of Uthman is contained in Bello, op. cit. pp. 24, 46. For some recent works on Uthman's life, his teachings and the Jihad, see D. M. Last, *Sokoto in the 19th Century—with special reference to the Vizirate*, Ph. D. Thesis, 1964, University of Ibadan, unpublished; Sifofin Shehu, 'An Autobiography and Character study of Uthman b. Fudi in verse', *Research Bulletin*, vol. 2, no. 1, January, 1966, Centre for Arabic Documentation, Ibadan; M. Hiskett, 'An Islamic Tradition of Reform in the Western Sudan', *Bulletin School of Oriental and African Studies*, vol. 25, 1962; and H. F. C. Smith, 'The Islamic Revolutions of the 19th Century', *Journal of the Historical Society of Nigeria*, vol. 2, no. 1, 1961.

25. Sultan Mohammed Bello, op. cit., pp. 19–22 and 122–25.

26. A. Burdon, 'The Fulani Emirates of Northern Nigeria', *The Geographical Journal*, vol. 24, 1904, pp. 636–51. The quotation is at p. 640. Correspondence

between Mohammed el Kanemi, Shehu of Bornu and Uthman dan Fodio suggests, in fact, that while Islam as practised in the Hausa States was imperfect, this did not justify a Jihad. See Bello, op.cit., passim.

27. D. A. Olderogge, Feodalizn v Zapaduom Sudane v 16–19 vv in *Sovietskaya Ethnographia* no. 4, 1957, pp. 91–103 (summarized in African Abstracts, vol. 10, no. 1, January, 1959, pp. 11–12). Unlike his article on Uthman dan Fodio already cited, Hodgkin in his *Nigerian Perspectives*, Oxford University Press, 1960, points out the religio-political and social aspects of the Jihad, pp. 39–40.

28. The Keri-Keri are one of the numerous small Tribes in Bornu. See C. K. Meek, *Tribal Studies in Northern Nigeria*, vol. 2, pp. 220–47 for an ethnographic description.

29. E. J. Arnett, *Gazetteer of Sokoto Province*, London, Waterlow & Sons, 1920, pp. 30–31. Accounts of the Jihad and the establishment of Fulani rule in Northern Nigeria will be found in the other provincial gazetteers, e.g. *Bauchi* by F. G. Gall, 1920; *Zaria* by Arnett; *Muri* by J. M. Freemantle, *Kontagora* by E. C. Duff; *Kano* by W. F. Gowers; *Nupe* by E. G. M. Dupigny; *Yola* by C. O. Migoed; *Bornu* by H. R. Palmer. There are two on Ilorin, the first by K. V. Elphinstone, 1921, and the second by H. B. Hermione Hodge, 1920; see also Bello, op. cit. pp. 23–29 and 51–109; Palmer, *Sudanese Memoirs*, vol. 3; see H. F. Backwell (ed.), *The Occupation of Hausaland 1900–1904*, being a translation of Arabic MS. found in the House of the Waziri of Sokoto, Bohari, no date; preface by H. R. Palmer, New Translation.

30. T. L. Hodgkin, *Nigerian Perspectives*, Oxford University Press, 1960, p. 41.

31. As for instance: F. L. Shaw, op. cit.; C. H. Robinson, *Hausaland*, London, 1896; M. S. Kisch, *Letters and Sketches from Northern Nigeria*, Chatto and Windus, 1910; A. F. Mockler-Ferryman, *British Nigeria*, Cassell, 1920; C. W. J. Orr, *The Making of Northern Nigeria*, new edition, 1911, Frank Cass 1965; *Northern Nigeria Annual Reports 1900–1902*.

32. For an elaboration of these, see D. M. last, op.cit., pp. 265, 270 and 277.

33. Sir (later Lord) F. D. Lugard, *Political Memoranda*, London, Waterlow & Sons, 1906, p. 129; C. W. J. Orr, The Hausa Race, *Journal of the Royal African Society*, 1908, pp. 278–83; M. G. Smith, *Government in Zazzau*, Oxford University Press for I.A.I 1960; C. W. Cole, *Report on Land Tenure*, Niger Province, Kaduna, Government Printer, 1949, expressed the point as follows: "In the reports on land tenure in the Kano and Zaria provinces, and in various memoranda and records submitted to the Northern Provinces Land Committee, there is repeated reference to the 'Habe Customs' with regard to land tenure and how they continue to prevail against outside influence in spite of the changes from Habe to Fulani", op.cit. p. 8. See also Dr. Last, op. cit. p. 160 et seq. and p. 305. Dr. Last has argued that offices in Sokoto seem initially to have been modelled after those of the early Caliphates as described in the Jihad literature e.g. Uthman's *Bayan Wujub al-hijra* and Abdullahis *Diya al-hukkam*. Also D. H. Bivar, 'Arabic Documents of Northern Nigeria', Bulletin *School of Oriental and African Studies*, vol. 22, 1959; and Hiskett, 'Kitab al-Farq', a work on the Habe Kingdoms attributed to Uthman dan Fodio, same journal, vol. 23, 1960.

34. Barth, *Travels in North and Central Africa*, Ward Lock, 1890, Minerva edition, p. 310. The complete text of Barth has been reprinted in three volumes with an introduction by A. H. M. Kirk-Greene by Frank Cass, 1966.

35. C. L. Temple, 'The Government of Native Races', *Quarterly Review*, October 1918, p. 312. A descriptive account of Kano in the nineteenth century is given by D. Whitlesley, 'Kano, A Sudanese Metropolis', *The Geographical Review*, vol. 27, no. 2, April, 1937.

36. Quoted in E. D. Morel, *Nigeria, Its Peoples and its Problems*, 1915, p. 135, new edition, Frank Cass, 1967.

37. See e.g. R. Robinson, J. Gallagher and Alice Denny, *Africa and the Victorians*, Macmillan, 1961, especially pp. 379–409.

38. Sir George Goldie has often been recognized as 'the founder' of modern Northern Nigeria. See R. S. Rattray, 'The Founder of Nigeria', *The Fortnightly*, April, 1935, pp. 443–54 and J. E. Flint, *Sir George Goldie and the Making of Nigeria*, London, 1960; D. Wellesley, *Sir George Goldie*, Macmillan, 1934.

39. Order-in-Council of December 27, 1899.

40. The details of British Occupation of Northern Nigeria will be found in *The Collected Annual Reports, 1900–1911*.

41. H. R. Palmer, *Sudanese Memoirs*, vol. 3, pp. 139–41.

42. "The Government utilizes and works through native Chiefs and avails itself of the intelligence and powers of governing of the Fulani caste in particular. If an Emir proves unamenable to persuasion and threats he is deposed and in each case a Fulani or other successor recognized by the people has been installed in his place". *Reports 1900–1911*, p. 26.

43. The full address is given in pp. 105–107 of the 1903 Report. Quoted section, p. 106.

44. This early attitude of the British subsequently led early social anthropologists to attribute the existence of 'chiefs' to such societies. See: A. J. N. Tremearne, 'Notes on the Kagoro and other Nigerian head hunters', *JRAI*, vol. 42, pp. 136–99; C. K. Meek, The Katab and their Neighbours, *Journal of the Royal African Society*, vol. 20, no. 112, July 1929 and his *Tribal Studies in Northern Nigeria*, 2 vols. But contra M. G. Smith, *Social Organization and Economy of Kagoro*,unpubl. MS., 1952, Colonial Office Library GN 653—39109F, and his, 'Kagoro Political Development', *Human Organization*, vol. 19, no. 3, 1960.

45. *Annual Report 1904*, p. 230.

46. Lugard, *The Dual Mandate in British Tropical Africa*, 1929, 4th edition pp. 205–7, Frank Cass 1965. It is obvious that 'Native Authority' is being used in two different senses. In one sense to refer to the Emir, in the other to refer to the administrative machine under the Emir.

47. Lugard, *Instructions to Political or other Officers on Subjects Chiefly Political and Administrative* (cover title: *Political Memoranda*, which is the title hereafter used), London, Waterlow & Sons 1906, pp. 190–202 (to be reprinted by Frank Cass). The 'traditional system' is discussed in the next chapter.

48. These 'gifts' became so problematic by the early 'fifties that the Government eventually was forced to abolish them. See *Report on the Exchange of Customary Gifts*, Government Printer, Kaduna, 1954.

49. Lugard, *Political Memoranda*, p. 92.

50. On the question of taxation as a whole, Lugard, op.cit. pp. 89–116.

51. Lugard, *The Dual Mandate*, p. 194. The standard work on Indirect Rule is M. Perham, *Native Administration in Nigeria*, London, 1937. See also, Hailey, *Native Administration in the British African Territories*, Part III, H.M.S.O. 1951.

52. Conference of Chiefs of the Northern Provinces, Summary of Proceedings, 1938 (Confidential), p. 20, 21.

53. Ibid., p. 31.

54. F. W. de St. Croix, *The Fulani of Northern Nigeria*, Lagos, Government Printer, 1944, p. 135.

55. C. F. Wright, ' "Indirect Rule", As an Afro-American Sees It', *West African Review*, Dec. 1943, p. 31.

56. M. Perham, 'Nigeria Today, The Rule of the Emirs', *The Times*, (London). 29th December, 1932.

57. R. H. Palmer, 'Future of the N.A.'s', *West African Review*, August 1939, p. 8; also R. H. Palmer, 'Indirect Rule in Nigeria—Growing Power of the Chiefs', *The African World*, 29th December 1928 and 26th January 1929; Rev. Dr. W. R. Miller, 'Criticism of British Administration in Nigeria—Wrong Attitude towards African Emirs', *West African Review*, Dec. 1943, pp. 29–37.

58. *A Day in the Life of a Nigerian Emir*, translated from an account by the Sultan of Sokoto, Commonwealth Leaflets no. 3, circa 1948.

59. Rules and Orders of the Legislative Council of Nigeria, Lagos, 1924, Article 41 (c) and (g). For details of Constitutional developments in Nigeria during this period see: J. Wheare, *The Nigerian Legislative Assembly*, Faber, 1950; K. Ezera, *Constitutional Developments in Nigeria*, Oxford, 1960; J. Coleman, *Nigeria: Background to Nationalism*, Berkeley, Los Angeles, 1958; O. Odumosu, *The Nigerian Constitution*, Sweet & Maxwell and African Universities Press, 1963.

60. Sir Ahmadu Bello, *My Life*, Cambridge, 1962.

61. The phrase is Miss Perham's, *Native Administration in Nigeria*, p. 326.

62. Lugard, *Political Memoranda*, p. 298.

63. M. Perham, op.cit., p. 327. It is not clear what Miss Perham means by "the good Resident", or what her "sense of chivalry" refers to.

64. Quoted from *A Note on Moslem Religious, Social and Political Movements in Nigeria*, Nigerian Secretariat, Lagos, 15th December, 1953, p. 5. Confidential.

65. M. Sai'd Hayatu is the son of Sai'd, who was a son of Sultan Bello and therefore grandson of Uthman dan Fodio. Sai'd I, disappointed on not becoming Sultan, quarrelled with his cousin, Sultan Abubakar Atiku, 3rd Sultan (1837–42) and went to Yola. The Adamawa Fulani took up his cause and have since become partisans of the Muhammed Bello branch. Hayatu, restricted by the British in 1923 first at Kano and later Buea in Southern Cameroons, was only released from exile in 1956. He now lives quietly in Kano.

66. See, G. J. F. Tomlinson and G. J. Lethem, *A History of Islamic Political Propaganda in Nigeria*, 2 vols., Waterlow & Sons, 1927.

67. *A Note on Moslem Religions, Social and Political Movements in Nigeria*, 1952. Unpublished, mimeographed.

68. Address to the Legislative Council, 6th March, 1933, published as *Supplement to Gazette Extraordinary 6th March 1933*, pp. 16–17. See also his, *The Principles of Native Administration and their Application*, Lagos, Government Printer, 1934.

69. Abubakar Imam, 'The Nigerian Constitutional Proposals', *African Affairs*, vol. 45, no. 178, Jan. 1964, p. 26. M. Imam is now the Chairman of the Northern Public Service Commission.

70. The North's representatives were: The Emir of Gwandu (Hon. Yahaya), Emir of Katsina (Usman Nagogo), Emir of Abuja (Sulemanu) the Attah of Igbirrah (Ibrahima) and Mallams Bello Kano, Tafawa Balewa, Iro Katsina, Aliyu Makaman-Bida and Yahaya Ilorin, the first to the fifth member respectively. In a letter to his District and Village Heads (quoted in the *Nigerian Citizen* (Zaria), 25th Feb. 1949), the Sultan of Sokoto queried the 'justice' of the North's representation despite the greater preponderance of the North's population. The question of representation is one not still satisfactorily settled as the dispute over the 1962/63 Census shows.

71. The four obnoxious bills were (i) The Minerals Ordinance 1945; (ii) The Public Lands Acquisition Ordinance; (iii) The Crown Lands (Amendment)

Ordinance; and (iv) The Appointment and Deposition of Chiefs (Amendment) Ordinance.

72. For details see, 'Nigerian Prospects', Pan-Africa, Oct.-Dec. 1947, pp. 101–102.

73. *Nigerian Daily Times* (Lagos), 20th September 1946.

74. Obviously, history was repeating itself in 1953, only then it had wider repercussions. See, *Report of the Kano Disturbances 16th–19th May 1953*, Lagos, Government Printer, 1953.

75. *Nigerian Daily Times*, (Lagos), 1st May 1947.

76. Legislative Council Debates, 24th March 1947, p. 212. Cf. also the speech by M. Aliyu Makaman Bida, the substance of which formed the Editorial of the *Daily Times*, 27th March 1947.

77. *Nigerian Citizen* (Zaria), 11th August 1949.

78. Contribution was in threepenny and sixpenny bits per person. By mid-December 1950, £23,000 had been collected. When the South gave way over the issue of representation, a 'Self Development Fund Committee' was formed to control the expenditure of the money collected in furthering education in the North. See *Nigerian Citizen*, 15th December 1950. Ultimately, a total of £47,697 4s. 9d. was collected, *Nigerian Citizen*, 2nd Aug. 1951.

79. Hicks and Phillipson, *Report of the Commission on Revenue Allocation*, Lagos, Government Printer, 1951.

80. Debates of the Eastern House of Assembly, vol. I, 1953.

81. Taking the per-capita income of the African population as an index of the level of capital formation, the position of the three regions is shown as follows:

	1950–51	1952–53
Northern Region	£15	£17
Western Region	31	34
Eastern Region	19	21

Source: The Economic Development of Nigeria—Report by the International Bank for Reconstruction and Development, Johns Hopkins, 1955, p. 398. See also Prest and Stewart, *The National Income of Nigeria 1950–51*, Lagos Government Printer, 1951.

82. For a 'Northern' viewpoint of these events, see, Sir Ahmadu Bello, *My Life*, Cambridge, 1962.

83. *Report on the Kano Disturbances*, Appendix B. p. 46.

84. *Population Census of the Northern Region of Nigeria 1952*, Lagos, Government Printer, 1953, pp. 10–11.

85. *Report of the Commission Appointed to Enquire into the Fears of Minorities and the Means of Allaying them*, Cmnd 505, 1958.

86. Nigeria adopted a Republican system of government in October 1963. The system described here is the pre-republican one. The change to Republicanism in no way affected the constitution of the Regions.

87. See S. A. de Smith, 'Westminster's Export Models', *Journal of Commonwealth Political Studies*, vol. I, no. 1, November 1961.

88. The Constitution provides for some Ministers to be chosen from the House of Chiefs.

89. The Provincial Commissioners Bill 1963. See also *Administrative Instructions to Provincial Commissioners and Provincial Secretaries*, Kaduna Government Printer, n.d.

90. See for a fairly concise account M. J. Campbell, *Law and Practice of Local Government in Northern Nigeria*, Sweet & Maxwell and African U.P. 1963.

91. Quoted from, *Nigerian Citizen*, 28th August 1950. The full speech is in Debates, N.H.A., 19th August 1950, pp. 91–98.

92. For a definition of these terms see, Native Authority Law 1954, section 2. Figures for 1950 are from, *Report on Local Government in the Northern Provinces of Nigeria*, by K. P. Maddocks, and D. A. Pott, Kaduna, Government Printer, 1951, and for 1958 and 1962 from M. J. Campbell, op.cit. For a description of the structure of the Native Authority, see pp. 242–44 below.

93. Northern House of Assembly, Debates, 11th March 1963, p. 152.

94. N.H.A., Debates, 13th March 1963, p. 275. President and Members of Native Courts, members of the N.A. Police Force and Prison Staff, may not contest elections. All other classes are allowed to.

95. Of the total of 1,667, traditional, nominated and elected members of the Native Authority Councils in the North, a total of 940, or over 50%, have been trained. This takes no account of the district, town, village, and outer councils. See Debates, 25th August 1962, p. 617.

96. See *Development Plan 1962–68*, Kaduna Ministry of Economic Plan, no date, for details of the new plan.

97. On the problem of unemployment amongst primary school leavers see A. Callaway, 'School Leavers and the Developing Economy of Nigeria' in R. O. Tilman & Taylor Cole (eds.), *The Nigerian Political Scene*, Duke University Press 1962.

II

Traditional Social and Political Organization

THE SOCIAL BASIS OF MODERN POLITICS

The current politics of Northern Nigeria cannot be understood without a background knowledge of the patterns of traditional social organization. This, immediately raises certain problems. The first and most obvious one is the considerable ethnic diversity to be found in Northern Nigeria. Besides the four main ethnic groups, the Hausas (or Habe), the Fulanis, Kanuris and Tivs, the 1931 census recorded over 200 other ethnic groups. This diversity entails differences in forms of social organization. Some principles of categorization will therefore be needed if any coherent description is to be given. Thus, the first problem turns on one of classification. For purposes of ease and economy in description, select groups, falling within the 'classes' delineated, may then be taken as paradigm cases of these classes. The second problem is one of orientation in description. Thus, the social anthropologist observing Tiv society for instance, may find himself concerned with Tiv kinship structure and coherence. For the political scientist examining the same society, the complexity and coherence of the kinship structure may be of a secondary importance to the actual location and use of power within the society. In the description of the traditional social systems, accordingly, emphasis will here be given to the 'political'.

I. ON CLASSIFICATION

It is now usual to begin discussions of the classification of African political systems from the first consistent attempt to do this by Fortes and Evans-Prichard. In their introduction to *African Political Systems*, they suggested a triple classification based on (a) societies in which there is a fusion of the political and kinship structure, (b) societies in which the lineage system forms a framework of the political system and (c) societies in which an administrative organization constitutes the basis of the political structure. But their main analysis concentrated on the latter two types, thereby effecting a simple dichotomy between societies with a 'state' organization (Type A) and those without, which were then named 'stateless societies' (Type B).[1] The differentiating criterion was seen to be the centralization of authority in the one, and non-centralization and diffusion of authority in the other.

Various criticisms have been made of this classification all of which turn on the interpretation of the term authority. Paula Brown, for instance, criticized the dichotomy on the grounds that it took too simple a view of the notion of 'authority' which Fortes and Evans-Pritchard interpreted principally as the exercise of political power. She made the point that there are various forms of authority, moral, ritual and legalistic and that other classifications are possible using these differing notions of the term.[2] M. G. Smith also pointed out the too easy identification between 'power' and the 'political' made by the editors of *African Political Systems*. This simple identification, he argued, ignores the differentiation between administrative procedures and political decision making. A lack of awareness of this differentiation obscured the fact that 'politics' is segmentary in character irrespective of the structural form which it assumes in society. Societies can therefore be classified in terms of the inter-relationship and interdependence between the various 'segments' of the political and the administrative.[3] Middleton and Tait, criticizing the A/B dichotomy noted that in societies lacking ranked and specialized holders of political authority, the relations of local groups to one another can be seen as a balance of power maintained by competition between them. On this basis they developed a typology of possible arrangements between lineages,[4] but as Dr. Mair rightly noted such a typology was scarcely an advance on that which they criticized as it was "without reference to the way in which each society conducts its political business".[5]

Other criticism of the A/B dichotomy has derived from the recognition that not all stateless polities without centralized government fall into the Class B category where the political structure is centred on the lineage framework. Eisenstadt drew attention to societies where 'age sets' and 'authoritative associations' are vested with political functions[6] while Lewis adopting a functionalist interpretation of politics would prefer to regard the Fortes and Evans-Pritchard classification as extremes on a wider continuum within which there are intermediary types.[7] Southall while accepting the dichotomy prefers the terminology of 'hierarchical power' societies and 'pyramidal social' societies.[8]

From the point of view of the political scientist, it would seem that much of the criticism of the classification in *African Political Systems* rests on a confused view of what is meant by politics and the main theme in politics, which, for our purposes, is taken as the study of 'power'.[9] Obviously, there is some confusion in the criticisms cited between political decision-making and various forms of social control[10] and if we take as the defining properties of a state such characteristics as territorial sovereignty, a centralized governmental system with specialized administrative staffs and the monopoly of the use of legitimate force,[11] it would follow that the analytical distinction made by Fortes and Evans-Pritchard is clear. Taking this definition of a state, we shall therefore in describing the 'paradigm' cases chosen, make a division between those societies with a state form and those societies without – the stateless societies. The first class is thus typified by the Habe–Fulani–Kanuri–Nupe 'states' where, on the whole, political and administrative roles are in different hands, and confined to certain sectors of the society. The 'stateless' society, on the other hand, is illustrated by the Tivs, the Bura, Pabir, Kagoro, Chawai, Ngizim, Kanakuru, Angas and many others.[12]

It is interesting to note, however, that before the Fortes and Evans-Pritchard classification was ever made, the ethnic diversity in Northern Nigeria prompted some attempts at a classification. Lord Lugard, for instance, attempted a categorization which closely parallels that found in *African Political Systems* though the principles of his classification were not explicitly stated. Thus he distinguished between the Centralized states, by which he meant the Fulani States and Bornu and the 'others' which he sub-divided into (a) independent states, chiefly pagan, ruled over by a 'responsible chief' such as the Boussa and Kiama in Borgu, Argungu in Sokoto and Gorgoran in West Bornu; (b) independent pagan states, "mostly in a low stage of development and owing allegiance to no single authority" such as the Bassa, and some of the peoples in Nassarawa, Muri and Yola provinces (these provinces no longer exist but are now 'districts' in Benue and Adamawa provinces respectively) and (c) pagan communities which were once under the Fulani but had thrown off the yoke of Fulani rule and refused to pay the tribute known as *Tawai*.[13] Lord Lugard, of course, based his classification on religious differences and existence or non-existence of a governmental system, for obviously the sub-division (a) but for religion, should have been included in the 'centralized states' while (b) and (c) would more properly constitute a class of 'non-centralized', 'stateless' societies.

Unlike Lugard, Meek adopted a tripartite classification into what he called "the unconsolidated" groups, "the consoldiated groups" and "class governments". For the unconsolidated groups, the village group was for all practical purposes autonomous and in general, "there was no central authority though it might happen that the heads of the various villages would meet for informal conferences under the presidency of the chief of the most ancient town. . . . But for all ordinary purposes the village group was politically independent, all disputes being settled by headmen and elders and all transgressions of tribal customs being punished by them."[14] Meek instanced the case of the pastoral Fulani or Fulanin Bororoje, whose migratory habits prevented anything like "regular political cohesion" and whose 'ruga' or encampment consisted usually of a few families, not always related.[15]

The consolidated groups were those who recognized "the authority of a central Chief". They might be grouped in a set of villages which was coterminous with the tribe or which form a single tribe. Alternatively, they might be a sub-tribe embracing different local groups or even different tribes. An instance of such a case with sub-tribes were the Tiv. Meek's use of the term 'tribe'[16] is not always clear and precise. In speaking of the Tivs as having 'sub-tribes', he is obviously confusing the word tribe with lineage segments of a tribe. Also, it is equally obvious that the distinction which Meek sought to make between 'the consolidated' and 'the unconsolidated' group is far from clear. The criterion, if any, of his distinction was one of the relative degree of cohesion within a given ethnic group. But in terms of the recognition of a central political force, there was no difference between the two groups, for he included the *Wajawa*, *Makangara* and *Kamuku* within the class of consolidated groups and noted that amongst them, there was "no supreme administrative authority" while "politically, they were independent". Each group recognized a head, the government being "analogous to that of the village".[17] It is equally obvious that, in our terms, both the 'unconsolidated' and the 'consolidated' groups come within the class of "stateless societies".

Meek's third category consisted of those who have reached a 'quasi-national stage', "a number of local tribes having lost their independence and become united to form kingdoms and empires".[18] They were "class-governments" because society was differentiated into royalty, nobility, commoners and slaves. Again, Meek makes no distinction between 'status' and 'class'.[19] The kingdoms could have either limited or absolute monarchy, though the latter was rarely to be found. Meek gave as examples of this group, the Jukuns, the Fulani Emirates and Bornu. By his reference to a 'quasi-national stage' of political development, Meek had in mind the defining properties of a state, as we have used it.

Summarily then, both Lugard's and Meek's classifications can be reconciled with that which is here adopted, one in fact which was current and formally recognised by, for example, Sir Donald Cameron when he wrote his 'The Principles of Native Administration and their Application'. By adopting this classification, we are thus keeping within known usage.[20] Empirically, there must be moments when a particular political system, in its development may be considered to be passing from one class to the other. But like all dichotomies it serves to bring out essential differences, which in effect forms its justification. In the following sections, an account of the centralized states will first be given, after which the 'stateless' societies will be considered.

II. THE CENTRALIZED STATES: THE HAUSA–FULANI EMIRATES

It has already been pointed out that with the Jihad, the Fulanis took over, though with some modifications, the old Habe systems of social and political organization. The pattern which they established and which is best known to us, is fairly uniform throughout the various Emirates. Though references will be made to the Bornu and Nupe social systems, the social organization of the Hausa–Fulani emirates will be taken as the paradigm of the centralized states of Northern Nigeria. To say that any particular structure is taken as the paradigm of such structures is to say that the particular system is being treated as a generalized model of such systems.

Social Stratification

Though the term 'Hausa–Fulani' Emirates has already been used without any specific distinction, it is important to note that in the Emirates with Fulani rulers, the Fulani use the term Habe (the traditional collective term for Hausa-speaking peoples) to distinguish non-Fulanis, and even extend this term to cover non-Habe pagan groups. In so using the term, Fulanis restate in ethnic terms the division between rulers and ruled common through the northern Emirates. But this is not to imply that all Fulanis fall within the class of the rulers and all Habes within the class of the ruled. Some Fulanis belong to the class of commoners and therefore the 'ruled' while some Habes are to be found in the group of the 'rulers'.

Both Fulani and Habe have a flexible kinship system, the stable elements of which as M. G. Smith pointed out, are the rigid application of the rule of male precedence, agnation as the basis of extended families and seniority by birth-order.[21] The household or compound is the familial unit, of which the head (*mai-gida*) is the senior male of the group. The mai-gida is formally responsible for all within the compound and the social placement of the individual within the society tends to be in reference to the status-position of the compound head. Children and women are regarded as legal minors and are therefore wards of any given, particular male.

The relative lack of social and political importance attached to women amongst the Fulanis and Habes is not, however, parallel in the other centralized states. Thus for instance, in traditional Bornu, one of the highest offices of state was held by the *Magira* who was the Shehu's 'official Mother'. She held one of the largest fiefs in the kingdom.[22] A roughly comparable situation was to be found in traditional Jukun society,[23] while in the pre-Jihad Nupe Kingdom, women held status-offices comparable to those held by men. Nadel pointed out that "the women rank-holders occupied an extremely influential position at the Court. They took part in the King's Council, they could join in the war with their own troops of slaves and serfs, they held fiefs and owned land."[24] These privileged positions have since disappeared. But in Bornu and Wukari (old Jukun) though not in Nupe, there is still evidence of some of the old authority vested in women.

In Hausa–Fulani society as a whole, certain basic distinctions are recognized, the most significant division is that between the nobility on the one hand (the rulers) and the commoners (or *takakawa*) the determinants of this bring birth and occupational differentiations. This distinction between rulers and ruled accordingly divides Hausa society into two clearly defined social strata, the one subordinate to the other.[25] The accident of birth determines whether one is a commoner or whether one belongs to the ruling class, a situation emphasized by the Hausa statement: "*Zuriyan Sarki ba talakawa ne ba*" ("The descendants of a chief never become commoners"). If, however, offspring of the nobility never become commoners, the children of the latter, through occupational preferments, may enter the ruling class and hence it is important to distinguish, within the 'nobility', or more appropriately, the notability, between the *Sarakuna* (or chiefs) and the *masu-sarauta* (or 'office-holders'). Membership of the Sarakuna is determined principally by birth, and the highest status is accorded to its members. Some of these may also hold 'offices' (*Sarauta*), such offices being usually hereditary. Hence, another distinction ought to be made between office-holders who inherit office (and therefore have 'ascribed status') *Karda*, and those who are freely appointed and recruited—*Shigege* (that is 'achieved status'). Obviously, *Karda* office-holders have a higher ranking than their *Shigege* counterparts and Hausa express this ranking by the term *Daraja* which may be rendered as 'prestige'. The correlation between *Daraja* and *Sarauta* also has significance in expressing social behaviour patterns. While pomp and an ostentatious display of affluence and influence is often to be expected of members of the *Sarakuna* and *Karda* office-holders, a similar display on the part of commoners who have been appointed to office is not looked upon with the same favour, distaste being expressed in statements such as: "*Yan fa talakawa ba dama; da sarauta su ke da gaske*" ("These commoners are quite impossible with the inflated airs they give themselves these days").[26]

The division of society into rulers and the ruled also has a parallel in the division based on the relative degree of servitude, and here the basic division is that between 'freeman' and 'slave'. In the traditional Habe systems, slaves played quite an important part in the political organization of the state. Smith pointed out that in Habe Duara in the nineteenth century, slave officials were powerful enough to effect the dismissal and appointment of chiefs as they pleased, and that in 1906 when the throne of the Fulani Daura fell vacant, slave officials of the royal houshold were able to select a successor without any reference to the free officials.[27] With time, however, they have lost their former importance, but two degrees of slavery may be noted. First, there were the domestic slaves or more properly, serfs—the *Churchenawa* or *Dimajai*. These quite often were descendants of slaves. They could farm on their own account but paid a 'tax' (*murgu*) to their masters or owning family (*Iyayengiji*), and could never be freely sold. Though freemen Muslims (*da* or *diya*) could not marry a slave by contract, they could take on 'slave-wives', the children in these cases being free.[28] Also, though slavery has been abolished in Nigeria, children of freemen (*yan tache*) and *dimajai* are still to be found connected by a relation of dependence and patronage to their former owners and masters, the latter referring to the former as talakawa (commoners), *bayi* (slaves) or *yanuwa* (kinsmen) depending on the context. '*Bayi*', the second group of slaves, were those who could be sold. They were treated as articles of exchange and used to form an essential part of the tribute paid by the various Emirs to their Sokoto overlord—the Sultan.[29] Their descendants today are to be found mainly as butchers, though this is not to say that all butchers are the descendants of slaves.

Status distinctions in terms of the nobleman and the commoner, the hereditary office holder and those appointed, freemen and slave, are not the only status gradations to be found in Hausa–Fulani society. Though agriculture is the main economic occupation of the people, large numbers are also engaged in commerce and industry. Generally, most occupations are hereditary, children following in the footsteps of their parents. The distinction made amongst political office-holders, between the *Karda* and the *Shigege* is thus equally applicable to economic groups. Hereditary occupations—and therefore relatively 'closed', being *Karda* pursuits—have a higher prestige (girma) attached to them than the self-chosen, *Shigege*, occupations.

Besides the *Karda* and *Shigege* distinctions, occupations are often ranked in terms of prestige (girma) which need not reflect economic success. The order of precedence, of course, varies from place to place, though there are certain common elements, as is shown in the following list[30] (precedence being shown in descending order).

Zaria	Bornu	Nupe
Attajirai (successful merchants)	Wealthy merchants	Wealthy merchants
Masu Sana'a (craftsmen other than those mentioned below)	Brokers, blacksmith	Brass-workers
Yan Kasuwu (small traders)	Leather workers	Carpenters & builders
Dillalai (brokers)[31]	Hunters	Barber-doctors
Manoma (farmers with unimportant subsidiary occupations)	Butchers	Bedworkers
	Drummer-entertainers	Leather-workers
Makira (blacksmiths)	Money-lenders	Weavers
Alaharba (hunters)		Butchers
Maroka and Makada (musicians and drummers)		
Mahanta (butchers)		

Each grouping has its own 'head' who in turn ranks higher than the other members of his occupational group. Traditionally, such a 'head' had the duty of collecting the occupational tax which was paid to the Chief. Thus in Zaria, Bornu and Nupe, wealthy merchants enjoy the highest prestige while in Zaria and Nupe, butchers have the least prestige. In Bornu this position is occupied by money-lenders. The difference here may be due to Fulani influence in both Zaria and Nupe, Bornu being Kanuri. There is a difference, however, between Nupe and both Zaria and Bornu. Occupational groups in Nupe tend to form more into craft guilds than in the other two areas named.

Thus, the 'glassmakers' guild—the oldest guild in Nupe—occupies a special place which does not appear in any ranking order. Similarly, Bornu has its own peculiarity. Though the 'shame' element (the rough converse of the prestige element) attached to any occupation increases as one goes down the scale of occupational grading, a distinction is made between those who take up these occupations out of economic necessity (*Khanziko*), which in a sense excuses the 'shame' attached to it, and those born into these jobs. The former thus enjoy a higher status than the latter and in these terms the situation in Bornu is diametrically opposed to that which obtains in the Hausa–Fulani Emirates, where *Karda* occupations have a higher prestige than *Shigege* or self-recruiting occupations.[32]

Taking 'office-holders' as an occupational group, and since such office-holding is one of the principal avenues towards acquiring wordly possessions, Hausas (as also Kanuris and Nupes) tend to rank office-holders with wealthy merchants and Koranic teachers or Mallams, who (in all three societies) form a fairly closed, hereditary, group in themselves.

In general therefore, one can, in terms of material wealth and economic pursuits, construct a three 'class' system of these societies. At the top will be the office-holders, the *Masu-Sarauta*, Mallams and wealthy merchants, and at the bottom, the butchers, musicians, drummers and in Bornu, money-lenders. The majority of the other occupations will then form the 'middle-class'. A model such as this is, as Smith noted, "consistent with several important patterns of Hausa Society. It embodies the popular distinction between the poor (Hausa–*Matsiyaci*; Kanuri, *Ngudi*), the moderately prosperous (Hausa–Madaidaici) and the rich or powerful (Hausa *Attajirai* and *Sarakuna*; Kanuri, *Galibu*)".[33] (There is no single Kanuri word for the moderately prosperous, a negation of both the 'poor' and the 'rich' giving the middle income person.)

It should be noted, however, that the boundaries between the classes and the status-orders within each class are not rigidly maintained. The main variables which determine individual membership in any class are birth or descent (Hausa–*Asali*) and wealth, the former being the more significant. Thus a man born of commoners usually remains a commoner, a craftman remains a craftsman and the ranks of the nobility are filled with men of noble birth. There exists, none the less, promotion within each status-order and a certain amount of inter-class mobility. The presence of relative inter-class mobility in fact prevents the system from being one of a hereditary caste. As Ginsberg has pointed out, the intensity of class cohesion is a function of the amount and case of social mobility within the class structure.

The negation of such mobility would turn social class into a caste structure.[34]

At this point, a note should be made that the varying status differentiations and the consequent class construct applies mainly to the urban centres. There is a greater lack of awareness of status differentiations in the rural or village areas.[35] In Nupe, for instance, "the higher and highest social orders were potentially attainable by all".[36] This difference in conditions in the urban and rural areas is also reflected in the attitude of urban and rural residents, the former tending to look down on the villagers, a point attested by Nadel when he wrote that "the commoners of the town, the people of no name or title, rank higher than the people . . . outside the capital, with their petty village titles and offices".[37]

A feature of this stratification which should be noted is that it is not only accepted, but also rationalized in the sense that attempts are made both to explain and to justify the structure. Here the central concept is the Hausa term *Arziki* (Kanuri *Arziyi*). Arziki, in general terms, may be translated as 'good fortune', a man's ability to have and to enjoy all that he desires without prejudice to others. A rise in the social scale is thus explained and justified by the possession of Arziki, while social failure or stagnation is due to the lack of the same Arziki. Thus, the term is used largely in two senses. In the first place, it is used to explain and to justify or validate the nature of the social structure itself. The two senses are obviously related and from this emerges a theory of society which, is 'holistic' with the individual having reference only in terms of the whole, a theory in many ways not unlike that of Bradley's in his essay on "My Station and its duties".[38]

Traditional Political Organization

The status orders which have already been noted were emphasized and enhanced by the political structure of the Hausa–Fulani State. In fact, it was this organization which lent meaning to the form of social stratification. In Hausa–Fulani society, the political structure and the system of social stratification were coterminous, the relations between the various strata being expressed, politically, in terms of clientage and fief-holding.[39] Structurally, the unit of organization was the compound or groups of compounds which composed the 'ward'. A village was then a collection of such wards while a group of villages, whether scattered or not, formed the fief which was held by a fief-holder. The totality of the fiefs within a definable area, together with the capital town—the seat of government—and the various vassal states, where these were to be found, was then the 'state', over

E

which the Chief, or Emir, ruled. Theoretically, the power of the Emir was absolute, but this was qualified where the state itself was a 'vassal' State of Sokoto, in which case, the ultimate reference of power lay with the Sultan. The complexity of relations which this 'model' gave rise to is best seen when each of the separate units is examined in some details.

As already noted, the minimal unit of organization was the compound, all members of the compound coming within the control of the compound head, or *mai-gida*. And just as the compound head was responsible for all within the compound, so was the ward head responsible, at one remove, for all members of the ward. But while the compound head was usually the most senior male of the compound, ward heads, or *Bulama*, as they were known in Bornu (Hausa-*Mai-Unguwa*) were appointed and dismissed by the village head, (Hausa-*Mai-Kasa*, Kanuri, *Lawan*,) who was the 'chief executive' of the village. His orders, which were binding on all within the village, were carried out by the respective ward-heads. The effectiveness of the role of the village chief thus depended on the extent to which he could control all factors of political significance within the village while ensuring support from his superiors. In order therefore to control the local community effectively, the village chief had to act, as much as possible, independently of the ward heads through the employment of personal, unofficial courtiers (*fadawa*) and retainers (*barori*) who in turn became clients of the local chief. In Hausa–Fulani society, the larger the number of clients—and therefore dependents and followers—an individual has, the greater is his prestige and the more he is esteemed. Thus, the chief's power *vis-à-vis* the village community was directly proportionate to the extent to which such intermediaries were used by him. Equally, to remain in their respective positions, ward-heads attempted to get themselves attached as much as possible to the chiefs intermediaries.

Nadel's statement that every Nupe village, as it constituted a separate community, also constituted a separate political system[40] is very much true of the Hausa–Fulani society. This means in effect, that at the village level, the various 'offices' of state (*sarauta*) were reproduced, 'ward heads' being appointed to such offices as *Makama*, Galadima and so on, the chief's closer associates being given the higher-ranking offices. The chief's power in appointing men to offices was not restricted only to 'offices' of state, but extended also to the headships of the various craft associations in the community. As such offices carried with them prestige and political influence, there was considerable competition for office which, paradoxically, acted as an integrative factor in maintaining the coherence and stability of the local community.

The chieftainship was thus the pivot around which the community revolved. Though in selecting chiefs overlords were not restricted to any one family and therefore exercised a considerable degree of freedom in the final choice, the office (*sarauta*) was open only to those families which in the past had supplied chiefs. In some areas the chiefship might be elective, though even here, the confirmation of the overlord was needed.

Some differences between the role of the village chief in Nupe on the one hand and in both Bornu and the Hausa–Fulani states should be noted. In all three cases, the village chief appointed his subordinate ward heads, but while in the latter areas, the power of the chief was total, in his own area subject to control from his superior, in Nupe the chief was aided in his administration of village affairs by a Council of titled elders (*Ticizi*) whose co-operation and advice he was bound to accept "as by a constitution in the modern sense".[41] Similarly, in the appointment of ward-heads, the village chief (*Zitsu*) in Nupe, had his freedom of action restricted in that "no 'house' may be excluded from the share out of village office, nor may one house own more than one title—at least not in theory".[42]

Just as the village head could, at will, appoint and dismiss the various ward heads, in like manner, he could also be appointed and dismissed at will by the overlord of the fief of which the village was a part. These fief-holders were the state officials, who generally resided at the capital of the state and were known as *Hakimi* in Kano, *Ubandaiki* in Zaria, *Kofa* in Sokoto, and *Ajia* in Bornu.[43] Because he was away from his district, the fief-holder supervised his holdings through staffs of titled subordinates or intermediaries (*Ajele* or *Jakadu*) whom he appointed and dismissed at will, and who were quite often given titles which defined the specific relationship between the intermediary and the fief-holder. Intermediaries dealt directly with the village heads and since these owed their status to the fief-holder, they invariably sought to maintain good relations with the intermediaries for example, through the presentation of gifts (e.g. *gaisuwa*, gifts or greetings). Intermediaries collected taxes of the village from the village head and as they generally were not paid for doing so, they retained a percentage of the taxes collected as their remuneration, just as the village heads themselves kept a fraction of the taxes they collected. In general terms, the function of the intermediaries was to supervise the fiefs and report certain classes of cases (crime and torts) to their superior. With the introduction of Indirect Rule which followed the British occupation of the North, this class of subordinate officials—the intermediaries—was abolished wherever possible, the fief-holders themselves, who then became District Heads, being required to reside in their districts and to carry out those functions which previously they delegated to their agents and clients.

Though fief-holders appointed intermediaries for the actual supervision of their fiefs, they in turn were ultimately responsible to the king or Emir for the well-being of their respective fiefs, and like the villageheads whom they appointed and dismissed at will, fief-holders were also appointees of the king and liable to dismissal by the king. It has already been noted that the fief-holders were state-officials but this does not imply that all state officials were fief-holders and hence the different categories of state officials should be distinguished. Certain features of the Kingship, however, should first be noted.

Generally, the Hausa–Fulani State was a mono-dynastic state, but this is not to say that all were monocratic states. Thus Kano, Sokoto, Katsina, and Bornu all had a single dynasty though with two segments (excluding Bornu) while Zaria had four and Nupe, three. Excluding Nupe for the moment, the existence of more than one dynasty (or more than one segment where there is a single-dynasty), would suggest dynastic (or segmental) rivalry for the throne whenever this fell vacant.[44] If rivalry was not to degenerate into open civil war, the existence of rules limiting dynastic competition would be an obvious presupposition, and M. G. Smith has noted for Zaria such a system of rules which he summarized as follows:

(a) Successive kings should not be chosen from the same dynasty.
(b) Only the sons of kings were eligible for promotion to the throne.
(c) Only those princes who had held or were holding territorial office were eligible for promotion.[45]

At this point, the difference between the main Fulani Emirates and Nupe may be noted. While the rules noted do not provide for any order of rotation of the kingship, Nupe maintained a strict 'order' of succession. Thus, of the three dynasties in Nupe, where one, at any given time, provided the Etsu-Nupe, his successor invariably was chosen from the second which happened to be the royal house of succession, the successor taking the title of *Shaba*. The head of the third dynasty or house then became known as *Kpotu*. On the death of the Etsu, the *Shaba* became Etsu, the *Kpotu* moved into the second line of succession and thus became in turn *Shaba*, while the head of the first house took the place of *Kpotu* thereby maintaining a rigid line of succession.[46]

However, for the purposes of delimiting the various categories of state officials, the rule which limited contenders for the throne to those princes who had held territorial offices suggests that every Emir on being chosen Emir, would appoint his own sons to the highest offices of state which went with control over one or more fiefs. And since the head of every dynasty sought to prevent segmentation of the dynasty while enhancing its cohesion, the practice of appointing the Emir's immediate relations to offices of state was carried further to include the various categories of relations. All such offices became restricted to members of royal nobility and three status orders of these may be differentiated. Those restricted to the Emir's sons (*sarautun 'yan Sarki*), those restricted to the Emir's patrilineal grandchildren (*ji kokin Sarki*), and those allocated to his affins (*dangi wajen mace*).[47] From this, it can be seen that every new Emir sought to appoint his own sons and kinsman to offices of state with the consequence of a high turnover in nearly all offices of state and discontinuity in administration. A bureaucratic organization in the sense of Max Weber[48] can hardly be expected to develop under such conditions, for bureaucracy, as currently understood, presupposes, amongst other things, continuity and impersonalization of office and fairly well known rules which govern promotion within the ranks of the bureaucracy. It is precisely these conditions, however, which the Fulani system lacked.[49] Even though part of British policy in the North was the stabilization of the status of native-authority personnel—the former officials—it can be seen from the statement of Sir R. Palmer already quoted (p. 17 above), that this did not succeed and that the old habits still continued. In '*Native Administration in Nigeria*', Miss Perham cited instances in Kano where the late Emir Abbas substituted his personal relations on succeeding to the throne. A similar policy was also followed by the ex-Emir, Sanusi of Kano, despite promises which he made on being elected Emir in 1954.[50] In Zaria, of the twenty-eight districts in the Emirate, the Emir's sons and relations controlled twenty-five, while Dr. Cohen showed that in Bornu, between 1900 and 1960, in four of the twenty-one districts which he studied, the range of tenure of office of District heads was five to nine years though tenure was supposed to be for life (under British administration at least till 1959) and that of the thirty-eight persons who had held office in the four districts 79% were dismissed and replaced, in each case by the Shehu's favourites.[51]

The second category of officials to be distinguished are the non-royal offices. These were held by freemen, Fulani and Habe, some of these holding fiefs. Such fief-holding offices were gradually transferred to kinsmen of the King. Occupants of such offices, however, were clients[52] of the King and as such were subject to the King. Within this category were the officials of the King's household who lacked fiefs. Slave officials who also lacked fief-holdings and who were gradually replaced by freemen were in this class. Finally, one should distinguish specialized offices which were held in particular lineages, such as the office or order of Mallams. Thus, either directly or indirectly, the King controlled all offices within the state, a power which tended to make him an absolute ruler.

The different categories of state officials which we have so far considered will be more properly shown when we consider for instance, the Nupe State where 'constitutional' principles were carried the furthest of all the centralized Emirates in the North. The first 'order' of officials, the royal nobility, headed by the Etsu, the *Shaba* and the *Kpotu* has already been mentioned. They conjointly formed the élite (the *Ena Gitsuzi*) of the state. Under them came those in the second category: the titled nobility who were not members of the royal lineages. This second category, the *Towni*, or turbanned officials were equal in political influence to, if they did not actually surpass, the *Ena Gitsuzi*, for while princes of rank were admitted to the *Nko*, the Council of state which advised the King (and whose advice the King was bound to accept), they exercised little influence upon the actual work of government.[53] This was entrusted to the *Rowni*, who were freely appointed officers of state. Whatever influence the *Ena Gitsuzi* had, came from the fact that they owned the larger and most of the fiefs in the State.

The *Rowni*, or titled officers of state, were in turn differentiated into the civil and military nobility (the *Sarakizi*); the judicial officers and the clergy (the *Ena Manzi*) and the court slaves (the *Ena Wuzi*). The first group, with some exceptions, was open to freemen commoners. Office was vested in the individual, promotion within the group being made by the King-in-Council. The Members, however, received no salaries but were given fiefs and landed property. Also since the 'order' was promotional and appointment made by the King, the significance of office, in terms of status-ranking, fluctuated.

As specialized knowledge was a prerequisite of office, the order of the *Ena Manzi*, unlike the *Sarakizi* tended to be rigidly hereditary. The members thus formed "a class between the classes, a mobile, privileged intelligentsia".[54] The *Ena Wuzi*, unlike the previous two 'orders', were a select group usually made up of members of the nobility of the other tribes who were captured. In the early part of the nineteenth century, some of these were appointed to the highest offices of rank in the 'order' of the *Sarakizi* and therefore owned land and fiefs, though, since the latter part of the nineteenth century, they have lost these privileges and become the lowest in rank. The *Ena Wuzi* is more comparable to the similar rank-order in the traditional Habe system which operated before the coming of the Fulanis, examples of which were to be found in the Habe Kingdoms of Abuja, Argungu and Daura.[55] (Since the Fulani conquest, however, the organization in these original Habe States has tended to follow the Fulani system.)

This account serves not only to bring out more clearly the categories of state officials but also points out some of the differences between the Nupe and the Hausa–Fulani systems. One such difference is the role of the Council of State in the political organization of the state. In the Fulani States, there was hardly any place for a 'Council of State. The Emir dealt directly with all the various classes of officials, relying on particular 'councillors' for advice, such councillors being the trusted office-holders of the King, but as these were very likely to hold different offices when a successor came to the throne, there was little opportunity for the creation of a Council similar to the Nupe *Nko* to develop. The only comparable situation to the Nupe was the Jukun Kings Council.[56] In Bornu where there was a Council (the *Nokena*—whose members were known as the *Kokenawa*)—the Council had no real power and was thus functionally different from the Jukun and Nupe Councils.[57] Bornu, like Sokoto, however, had a characteristic peculiar to it. Unlike the other states where power was centralized in the King, the situation in Bornu and Sokoto approached more to a dual monarchy, the Waziri or Prime Minister sharing power with the Sultan or the Shehu as the case may be. Though ultimate power rested with either the Sultan or the Shehu the control of the administration, appointment of fiefs, promotion and dismissal, was done largely by the Waziri who thus became the next most powerful individual in the state.[58]

In the other Fulani States, the power of the King or Emir was qualified, in their external relations, only by their relation to Sokoto or Gwandu. Towards the end of the nineteenth century even Gwandu had come to recognize the suzerainty of Sokoto in both political and religious contexts as the letters from Umaru Bakatara, tenth Emir of Gwandu (1888–97) to Sarkin Mussulumi Abderrahman, 11th Sultan of Sokoto (1891–1902) show.[59] The suzerainty of Sokoto was recognized by annual tributes from the various Emirs to the Sultan, the appointment[60] and confirmation in office of Emirs by the Sultan, and his right to arbitrate disputes between Emirs and decide matters of succession.[61] The relation was actually one of vassal and overlord. As has already been pointed out in the previous chapter, the extent to which this relation survived during the nineteenth century up till the coming of the British has very often been underestimated.

In this account of the traditional system of political organization, we have so far ignored the place of the 'vassal' territories within the main structure of the Fulani State, a relation not dissimilar to that between the Emir and the Sultan of Sokoto. These vassal territories were usually areas inhabited by the non-Hausa–Fulani peoples conquered by the Fulani. Here a distinction should be made between areas on the periphery of the state, and those which were closer to the capital. In Zaria, for instance, examples of the former would be Keffi, Idoma, Nassarawan kwotto, Jema'an Dororo and Bagaji, while instances of the latter were Kajuru, Fakita, Kagarko Lere and Durum. There were some differences between the two. Two such differences may be noted. Firstly, though the chieftains of each of these areas resided in their respective territory and were indigenous, the chieftains in the proximate vassal areas exercised more limited powers than those in the peripheral territories. Secondly, heads of proximate vassal areas, unlike the peripheral, were chosen and dismissed by the Emir and, not infrequently, were placed under the over-all supervision of some fief-holder. The distinction between peripheral and proximate vassal territories was not only to be found in the Fulani States, but was also applied in the Bornu Empire where the practical independence of areas like Kotoko and Logon distinguished them from others like Keri-Keri, Gummel and Bedde.[62]

Summarily, the Hausa–Fulani States were centralized, hierarchically organized, feudal states[63] with the King or Emir (ignoring Sokoto) as an almost absolute autocratic ruler. He relied on a body of state officials who exercised powers similar to that of the Emir, though delegated, for the day-to-day administration of the state.

The corollary of the power-structure was an almost equally absolute duty of obedience on the part of the mass of the citizens, a duty which was in no way abated by Islam, which enjoins on its members a seemingly unconditional subservience to the ruler.[64] The society, though structurally differentiated in status and class terms, was, nevertheless, closely knit by the ties of vassalage and clientage. State and society rested on the framework of the separation of political power (centralized in the king) from the administration with its elaborate fiscal machinery and separate judiciary. Social relationships were thus defined mainly in terms of relations between superior and subordinate, master and dependant.[65] These socio-political relationships have important consequences for modern developments which will be taken up later in this chapter. Attention will, however, next be directed to the 'dispersed' societies of the North.

III. THE NON-CENTRALIZED, DISPERSED SOCIETIES OF THE NORTH

If in their social and political organization, the centralized societies of the North reveal a considerable degree of structural uniformity, such a symmetry is not to be found amongst the dispersed societies, the only factors common to all of them being their structurally loose organization and the amalgamation of, or rather the lack of, a distinction between the 'political' and the 'social'. The variation in structural form is only paralleled by the differences in population size to be found amongst the various groups—sizes which range from the Owe (551 total) of Kabba Province, the Bussawa (8,021) and Bura (13,709) of Ilorin and Bauchi provinces respectively to the Igbirra (147,630), Birom (116,212) of Kabba and Plateau provinces and the largest—the Tivs (718,619) of Benue[66] province. The size of the Tiv population may be taken as a justification for constituting them the paradigm of such societies. If any further justification seems to be needed, the fact that they are the best documented of all such societies and also, the fact that they, almost alone, constitute at present the one single ethnic group in opposition to the Hausa–Fulani–Kanuri triumvirate of the North, may be cited.

Social and Political Organization

Probably the most noted fact about the Tivs is their extreme individualism, an attitude to be found, to the same extent, only amongst the Ibos of Eastern Nigeria.[67] Structurally, they are organized into septs of which there are five, while each sept is made up lineally of 'clans', kindred groups or sub-clans and finally a family or groups of families.[68] The basic organization, however, is in terms of a lineage system which is formulated in genealogies running back patrilineally from any one individual to the original Tiv. The genealogy represents a lineage system, segments of which can be considered from two points of view: in terms of span, composed of living people (*nongo*) and in terms of a unilateral descent group (*Ityo*). Ityo is a personal and particularistic concept which serves to identify the place of the individual specifically, within the complex web of Tiv social relationships.[69] Nongo on the other hand is an impersonal term referring to any lineage span and to the lineage group. It thus defines and places the living members of any given lineage segment (*Uipaven*). The terms Uipaven and Nongo can both be applied to any segment, but while there can be fission within the segment Uipaven, segmentation cannot take place in a Nongo, as this unit has no land of its own. The minimal unit or community associated with a territorial space (*Tar*) is thus the Uipaven. The *Tar*[70] is the territorial segment and therefore has political relevance. It should be noted, however, that the territorial community is not composed only of members of the same agnatic lineage. It also includes kinsmen and strangers—non-Tivs who have been given temporary rights of residence and cultivation. Also while fission can take place within the territorial segment two minimal segments (*Utar*) which adjoin each other can also fuse to form a larger, more inclusive unit which is then named after the common ancestor. (Each segment gets its name from its immediate lineage ancestor.)

The process of fission and fusion and cross-kin membership which is consequent on the segmentary lineage structure has the effect of maintaining the whole system in equilibrium at any given time and as Melvin Ember has written, in a different context, the lineage structure "implies a non-centralized distribution of political authority on a local level, it likewise implies a non-centralized distribution of authority on a supra-local level."[71] The authority of any one individual is thus restricted only to his lineage segment, the 'elder' of the segment having authority only over those members of his lineage segment. Segmentary competition and conflict is thus the rule rather than the exception, this lineage rivalry being suppressed, though never absent, only in times of stress, as for instance, during times of external aggression, when the whole of Tiv come together and act as a unit. This competition and rivalry limits the authority of the 'elder' or leader to the internal affairs of his segment only, the extent of the limitation varying with the contexts of action. A diagrammatic representation[72] will serve best to illustrate how far this limitation can be carried. Thus as against A, X is the 'leader' of B, and to A, X represents B. Within B, however, X represents only '4', while within '4', he represents only 'h'.

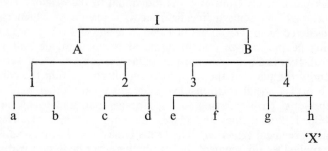

Such an extreme fragmentation of authority can hardly allow for the development of a chief. As Akiga put it "the conception of executive Chieftainship is foreign to the Tiv".[73] In Tiv terms therefore, one can only legitimately talk of a 'leader' and hardly ever of a 'chief'. But if Tiv social organization makes it impossible to use the term 'chief' meaningfully, it also poses certain dilemmas for leadership, as the Bohannan's have shown. Firstly, there is the 'individual dilemma'. "A leader immediately becomes the object of attention and in a society where magical beliefs are still prevalent, he becomes a possible target of mystical and physical malice." The Bohannan's emphasize this point by noting that "Tiv egalitarianism is more concerned with whittling everyone down to the same size than with giving every one the same chance."[74] The second dilemma is a social one, and here, the segmentary principles inherent in Tiv social structure which places in opposition groups of equivalent size, militates against the internal unity of any single segment.

From the account so far given, it should be obvious that any form of socio-political stratification in terms of birth, status-ranking, occupational differentiation, ethnic identity, patterns of urban-rural residence such as characterize Hausa–Fulani society, will be foreign to the Tiv. Equally, the distinctions between the political and administrative, between the social and the political, would be unintelligible to the Tiv. Leadership becomes not a function of certain socially recognized and predetermined variables, but of individual merit and ability coupled with a knowledge of ritual processes and functions. The conception of 'office' in Max Weber's terms[75] and as known in the centralized states is thus unrecognized in Tiv society.

However, to say that there is no specifically recognized set of variables determining socio-political stratification is not to say that Tivs recognize no distinctions in their society, however, elementary. Thus, they distinguish between 'elders' and 'men of affluence and prestige'. Such distinctions are in fact common to almost, if not all, African societies. The Elders are, as the term suggests, the older members of the local community who are duly respected because of their age, though they may have little or no influence whatsoever. Due to their age, they are supposed to be possessed of ritual knowledge which in itself entitles them to recognition and certain privileges. Though they exercise little, if any, political power, collectively and individually, they are sought after for advice on problems affecting the community as a whole. In times of stress from external sources affecting the whole of Tiv, from the elders may be chosen, or they may choose, a 'chief' to lead the entire people. (It is this practice which the early British administrators misinterpreted to mean that the Tivs had a chieftaincy system). Even under such conditions, to quote Akiga again, "they (the elders) had no intention that he (the chief) should usurp their 'authority' but simply that he should be the instrument by which this 'authority' would be enhanced. . . . They took pains to ensure that their protégé should not lose sight of his true position as (one) who held 'office' only by their grace and whose behaviour was strictly subject to their control".[76]

Besides the 'elders' then, there are the men of affluence and prestige. But it is characteristic of the Tivs that wealth must be displayed, for stinginess is something abhored. Through wealth, the individual may acquire slaves and dependents. These add to his physical force but never his 'authority', this being a correlative of office and a hierarchical form of organization—properties which, as we have seen, were not a feature of the society.

Though Tiv was taken as the paradigm of the dispersed, un-centralized, non-hierarchically organized societies, it is worth repeating that it is not being suggested that all the societies grouped under this category exhibit precisely the same characteristics. Some of these societies share the same segmentary principles, which are comparable in content with Tiv, others not. In each case, the political significance of these principles varies from one group to the other. All such societies, however, lack any recognized system of chieftaincy as this is understood in the Hausa–Fulani states. Of the Ngizim of Bornu, Chawai of Zaria, Bura and Pabir, and the Mambila of Adamawa,[77] certainly there is no known chief, nor any formal system of social stratification in terms of status orders or 'class'. Possibly the only way of showing the variability of social systems grouped under this category is by discussing briefly the social organization of some of the ethnic groups classed under this category of dispersed societies. The Biroms and Idomas may be selected for this purpose, not only because they are again fairly large groups, but also because they (especially the Biroms) are in some degree, in a 'transitional stage'. As has already been pointed out, while the analytical distinction between the two classes of centralized and non-centralized societies is clear, empirically, some societies will be found to be in some sort of a transitional stage, when they may be considered to pass from one to the other. The criterion of passage, as Southall rightly pointed out, must be Weber's concept of legitimacy.[78] It is in this context that Birom social and political organization is particularly interesting.

The Idomas, who are to be found in Benue province, are made up of a congeries of small ethnic groups, the common characteristic of which is the similarity of language and customs.[79] Like that of the Tivs, who are their near neighbours, Idoma social organization is based on a lineage system, the basic structural unit being the extended family in which the 'elder' is directly responsible for all the members of his compound. The lineage structure, however, makes the internal unity of the lineage segment problematic, with the result that fractionalization is characteristic of all Idoma groups. Social differentiation therefore tends to be in terms similar to that of the Tivs—distinctions being based on age and personal attributes. Contrasted with the inhabitants of the Hausa–Fulani States with their elaborate social stratification system, the structure of Idoma society in these terms is rather simple.

What is interesting, however, is that not being strictly a homogeneous group like the Tivs, for instance, the pressure of external forces and competition for land use, have resulted in concern with unity and consequent attempts at evolving a system of chieftaincy. Hence a strong concern with chieftaincy as an institution—with an elaborate ideology on the subject—is common with the Idomas. But, as Armstrong noted, "fractionalization makes it improbable that the Idoma had any chiefs as such".[80] A chieftaincy system implies the recognition of an individual as the chief and the legitimation of the power exercisable by that individual acting in his official capacity. It is precisely this attribute which is lacking amongst the Idomas. The main contrast with the Tivs on this subject has been that with the policy of Indirect Rule of the British, the attempt to create a chief has been more readily acceptable to the Idomas than to the Tivs, the possible explanation being the existence of an ideology of chieftaincy amongst the Idomas but not the Tivs.

The Biroms of Plateau Province are scattered through some eighty villages in the Birom tribal areas, but they were only federated into a single unit in 1935. Though there was unity through language, customs and other forms of culture, there was traditionally no integration between the villages. Nevertheless, some villages had closer ties than others, and it is possible therefore to group the villages into three sectors—an east, west and southern sector, a division which Birmos themselves recognize.[81] The basic unit of political organization was thus the village, while the only wider unit was the village sector.

Though kinship was based on a lineage system, unlike the Tiv, this was not internally differentiated along lines of structural subdivision. The Biroms lack any formal hierarchical organization, the social unit being the extended family consisting of members of an agnatic lineage which in some cases are localized to form a clan but as Tanya Baker pointed out, such clans "are not linked to one another by genealogical or fictional ties and tend to be small".[82] Unity between the clans in any village was maintained not by lineage or affinal ties but through the common recognition of the village head, the village spirits and priests, though, not infrequently, the village head and the village priest were one and the same person. In such a case, his role as a 'head' was secondary to his role as a priest. But in no case was there any recognition of a political authority inherent in the role of the village head. This is clearly illustrated in the cases of succession to the village headship or chiefship.

Succession was within the lineage. In some cases, brother succeeded in order of birth in which case there was no question of choice. In others, sons succeeded their fathers, while in sub-villages, succession had to be confirmed by the chief of the senior village. The confirmation was, however, of a ceremonial and ritual nature. To quote Dr. Baker again, there was in any case "no suggestion of political authority in that recognition".[83] The true role of the chief is in fact suggested in the terminology adopted by the Biroms. The Chief was Da Gwom (Da = father and Gwom = Chief), the chiefly role being a recognition of an associated priestly office. The chief was therefore more properly described as the 'elder' of the village and not the political authority.

In this respect, Biroms can be seen as evolving towards a chiefly system. Such a role can only be said to exist when the office of the chief is recognized in terms of stated authority. This comparative lack of stated authority explains the fact that though village headship is inherited, Biroms make no distinction between members of chiefly lineages and those of others, and Biroms have no word comparable to the Hausa *Talakawa*. That word was borrowed in recent times from the Hausa. The dispersed nature of Birom political and social organization is seen, lastly, in the fact that no organization united all the villages into one integrated unit. "The political units of the Birom were therefore smaller than the tribe."[84]

Summarily, the essential characteristics common to all the societies discussed here, in spite of their different social systems, are seen to be a lack of role differentiation and a non-hierarchical social structuring. As Dr. Apthorpe has put it, in these societies "political and administrative roles are most commonly not allocated to this or that sector of society. Not least is this because the egalitarian principles which inspire such societies lead to a lateral repetitiveness of form rather than a society with hierarchical structure."[85] The differences between the centralized and non-centralized societies have certain implications for social and political change. With the impact of modernity on these societies, changes in the economy, educational influences, political development and so on, it is hardly to be expected that the reaction of these two types of societies will be similar. The implications which these differences have for socio-political change is thus a question which has to be considered. The tentative suggestions which will be offered may in fact be regarded as hypotheses to be verified or refuted by the subsequent analysis of current political institutions and practices.

One may take as a starting point, the contention by Lloyd Fallers that "the societies with hierarchical, centralized political systems incorporate the Western type of civil sevice structure with less strain and instability than do societies having other types of political systems, e.g. segmentary ones".[86] This contention ignores the nature of the changes being introduced, the impact of such changes and the level of social mobilization found in any of the societies, variables which in themselves will obviously influence the relative degree of receptivity and adaptability of either type of society to socio-political change.[87] In fact, the argument rests on the premise that the existence of role-differentiation, for instance, between administrative and political authority, makes the centralized societies more adaptable to the introduction of modern bureaucratic systems which presuppose such a differentiation of roles. This is the underlying assumption of Apter's argument which sought to demonstrate that the centralized type of polity is "highly resistant to political rather than other forms of modernization and in particular cannot supplant easily the hierarchical principle of authority with a representative one".[88]

However, neither Fallers nor Apter have provided any empirical evidence to support their contentions. There is no logical or empirical reason why the existence of role-differentiation by itself, should make any one society more adaptable to innovation than any other, and Apter's hypothesis that a hierarchical authority stemming from a single king can innovate much more easily than any other type of authority is highly disputable. As has already been noted, the centralization of power in the hands of the Emir which places him in a position to control all appointments in the state, the relations of clientage and vassalage which are necessarily associated with the hierarchical organization found in such societies and which place a premium on loyalty to the exclusion of other considerations, the toleration of maladministration but not impartiality, all of these militate against and are dysfunctional of, a bureaucratic system (at least within the local structure). Such a structure as has already been pointed out presupposes inter-alia, continuity in office, impartiality in official promotions and the impersonalization of office, a premium being placed on administrative efficiency rather than on personal loyalties as such. Given considerations such as these, it might be more plausible to suggest that the dispersed societies are much more receptive to change than the centralized polities. Such a supposition would seem more probable when note is taken of Apthorpe's suggestion that the non-centralized states at least have the advantage that their lack of an ordered hierarchy (or hierarchies) would offer no rival structure to that being sponsored, a circumstance which facilitates receptivity to change.[89]

Whatever may be the merits of either argument, it is nevertheless true that if an organization is established for the explicit purpose of realizing specified objectives, it is expected to be governed by the criterion of efficiency. An organization so governed can be defined as a bureaucracy,[90] for bureaucratization implies that considerations of efficiency outweigh all others in the development and formation of the organization. From this standpoint, it can legitimately be claimed that the argument of adaptability as posed by the proponents is misguided. Neither argument obviously can be empirically demonstrated if only because the rationale of the arguments has been geared to a consideration of the formal characteristics of a bureaucratic system without any objective criterion of judgment being proposed. In the subsequent discussion of grass-roots politics, the criterion of efficiency will be adopted in assessing the performances of local, that is, Native Authority organizations. It should then be possible to decide whether there is any correspondence between social structure and the efficiency of a given organization—all other factors being taken as constant.

Other issues can be envisaged, for instance, the nature and stability of leadership. With non-centralized societies, as has already been shown, this tends to be collective rather than personal. In a party political context, this would have the effect of producing incessant conflicts and differences of opinion amongst the ranks of the leadership, with the constant fractionalization and splintering of ranks. Since the authority of the individual leader is limited to his immediate followers and supporters and does not extend to cover other members of the party, the crisis of party leadership will pose the problem of party loyalty which will be intensified where the party embraces more than one ethnic group. As leadership comes to be institutionalised, or rather legitimised, these problems would tend to decrease. One can therefore generalize and say that the level of party cohesion in such circumtances would be functionally related and directly proportional to the degree to which an institutionalised leadership has been attained. With centralized societies on the other hand, because leadership tends to be personalized, be it in one person or group, the possibility for taking quick and effective decisions is greatly enhanced. Conflicts, either within the leadership or amongst the rank and file, are more easily resolved, the leadership being relatively unfettered by prearranged rules.

The problems of leadership are immediately relevant to the question of the structure and nature or more simply, the typology of parties. Because of the egalitarianism of the non-centralized areas parties in such societies would tend to be of the 'mass' type. There is thus an emphasis on party membership, regular meetings and elections of leaders. With the centralized states, the structuring of the society would tend to produce a party based on 'status' differentiations. Weber makes the distinction between parties based on 'status situations' and those based on 'class situations', though both may be combined.[91] 'Status' based parties tend to terminate their structure with the adherence of the influential members of the society, influence being defined in economic (wealth) and political (power or authority) terms. These invariably are the 'chiefs' and, or their direct representatives. Emphasis thus turns on the inclusion of such chiefs and not on the party, as a collectivity. With a change in emphasis which concentrates attention on the party as such, a status based party would be confronted with conflicts between the 'traditional' and the 'modern' elements within it. Though such conflict situations may be inherent in the status-based parties, it will readily be appreciated that this type of party, unlike the 'mass' type provides hardly any setting in which opposition is possible. Where such opposition exists, its ideological expression tends to be formulated in status and class terms. In general, political participation amongst such opposition groups tends to be more negative than positive in character.[92]

Finally, while it may be accepted that disaffection within the ranks of the mass-type party may lead to a weakening of the party, the suggestion that in the status based parties, this will lead to a disintegration of the party cannot be taken too seriously.[93] Though this may be a possible consequence, it can only be one amongst other possibilities. In practice it seems much more probable that in status-type parties disaffection may lead to a functional restructuring of the party.

These themes, or rather hypotheses, will be developed and tested in subsequent chapters. The immediate question is to see how parties developed in these societies, for as Avery Leiserson noted: "The political party, or party system, provides the major connective linkage between people and government, between separate, formal agencies and officials of government, and between official and non-official (extra-governmental) holders of power".[94] The development of the party system and the role of parties within the political structure will thus be the topic of the remaining chapters.

F

NOTES

1. E. E. Evans-Pritchard and M. Fortes, *African Political Systems*, Oxford, 1940, pp. 6–7.
2. Paula Brown, 'Patterns of authority in West Africa,' *Africa*, vol. 21, 1951, pp. 261–78. Also Phyllis Kaberry, 'Primitive States', *British Journal of Sociology*, vol. 8, 1957, pp. 224–34.
3. M. G. Smith, 'On Segmentary Lineage Systems', *Journal of the Royal Anthropological Institute*, vol. 86, 1956, pp. 38–80.
4. J. Middleton and D. Tait, *Tribes Without Rulers*, Routledge and Kegan Paul, 1958, Introduction, pp. 1–31.
5. Quoted from J. Apthorpe, 'The Introduction of Bureaucracy into African Politics', *Journal of African Administration*, vol. 12, no. 3, July 1960, pp. 130. Dr. Apthorpe accepts the analytical distinction made by Fortes and Evans-Pritchard. See his 'Political Change, Centralization and Role Differentiation', *Civilizations*, vol. 10, no. 2, 1960, pp. 217–22.
6. S. N. Eisenstadt, 'African Age Groups', *Africa*, vol. 24, 1954, pp. 100–13. Also his, *From Generation to Generation*, Routledge and Kegan Paul, 1961.
7. I. M. Lewis, 'The Classification of African Political Systems', *Rhodes–Livingstone Journal*, no. 25, March 1959, pp. 59–69.
8. A. Southall, *Alur Society*, Cambridge University Press, no date, pp. 250–52.
9. Lasswell and Kaplan, 'The Science of Power ... is the Science of politics,' *Power and Society*, London, Routledge, 1952, p. 82.
10. See E. Coulson, 'Social Control and Vengeance in Plateau Tonga Society', *Africa*, vol. 23, 1953, pp. 199–212. The distinction Coulson seeks to make between 'Social Control' and 'political control' is also brought out by D. Forde in *The Native Economies of Nigeria*, M. Perham (ed), p. 121, footnote 1 and C. K. Meek, *Law and Authority in a Nigerian Tribe*, Oxford University Press, 1950, Introduction p. xiv. The distinction can also be expressed in terms of the difference between Weber and Durkheim in their use of the term 'social control'.
11. Cf. S. F. Nadel, *A Black Byzantium*, Oxford University Press, 1942, p. 69.
12. The literature in these societies in Northern Nigeria, is now fairly extensive. See some of the references cited in footnote 6, chapter I. Others not shown there are A. J. N. Tremearne, 'Notes on the Kagoro and other Nigerian Headhunters', *Journal of the Royal Anthropological Institute*, vol. 38, 1908, pp. 58–98; T. M. Baker, 'Social Organization of the Birom', unpublished Ph.D. Thesis, London 1954; E. S. Fegan, 'Some Notes on the Bachama Tribe', *Journal of the African Society*, vol. 29, no. 115, 1930 and no. 116, 1931; R. Mohr, 'Social Organization of the Angas', *Anthropos*, vol. 35, nos. 3 and 4, 1958, pp. 457–72; C. K. Meek, 'The Kulu in Northern Nigeria', *Africa*, vol. 7, 1934, pp. 257–69, and 'The Katab and their Neighbours', *Journal of the African Society*, vol. 28, no. 112, 1929; M. G. Smith, *The Social Structure of the Northern Kadara*, Unpublished manuscript, 1952. This is a select list.
13. Lugard, *Political Memoranda*, p. 122.
14. C. K. Meek, *Northern Tribes of Nigeria*, London University Press, 1925, vol. I, p. 248.
15. On the Pastoral or Bororoje Fulani, see D. J. Stenning, *Savannah Nomads*, Oxford University Press, 1959, and C. E. Hoppen, *The Pastoral Fulbe Family in Gwandu*, Oxford University Press, 1958; F. W. de St. Croix, op.cit.
16. For C. K. Meek's definition of tribe see Meek, op. cit. pp. 241–42.
17. Op. cit., p. 250.

18. Op. cit., p. 226.

19. W. G. Runciman, *Social Science and Political Theory*, Cambridge University Press 1963, pp. 135–47.

20. See also K. Buchanan, 'The Northern Region of Nigeria —The Geographical Background of its political Duality', *The Geographical Review*, vol. 43, no. 4, 1953.

21. M. G. Smith, 'The Hausa System of Social Status', *Africa*, vol. 29, 1959, p. 243. See also M. G. Smith, 'Kebbi and Hausa Stratification', *British Journal of Sociology*, vol. 12, 1961, pp. 52–61, which is a reply to Miss E. R. Yeld's, 'Islam and Social Stratification in Northern Nigeria', same journal, vol. II, 1960, pp. 112–28.

22. C. K. Meek, op. cit. p. 254. *The Encyclopedia of Islam*, Luzac, 1913, vol. I, pp. 747–54.

23. C. K. Meek, *A Sudanese Kingdom*, Routledge and Kegan Paul, 1931, p. 334 seq., and *Northern Tribes*, vol. I, p. 256.

24. S. F. Nadel, *A Black Byzantium*, Oxford University Press, 1942, p. 147.

25. M. G. Smith, 'The Hausa System of Social Status', op. cit. p. 247.

26. See for instance A. H. M. Kirk-Greene, *Traditional Authority and the New Leadership Cadres*, Mimeographed, n.d.

27. M. G. Smith, 'The Hausa System of Social Status, op. cit. p. 242.

28. On this point see F. H. Ruxton, *Maliki Law*, Luzac, 1916, p. 367.

29. W. S. Trimmingham, *Islam in West Africa*, Oxford University Press, 1959, p. 132.

30. The Zaria list is from M. G. Smith, 'The Economy of the Hausa Communities of Zaria', *Colonial Research Studies* no. 16, 1955, p. 16; Bornu, from R. Cohen, *The Structure of Kanuri Society*, University of Wisconsin Ph.D. thesis 1960, Unpublished, University Microfilms, University of Ibadan Library, pp. 196–97, while that for Nupe is from S. F. Nadel, op. cit., p. 103.

31. Strictly speaking *dillalai* (Hausa, sing, dillali; Arabic = *dillal*) are auctioneers and commission merchants. G. P. Bargery, *A Hausa-English Dictionary and English-Hausa Vocabulary*, Oxford University Press, 1934, translates *dillalai* as 'a broker', and the 'trade of brokerage' as *dillanci*. The terms 'brokers' is retained in the text simply to follow the seemingly now common translation given by Arnett, (*A Gazetteer of Zaria Province*, 1920, p. 16. The *dillalai* at the time of the British occupation of Zaria paid tax, i.e. *kurdin dillalai* of 5,000 cowries per man per year, roughly four pounds sterling), Bargery, Smith and others. It should not be understood in the sense in which it is used of a modern complex money market.

32. R. Cohen, op. cit., p. 196.

33. M. G. Smith, op. cit., p. 249.

34. M. Ginsberg, *Sociology*, Oxford University Press, 1934, p. 163.

35. Miss E. R. Yeld, op. cit., passim.

36. S. F. Nadel, op. cit., p. 133.

37. Ibid., p. 131.

38. F. H. Bradley, *Ethical Studies*, Chapter V. On the use of Aziki see M. G. Smith, 'The Economy of Hausa Communities in Zaria', *Colonial Research Studies*, no. 16, 1955, pp. 14–15; R. Cohen, op. cit., pp. 227 and 228.

39. In using the term 'fiefs', it should be noted that its context is the Fulani practice and that under the Habes, the system of fiefs was different, a difference which, in part distinguished the Habe and Fulani approaches to political organization. See C. W. Cole, *Report on Land Tenure—Niger Province*, Kaduna, 1949, pp. 48–49.

40. S. F. Nadel, op. cit., p. 44. See also his 'Nupe State and Community', *Africa*, vol. 8, 1935, pp. 257–303.

41. S. F. Nadel, op. cit. p. 56. The Nupe emphasis on 'constitutionality' was noted by Lady Lugard who wrote that "The Constitution of Bida . . . is one in which the principle of Constitutional government was carried . . . to its most complete expression". F. Shaw (Lady Lugard), *A Tropical Dependency*, pp. 405–06. The similarity of structure at this level of government between Nupe and Jukun may also be noted: see C. K. Meek, *A Sudanese Kingdom*, pp. 343–44. Meek also noted the similarity with Benin, Oyo and Buganda, ibid,. p. 346.

42. S. F. Nadel, op. cit., p. 46.

43. Lugard, *Political Memoranda*, pp. 95–96. M. G. Smith, *Government in Zazzau*, Oxford University Press, 1960, uses the term Hakimi for Zaria fief-holders.

44. On the 'integrative' role of dynastic rivalry see M. G. Smith, op. cit., pp. 104–07, 120–23.

45. M. G. Smith, op. cit., p. 110.

46. S. F. Nadel, op. cit., pp. 93–95.

47. M. G. Smith, op. cit., p. 112.

48. M. Weber, *Essays in Sociology*, London, 1948, 3rd impression, translated by Girth and Mills, pp. 198–204, 224–35, 240–44.

49. Contrast Meek's statement about the Jukun Kingdom: "As government was almost entirely in the hands of members of the royal family, bureaucracy was more developed among the Jukun than among any other peoples of Nigeria." Meek, *Northern Tribes*, 1925, vol. I, p. 255. Two comments may be made. Firstly, Meek is using the term bureaucracy in a very loose sense. Secondly, his statement is not strictly accurate as there was an emergent bureaucracy in Habe Zaria and Abuja—see M. G. Smith, *Government in Zazzau*, pp. 68–70.

50. See *Nigerian Citizen*, Zaria, 30th November 1957. The examples by Miss Perham are at p. 106.

51. R. Cohen, 'The Analysis of Conflict in Hierarchical Systems', *Antropologica*, vol. 4, no. 1, 1960, pp. 87–120. The case cited is on p. 97. See also A. Rosman, 'Social Structure and Acculturation among the Kanuri of Bornu Province', *Transactions of the New York Academy of Sciences*, Ser. II, vol. 27, no. 7, pp. 620–30; and also A. H. M. Kirk-Greene, op. cit.

52. M. G. Smith, *Government in Zazzau*, passim, has defined the relation of clientage as a total relation which was economic, political and social and which held between the superior and his subordinate. He points out that "clientage . . . is coterminous with Hausa Society", ibid. p. 260; "it is the characteristic medium of Hausa political relations", p. 245.

53. S. F. Nadel, op. cit., p. 95.

54. Ibid., p. 102.

55. M. G. Smith, op. cit., pp. 42–66, and M. Hassan and Shu'aibu, *A Chronicle of Abuja*, translated by F. Heath, University of Ibadan Press, 1952.

56. C. K. Meek, *A Sudanese Kingdom*, 1931, p. 333.

57. *Encyclopedia of Islam*, vol. I, p. 750. "The ruler exercises despotic authority and combines in his person both spiritual and temporal power; he disposes at will of the lives and goods of his subjects." Loc. cit. Composition of the Council is given as the heir presumptive—Yerima, sons and brothers of the Shehu, his relatives or *Maina* and the great nobles and certain captains commanding the troops. On the authority of the Shehu, however, contra Barth, op. cit. p. 310.

58. M. G. Smith, 'Political Organization in Hausaland', *Institute of Commonwealth Studies*, University of London, Postgraduate Seminar Session 1959/60,

P1/59/4, and also, the *Encyclopedia of Islam*, vol. I, pp. 750–51. The power of the Waziri of Sokoto even extended to the confirmation of appointment of Emirs as evidence by the case of Tukr, Emir of Kano, who was appointed by Buhari, Waziri of Sokoto in 1893. In Sokoto the division was such that the Waziri was in charge of Kano, Zaria, etc., while the Galadima was responsible for Katsina and the territories to the West, W. F. Gowers, *Gazetteer of Kano Province*, 1921, p. 19. See H. F. Backwell, op. cit., p. 76.

59. H. F. Backwell, op. cit. pp. 16–17. The first five letters quoted in Backwell were dated between 1891 and 1897.

60. Selection of the Emir was done by a traditional Council of Electors. The electors chose from a number of eligible candidates stating the order of preference. The actual choice of a candidate was than left to the Sultan.

61. H. F. Backwell, op. cit., pp. 21–73. See also E. J. Arnett, *Gazetteer of Sokoto Province*, 1920, p. 33.

62. The Bornu Kingdom was comprised of two fairly distinct areas: Bornu proper or Bled (Bilad) Kuka, administered directly by the Shehu and the vassal sultanates governed by 'native' chiefs.

63. J. Goody, 'Feudalism in Africa', *Journal of African History*, vol. 4, no. I, 1936, pp. 1–16, has suggested that the term 'feudalism' as applied to African societies is misleading as this tends to blur the differences between the conditions in Europe, where the term originated, and those in Africa. This, however, is a matter of opinion. In Marc Bloch's usage (*Feudal Society* translated by M. M. Postan, 1961, Chapter 32,) the term as used here would not seem to be improper.

64. Cf. the Hausa saying, "Addinimmu addinin biyayya ne", "our religion is a religion of obedience". See also, D. P. L. Dry, 'The Hausa Attitude to Authority', Proceedings of the First Annual Conference, W.A.I.S.E.R., University of Ibadan, 1952. There are of course other interpretations of Islam with a more radical and egalitarian spirit. In Northern Nigeria such interpretations are associated with the Tijaniyya brotherhood (footnotes 97 and 98, p. 198 below) which, however, has not gained as many adherents as the Kadiriyya, the dominant conservative tradition upheld by the Sultan of Sokoto and most of the Emirs. J. E. Means' claim, A Study of the Influence of Islam in Northern Nigeria, Unpublished Ph.D. thesis, Georgetown, 1965, that Tijaniyya is the dominant brotherhood in the North is grossly wide of the mark.

65. In the 1931 Census, 47.5% of the total population of the North were classified as 'dependants'. Taking the Emirates alone, the percentage must surely have been higher. C. K. Meek, *Northern Tribes*, vol. 2, p. 213.

66. See Population Census of Northern Nigeria 1952.

67. D. Forde and G. I. Jones, *The Ibo and Ibibio Speaking Peoples of South-Eastern Nigeria*, Oxford University Press for the I. A. I., 1950.

68. On the Tivs in general see R. C. Abraham, *The Tiv People*, London, 1940; R. M. Downes, *The Tiv People*, Kaduna, 1933; *Akiga's Story*, translated by A. M. East, Oxford, 1939; Laura and Paul Bohannan, *The Tiv of Central Nigeria* I.A.I., 1953; and P. Bohannan. *Justice and Judgement among the Tiv*, I.A.I. 1957.

69. L. Bohannan, 'Political Aspects of Tiv Social Organization' in J. Middleton and D. Tait, op. cit., pp. 37–39.

70. For the importance of this Tiv concept see P. Bohannan, 'A Tiv Religious and Political Idea', *South-western Journal of Anthropologist*, vol. II, no. 2, 1955, pp. 137–49.

71. M. Ember, 'Political Authority and the Structure of Kinship in Aboriginal Samoa', *American Anthropologist*, vol. 64, no. 5. 1962. p. 969.

72. This diagram is taken from L. Bohannan, op. cit., in Middleton and Tait, op. cit., p. 59.

73. R. M. East, op. cit., p. 363, 365.

74. Laura and Paul Bohannan, op. cit., p. 31.

75. M. Weber, *The Theory of Social and Economic Organization*, translated by Talcott Parsons. p. 302.

76. R. M. East, op. cit., p. 366.

77. On the Ngizim, Chawai, Bura and Pabir and Mambila, see C. K. Meek, *Tribal Studies in Northern Nigeria*, 1931, vol. II, p. 250, 148; vol. I, p. 141, 533–36, and F. Redfisch, 'The Dynamics of Multilineality on the Mambila Plateau', *Africa*, vol. 30, 1960, pp. 246–61; C. L. Temple, ed., op. cit., pp. 72–74. Meek should however, be read with caution. Thus, while he asserted of the Kagoro, vol. 2, p. 96 (also Temple, p. 188), that they had a chiefly system, Cole, *Report on Land Tenure in Zaria*, 1949, reported that "when living in their stronghold in the Kagoro hills, the Kagoro had no single chief", op. cit., pp. 12, 13. Cf. in this instance, M. G. Smith, *Social Organization and Economy of Kagoro*, Colonial Office, GN 653–391091, 1952, and contrast A. J. N. Tremearne, 'Notes on the Kagoro', *Journal of the Royal Anthropological Institute*, vol. 42, pp. 136–99. In fact, the accounts given by both Meek and Temple are often inconsistent, one with the other. Cf. here the accounts by Meek on the Bolewa, vol. 2, pp. 290–92, and the Chamba, vol. I, pp. 338–79 and Temple, pp. 62–68 and 79–84 respectively. This is not to suggest that Temple is any more accurate than Meek. Compare, e.g., Temple's account of the Angas of Bauchi Province, pp. 8–17 with R. Mohr, 'Social Organization of the Angas', *Anthropos*, vol. 53, 1959, pp. 457–72. In general, accounts to be found in the Ethnographic Survey of Africa series e.g. those by H. D. Gunn, 1953; Gunn and Conant, 1960; D. Forde, P. Brown and R. G. Armstrong, 1955, are more reliable than the older accounts by Meek, Temple and others.

78. A. Southall, op. cit., p. 252. For Weber's concept of 'Legitimacy', M. Weber, *The Theory of Social and Economic Organization*, translated by Parsons, p. 114; S. Bendix, op. cit., pp. 295–96, 297–99, 322 and 413–14.

79. See R. G. Armstrong in Forde, Brown and Armstrong, *Peoples of the Niger—Benue Confluence*, I.A.I., 1955, p. 102.

80. Ibid., p. 95. The existence of an ideology of chieftancy may be accounted for by C. L. Temple's suggestion that some time in the past, the Idomas, or rather, Idoma proper, had a traditional Chief who was known as the Oni. Temple noted that there were "three or four branches" of the "royal family", but "no chief had control over the other royal families". Temple, op. cit., pp. 142–47. Quotation is on p. 142.

81. T. M. Baker, *The Social Organization of the Birom*, unpublished Ph.D. thesis, University of London 1954 (Ibadan University Microfilms); also H. D. Gunn, *Peoples of the Plateau Area of Northern Nigeria*, I.A.I., 1953. In an interview with Mr. Patrick Dokotri, former Administrative Secretary of the Jos N.A. and a Birom, he pointed out, however, that Biroms recognized only a dual and not a tripartite division, other interviews yielded the same information.

82. T. M. Baker, op. cit., p. 274.

83. Ibid., p. 66. See also T. M. Baker, 'Political Control Among the Biroms', Proceedings of the Fifth Annual Conference, W.A.I.S.E.R., Ibadan, 1956.

84. Ibid., p. 67.

85. R. Apthorpe, 'Political Change, Centralization and Role Differentiation', *Civilizations*, vol. 10, no. 2, 1960, p. 221.

86. Lloyd Fallers, *Bantu Bureaucracy*, Cambridge for the E.A.I.S., E.R., n.d. p. 242.

87. K. W. Deutsch, 'Social Mobilization and Political Development', *The American Political Science Review*, vol. 55, no. 3, 1961, pp. 493–514. See also his *Nationalism and Social Mobilization*.

88. D. Apter, 'The Role of Tribalism in the Political Modernization of Ghana and Uganda', *World Politics*, vol. 13, no. I, 1960, pp. 45–68. Apter, however, makes hardly any reference to segmentary societies. His 'Pyramidal' societies, a term borrowed from Southall, is in fact used to describe structures widely different from those intended by Southall. See in this context, Apter's, *The Political Kingdom of Uganda*, Princeton, 1962.

89. R. Apthorpe, op. cit., passim. J. S. Coleman, 'The Politics of sub-Sahara Africa', in G. A. Almond and J. S. Coleman, (eds.), *The Politics of Developing Countries*, Princeton, 1960, pp. 255–660.

90. P. M. Blau, *Bureaucracy in Modern Society*, N. Y. Random House, 1961.

91. Max Weber, *Essays in Sociology*, pp. 194–95. T. L. Hodgkin in his *African Political Parties*, Penguin, 1962, makes a distinction between 'mass' and 'patron' parties. Weber's terminology is here used in preference to Hodgkin's as the term 'patron' seems to carry the suggestion of one, the 'patron' who need not be connected directly with the party. In the context of Northern Nigeria, such a suggestion would be unrealistic. For other classificatory terminology see M. Duverger, *Political Parties*, Methuen, 1954 and Appendix I.

92. E. L. McDill and C. Ridley, 'Status, Anomia, Political Alienation and Political Participation', *American Journal of Sociology*, vol. 68, no. 2, 1962, pp. 205–13.

93. See R. Schacter, 'Single Party Systems in West Africa', *The American Political Science Review*, vol. 55, no. 2, 1961, p. 295.

94. A. Leiserson, 'The Place of Parties in the Study of Politics', *The American Political Science Review*, vol. 51, no. 4, 1957, p. 948.

III

The Emergence of Political Parties in Northern Nigeria

The political and social history of the North outlined in the first chapter revealed not only certain features which can be said to be peculiar to the North, but also some essential differences in outlook between the North and the South. These differences and characteristic features can be accounted for (to a large extent) in terms of the effects of British administrative policy in the North. To understand why political parties developed[1] when they did it will be necessary, then, to examine in some more detail certain aspects of British policy.

I. THE SIGNIFICANCE OF BRITISH POLICY

One of the criticisms often brought against British rule in the Colonial territories is their policy towards education in these areas. In Nigeria, nowhere is this criticism probably more justified than in Northern Nigeria. In pursuance of the promise made by Lugard to the Sultan after the conquest of Sokoto not to interfere with the local customs and the religion of the people, it became part of British policy to keep out of the North the various Christian missions, as it was thought that to allow them would be contrary to the promise made by Lord Lugard. While the South was left open to missionary influence, the North by and large remained free from such influence.[2] And one must remember that Western education was not infrequently left by the government to individual entreprenuers and missionary organizations. The practical effect of this policy can be seen in the following table, which contrasts the secondary education situation in Northern Nigeria with that in the South.

No secondary school existed in the North until the founding of the Katsina College in 1922, which started as a teacher training college. By 1952 only 2% of the total population of the North (of the ages of seven and above) was literate in English[3] as against 17·4% and 16% in the West and Eastern Regions respectively. The

TABLE 2

Secondary Education 1947 and 1950
Government and Native Authority

Region	Year	No. of Schools	Total Enrolment
South	1947	7	1,304
”	1950	7	1,053
North	1947	1	162
”	1950	13 (*a*)	2,148

Voluntary Agency (*assisted*)			Voluntary Agency (*unassisted*)	
No. of Schools		Enrolment	No. of Schools	Enrolment
South	36	1947	8,353	(*b*)	(*b*)
”	52	1950	9,307	51	4,900
North	2	1947	89	Nil	Nil
”	3	1950	222	Nil	Nil

NOTES: (*a*) Includes 11 Middle Schools, i.e. two years post-primary. These in fact should more properly be regarded as primary schools.

(*b*) Not available.

Figures for 1947 from *African Education: A Study of Educational Policy in British Tropical Africa* (O.U.P., 1953) p. 48. Those for 1950 from Hicks and Phillipson: *Report of the Commission on Revenue Allocation* (Lagos, 1951) p. 109.

mental attitude this comparative lack of a Western type education engendered on the part of the people of the North has been very well put by Dr. R. M. East when he wrote that in the North: "A line of Arabic in an article, a quotation from a Hadith or even from a modern Sheikh, is more effective than any amount of logic in convincing a Hausa Moslem that the writer's opinions are sound."[4] In a predominantly Moslem North, where power was apparently vested in the hands of the ruling Emirs, the lack of education thus had the effect of creating a relatively complacent attitude amonst the people who seemingly felt satified with the *status quo*.

James Coleman has drawn attention to the relevance of education for the development of a nationalist feeling, and thus, for the emergence of political parties.[5] British policy with regard to education can be seen, by implication, as having the effect of retarding the growth of the party system in Northern Nigeria. As will be shown shortly, this retardation is to be thought of not only in negative terms such as is suggested, but also more positively, in action geared towards the elimination of an emergent nationalism.

Satisfaction with the *status quo* is, for example, clearly brought out in the replies suggested in 1942 by the Sultan of Sokoto to proposals for political changes put forward by the West African Students Union—an organization of students based in London.[6] Thus, to the proposal that the constitutions of the Legislative Councils in the British West African territories be altered to allow for an unofficial African representation equal to the official, the unofficial members being elected on an adult franchise, the Chiefs of the North replied: "We think the Governor is fully able to deal with all matters concerning Northern Nigeria." They were accustomed to meeting the Chief Commissioner to discuss matters concerning the North which were to be debated in the Nigerian Legislative Council. With this arrangement they were satisfied and did not think that "in the territories of Northern Nigeria there is a single man who is sufficiently qualified to enter the (Governor's) Executive Council" when it was proposed that at least six Africans in each colony should be chosen to sit on the Executive Councils.

The same conservatism is revealed in the replies made to suggestions for a wider scope of opportunities for Africans to be appointed to the higher levels of the administration and the institution of more schools, colleges, and universities. The former suggestion was attributed by the Chiefs simply to ignorance for to them "Africans (were) already holding the higher appointments" such as those of Chiefs, native judges and district heads. This showed the concern with the local administration to the almost complete exclusion of everything else. The administrative civil service was not their concern. This they regarded as the special preserve of British officials because "they alone are qualified to do the work required". There was no thought of training the indigenous people to hold such offices, hence, in reply to the latter proposal, the Chiefs replied that "In Islam there are ways of fitting a man in character for any kind of work and position in life according to his ability. But it is character and worth which matters, and what we are looking for."[7]

These replies by the Chiefs point to another feature of British policy—the concentration of political power in the hands of the Emirs. Not only had the Emirs become increasingly powerful, but with the institution of annual Meetings of Chiefs, they became the only organized indigenous group in the North with a separate interest, that of maintaining their position. To do this effectively meant being able to control all forms of criticism of their regime.

The first 'experimental' news broadsheet was published by the

Government in 1930. This was essentially a Government hand-out which sought to bring to the notice of the Emirs the various activities of the Government. The first 'newspaper'[8] was, however, not published until 1939, and even then, it appeared only fortnightly. When it was suggested that members of the public might be encouraged to express their views in letters and articles to the paper, the Emirs objected. The Emir of Kano, to cite one example, was of the opinion that the Chiefs would only allow such a move if all articles and letters were first sent to them for censorship. Not until it was suggested that any items containing references of any kind to the Native Authorities should be so treated did the Chiefs agree to the public expression of opinion in the newspaper. But since the average Northerner lived his whole life within the orbit of the Native Authority, this policy in effect meant the suppression of all forms of criticism.[9]

The authoritarian tendencies of the Chiefs extended not only to the suppression of critical opinion, but also the repression of radical or quasi-radical movements. This is probably nowhere better illustrated than by the attitude of the Chiefs to the first nationalist movement formed in the North.

The influence of the NCNC delegation in introducing some political awareness amongst Northerners has already been noted. Related to this awareness was the fact that some Northerners such as M. Sa'ad Zungur, and Raji Abdallah, became closely associated with the NCNC for some time. Experience gained by them during this period subsequently led to the formation in Kano under the leadership and direction of Raji Abdallah, of the Northern Elements Progressive Association (NEPA) in 1947. Although without a clearly defined policy, NEPA aimed at bringing about a much more critical attitude amongst Northerners to the political situation of the North. Though not strictly a political party, NEPA was none the less suspect and through a member of its executive, who was also a civil servant, a Mallam Howeidy, the names of the other leading members of the association became known both to the British Resident in Kano and the Chiroma—the heir apparent to the Emir of Kano, and head of the Kano Native Administration. Under the pretext that these men were engaging in 'political activity', those of them who were civil servants—including Abdallah himself and M. Zukogi (now Secretary-General of NEPU)—and who refused to dissociate themselves from the Association were dismissed from the Service. Others who preferred to remain in their employments were transferred from Kano. If the Administration could justify their action on the grounds that membership of such an association was a contravention of the

General Orders (40b) which proscribed political activity amongst civil servants, such a plea was not open to the Native Authority. This, however, did not prevent the N.A. from following the action of the Resident and similarly dismissing people like M. S. Darma. NEPA nevertheless maintained a precarious existence in Kano until it was superseded by and absorbed into the Northern Elements Progressive Union in 1950. It was resuscitated in places like Agege, near Lagos as the 'Jam'iyyar Al'Ummar Nigeriya ta Arewa' (literally the Northern Nigerian Peoples' Society).[10]

Such policies and actions, however, cannot but eventually lead to some counter-action. Arbitrary treatment of N.A. employees, such as the imprisonment, under supposedly false charges, by the Sultan's Court of the Sardauna of Sokoto,[11] was to generate a questioning attitude amongst the younger members of the society,[12] who did not even feel satisfied with their prospects under the N.A., about the only major source of employment open to the few educated Northerners. As against their Southern counterparts employed in the Regional bureaucracy, there was limited scope for advancement in the N.A. structure. In 1928, for instance, the Conference of Residents of the North negatived the principle of annual incremental rates of pay for native authority employees "as being foreign to native ideas in the Northern provinces" and recommended instead an increased number of grades on fixed salaries.[13] This policy was only amended when, as a result of dissatisfaction amongst the graduates of Katsina College, the government accepted a suggestion of a triennial system of increments instead of an annual one.[14]

But such piecemeal action could hardly be expected to solve the problems inherent in the political structure. As a Northerner later put it: "the number of educated men was growing but despite their qualifications they were always relegated to the back row in the Native Authority services. They became conscious of this and the result was friction between the educated men on the one hand and the native authority and Europeans on the other."[15] The Resident of Bauchi Province was more specific in his report for 1939. "Signs are not now lacking", he wrote, "that the younger generation, many of whom have graduated at Katsina College,[16] are gradually becoming dissatisfied with this comfortable, but unambitious programme, and that the time has arrived to prepare for a new régime, the coming of which is unlikely, in Bauchi itself at all events, to be much longer delayed."[17]

There were other dimensions in the growing resentment of the implications of Indirect Rule. One of the props on which the system rested was the misguided theory that there must be a definite person, preferably a Chief wherever this was possible, who should be held directly responsible to the Administration for the management of any group of people. With no system of chieftaincy amongst the mass of the peoples of the Benue, Plateau, Niger and Southern Zaria provinces, with the extension of the Native Authority structure to these areas, Hausa–Fulanis were invariably brought in to hold the main offices in the Native Authority. Thus in Jos, for example, until 1952, the Magajin Gari, the immediate head of the Native Authority was a Hausa man from Kano, with the result that there was resentment amongst the Biroms, the indigenous people, who felt that the direction of Jos affairs should be in their hands, or at least, by someone, nominated by them. In Markurdi, in the Tiv area, the Administration's 'contact' with the Clan heads up till 1946, was a Yoruba Muslim, a M. Audu Dan Afoda, who gradually arrogated to himself more than necessary powers. When Afoda died in 1946 the attempt to appoint his son as the successor was halted as a result of protests by the local inhabitants. Instead, Afoda's son was appointed the Wakilin Makurdi, a deputy, his father's 'office' being left vacant. Incensed by the seemingly obvious disregard of their interests, some Tiv ex-servicemen roused the populace in protest, thereby creating the conditions which gave rise to the Tiv disturbance of 1948. In general, offices such as those of the Native Authority Supervisor of Works, the Treasurer and the Chief Scribe, the principal offices within the Native Authority which were handed over to Hausa–Fulani men, caused deep resentment. It was practices of this sort which impelled the Kilba of Adamawa, to demand separation from the Fulani dominated Adamawa Native Authority,[18] demands which were to gather momentum with the political changes affecting Nigeria as a whole, and to lead to separatist movements.

II. THE EMERGENCE OF POLITICAL PARTIES

In considering certain aspects of Indirect Rule in the North, at least one significant point emerges: whereas in the South nationalist criticisms were directed against the Colonial system, criticisms which sometimes took the form of a demand for independence, in the North criticism was directed to the application of the principle of Indirect Rule, and only by extension, if at all, to Colonialism as such. Thus, if in the South, critical opinion demanded the abolition of the Colonial system, in the North, similar opinions were essentially reformist. But there was disagreement as to what direction reform should take. It was disagreement on such issues which distinguished the early associations which began to emerge, and which, to take one example, marked the Bauchi General Improvement Union, (BGIU) from its rival organization the Bauchi Discussion Circle (BDC).

The BGIU was formed some time between 1943 and 1944 by M. Sa'ad Zungur, who, at one time, was a teacher at the School of Pharmacy in Zaria. While in Zaria, Zungur formed the Zaria Friendly Society which very soon became defunct when he found that its members were, unlike himself, not prepared to use the Friendly Society as a platform for attacking and criticizing the Native Authority. When therefore the BGIU was started, it took the form of a radical movement directed against the Native Authority and included men like Aminu Kano, then a teacher at the Bauchi Middle school.[19] It was to counter the radicalism of the BGIU that, under the supervision of the District Officer, the BDC was formed, a 'moderate' organization, the members of which met periodically to discuss pressing questions of the day. It included in its membership, both the present Prime Minister, Abubakar Tafawa Belawa and Yahaya Gusau, who is now a Permanent Secretary in the Northern Civil Service and former member of the Northern House of Assembly.

Similar associations soon cropped up in the far North. Thus, in Sokoto, the Youth's Social Circle was formed in 1945 by people like Shehu Shagari, Ibrahim Gusau, with the Sardauna of Sokoto on the periphery. In Kano, there was the Kano Youth's Association, formed in 1948 by Sani Darma (a former founder member of NEPA), Abudukadiri Ajaiyi and Maitama Sule, now an NPC Federal Minister. More radical in tone was the Tarau Masu Zumunta (Fraternal or Friendship Association) formed also in Kano by Abba Maikwaru (again, a founder member of NEPA) in the same year. In Zaria the Zaria Youth's Association took the place of the former Friendly Society. An attempt to unify these into a single region wide association which started with the invitation by the Zaria Association to the Kano and other groups to meet in Kaduna, was, however, a failure.

One characteristic feature of these associations was the preponderance of school teachers in their membership. In a sense this was to be expected, as these teachers constituted the main base of the educated minority in the North. Though a Northern Teachers' Association was formed in London in 1947 by Aminu Kano, who was on a teacher training course at the University of London, when the NTA was transplanted to Nigeria, it was denied recognition by the Government as a corporate group.[20] Refused the possibility of legitimate action in an organization of their own, the friendly societies, discussion groups and youth associations became the only instrument of criticism open to them and by the same token, provided them with a platform for the expression of their political views.

If, however, the attempt by the Zaria Youth's Association to form a region-wide organization proved abortive, the imminence of Constitutional changes already promised by Sir John MacPherson, made the institution of some region-wide organization seem imperative. The first tentative steps were taken when in September 1948 Dr. R. A. Dikko of Zaria and Mr. D. A. Rafih of Kaduna summoned meetings to discuss the forthcoming changes to the political structure of Nigeria. These meetings led to the formation of the Jam'iyyar Mutanen Arewa (Northern Peoples Congress) in Zaria in October by Dr. Dikko and M. Abubakar Imam, while in Kaduna, Rafih started the Jam'iyyar Mutanen Arewa A Yau (the Society of Northern Peoples of Today). A meeting of both organizations led to their amalgamation in October 1948 with the new name of Jam'iyyar Mutanen Arewa (JMA). Unlike the earlier associations the JMA was intended to cover the whole region and at a meeting in April 1949 between the NTA and the JMA, the former was exhorted to start branches of the JMA in their respective areas where such did not exist.[21] When therefore, the inaugural meeting of the JMA was held at Kaduna in June 1949, it was attended by over 500 delegates and it was stated that the JMA was strictly a cultural organization.[22] To emphasize its 'Northern 'outlook, it was also decided at the inagural meeting that the Hausa title of the organization was to be retained and not translated into English.

The JMA held its first 'general meeting' in Kano in December 1949 and was told by the General Secretary "In June we counted our members in hundreds now . . . we do so in thousands".[23] Over ninety delegates attended who were later entertained by the Emir of Kano; and at the end, the meeting decided to create some 'committees' to deal with specific problems, the first three being committees on finance and education and a 'newspaper Committee'.[24] At the Kano meeting, those members of the *Taron Masu Zamunta* and the Kano Youth's Association who had not already joined the JMA became members, the TMZ and the KYA being formally affiliated to the JMA.

But this immediately created problems for the JMA, as the Kano contingent, being much more radical in outlook, wanted the JMA declared a 'political party'. Caution, however, dictated differently, for as Yahaya Gusau later remarked in the Northern House of Assembly, when the JMA was founded "it was sheer madness to talk of politics" openly.[25] At the inaugural meeting, the JMA received congratulatory telegrams from the Sultan of Sokoto, the Emirs of Kano and Zaria amongst others. But curiously, in another telegram to the editor of the 'Gaskiya Tafi Kwabo'[26] a few days later, the Sultan demanded not to be associated with the JMA in any way. It is not improbable that this may have been due to some pressure from the British authorities who had sent a Captain C. D. Morney to observe the proceedings and to enquire into the aims and orientations of the JMA.[27] With the example of the Sultan before them, the JMA leadership were not prepared to accept the Kano demands.

To the Kano contingent, the refusal to declare the JMA a formal political party seemed unnecessarily cautious and on 5th August 1950 the leadership decided to merge the TMZ and the KYC into a new organization and to declare it a political party which became known as the Northern Elements Progressive Union (NEPU, or in Hausa, Jam'iyya Neman Sarwaba) with Abba Maikwaru as President. But NEPU members still regarded themselves as members of the JMA. The duality in orientation was not resolved until the Second Conference of the JMA held at Jos in December 1950. Here NEPU demanded that the JMA should be converted into a political party, the intention being to use such a party as a platform to contest the forthcoming elections under the proposed new Constitution. Unable to come to an agreement, NEPU decided to sever relations with the JMA, which continued a 'cultural' organization.[28]

NEPU entered the field of practical party politics when, at a meeting in Kano on 3rd-6th April, 1951, attended by "all branches, some tribal unions and trade union organizations" it came out with a declaration of 'objectives' which was concluded in general terms and aimed at the emancipation of the *Talakawa*, the progressive reform of the native authority system and the provision of better welfare services in the North.[29] In September 1951 it recorded its first success when it contested and "topped the primaries" in Kano, Zaria, Jos, Minna, Maiduguri, Kaduna and Nguru.[30] Of the 26 seats for the five areas in Kano, NEPU won 12 seats; the NCNC, which had an 'electoral' understanding with NEPU, won 5; Native Authority officials (the N.A. nominated more candidates than there were seats, thereby splitting their vote) 6; and Independents 3.[31]

These successes were not without immediate effect. As an editorial in the *Nigerian Citizen* was later to put it, it showed "the red light" for "the most stringent heart-searching particularly at the top" and with NEPU's 'objectives' already known, the question was whether the Native Authorities and the Regional Administrative Authorities would heed the "warning" "before it is too late".[32] It is probable, as M. Nuhu Bamali has suggested,[33] that it was the intention of some of the members of the Northern House of Assembly, including Abubakar Tafawa Balewa, Sir Ahmadu, Sardauna of Sokoto, Alhaji Aliyu, and Makaman Bida, to form a political party to represent the North. Though there is no evidence to substantiate this, it is certain that by late 1951 such a move was already impracticable in the face of NEPU successes. Hasty consultations between these men and the JMA therefore followed. The first of these was a meeting in the Northern House of Assembly, 29th September. Here the JMA leadership was supposed to have opposed the membership of the Sardauna and Balewa should the JMA be converted into a political party. This opposition possibly derives from the fact that when the JMA was formed, the invitation to Balewa to join the JMA was turned down while the Sardauna promised financial support but did not commit himself to membership of the organization. Not until the Chiefs intervened, it is said, was this deadlock resolved.[34] At an emergency meeting of the JMA which met on the 30th September at Zaria, the decision was finally taken to declare the JMA a political party as from the following day, 1st October 1951, when it became known as the Northern People's Congress (NPC). Though at the emergency meeting it was also decided that the NPC should contest the elections, at the intermediate stage it never was actually able to do so. Nevertheless, all those elected subsequently declared their support for the NPC.[35] As these were in the main Native Authority officials, district and village heads, and a good number of the relations of the Emirs, the party and the traditional aristocracy became welded into a single network.

From this confused beginning the NPC gradually spread its network through the North. At the Second Conference of the party in December 1950, while it remained the JMA its Secretary pointed out that membership was now over 6,000, 21 new branches having been formed that year to bring the total to 57. At the time of the JMA's conversion, the number of branches was said to have risen to 65. When the first Convention of the NPC (as a political party) was held in Kaduna in July 1952, the Administrative Secretary told the Convention that there were now over 10,000 members with 76 branches. The popular interest in the party, the Administrative Secretary said, was shown by the fact that over 1,548 letters "passed through the Congress Secretariat". In order to popularize the party, the Convention discussed the question of appointing "Field Secretaries" but this proposal was shelved "until the cost could be worked out". To meet the pressing demands for funds to carry out party work, however, the suggestion that parliamentary members contribute a percentage of their salaries to party funds was accepted.

G

The rigorous extension of the party began in 1952 when Ibrahim Imam, its General Secretary, and Isa Kaita, its Financial Secretary, toured the North for three months beginning towards the end of August. The aims of the touring team were the 'reorganization' of the party, membership drive, fund collection, and the publicizing of the proposed amendments to the party manifesto. The success of the team was soon shown when after it had visited Katsina, Sokoto, Kano and Zaria provinces, it was reported that over 4,400 new members had been enrolled in these provinces, while in a report to a U.K. Labour Party delegation to Nigeria at the end of the year, the NPC pointed out that its membership was over 45,000 in more than 100 branches (The *Party List* dated 16th January 1953 showed a total of 120 branches throughout Nigeria, Gold Coast, now Ghana, and Sierra Leone of which 85 were entered in Northern Nigeria). When the Convention of the party was held in Jos in April 1954, 332 branches were represented. Four years later, this had risen to 480 branches registered with the party headquarters with another 175 known to exist though not registered. There had been a considerable increase in the number of branches established since 1952, but contact between them and party headquarters, measured by the volume of correspondence, had not increased to the same extent, for in his report to the Party Convention in 1958, the General Secretary, Abba Habib, stated that the party headquarters received only 1,389 letters from the various branches between April 1957 and January 1958. But as against this, the party sent out 1,777 letters and circulars.[36] After the Federal elections in December 1959, the Principal Organizing Secretary—Mallam Raji Abdallah (now the Party Manager)—admitted that though no accurate records were kept, membership of the party was about 4,000,000 in over 5,000 branches. Though it is almost impossible to say what the term 'member' of a political party means in Nigeria, it is very probable that the figure of 4,000,000 is an exaggeration, for at the election in that year, of the 3,258,520 people who voted in the North, only 1,994,045 voted for the NPC. Admittedly, voting figures cannot be said to show the 'membership' strength of any political party. Nevertheless, they do provide a rough approximation of the 'support' given to any one party, and in Nigeria as elsewhere no hard line can be drawn between a 'supporter' and a 'member'. In two elections in the North in which voting was direct, the NPC polled 60·8% of the total vote cast in the North and won 77% of the seats at the 1959 Federal Elections, while in the 1961 regional elections (excluding Sardauna Province, the former Northern Cameroons) it polled 69·1% of the votes to win 94·1% of the seats.

The widespread influence of the NPC can be easily explained. It derives from several factors of which a few need to be noted. In the first place, there is the role of those members, elected in 1951, who later became members of the party. These invariably were N.A. officials and relations—sons, brothers and nephews—of the ruling Emirs. As members of the Native Authority, they did not hesitate to bring the whole machinery of the Native Authorities behind the party. This operated in two ways. Positively, by an identification of the Party with the Native Authority, as for instance when the Sardauna of Sokoto, Ahmadu Bello, Deputy President of the party, meeting NPC officials in Gusau in 1952 told that them the NPC "will work hand-in-hand with the Adult Education Department to avoid duplication".[37] It was intended that in this campaign the NPC, within a period of six months, would help train 200,000 illiterates who would also be new members of the party. The department of Adult Education thus became a propaganda wing of the party. Negatively, the identification took the form of victimization of members of other parties. To take one instance, in October 1952, eight known members of NEPU were each jailed for six months by the Alkali (Native Judge) of Giwa (Zaria) for summoning and attending a political meeting allegedly in contravention of the Zaria N.A. (Control of Processions and Assemblies) Rules 1949. But the chief crime of the eight seems to have been stated by the District Head of Giwa and the Village Head of Kaya who reported, in evidence before the Alkali, that "the men were no longer respectful".[38]

Secondly, the NPC also had the backing of the Chiefs. At the 1952 Convention the Deputy President, Ahmadu Bello, assured members that all Emirs were behind the party. In 1954 when the Emir of Kano died, the Secretary of the Working Committee of the NPC, Nuhu Bamali, writing on the instruction of Ahmadu Bello, now President General, to express the condolence of the party to the Emir's son and successor (resigned 1963) concluded: "At the same time we are congratulating you on your installation as the new Emir, we hope the NPC will receive the greatest help from its old active member."[39] In October 1952, the Sultan of Sokoto agreed to become patron of the Party and as he is the religious head of all Muslims in the North—excluding Bornu, his identification with the party is most unlikely not to have a favourable effect in winning support for the party. The role of the chiefs in this respect, however, is most clearly seen in the report to the NPC General Secretary, Abba Habib by Mr. Abutu Obekpa, Minister of State after his tour of Idoma Division, in 1958, in which he pointed out that "the NPC Divisional Conference held on the 24th July 1958 where all the District Heads and personalities of Idoma were invited made the NPC to gain full support in Idoma Division. . . . The Chief of Idoma helped greatly for the elections of the District Councils and also in advising the entire people of Idoma to join the NPC. It means that all the supporters of the Chief in the whole Division are supporters of the Northern Peoples' Congress." He added that "if steps are being taken in accordance with the minutes of the NPC Idoma Divisional Conference . . . then I should boast that the land of Idoma Division will be for the Northern Peoples' Congress for ever".[40]

Other factors helped to foster the growth of the NPC but those will be dealt with later. It will only be necessary to note, in addition to what has already been said, the role of the British administrative officers. Having initially attempted to check the development of parties, as the example of NEPA and the JMA illustrate, with the formation of NEPU, they now turned to view the JMA as the lesser evil. If they did not actually contribute to the spread of the NPC, they were nevertheless known to be sympathetic towards it. It has also been suggested, though there does not seem to be any verificatory evidence, that the Governor of the North was largely responsible for bringing the Emirs and Chiefs to support the NPC during the period 1952 to 1953.

The same influences which helped the growth of the NPC equally explain the relative decline of NEPU. When NEPU was inaugurated, its radicalism, its opposition to "the Family Compact rule of the so-called Native Administration in their present autocratic form" won it considerable acceptance which made itself felt during the 1951 elections even though the electoral regulations eventually operated against it. Without the support of the Chiefs, Emirs, and Native Authority officials to aid it, NEPU in its early stage relied mainly on the exploitation of economic dissatisfaction for its expansion. In Kano, NEPU's electoral success and early influence is not unconnected with the N.A.'s proposal in 1951 to increase the rate of taxation following the rise in incomes caused by rising commodity prices. Groundnuts, for instance, had risen from £22 16s. 0d. per ton to £33; cattle price had also risen. But the rise in personal incomes was not equally felt throughout the society. Teachers and Native Authority employees, like others with fixed incomes, certainly suffered from the equally rising prices for consumption goods. The small peasant farmers who sold his crop to middle-men equally did not benefit from the rise in prices, neither did the 'petty-trader', the bicycle-repairer and the small butcher—the class from which NEPU derived its membership. Equally important also was the proposal by the Kano Waje Town Council under the Sarkin Shanu to increase the water rate from 11s. to £3 per compound.

A similar dissatisfaction in Zaria was exploited by Gambo Sawaba—a dealer in kola-nuts who was responsible for establishing NEPU on a firm basis there. The Water-works (Zaria Assessment) Order 1954 stipulated that in Tudun Wada, the owner or occupier of a tenement was to pay 12s. per annum for each "sleeping quarter situated within the tenement"; in Zaria City the rate was fixed at 6s. per male over 16 years and 2s. per female, also over 16 years, resident within a tenement; while at Sabon-Gari, the rate was 20s. per annum for each sleeping quarter. These rates were increases from 2s. 6d., 1s. and 6s. respectively for the three places. As compounds or tenements of those with low incomes contained more "sleeping quarters", the new rates caused greater hardship on members of this class and they therefore tended to support NEPU, in opposition to the NPC with which the Native Authority was associated.

Other practices provided NEPU protagonists with organizational weapons. Rural grievances such as the commandeering of corn by district and village heads on the pretext that the Emir required it "to entertain his guests", and the exploitation of unpaid labour, as for instance, people being called upon to help rebuild or repair compounds of district heads and Chiefs, were the sources on which NEPU relied. Opposition to policies which were urgently needed were on occasion made to serve NEPU needs, as for example in Bida where on the advice of the Health Authorities the Emir forbade the planting of corn in compounds in order to lessen the incidence of mosquitoes.

As those with low incomes and therefore low status were also, in the far North areas, predominantly Habes or Hausas, an ethnic element was equally involved which NEPU exploited. The resentment felt has been very well expressed by Baba of Karo when she said "when the Europeans came the Habe saw that if you worked for them they paid you for it, they did not say like the Fulani 'Commoner, give me this! Commoner, bring me that' "[41] The rough correlation between being of low status, being within the low-income group, being a Habe and being a member of NEPU could create the impression that the line of division between NPC and NEPU is one between being Fulani and being Hausa. Such a conclusion would be unwarranted. The lines between the two are already blurred by inter-marriage, and the NPC has as many Hausa members as NEPU's total membership which according to both the President, Aminu Kano and the General Secretary, Abubakar Zukogi, was estimated to be about 500,000 in 1960. The party has never kept any satisfactory records of its membership so that it is literally impossible to say what the figure is. It is probable that the quoted figure is an exaggeration.

In the Party's Memorandum to the Secretary of State for the Colonies in 1952, it claimed to represent "the mass of the people of Northern Nigeria" a claim which brought forth an editorial in the *Nigerian Citizen* of 31st July 1952 that far from representing the "mass", it was only true to say that NEPU represented "a not very large group of dissatisfied and vociferous intelligentsia". But while this may have been true of the leadership at that period, it was not true of its 'general supporters'—the rank and file of the party—and it is not even true of the party's leadership today. The low social strata from which NEPU derives its members and supporters may in part explain why it has been difficult to estimate the actual strength of the party. Determining the number of members, branches and so on, depends on the proper keeping of records. This in turn depends on a certain level of literacy which most of its supporters lack. In February 1956 the files of the organization department in the party headquarters showed an 'estimated' membership of 58,000. A report of the same department in October 1961 noted that "only about 65% of branches respond to circulars". Of the 646 branches entered in the 'Register Book' of the organization department as having been formed in 1959–61, only 63 were formally registered in the sense of having paid 'registration dues', most of these being in Katsina, Benue and Bornu provinces. And of the 63 so registered, only 4 made the monthly contribution of 10s. 6d. to the party headquarters once during the whole period, while only one branch made the contribution twice. Only 6 of the 63 'registered' branches paid the 'certification fee' of 7s. 6d. to the party headquarters.[42] No figures of membership, however, was shown in the 'Register Book'. With the tendency for NEPU 'members' to switch over to the NPC, it is even doubtful if any significance can be attached to that term. Presumably, it is a recognition of this fact that has led the party to insist on a legal bond between its prospective candidates and the party itself for local, regional and federal elections. But whatever support NEPU may have in the North it has been very much under-represented. It had no representation in the Northern House of Assembly until 1956 when with its affiliates it won nine seats in the regional election of that year; two of these were in Bornu where the constituencies were contested by Bornu Youth Movement candidates. In the federal elections, with the NCNC, it polled 16·1% of the votes but secured only eight seats in the House of Representatives as against the NPC's 60·8% of the votes for 134 seats, while in the Regional elections of

1961, it polled 14% of the votes but failed to win a single seat. (The one seat (Jos Central) which could be claimed by the party was won by an NCNC candidate.) This again compares unfavourably with the NPC's 69·1% of the votes and 160 seats.[43]

The NPC has since 1951 formed the government of the North with NEPU as the main opposition party. Within the North, both constitute the two main parties and have been subjected to much less internal strife and dissension than most of the 'minor parties'. But they have not been totally devoid of internal conflicts. The nature of these conflicts will be dealt with in detail later on. Some of them, however, have led to the formation of breakaway groups which subsequently constitute themselves into new parties. As we are here concerned with the emergence of parties, it will be convenient to mention these dissident groups. With NEPU the problem has always been one of leadership, a problem which is characteristic of "mass organizations" in status-based societies.[44] The first clear indication of this was provided in 1954 when a section of the leadership, dissatisfied with the party's inflexible antagonism to the Chiefs which they regarded as unrealistic, decided to break way, and formed the United Nationalist Movement in May of that year.[45] A similar crisis in the leadership of NEPU in 1960–61, this time over the misuse and misappropriation of party funds[46] and the party's continued alliance with the NCNC, led on 8th August 1961 to the formation of a splinter group, which styled itself the Nigerian Elements Freedom Organization.[47] NEFO, during its short existence of only one year was based mainly in Zaria. It ceased to be a separate organization when most of its members either returned to NEPU or became, formally, members of the Action Group. Kano which gave birth to NEPU, also saw the emergence of the first dissident group within the NPC when in September 1960, a group of NPC rank and file members and some of the local party organizing secretaries, dissatisfied with the way the party was being run, decided to break away and to form the Northern Youths' Movement. With very little support, the NYM has since its formation only succeeded in maintaining a twilight existence in Kano.[48] Probably more significant than the NYM is the Kano Peoples' Party (KPP). It has already been suggested that the Northern Peoples' Congress, since its existence as a political party, has become identified with the Chiefs and Native Authorities. Much of its support thus derives from the traditional support of the masses for their Emirs. When after the Report of the Commission to enquire into allegations of corruption and financial mismanagement in the affairs of the Kano Native Authority,[49] the Government asked the Emir to resign, it was not surprising that some of his supporters defected from the Party with which the Emir was identified—the NPC.[50] It was this defection which led to the formation of the KPP on 16th April 1963. The KPP is so far the only important threat to the NPC in Kano, where it claims that it already has the support of the peoples of twenty-four districts out of the twenty-six which make up Kano Province. The party also claims to have some supporters in Zaria, Katsina, Jos and Adamawa, but it is as yet impossible to say how it will fare in the face of NPC opposition.[51]

The type of opposition to the Native Authority system on the part of the younger generation which gave rise to both the NPC and NEPU was not restricted to the essentially Hausa–Fulani areas of the North. The same opposition was also to be found in Bornu, where opposition was directed not only to the authoritarian structure of the system, but also to certain privileges traditionally enjoyed by the Shehus, privileges which were regarded as anachronisms in the twentieth century. It is curious to note, for example, that though Bornu, at certain times of the year, is the hottest area in the whole of Northern Nigeria, the indigenous people were forbidden to use open umbrellas, this being a privilege of the Shehu. Equally, no one was allowed to build a two-storey building in Maiduguri, the capital, as this would be to compete with the Shehu. Even as late as 1953, an Alhaji Meshari had been expelled from Maiduguri for contravening this customary privilege. It was, in part, against such privileges that the Bornu Youth Improvement Association was formed in 1949 by Alhaji Ibrahim Imam who was then an engineering assistant in the Bornu Native Authority. Like Aminu Kano, Imam has never associated himself with the aristocratic tradition of his family. Three of his half-brothers sat on the Shehu's Council, one as the District Head of Yerwa (Maiduguri), the other a Legal Adviser to the Shehu's Court and the third as another District Head (formerly a master at the Provincial Secondary School). Thus, though closely connected with the aristocracy of Bornu, Imam had encouraged the Native Authority workers in their strike in 1950, an association which subsequently helped him towards being appointed Supervisor of Works in 1950.[52] In 1951 he defeated both the Waziri Mohammed and his elder brother Shehu Bugari and got elected to the Northern House of Assembly.[53] With his new commitments, the Bornu Youth Improvement Association was deprived of his leadership and rapidly ceased to function soon after its formation.

The gap created by the cessation of the BYIA led in January 1951 to the formation of a branch of NEPU in Maiduguri by Alhaji Waziri Ibrahim, later NPC Federal Minister of Economic Planning.

The close association betweeen NEPU and the Hausa Community of Maiduguri, alienated the Kanuris from supporting the party.[54] This led to the formation of the Bornu Youth Movement on 26th June 1954 supposedly under NEPU initiative by a group of young Kanuri men led by M. Binwafe, a former NEPU party auditor. The immediate impetus, however, was provided by the scandal in the Bornu Native Authority in 1953 which led to the resignation of the Waziri and the appointment of the Wali, M. Muhammed, then the Federal Minister of Natural Resources, as the new Waziri. But if, as NEPU maintains, the initiative to inaugurate a Kanuri party may have come from NEPU, the BYM as soon as it was founded, declared its independent stand in stating that it believed that the interests of Bornu, Adamawa and Plateau provinces could not be adequately served in the existing political set-up unless these provinces were to become a separate state in the Northern Region.[55]

In its first two years of existence, the BYM had little effect. The spur to Kanuri nationalism provided by the party led to the formation of separate groups, such as the Kanuri wing of the United Nationalist Movement which called on Kanuris to support the NPC;[56] the Bornu State Movement was also formed in 1954 to foster Bornu claims in the regional government.[57] Ethnic separatism also became noticeable with the formation of the North-east Convention Peoples Party (NECPP) to promote the claims of the Gizmawa of Potiskum in the Fika Division of Bornu.[58] All of these were separately affiliated to the NPC which was, at this time, hardly organized in Bornu, though these alliances were subsequently broken, individual members returning to the NPC.[59] With the exception of the BYM, none became an effective force in Bornu local politics.

On the formation of the BYM, both Ibrahim Imam, who had resigned from being the General Secretary of the NPC, on office to which he was 'nominated' in 1952,[60] and Zannar Bukar Dipcharima[61] were invited to become patrons of the party: both declined. In 1955 BYM entered into an understanding with NEPU, an understanding which became formal with the signing of a 'bond' between both parties in November 1956.[62] BYM's main start came with the further financial scandal in the Bornu N.A. in April 1956 which led not only to the resignation of the Waziri-Mohammed (appointed after the 1953 scandal) but also to an extensive purging of other officials of the Native Authority. This crisis both discredited the NPC with which the Native Authority was associated and swung massive support in favour of the BYM which was now looked on as a reformist party.[63] It also created the atmosphere which led to BYM winning the seats for Yerwa in the 1956 regional elections.[64] Before the elections Imam who was then a building contractor at Bama was once again invited to become the Party's patron, an invitation which he this time accepted.[65]

The BYM attained its height of popularity and effectiveness in 1956. In the elections to the Yerwa Town Councils in 1957 it won only 8 seats to the NPC's 23.[66] The principal cause for its decline can be attributed to the sudden emergence of the NPC to a commanding position in Bornu. Much of this new ascendancy can be attributed to the active role which the Native Authority under the new Waziri adopted in party politics after the 1956 purge,[67] when the whole N.A. machinery was employed in furthering the expansion and control of the NPC.[68] At the same time, the local party leaders issued directives, in June 1957, forbidding all contact between NPC and BYM supporters, directives which were reissued in 1961 in the form of an eighteen-point resolution.[69] The practical effect of these, was the intimidation of BYM and NEPU members into either leaving the party to support the NPC or to leaving Yerwa itself.[70] By 1961 the BYM (and NEPU) had ceased to exist as a political force in Yerwa.[71] At the regional elections in May of that year the BYM contested under the AG platform, by which time it had not only broken its alliance with the NEPU[72] but had been absorbed by the Action Group. It is significant that the leader of the party did not contest the regional elections from a constituency in Bornu, but was found a constituency in Tiv Division by the Action Group.

III. THE 'LOWER' NORTH

If the NPC and NEPU were in different respects part of the reaction to certain implications of Indirect Rule—the authoritarianism of the Emirs and the N.A. system—this general reaction, it has been suggested, also had other dimensions. One of these, was the growth of separatist movements in different parts of the North. The motivational orientation of these movements vary, but basically, they were all directed against the Hausa–Fulani hegemony in the North. Thus, while in the Benue Niger, Plateau, Bauchi Provinces and Southern Zaria—the area often referred to as the Middle Belt—this opposition took the form of a demand for a separate state, in Ilorin province it eventually led to a demand for the amalgamation of that area with the Western Region of Nigeria. Reinforcing the demands of these areas, especially the Middle Belt was the question of religious differences, a point graphically put by Abba Habib, the NPC General Secretary, when he said that the United Middle Belt Congress

(UMBC) "is only an ideology infused by the Christian missionaries against the expansion of the Moslems in Northern Nigeria". The UMBC, as will be seen shortly, is the party which eventually emerged to provide organizational direction to the demands of the people of the Middle Belt area.

The pattern which political opposition took was, however, dictated not only by a general resentment against Hausa–Fulani domination but also by local conditions. It was the local conditions which provided the matrix around which attitudes and alignments crystallized. Thus in Adamawa, in Wurkum division where the people had been under a Fulani Chief since about 1926, latent resentment led to the formation of the Wurkum Tribal Union in 1951 which spearheaded an anti-Fulani campaign, a campaign which gradually crystallized into opposition to the Native Authority.[73] In the Magdali district, opposition to the Native Authority started not from the subject population, but from within the ruling Fulani. Here as in most other Emirates the appointment of the District heads was the Lamido's prerogative. The family of Haman Yaji have since 1927 provided the District heads of Magdali District, but in 1952, when the Lamido was deposed, the new Emir appointed the son of the Galadima, to the District headship of Magdali. The result was the initiation of an opposition to the Native Authority by the family of Yaji who had the backing of the ex-Lamido.[74]

In the Wukari division of Benue Province, where the Jukun and Chamba occupy the key positions, the opposition came from the Donga and Kentu groups who questioned the traditional right of the Chamba minority to the principal offices in the Native Authority, the Chamba on the other hand, providing the nucleus of an opposition to the Native Authority in the Takun division where, in the early years of British administration, the 'chieftaincy' was taken from the Chamba minority and given to the Kuta who constitute the major ethnic group in the area.

In the Idoma Division the attempt to raise the status of the people led to the formation of the Idoma Hope Rising Union (IHRU) in 1944. Soon after its formation the Idomas, who, as was shown in Chapter II, have been much concerned with questions of Chieftaincy, appealed to the Government to have a Chief of Idoma—Och'Idoma —created. In 1947 Ogiri Oko was appointed the Och'Idoma, but as he was considered an unsatisfactory candidate, being an illiterate, the IHRU immediately went into opposition against the Native Authority which the new Och'Idoma headed, with the result that at the 1951 elections, the IHRU supported NEPU. Like the IHRU, the Tiv Progressive Union, about the oldest 'tribal' union in the North, was formed in 1938 with the same aims the 'general improvement of the Tiv People'. In 1947, at the same time as the Och'Idoma was appointed, Makere Dzakpe was appointed Tor Tiv. His determination to assert his authority, coupled with the traditional individualism of the Tivs, was to lead to dissatisfaction amongst the Tivs, and to force the TPU into opposition to the Tiv Native Authority. In the 1951 election, the Tivs won all eight seats for Benue Province, but three of these successful candidates later supported the NPC. With the growing dissatisfaction with Tiv affairs, the TPU requested the Lieutenant Governor of the North to institute a commission of enquiry into Tiv affairs and the failure of the Tiv representatives to support this move led to the TPU becoming actively anti-NPC,[75] a position which it has consistently maintained ever since.

In most, if not all, of these areas, the opposition groups were invariably drawn from the younger elements, teachers and ex-Servicemen, with a handful of Native Authority employees. It was also this class which provided the mainstay and initiative of the Igbirra Tribal Union, a group in opposition to the authoritarianism of the Atta of Igbirra and the Native Authority.[76] It was they who also formed in 1945 the Birom Progressive Union, an organization which aimed at uniting all Biroms and securing fair compensation from the mining companies for land over which they held leases.[77] But the BPU also had political motivations. Jos, which is the main centre in Plateau Province, has since the establishment of British rule been under a Hausa Chief. The Biroms, who claim to be the original inhabitants of the area, objected to this. The BPU was thus from its inception opposed to the Hausa-dominated Jos Native Authority and as a result of petitions to the Government, a Chief of Birom was appointed in 1947. Though moved from Rium to Jos the same year, his authority was restricted only to Biroms who wanted him made the Chief of Jos. The Chief of Birom, Rwang Pam, had in one of the annual meetings of the BPU in 1946 been elected Treasurer of the Union but later resigned his office because of the pressure brought to bear on the organization by the authorities owing to its incessant representations to the Native Authority and to the government over compensation for lands acquired for mining. This not only made the BPU elect non-Native Authority men, but also forced it into direct antagonism to the Native Authority.

The organizational direction to these 'protest' or 'oppositionist' groups was provided in 1950 with the formation, under Birom initiative, of the Northern Nigeria Non-Muslim League which was aided by the Christian missions, principally the Sudan Interior Mission and the Sudan United Mission. In 1951 the Middle Zone

League was formed, again under BPU initiative.[78] It was the intention of the leaders of the non-Muslim League to organize an Association of non-Muslims in the North to counter Islamic expansionist moves.[79] But this raised two problems. There are non-Muslims, the Maguzawa, in the predominantly Muslim areas of the far North—Kano, Katsina, Sokoto, Bornu and Northern Zaria. The non-Muslim League was not intended to include these. It was more narrowly restricted, the intention being to make it inclusive only of those peoples of the Middle Belt. The idea of a non-Muslim League therefore needed redefining. Secondly, the League through its association with the Christian missions, raised certain doubts. When the BPU was first formed, the inaugural meeting was held at the Roman Catholic Mission School in Jos. As its membership grew, there also developed the suspicion that the organization was a camouflage intended to get its members to become members of the Roman Catholic Church. To allay these fears, the BPU moved its meeting place to Dahwol Kanang, close to Bukuru. This experience suggested that if the peoples of the non-Muslim areas of the Middle Belt were to be united, an organization not so obviously associated with the Missions was needed. This was the origin of the Middle Zone League, which immediately superseded the non-Muslim League—though this did not prevent the President of the former, Pastor David Lot of the S.I.M., becoming the leader of the MZL, which set out with the ostensible aim of demanding a separate state.[80]

With its formation, most of the 'progressive', 'tribal' and 'state' Unions became allied to the MZL; for example, the Yergam Union, Nzit Tribal Union, Bachama Progressive Union of Adamawa, and Katagun Peoples' Union; others, the Igbirra Tribal Union, Tiv Progressive Union, and Idoma Hope Rising Union, were sympathetic even if they were not allied to it formally: but the core of the MZL was the BPU. With its affiliates the MZL won about twelve seats in the 1951 elections, though these were won by people who contested the elections as members of one particular union or the other. Party allegiances were unknown until the House of Assembly met in 1952, when it became clear that the NPC were in the majority.[81] The NPC's 'motto' declared when the JMA became a political party was (and still is) "One North, one people irrespective of religion, rank or tribe", but how strongly the NPC held to the idea of 'one North' was not known. In retrospect, one would probably think the MZL naïve for not seeing any inconsistency between the aim of a separate state and the NPC's motto of 'One North', but then at the various conferences which preceded the 1951 Constitution, there had been considerable division of opinion as to whether areas like Ilorin and Kabba should be allowed to go to the West. If there were then no strongly held views on the Ilorin–Kabba issue, was it unreasonable to expect that the NPC would have strong objections to a 'Middle Belt State' within the 'One North'? These and similar questions were debated by the leaders of the MZL, who with the backing of the Chiefs of Kagoro and Birom decided to form an alliance with the NPC in 1953. Whatever may have been the views of the rank and file, two principal reasons were given to justify the alliance. In the first place, with the general identification of the NPC with the Chiefs and Native Authorities, it was thought that such an alliance would minimize the growing victimisation which the NPC through the Chiefs and Native Authorities was bringing to bear on non-NPC party members. Secondly, it was felt that the alliance would give the MZL an insight into the workings of the NPC government, an experience which would be invaluable to the party when it succeeded in getting the proposed state created. Thus, expediency and not principle decided the MZL on the alliance with the NPC, but it was at a cost, for it discredited the MZL with those peripheral groups that had supported the party.

The alienation of these groups, the Tiv Progressive Union, the Ijumu Progressive Union, and the Igbirra Tribal Union to name the significant ones, led to the formation in July 1953 of the Middle Belt Peoples' Party (MBPP) with E. G. Gundu, a founder of the Tiv Union, as the President.[82] The Tivs were in fact the largest and most significant group in the MBPP. The TPU has since 1944 been loosely connected with the NCNC. Bello Ijumu, one of the leaders of the Ijumu Progressive Union was the first secretary of NEPU which is an ally of the NCNC. It was to be expected therefore that the MBPP would move towards NEPU.[83] Within the MBPP, however, the dominant influence of the Tivs caused some resentment. Idomas, with whom the Tivs have been involved in incessant disputes over land ownership, began making overtures to the NPC, while with the Igbirras, a split developed in the Igbirra Tribal Union, the majority faction supporting the MBPP, while the minority went over to the NPC.

With the approach of the 1954 Federal Elections, there were moves to unite the MBPP and the MZL.[84] A proposed meeting between the two parties, NEPU and some tribal organizations scheduled for the end of June 1954 failed, but in July, the MBPP and NEPU entered into an 'alliance'. In August, the MBPP Conference at Jos was told that a committee comprising members of the MBPP and MZL had examined the question of merging both parties and had agreed on the United Middle Belt Congress (UMBC) as the name of the new party, and that a further meeting was scheduled for September. Bello Ijumu was delegated later to put to the MZL at this meeting the choice of either joining the MBPP or the MBPP/NEPU alliance.[85] Still, agreement was reached and by mutual consent the question of merging both parties was postponed until after the elections. Various reasons can be adduced to explain this failure to merge the parties, but the most likely explanation, which the subsequent events show to be the most probable, is the inability to agree on the leadership of the new party and the strategy to be followed.

The MZL and the MBPP contested the 1954 elections under separate platforms, the former securing three seats while the latter won one. The Birom Progressive Union which contested separately from the MZL won one seat.[86] After the election, another attempt at merging both parties was made. At a meeting in Kafanchan in June 1955, both parties were united to become the UMBC and it was then agreed that the UMBC should not be affiliated to any other party and that those who were members of other political parties were to resign their membership of these parties.[87] But this was hardly practicable as the new union had scarcely any funds on which to run the party.[88] Some members of the party in the Federal Legislature then contacted the NPC to explore the possibility of an alliance between the two. J. S. Tarka, the member for Benue, however, objected suggesting that before any such agreement was made, the UMBC should get the NPC committed to the creation of a Middle-Belt State, ensure that the UMBC was represented at the 1956 Constitutional Conference in London and finally, agree not to contest constituencies where there were UMBC men standing.[89] The NPC could scarcely be expected to accept the first point. Nevertheless, without the knowledge of his party, the leader of the UMBC, Pastor David Lot, summoned some of the old MZL leadership on September 17th to a meeting in Kagoro where the decision was taken to ally the UMBC with the NPC.[90] Lot, as a result, was appointed a Minister of State in the Northern Regional Government while Patrick Dokotri, his next in command, accepted the office of Parliamentary Secretary to the Federal Minister of Mines and Power. At a meeting of the Party in Jos, a group opposed to the agreement with the NPC, led by Moses Rwang, and Ado Ibrahim, moved the expulsion of Lot and Dokotri from the UMBC.[91] The Party then broke into two factions, one wing led by Rwang, the other by Pastor Lot.[92] Both factions, each claiming to be the UMBC, held conferences simultaneously at Ilorin in November, but it was obvious that the majority of the members supported the Rwang wing which then elected H. O. Abaagu, a Tiv, as President. Besides adopting the "Constitution and Bye-Laws"[93] of the party, it also passed a number of resolutions to the effect that the party would, (a) maintain a firm stand for the creation of a 'Middle Belt State', (b) enter into no alliance "with any party at present"; (c) demand representation at the 1956 Constitutional Conference where a formal request for the creation of the "State" would be made. It also resolved not to associate itself with the NPC's "alleged plan to secede from Nigeria and join the Sudan"; objected to the NPC's proposed autonomous provincial administration and associated itself with NEPU's demand for electoral reform and universal adult suffrage.[94]

The split in the UMBC was on the old lines of the MZL and the MBPP and brings out the suggestion already made that the inability of both to unite in 1954 was due to difference of opinion on party strategy which, in itself, is a reflection of a failure to agree on a common leadership. The alliance between the Lot faction and the NPC was, however, shortlived. The predominant group in the MZL had, from its formation, been the Birom Progressive Union. In mid-1956, its Secretary, Bitrus Rwang Pam, who was also the General Secretary of the UMBC (Lot wing) son of the Chief of Jos, and Divisional Secretary of the Jos Native Authority, felt compelled to warn the NPC to urge the local (Jos) NPC to desist from instigating the Rububas, mainly Hausa, to break away from the Jos Native Authority. Besides, the Jam'iyyar Hausawa—the Hausa Tribal Party—were demanding of the Government (the NPC) that a Hausa Sarkin Jos (Chief of Jos) should be appointed (the Chief of Jos before 1947 had been a Hausaman). The tensions between Hausas and Biroms, heightened by the enquiry, conducted by an NPC official before the Senior District Officer, into the conduct of affairs by the Chief of Jos and the alleged imprisonment of the pagan peoples of Bauchi for refusing to accept a Hausa man as their Chief,[95] led to the final break between the Lot-UMBC and the NPC and just before the 1956 elections, both the President and Vice President, Lot and Dokotri, resigned their governmental offices with the NPC.

The break with the NPC was approved by the executive meeting of the party held in Jos at the end of November. This was followed by a reunification of both factions, H. O. Abaagu being appointed as a temporary chairman.[96] Finance, however, remained an ever-pressing problem. To meet this, a section of the leadership—Bello Ijumu, Moses Rwang, E. G. Gundu, Akase Dowgo and Ewoicho Omakwu, contacted the Action Group leadership at Ibadan, while the chairman, on behalf of the party, made representations to

NEPU.[97] These conflicting approaches came to a head at the Party's Conference at Lafia in January 1957. The Conference not only revealed the characteristic weakness of the UMBC—one of leadership—it also marked the terminal period of the several attempts to unite the peoples of the Middle Belt into a single, all-embracing political party. First, those who had approched the AG were accused of "subversive action" against the party, and walked out of the meetings, a move which resulted in their expulsion. Next, four candidates were nominated for election as President, Achiga Abuul, Jonas Assadugu, Abaagu and J. S. Tarka. All but Assadugu were Tivs, a point which marks the overwhelming place of the Tivs at the Conference. The order of preferences, when the returns were declared, was in the same order as the nomination, Abuul winning an over-all majority. As the new President, his inability to address the Convention in any language other than his native Tiv drew from Dokotri— the General Secretary of the Conference—a refusal to serve "under an illiterate President". In the intervening confusion, the Tivs decided to put forward Abaagu who, however, declined on the grounds that Abuul was "democratically elected". When order was restored, Assadugu decided to withdraw his candidature. As a Bachama with the rejection of Abuul he stood little chance against Abaagu and Tarka. But with Abaagu's refusal to accept nomination, Tarka was declared President. Abuul then walked out of the Conference to join the Rwang-Ijumu faction. This group later formed the Middle Belt State Party.[98] The MBSP contested two constituencies at the 1959 elections but failed to win any seats. With the withdrawal of some of its members from party politics and of others to join NPC, it had by 1961 ceased to exist.

Meanwhile, the Action Group had approached the UMBC with offers of financial support and the promise to raise the question of a Middle Belt State at the 1959 Constitutional Conference in London. In return, the UMBC was to support the Action Group's demand for the merging of Ilorin and Kabba provinces with the Western Region. The Tiv Divisional Conference of the UMBC which met in November was persuaded by Tarka (who had been chosen by the Action Group as one of its representatives at the London talks) and his immediate followers to accept the AG offer. The result of this new alliance was another split in the UMBC. This time Abaagu broke away to form his Benue Freedom Crusade to oppose any move to merge Ilorin and Kabba with the West. Like the MBSP, the Crusade had a very short life. Its leader, early in 1959, joined the NPC and with him went his supporters.[99]

With the breaking away of the various groups that once supported

H

the party, the UMBC has tended to become more and more a protest movement of the Tivs.[100] The Idomas, Igbirras, Igalas, Jukuns with the patronage of their respective Chiefs, the Ochi, Ohinoi, Atta and Aku-Uka, have all found it 'convenient' at least, at the level of regional government, to support the NPC. Most of the former leaders of the party have equally swung over to the NPC—Bitrus Pam, after serving his sentence in jail for misappropriating Native Authority property, Abaagu, even Moses Rwang who contrary to his previous beliefs and public statements joined the NPC in 1959, stating that "it is the only stable political party in the country catering for the common man". Various reasons can be found to explain the gradual decline of the UMBC which in 1960 existed only in the Lafia and Tiv divisions of Benue Province;[101] in part, this can be traced to the growth of Tiv influence within the party;[102] in part it is also due to the beneficent 'father figure' image which the NPC, with its control of the Government creates, an image well shown in the speech of an opposition member of the Assembly in 1959: "I should now turn to the NPC who are like our fathers. They should bear in mind, while distributing the estates, that the people of my area have been struggling for the past thirteen years to get what they want. . . . I know that the NPC Premier and his Minister appreciate this but their provincial branches do not";[103] and later when the same member had joined the NPC: "At that time (1952) (I was) just wearing a short pair of trousers and a shirt, appearing as a hooligan for no other reason than of politics. But when God has given me an opportunity I declared for the NPC in 1960. I raised my dignity thereby . . . and has become a man, and my people have become *good* people."[104] Equally important has been the party's inability to develop a common leadership, a failing which the party has also carried into the House of Assembly.[105]

The UMBC was an attempt to unite the peoples of the 'Middle-Belt' in opposition to the possible domination by Moslem Hausa–Fulanis of the 'Far North'. In its early stage as the MZL, it had set out with a fairly consistent aim—the demand for a separate state. Not so, however, the Ilorin Talaka Parapo—The Ilorin Commoners Party—which was founded in 1954. Ilorin, unlike a good many of the other provinces in the Middle-Belt, is, in its ethnic composition, fairly uniform, the inhabitants being mainly Yoruba who constitute 91% of the total population. The opposition to Native Authorities which, as has been shown, led to the formation of the various 'progressive' and 'tribal' unions, similarly explains the formation in Ilorin of the ITP. Its first Secretary, Mr. J. S. Emoeko, had stated that the aims of the party were the elevation of the 'status' of Ilorin, the eradication of primitiveness and corruption amongst, and the infusion of educational, political and social consciousness into, the people. It also aimed at arousing 'patriotism among the Ilorin people'. It was thus concerned, as the Report of the Minorities Commission[106] put it "with domestic issues—economic, social and political, hoping above all for a more democratic system of local government". But the approach to these questions only became clearer as the party developed. In its early stage, the Provincial Annual Report noted, the party was timid and traditional, demanding for instance, a return to indirect elections on a three-tier system and non-elective seats for the hereditary ward heads on the Town and Ward Councils.[107] This traditionalism it later shed, when, to quote the same report, "the ITP movement saw itself as a revolt of the underprivileged and of an emergent middle-class against the concentration of political and administrative power in the hands of the traditional leaders of the Native Authority and of their families. It was at this point that the ITP began to spread its attentions from Ilorin Town to the 'metropolitan districts' which were administered by district heads representing the traditional ruling families of Ilorin Town on the North Regional pattern".[108] This change, however, was not the result of a conscious reorientation. It was forced on the ITP by circumstance. Ilorin like most of the provinces of Northern Nigeria is divided into some thirty-one districts, those to the North being placed under Fulani district heads. Ilorin itself is administered by the Emir assisted by the Magaji Are, Baba Isale (all Yorubas) the Magajui-Gari, who supervises the Emir's 'quarter' and the four 'quarter' heads—Baloguns, the Balogun Gambari, Ajikobi, Alananu and Balogun Fulani. Only two of these, the Baloguns Ajikobi and Alanumu are Yorubas. These men dominated the Native Authority. Below them were the 'ward heads' who were all Yorubas, who in those quarters under the Baloguns Gambari and Fulani, resented being placed under non-Yorubas.[109] They therefore supported the ITP, as an expression of this resentment, a move which was enhanced when in April 1955, the Native Authority proposed that only literate councillors should be appointed chairman of committees.

By June 1955 then, the ITP had become of some importance in Ilorin. It then applied to the NPC for affiliation.[110] Here difficulties began to emerge which were to push the ITP into adopting an increasingly radical attitude. Meanwhile, the Action Group, having lost Lagos which was excised from the Western Region with the introduction of the 1954 Constitution and with the 1956 Constitutional talks in view, had increased its propaganda in the Ilorin and Kabba provinces demanding that, as these areas were essentially

Yoruba areas they should be merged with the Western Region. This demand won support amongst some of the ITP members, who tended therefore to be sympathetic towards the Action Group. On the other hand, the NPC to whom the ITP had applied for affiliation, referred the latter to the local branch of the NPC which since its formation was dominated by Sa'adu Alanamu the Chief Scribe of the Ilorin Native Authority and the son of the Balogun Alanamu, one of the four 'quarter' heads. In the local branch, however, there has been friction between the leader, Alanamu and Yahaya Ilorin, a former teacher at the Ilorin Provincial Secondary School and an NPC Minister of Health in the Northern House of Assembly. Both were rivals for the leadership of the local branch. As a result of this rivalry, Yahaya was accused by the branch executive of supporting the ITP and given three days to declare his stand. A meeting was then convened which was to be attended by Yahaya, the branch executive under Alanamu and the ITP leaders. But simultaneously with this, another meeting of the NPC allegedly instigated by Alanamu met under one S. A. Nagode and resolved not to compromise with the ITP or Yahaya until the latter declared unequivocally his stand.[111]

The extension of these cross-currents was the propagation by the local NPC that the ITP was Action Group inspired, while to the traditional leaders of Ilorin, the AG was portrayed as a party without any respect for Chiefs, the instance of Oyo, where the Alafin had been exiled in late 1954 by the AG controlled Western Nigeria Government, being cited to substantiate this claim. A direct follow-up of this, as the Annual Report noted, was that the traditional leaders "closed their ranks and prepared to resist what they regarded as alien and dangerous influences with every weapon that lay to their hands. In particular, they mobilized the Native Authority and set it to work to serve their purpose. . . . They also tended to resist changes in local government affairs desired by the people and approved by the Government. . . . They were on the defensive and therefore aggressive."[112] The victimization by the Native Authority of ITP supporters entailed, since the Native Authority was associated with the NPC, that the ITP became more and more critical of the NPC. Thus though the two parties did eventually enter into an agreement, this was no sooner concluded than it was abrogated,[113] with the result that the ITP now openly came to support the Action Group.

The undisguised antagonism between the ITP on the one hand and the Native Authority and NPC on the other led to the ITP's reversal of its former stand. With the approach of the elections to the local councils in June 1956, the ITP demanded that the elections should be direct with secret ballot. The electoral regulations provided for a 37% injection of traditional members at the primary stage and a 31% injection at the secondary stage. This the ITP rejected, insisting that only the six traditional ward heads should be allowed in the Town Council. All other traditional members were to be eliminated. But the traditional members were not to be denied the privilege allowed them by the electoral regulations preferring to have no Town Council rather than one directly elected. When it became known that the ITP had won 53% of the seats at the primary stage, the Emir and the Native Authority Council, now thoroughly alarmed, cancelled all local elections. The dispute between the ITP and the Native Authority thus took the form of a challenge to traditional privilege by the under-privileged.

The Emir and the Native Authority Council could only suspend the local elections for a limited period. They could not do so for all time. The changing conditions were revealed at the regional elections of 1956 when the ITP, now backed financially and administratively by the Action Group, won the four seats for the province.[114] When the local elections were finally held in April–May 1957, the ITP/AG won a majority of seats to control the Ilorin and Offa Town Councils and enough seats to control 22 of the 31 district councils. On the whole, the party won 246 seats to the NPC's 149. With its control of the Ilorin Town Council, the ITP at the first meeting of the Council on 8th May, succeeded in getting a motion expressing the wish of the people to be merged with the Western Region passed—"a major blunder" which "naturally incurred the displeasure of the Regional Ministers" as the 1958 Annual Report put it. The resolution, however, was followed with an instruction to two of the ITP/AG members—J. S. Olawoyin and Alhaji Maito—to press for the transfer of the province to the Western Region. This and other intemperate measures[115] adopted by the ITP soon alienated some of its supporters and split the leadership. Some of these, such as Jimoh Ajikobi, a member of one of the four traditional ruling families in Ilorin and a chairman of the party, soon resigned to join the NPC. He was followed by Ibrahim La'aro, an ITP member of the Northern House of Assembly, who later went over to the NPC. The ITP's virulent attacks on the Emir brought from an NPC supporter, Sani Okin, the Vice-President of the local branch, the statement that "anybody who denounces the Emir of Ilorin denounces God". If 91% of the people are Yorubas, most of these, 64% of the population, are also Muslims, a religion which makes obedience to constituted authority a cardinal doctrinal principle.[116]

In January 1958 the ITP, which was more or less now absorbed by the Action Group, suspended the six traditional ward heads from the Council. They were immediately reinstated by the Emir on his own authority. This and previous uncontrolled acts of the ITP resulted in a "solemn warning" by the NPC Government of the Northern Region. They did not realize the "limits which they should set themselves should they wish to survive" in a region in which they formed the opposition. And the Government in May instituted a Commission of Enquiry into the affairs of the Native Authority Council which was finally dissolved on 28th July 1958.

The ITP's influence derived from its control of the Town Council which gave it a significant role in the Native Authority Council. With the dissolution of the Town Council also went the party's political future. In place of the original council, the Government appointed a Caretaker Council which consisted of selected traditional title holders, district heads, Native Administration officials and a prominent Muslim—all known NPC members or sympathizers.[117] Reaction soon set in. The traditional titleholders had in the past preserved their privileges by "every legal and illegal method". Challenged by an emergent middle-class, they had lost these for a short period. With a sudden reversal of their fortunes, it was therefore to be "expected", as the 1958 Annual Report noted, that they would not act "with absolute impartiality". "The resources of the Native Authority machine, including the police, the Courts and the officials of the Forestry and Health Departments" were now brought in to bolster their authority and to bring pressure to bear on the opposition.[118] The methods proved successful. At the 1959 Federal Elections, unlike the 1956 Regional elections when it won all the seats for the province, the party won only one of the six seats. Even this was lost during the 1961 regional elections when the NPC won all the six seats. By the time of the regional elections, the ITP had ceased to exist as a separate party, having lost its identity to the Action Group. The crisis in the latter party in 1962[119] not only may have spelt the end of ITP in what ever form it existed in Ilorin, it also resulted in the leaders of the ITP seeking membership of the NPC.

One interesting sociological fact arising from this account of the emergence and growth of political parties in the North is that they have in all cases had their origins in the main towns—the NPC in Zaria, NEPU in Kano, MZL and UMBC in Jos, BYM in Maiduguri and the ITP in Ilorin. In a sense this is to be expected as urban conditions tend to produce not only new social relationships and a wider opportunity for social action and interaction, but also different and conflicting value systems and social orientations. In a markedly stratified society, individual awareness of status within the stratification system is much more noticeable in an urban than in a rural setting. This awareness creates conflict situations which are a necessary condition for social action—a political party being merely a mode of such action. From this, it would seem to follow that the higher the level of urbanization, the greater the degree of political involvement, which, in part, would explain the apparent difference in party political activity between the Northern Region and that in the South.[120]

The account so far has been in terms of the development of the party system. But to talk of a party 'system', is to imply that the parties each exhibit a structural form which makes it meaningful to talk about them as constituting a 'system'. This will be the subject of the next two chapters. By 1962 both the ITP and the BYM had been absorbed into the AG. The UMBC so far resisted this move. Since we are here concerned strictly with Northern Nigeria, subsequent analysis will therefore be limited to the NPC, NEPU and UMBC. References to 'Southern' based political parties will be made only in so far as these help in the description of the parties named. Before this is done, however, some consideration will be given to the nature of party alliances and affiliations.

IV. THE NATURE OF PARTY ALLIANCES

The history of the various parties presented so far has revealed a bewildering tendency for the different parties to affiliate or form alliances with one another. Thus, the UMBC was for a time affiliated to the NPC then NEPU and finally the Action Group. NEPU itself is affiliated to the NCNC. Mr. Post,[121] in considering this question, carried out his analysis principally from the viewpoint of the AG and the NCNC both trying to gain a 'foothold' in the Northern Region. He did not concern himself, however, with the nature of such alliances, neither does the account which he offers help in the understanding of the form of party affiliations in any one Region, the orientation of his analysis being in terms of a "balance of power".

A consideration of the 'agreements' entered into between the parties shows, however, that they fall into the two categories differentiated by Duverger who made the distinction between 'electoral' and 'parliamentary' alliances. In general, relations between the NPC and its affiliates have tended to be of the 'parliamentary' type. Thus after the 1954 federal elections, the NPC accepted the Igbirra Tribal Union candidates on a parliamentary basis. But at the local level, the ITU is in opposition to the NPC. In 1956 the ITU defeated the NPC candidates in both Igbirra North and South constituencies. Both the ITU men later declared for the NPC. One, later appointed a Minister in the North Regional Government, Mr. George Ohikere, decided to contest Igbirra South in 1959 as an NPC candidate but was defeated by the ITU candidate Muhammadu Kokori Abdul, who, after the elections declared his support for the NPC. In the 1960 elections to the Okene Town Council and four other District Councils in the Igbirra Division, the NPC candidates were all defeated by their ITU counterparts. In the Igala Division, both the Igala Union and the Igala Divisional Union, who are opposed to each other at the local level (the Igala Union being against the Native Authority, which the IDU controls) are at the 'parliamentary' level, affiliates of the NPC. Though in the 1956 regional elections, the NPC had contested against the IDU, in 1959, it had refrained from so doing. Presumably, the case of Igala is the exception to the rule, but this is not to say that the rule does not hold. Between 1951 and 1955, the MZL was in alliance with the NPC in the regional Assembly, but during the 1954 elections, the NPC had contested the same constituencies against MZL candidates. After the split in the UMBC in 1955, the faction that supported the NPC (UMBC Lot faction) was in the 1956 regional elections opposed by NPC candidates. At the level of federal politics, having earlier resolved not to enter into any alliance with a 'Southern based' political party, the NPC in 1958, decided against this policy. It then declared its preparedness to "co-operate" at the parliamentary level with any political party or individuals "interested in our ideology". After the 1959 Federal Elections, the NPC and the NCNC agreed to form a coalition government, but both had opposed each other during the elections. NEPU as an ally of the NCNC thus became a partner in the federal coalition though it is in opposition to the NPC in the North.

Being firmly entrenched, the NPC can possibly afford to ignore, or disregard electoral agreements in the full knowledge that successful candidates would nevertheless support it in the Assembly. Not so NEPU. It has been noted that NEPU has tended to be under-represented in Parliament. With a firmly established NPC, NEPU's chances therefore lie very much in electoral arrangements if the votes of the 'opposition' are not to be split. Hence, unlike those of the NPC, the alliances entered into, and agreements made, by NEPU are of the 'electoral type'. Thus, clause one of the 'Bond' between NEPU and BYM stipulates that "during any either local or national election the parties should decide amongst themselves that the party that has the bigger following should be backed by the other party which commands the minority following. That is, in an election where one party has ten members and the other has seven then the latter should render its vote to the former." Clause two of its agreement with the 'Habe Alliance' led by Ibrahim Dimis stated that in the event of an election whether local or national, the two parties will join forces to fight the election and that all chosen candidates from either side will contest under the platform of NEPU". Similarly, the party's alliance with the Adamawa National Congress, signed on 1st January 1958, after stating that "either party is an entity enjoying its sole right to spread its branches", specified that "at the time of elections, both local and general, both parties will agree on candidature".[122]

Though, as Duverger noted, the 'electoral' and the 'parliamentary' type of party affiliations can be combined, at the regional level, this has rarely been the case with NEPU. Its 'electoral' agreements have often not been extended to cover co-operation at the parliamentary stage. Thus, despite its understanding with the UMBC, after the regional elections, that party refused to accept Ibrahim Imam, a BYM/NEPU member, as the leader of the opposition in the House of Assembly. Even when all these, BYM, NEPU and UMBC later agreed to have Bitrus Rwang Pam (UMBC) as the leader, the agreement was short-lived, each party taking different stands in the Assembly.[123] The fact that 'opposition' members tend, sooner or later, to cross over to the Government—the NPC—actually makes a 'parliamentary' alliance problematic. Hence the recent move by NEPU to make those the party intends to sponsor for elections undertake that in return for financial help or other aid, should the candidate later default to the NPC, he will be liable to a 'fine' of £1,000 for a breach of contract. So far, no test case has yet arisen to decide the validity of such agreements. If accepted, however, their implications would be far-reaching as it would introduce a different interpretation of the status of the member of Parliament, a question supposedly determined by Burke.

NOTES

1. On the Development of Political Parties in Nigeria, see J. Coleman, *Nigeria Background to Nationalism*, Berkeley, 1958; 'The Emergence of African Political Parties' in *Africa Today*, C. Grove Haines, (ed.) Johns Hopkins, 1955; N. Azikiwe, *The Development of Political Parties in Nigeria*, London, 1957; P. C. Lloyd, 'The Development of Political Parties in Western Nigeria', *The American*

Political Science Review, vol. 44, no. 3, September 1955; R. L. Sklar, *Nigerian Political Parties*, Ph.D. Thesis, Princeton, 1961; K. W. J. Post, *The Nigerian Federal Election 1959*, Oxford University Press for N.I.S.E.R. 1963.

2. Missionaries were allowed into the non-Moslem areas of the 'Middle-belt' of the North.

3. According to the 1921 Census, literacy figures for the main ethnic group of the North were: Kanuri, 5·3%, Fulani 3%, Hausa 2·6%, Nupe 1·57%, Yoruba 1·06%, others 0.58%. Average literacy rate for the North as a whole was 1·94%. See C. K. Meek, *Northern Tribes*, 1925, vol. 2, p. 258. In 1953 the Regional Minister of Education and Social Welfare, quoting from the 1952 Census figures, gave the following literacy figures on a provincial basis: Benue 1·9%, Kano 0·9%, Katsina 1·6%, Zaria 5·6%, Niger 2·8%, Plateau 5·1%, Bornu 0·9%. The corresponding figures for literacy in Arabic were Benue 1·0%, Katsina 4·8%, Zaria 10·8%, Niger 4·0%, Plateau 2·2%, Bornu 2·1% and Kano 8·0%. See *Debates of the Northern House of Assembly*, 15th January 1953, p. 29.

4. R. M. East, 'Recent Activities of the Literature Bureau', *Africa*, vol. 14, 1943–44, p. 75.

5. J. S. Coleman, 'Nationalism in Tropical Africa', *The American Political Science Review*, vol. 48, 1954, pp. 404–25, and also his *Nigeria Background to Nationalism*, See also T. L. Hodgkin, *Nationalism in Colonial Africa*.

6. *Report of the Conference of Chiefs and Emirs of the Northern Region*, Kaduna, 1942, pp. 52–57.

7. Loc. cit.

8. The paper *Gaskiya Tafi Kwabo* (Truth is Worth More than a Penny), was in Hausa. In its first year, it had a circulation of 15,000 copies per month. See *Annual Report of the Northern, Western and Eastern Provinces and the Colony*, 1939, p. 2.

9. *Report of the Conference of Chiefs and Emirs*, 1939, pp. 20–21.

10. J. Coleman gives the date of the founding of NEPA as 1945. Post and Sklar both gave 1946 while Segal: *Political Africa*, passim, quotes 1947. The documents of this organization in the possession of Raji Abdallah and Sani Darma show the date as 1947. Most comments on NEPA tend to suggest that it became defunct soon after its formation. This is certainly incorrect.

11. See Sir Ahmadu Bello, *My Life*, Cambridge, 1962, passim.

12. Cf. Sir Bernard Bourdillon's speech to the Conference of Chiefs 1939, about the challenge of youth and the educated, who "will demand to have some say in the management of their own affairs. . . . If you ignore it, you will be laying up trouble for yourselves, for it will grow and spread underground, unseen and uncontrolled, until it becomes a strong movement of revolt. . . . And so my advice to you is to encourage a free expression of opinion . . .". Ibid., pp. 5–6.

13. Northern Provinces Advisory Council, *Summary of Proceedings*, Kaduna, 1932, p. 20.

14. The Revision of the Scale of Salaries of Graduates of the Higher College, *Report of the Committee under the Chairmanship of the Resident, Benue Province*, 1932.

15. Nuhu Bamali, 'How the NPC was Founded', *Nigerian Citizen*, Zaria, 15th May 1959.

16. A good number of the political leaders of the North have gone through Katsina College, men such as Tafawa Balewa, Ahmadu Bello, Isa Kaita, Aliyu Makaman Bida, Ahman Pategi, Aminu Kano and many others. Nuhu Bamali, op. cit., suggested that the NPC was actually a direct lineal successor of the Katsina Old Boys Association formed in 1939. There is, however, no evidence to

substantiate this besides the mere fact that most of the present leaders of the NPC were products of Katsina College.

17. *Annual Report for the Northern, Western, Eastern Provinces and the Colony*, 1939, p. 15.

18. One of the few exceptions to the practice of appointing Hausa–Fulanis to positions of authority was that of M. Abubakar Gardu, a Jukun of Wukari who held the office of Treasurer of Wukari N.A. from 1922–52. His appointment, however, was due largely to pressure from the Sudan United Mission (SUM). Kilba separatism was quickly followed by similar moves from the Batta and Chamba. To quieten down this move, the Lamido hastily appointed the District Heads of these areas to his Council. See *Annual Report*, 1952, p. 5.

19. For a profile of Aminu Kano, see *West Africa*, 19th July 1952 and 15th December 1956. Not only had Aminu Kano written critical articles about the North in the *West African Pilot*, Lagos, he also wrote an inflamatory pamphlet entitled, *Kano Under the Hammer of Native Administration*, Kano, n.d., c. 1947.

20. In a speech in the Northern House of Assembly (reported in the *Nigerian Citizen* 14th January 1949), Tafawa Balewa pointed out that "we made application (to have the NTA recognized) only two months ago. Two months ago, we got it from the government that it is the policy to discourage Trade Unions in Northern Nigeria."

21. *Nigerian Citizen*, 8th April 1949.

22. This is highly misleading, for the JMA had definite political orientations; see B. J. Dudley, 'The Nomination of Parliamentary Candidates in Northern Nigeria', *Proceedings of the 8th Annual Conference of NISER*, Ibadan, March 1962, reprinted in the *Journal of Commonwealth Political Studies*, vol. 2, no. 1, November 1963. Nuhu Bamali, op. cit., in fact states that the JMA "was intended to be a political party but cloaked as a cultural organization".

23. *Nigerian Citizen*, 30th December 1949.

24. For details and composition of the Committees, see *Nigerian Citizen*, 6th January 1950.

25. Debates of the Northern House of Assembly, 22nd May 1953, p. 19.

26. Telegram dated 4th July 1949. I am indebted to Alhaji Ibrahim Iman for a photostat copy of the Sultan's telegram.

27. See Nuhu Bamali, op. cit.

28. Sklar, op. cit., p. 146 asserts that the severance of relations between NEPU and the JMA was due to a motion from the conservative Sokoto YSC. There is no evidence that the Sokoto YSC was represented at the Meeting. The list of delegates, NPC Headquarter File No. JMA/1250/212, of 1st December 1950, compiled by M. Yahaya Gusau and sent to Mr. A. Akilu of the North Civil Service show no representation for the YSC or Sokoto as a whole.

29. See Memo. to the Minorities Commission by M. Aminu Kano, NEPU Headquarter File No. 00221. The 'objectives' became the basis on which the October 1952 Declaration of Principles was formulated.

30. Loc. cit. Percentage registration of electors in some of these towns were Kano Township 10%, Kano Sabon-Gari 27%, Kaduna 52%, Zaria 31%, Jos Township 29%, Jos Native Town 41%. See *Nigerian Citizen*, 16th August 1951 and 23rd August 1951.

31. *Nigerian Citizen*, 25th October 1951.

32. Loc. cit.

33. Nuhu Bamali, op. cit.

34. Information supplied by M. Garba Abuja, M. Abuja was the first Administrative Secretary of the JMA, having been appointed to that office on the first

of September 1951 (Dr. Dikko writing from Bauchi to Yahaya Gusan, Secretary of the JMA (letter dated 11th September 1951) pregnantly ended with the caution "Do not listen nor yet pay any attention to rumours"). This information has been repeated by other people interviewed by the writer. M. Abuja broke with the NPC in 1960 and took away with him a good number of the NPC Headquarter's files, which he kindly allowed me to use. I am indebted to him for this and other help.

35. When, for instance, the eight representatives for Katsina were elected, a 'spokesman' for the NPC said all of them would indicate their support for the party, *Nigerian Citizen*, 8th November 1951. Later, Ibrahim Imam, the party's General Secretary at this time, was to say in a speech at Zaria, that the 1951 elections were not fought by the NPC on its platform. "Members of the House were therefore not bound to be loyal to the Party," *Nigerian Citizen*, 16th October 1952. On becoming a political party, the civil servants within the party resigned; both Balewa and the Sadauna became members of the party as from the day it became a political party. Sklar, op. cit. gives the date of conversion, first, as 5th July, footnote I, p. 581 and secondly as 1st October, p. 147.

36. See *Nigerian Citizen*, 15th January 1958.

37. *Nigerian Citizen*, 2nd October 1952. The relationship between the Native Authorities and the NPC will be dealt with in greater detail in subsequent chapters.

38. *Nigerian Citizen*, 23rd October 1952. In May 1962, the village head of Kakumi, Alhaji Mogagi was fined a total of £71 at the Kano Chief Magistrate Court for the illegal imprisonment of a NEPU, Malam Tudu, in August 1959. M. Tudu claimed that on being invited by the village head, he was 'ordered' to declare himself an NPC member and that for refusing to do so, he was bound in chains and locked up in a school room. See *Daily Express* (Lagos), 7th May 1962. It has been claimed that over 7,000 NEPU and other opposition party activists have been imprisoned for their political belief by NPC-N.A. functionaries —see Debates of House of Representatives, Lagos, 12th April 1960, vol. I, col. 1133. This, however, is hardly credible as the total number of prisoners in Northern Nigeria in June 1960 was only 8,545. See Debates of the N.H.A., 22nd August 1962, col. 493.

39. Letter dated 16th January 1954 from Nuhu Bamali, Secretary to the NPC Working Committee.

40. 'Political Touring Reports 18th July—28th July 1958', by Abutu Obekpa Minister of State. Unpublished.

41. Mary Smith, *Baba of Karo*, London, 1954, p. 66–67.

42. *Report of the Organization Department*, October 1961 dated 23rd October 1961, File 0138 NEPU H.Q. Files.

43. For results of the Federal Election see *Report on the Nigerian Federal Elections*, Lagos, 1960, Appendix I, p. 24, and for the 1961 Regional Elections, *West Africa*, 20th May 1961.

44. See R. Michels, *Political Parties*, translated by Eden and Cedar Paul, Dover, 1959 (reprint of the 1915 translation); and also Michels, 'Some Reflections on the Sociological Character of Political Parties', *The American Political Science Review*, vol. 21, no. 4, 1927; G. Mosca, *The Ruling Class*, translated by H. D. Kahn, edited by A. Livingston (McGraw-Hill, 1939); and also M. Duverger, *Political Parties*, Methuen, 1954.

45. Soon after its formation, the UNM became absorbed into the NPC— see *Nigerian Citizen*, 27th May, 17th June, and 1st July 1954.

46. Report of the Board of Auditors Appointed by the National Executive

Committee of NEPU, dated Kano, 27th January 1961. The report is in Hausa and its full title in Hausa is: Report na Board of Auditors Wand NEC Na NEPU Ta Nada A Taronta Na Jos Ran 18/9/60 Don Bie Inken Yan Finance Committee Da Ake Tuhuma Bisa Muguwar Hanya, I am indebted to M. Aluyu Mahmud, a member of the Board for a copy of its Report (Unpublished).

47. By November 1961 NEFO claimed it had 1,727 members in Plateau Province, 1025 in Katsina and 1508 in Zaria. It had a following also in Kano, Adamawa, Bauchi and Sardauna Provinces but the exact numbers were unknown. Information supplied by M. Gambo Sawaba, a founder member and one of the leaders of NEFO in Zaria.

48. Following attempts to bring the leaders of the NYM back to the NPC, the former submitted a fourteen-point claim (in a letter dated 8th November 1960) to the General Secretary of the NPC Kano Province as a basis of negotiation. The failure to agree on this fourteen-point programme led to a formal break of the NYM with the NPC. On 19th March 1961, the NYM sent a formal application to the Electoral Commission to be registered as a political party with the 'groundnut' as its party symbol. The reply CREO/180/VII/187 of 23rd March 1961 curiously stated that the Commission could not register the NYM as a party for under Reg. 90 of the Northern Electoral Regulations, the Commission only registered political parties. An appeal to the Chief Regional Electoral Office brought a further reply CREO/180/VII/240 of 25th October 1961 that the Commission was an independent institution and not subject to the authority of the CREO, citing Reg. 5 of the Elections (NHA) Regulations 1960 established under Section 36A of the Nigeria (Constitution) Order in Council 1954.

49. Mr. D. J. Muffett was appointed the Sole Commissioner and the Enquiry thus became known as the Muffett Enquiry. Though the Government had decided not to publish his findings, a 'statement' by the Government after the Enquiry is given in full in the *Nigerian Citizen*, 1st May 1963.

50. Cf. for similar situations in Western Nigeria: P. C. Lloyd, op. cit.

51. A month after its formation the KPP had on its register 36,423 members all of which were in Kano Province—information supplied by the General-Secretary M. Ali Wazirichi who showed the writer the Party's membership register. The President of the party is M. Bello Abdulkadiri a former N.A. Lance-Corporal of the Political C.I.D. branch. In June 1963 the executive members of the party were sentenced to varying terms of imprisonment by the Alkali Court for using "annoying language" in references to the Premier Sir Ahmadu Bello.

52. The strike led to the removal of the former Supervisor of Works, one M. Barma, from office. With his removal, the strikers insisted on being involved in the choice of his successor and Imam was nominated by them.

53. Imam in fact scored only two votes less than Shettima Kashim (67 to 65) who was to become Waziri in 1956 and Governor of the North (now as Sir Kashim Ibrahim) in 1962. For a 'portrait' of Imam, see *Nigerian Citizen*, 31st March 1956, *West Africa*, 11th April 1953, and 8th September 1956.

54. The following were responsible for creating a NEPU branch in Yerwa: Alhaji Waziri Ibrahim (a Kanuri from Konduga an employee of the United Africa Co.); Alhaji Audu, Habe, motor garage passenger collector; Ahmadu Zaria, Habe, letter writer; Garba Kano, Habe, trader; Balla Dambatta, Habe, trader; Gogobiri Masha, Habe, kolanut trader; Umaru Orante Adamu Gombe, Adamu Bokin ba'agale, Ali Dan Alhaji, Garuba Hadeija, Alhaji Mikoall, Habes and traders in kola-nuts; Inuwa Maitakara, Kanuri, hotelier; Abubakar Meskin Kanuri, Arabic teacher; and Aminu Zaria, Habe, garage passenger collector

(Dan Commission). Thus of the fifteen founders, only three were Kanuris. The preponderance of petty-traders amongst the founders is illustrative generally of the strata of society from which NEPU drew its supporters.

55. *Nigerian Citizen*, 1st July 1954.

56. The UNM was formed in Maiduguri in September 1954, when it reported that over 100 youths joined the party. The Deputy President was Sabo Bakinzuo, formerly a NEPU member. See *Nigerian Citizen*, 7th October 1954.

57. The Bornu State Movement was for a long time led by M. Abba Gana. It was used to pressure the NPC into providing jobs for Kanuri youths in return for not pressing the demand for a Bornu State. Its leader, then an organizer with the University of Ibadan Extra-Mural Department in the North was later appointed the High Commissioner for the North in Britain and on being recalled, was made the Chairman of the Gaskiya Corporation.

58. It was the Gizmawa Tribal Union, formed in 1953, which converted into the NECPP. Sklar, op. cit., p. 623, claimed it was formed to unite the Karekare, Bolewa, Ngawa and Ngizima (Gizmawa) but that the task was difficult because while the Karekare and Gizmawa incline towards NEPU, the Bolewa and Ngama, being conquering tribes tend to support the NPC. In fact, the NECPP was essentially a Gizmawa party. It supported the NPC in the hope that the NPC would accede to the demand for a separate Bornu State; cf. its resolutions to the NPC Maiduguri Convention of 1955. *Nigerian Citizen*, 9th June 1955. In 1956 it broke off relations with the NPC and its members became absorbed by NEPU. The Gizmawa and Karekare of Fika, Badawa of Bedde Division, Babera and Bra in Biu Division and the Fadawa in Dikwa Division all claim to be real Kanuris.

59. In July 1955 the UNM broke its association with the NPC because the latter failed to commit itself to self-government in 1956, *Nigerian Citizen*, 21st July 1955, while the NECPP broke off with the NPC for failing to agree to separate Bornu State; cf. letter in *Nigerian Citizen*, 26th May 1956.

60. For Imam's reasons for resigning from the NPC see *Nigerian Citizen*, 29th April 1954, which gives quotations from Imam's two-page letter of resignation dated 24th April 1954 addressed to the Sardauna. BYM members claim that though Imam was independent, having declined the invitation by BYM, he nevertheless gave the party financial support. Sklar, op. cit., p. 538, incorrectly stated that Imam was a founder-member of BYM. Besides Binwafe already mentioned, the other founders of the BYM were Abba Matidan, N.A. official, now assistant editor *Morning Post*, Messrs. Baba and Aba'aji, both N.A. employees and M. Baba Carpenter, an N.A. carpenter.

61. Dipcharima who was at one time President of the Zikist Movement joined the NPC in August 1954 when he stated: "I have accepted the Presidentship of the Bornu NPC. I have taken over full responsibilities of the branch." See *Nigerian Citizen*, 2nd September 1954.

62. The 'Bond' dated 2nd November 1956 was to the effect that (a) both parties should not contest the same seat, the size of the following of either party in each constituency being the deciding factor as to which party's candidate would contest the constituency; (b) weekly consultative meetings to be held between both wherever they were represented in the same area; (c) one member of the BYM should represent it at NEPU Headquarters "as is now the case"; (d) whenever, in any constitutional Conference, NEPU was allocated more than one seat, one of these should be made available to the BYM; (e) there should be no public criticism by either of the two parties. The Bond was signed on behalf of BYM by its President and Vice-President, Sanda Na Alhaji Hanuza and Alhaji Sherif respectively.

63. *The Provincial Annual Report for 1956* noted that Imam and the BYM were "capitalizing on the corruption of the N.A. in 1953/54 and 1956".

64. Though the elections were indirect, in 19 Urban Constituencies it was "direct" on an adult taxpayer suffrage. These were: Kano 4 seats; Sokoto and Yeruwa 2 each; Gusau, Kaura-Namoda, Katsina, Nguru, Ilorin, Offa, Bida, Jos, Okenne, Zaria, Kaduna, one seat each. On the whole the NPC won 10, NEPU 4, BYM/NEPU 2, A.G. 1, Igbirra Tribal Union/NPC 1, Ilorin Talaka-Parapo/A.G. 1. For details, see *Nigerian Citizen*, 5th September and 17th November 1956.

65. Imam was informed in a letter dated 3rd September 1956 that BYM/NEPU would only support a member of the party in the elections and not an Independent candidate. Imam joined the party the following day. Before the elections, the party nominated Imam for Yerwa North and M. Garba Kano for Yerwa South, but Imam demanded to be allowed to stand for Yerwa South. Not only was there a stronger concentration of BYM supporters in Yerwa South, but the new Waziri, Shettima Kashim was standing in Yerwa North for the NPC. The rejection of Imam's demand led to Sani Darma being sent from NEPU Headquarters to Maiduguri to settle the deadlock. Darma succeeded in getting the BYM to accede to Imam's demand, but now, Garba Kano who was to contest Yerwa North decided to withdraw, not being a Kanuri himself. The party then nominated a M. Basharu, an N.A. driver to stand for Yerwa North and later to defeat his boss, the Waziri, who was before the elections, a Minister in the North Regional Government. The defeat of the NPC in Yerwa should not be attributed principally to the corruption of the N.A. The NPC spoilt its chances when it allowed thirteen different people to contest the two seats for Yerwa. See *Nigerian Citizen*, 27th October 1956.

66. See *Provincial Annual Report for 1957* which attributed NPC's successes to the reconstruction of the Native Authority after the exposure of abuses, a point which unwittingly tied the N.A. with the NPC.

67. In 1960, 30 gold medals, 140 silver medals and signed certificates were presented to Bornu NPC men which included Shettima Kashim, the Waziri, and head of the N.A., Bukar Batulbe, a trader and Provincial President of the NPC, Mallam Ja'afar, N.A. Health Inspector and Provincial Secretary, Mr. H. A. Zanna Mustafa Laisu, Councillor for Local Government and Works, and Galadima Kiari, D. H. Nguru, Yerima Mustafa, D. H. Geidam, Madu Alkali, N.A. Information Officer, "for loyalty and hardwork". See *Nigerian Citizen*, 13th July 1960.

68. See e.g. Debates of the Northern House of Assembly 2nd March 1957, p. 464 and 7th April 1960, cols. 38–39.

69. For the June 1957 directives, see *Nigerian Citizen*, 6th July 1957. The 1961 eighteen-point resolution was dated 27th July 1961 and signed by Alhaji Mustapha Haruna, President of the Hausari NPC branch. As a result of the latter resolution, NEPU petitioned the Governor-General of Nigeria, the Governor of the North, the Premier and the Waziri. This led to a meeting between the Waziri, NPC and NEPU representatives, at which meeting the Waziri made the NPC representatives admit the Resolution was taken without the knowledge of the Native Authority. NEPU reported having told the District Head of Yerwa about this on three separate occasions. Apparantly no action was taken. However, as a result of the meeting with the Waziri, the local rediffusion service made a broadcast saying there was no restriction on social contacts in Yerwa.

70. See Elections in Sardauna Province, *West Africa*, 9th December 1961, contributed by the writer.

71. In the 1959 Federal elections in Yerwa BYM/AG polled 7·2% of the total

votes, NEPU 12·2%. In 1961 the figures were AG 2·3%, NEPU 5·6%. When the author visited Maiduguri in December 1961, there was virtually no AG/BYM branch existing there, while of the 184 NEPU branches supposed to exist in Bornu Province, only one was in Yerwa. The NPC candidate for Yerwa polled the next highest vote 92·1% (the highest was 98·6% in Maradun-Sokoto Province) in the regional elections.

72. A split occured in the ranks of the BYM when Imam, unknown to the BYM executive, negotiated an alliance between the party and the AG in 1958. At a meeting of the party summoned by Tanko Yakassai a NEPU headquarter official sent to Maiduguri, the decision was taken to expel those leaning towards the AG. This caused a split of the party into two factions, BYM/AG and BYM/NEPU. For the ostensive reasons of the break, see the press release by Ibrahim Imam, Alhaji Sheriff and M. Basharu, quoted in full in *Nigerian Citizen*, 21st June 1958.

73. *Provincial Annual Report* 1954, pp. 3–4.

74. *Provincial Annual Report* 1953, p. 5. Not surprisingly, the opposition quickly allied with NEPU.

75. Benjamin Akiga, Makondo Igbon, Chia Aka who supported the NPC refused to support the demand for an enquiry. At a mass meeting of the TPU in Makurdi in July 1952 a vote of no confidence was passed on the three thereby signifying the break with the NPC. See *Nigerian Citizen*, 7th August 1952. In 1944, TPU became an affiliate of the NCNC, 'Two Nigerian Lists', *African Affairs*, vol. 44, no. 177, October 1945, p. 165.

76. In 1955, the Chief of Birom, Rwang Pam became the Chief of Jos; the ascendancy of the Biroms in Jos led in 1956 to the formation of the Jamiyyar Hausawa or Hausa Tribal Party "to protect the interests of the Hausa elements in Jos area", *Nigerian Citizen*, 5th May 1956 and 28th August 1956.

77. J. Davies: *Gyel Farm Survey*, pp. 196–212, reported that in 1944, 10·3% of the original arable land was already destroyed through the operation of the mining companies; 2·2% was taken over for occupation by the miners; 86% was under mining leases of some sort or the other though not all were necessarily taken up; 4% was settled and farmed by strangers employed in the mines. The land situation was complicated by the fact that the best tin-bearing lands were also the most fertile areas.

78. M. G. Smith has pointed out that the MZL was formed on Kagoro initiative and that the inaugural meeting brought together representatives of ninety-eight pagan tribes. The question as to whether the initiative came from Kagoro or the Birom may be academic as both the Chief of Birom and the Chief of Kagoro supported the MZL. There is, however, no question as to the greater political awareness of the Biroms. Smith, 'Kagoro Political Development', *Human Organization*, vol. 19, no. 3, 1960, p. 146. Sklar, op cit., pp. 546–47 states that the non-Muslim League was converted to the MZL but gives no reasons for this. Smith pointed out that the headquarters of the MZL was at Jos. This is incorrect. The headquarters was moved to Jos from Bukuru only in July 1954; see *Nigerian Citizen*, 15th July 1954.

79. Even as late as 1955, in a debate on the N.A. (Amendment) Law 1955, the Premier of the North, Ahmadu Bello, told the Assembly: "The right traditions that we have gone away from are the cutting of the hands of thieves. . . . That is logical and it is lawful in our tradition and custom here. . . . It is because *the Moslem power is not strong here* that we have not got slaves to sell." Debates of the House of Assembly 10th March 1955, p. 6. Also ibid., 4th March 1955, p. 15.

80. The area involved in a Middle Belt State has never been clearly defined by

its protagonists. Article three of the UMBC 'Constitution and Bye-laws' gives it as "Kabba, Ilorin, Niger, Benue, Plateau, Adamawa, Southern Zaria and Southern Bauchi provinces". The UMBC Lafia Conference 15th–17th January 1957, gave the same area, *Nigerian Citizen*, 23rd January 1957. Slightly different 'definitions' were given by Bitrus Pam and Ibrahim Imam respectively; see Debates of the N.H.A. 26th February 1957, p. 250, 6th March 1956, p. 179.

81. In a list prepared by NPC headquarters staff officials dated 18th November 1953, of the ninety members of the House, sixty-two were shown to "have declared their party loyalty to the Northern Peoples Congress".

82. See *West Africa*, 8th August 1953. The aim of the MBPP when inaugurated was the creation of a separate Middle-Belt State.

83. Sklar op. cit. p. 546 stated that the MBPP was organized "as an affiliate of the NCNC". This does not seem to have been borne out by the President, who in a public release stated that "the fact that some members of the MBPP are also members of NEPU, NCNC, etc., does not prove that the MBPP . . . is already affiliated to any of these parties". *Nigerian Citizen*, 18th February 1954.

84. Anta Ninzam, an MZL member of the House of Assembly said that the move to merge with the MBPP was suggested by one of the MZL leaders who was threatened with expulsion for embezzling the party's funds. See Debates of the House of Assembly 6th March 1956, p. 210.

85. Minutes of the Tripartite (NCNC/NEPU/MBPP) Election Committee held in Kaduna at the Owerri Hall 30th August 1954 in NEPU Headquarter File no. 0127.

86. The other results were NPC 80 Seats, NCNC 2, AG 1, Idoma State Union 2, Igbirra Tribal Union 1 and Independent 1. The Idoma and Igbirra representatives later declared for the NPC.

87. The meeting took place on 1st June 1955; Sklar op. cit. passim gave 10th June, see *Nigerian Citizen*, 16th June 1955.

88. In his Report to the 1st Annual Conference of the UMBC held at Ilorin 19th November 1955, the General Secretary, Ado Ibrahim, son of the deposed (1954) Atta of Igbirra, pointed out that party expenditure ran to £600 for the period under review, but as a result of lack of funds, only the party Propaganda Secretary was paid, all others remained unpaid. See *Nigerian Citizen*, 24th November 1955.

89. Tarkar's conditions were given by the '*Citizen*' *Report* (29/9/55) which announced the agreement with the NPC.

90. See the letter by Bello Adedokun, UMBC Kaduna Branch President to the *Nigerian Citizen*, 13th October 1955.

91. A different interpretation is given by Ninzam in Debates N.H.A. 6th March 1956, p. 211 where he stated that it was Rwang and Ibrahim who were expelled and that they (Lot, Dokotri etc.) had approached the NPC and expressed their "complaints". "They (the NPC) then assured us that they would *continue* to help us".

92. Later, a small section, drawn principally from Offa Yorubas, led by Malomo Babatunde, an organising secretary of the Rwang faction broke off to form the Middle Belt Democratic Party which subsequently was affiliated to the NPC because "it is the party to be reckoned with". See *Nigerian Citizen*, 22nd February and 29th August 1956.

93. Dokotri, in his Vice-President's address to his faction stated that the split was due, in part, "to the fact that we have lived without any laws to govern and direct us" referring to the lack of a party Constitution. *Nigerian Citizen*, 24th November 1955.

I

94. *Nigerian Citizen*, 24th November 1955.

95. See Debates of the Northern House of Assembly 26th February 1957, p. 252 *et seq.*

96. See *Nigerian Citizen*, 5th and 12th December 1956.

97. The condition was that NEPU should support the demand for a Middle-Belt State. To which Aminu Kano replied: "NEPU does hereby reaffirm its pledge to stand by you to the end and that at any Constitutional Conference, the party will support the creation of a Middle Belt State. It is now left with your party leaders to show the viability of such a state in terms of the unity of the Nigerian Federation". Quoted in the *Nigerian Citizen*, 19th December 1956.

98. See *Nigerian Citizen*, 23rd and 30th January 1957; 6th and 8th February 1958; 16th and 30th April 1958; 4th and 11th June 1958.

99. See *Nigerian Citizen*, 5th March 1958. I am indebted to Mr. B. N. Nyiwo, a Tiv agricultural assistant, who helped me as a research assistant for two months, for some of the details of the Lafia Conference and its aftermath. M. Nyiwo prepared a report for me based on personal interviews with Tiv leaders and copies of letters and memoranda which he was given. His findings however, only supplemented and confirmed my own reading of the *Nigerian Citizen* and other interviews, principally with men like Hon. Vincent Orjime, UMBC, Mr. Patrick Dokotri, Birom UMBC and Senator Abaagu Tiv, NPC.

100. The Tivs have gradually become the only ethnic group which has refused to co-operate with the NPC. Senator Abaagu has tried to explain this, in an interview, by the fact that the Tivs were never conquered by the Fulanis and have never been brought under Fulani control. Tiv egalitarianism may also be another factor and the use of the Native Authority—the Tov Tiv and 'elders' as an instrument of coercion by the NPC may be very significant. (See the letter by Ayilla Yough, a UMBC, dated 18th July 1960 to the District Officer in charge Gboko—UMBC Headquarter's File no. UMBC/AG/BPC/2–2).

101. See Debates of the Northern House of Assembly 7th April 1960, cols. 57–59, and 19th April 1960, cols. 314–15.

102. The APA National Congress (the former Kwararafa Congress) made up of Igalas, Igbirras, Idomas, Jukuns, Ankweis, was told by its President at the Convention of the Congress held at Oturkpo in January 1959 that "the greater part of the Middle Belt belong to their warrior ancestors and is now being claimed by settler groups—Tiv".

103. M. Maude Gyani (Member Zaria S. W.) in the debate on the Speech from the Throne; Debates 17th February 1959, col. 35.

104. Maude Gyani, who has been appointed Wakilin Jaba in the time since becoming a member of the NPC; Debates 9th March 1963, col. 129.

105. Debates of the N.H.A., 12th March 1957, p. 883, 16th September 1957, pp. 1078–79 and 17th September 1957, pp. 1144–47.

106. *Report of the Commission Appointed to Enquire into the Fears of Minorities and the Means of Allaying them.* Cmnd. 505, 1958 passim.

107. *Provincial Annual Reports* 1956, p. 50.

108. Ibid., p. 51.

109. H. B. Hermione-Hodge, *Gazetteer of Ilorin Province*, 1929, pp. 202–3. Fulani district Heads were, early during the period of British Administration withdrawn from the areas to the East and South.

110. *Nigerian Citizen*, 11th August 1955.

111. *Nigerian Citizen*, 15th and 22nd December 1955. The meeting referred to was to have been held at the Baboko N.A. School on 18th December 1955. In a letter dated 29th September 1956, the Premier of the North, Sardauna of Sokoto, requested the officer administering the Government, Mr. K. P. Maddocks, to

declare Yahaya's seat, then still a Minister of Health, vacant. This was due to Yahaya's decision to stand against Alanamu who was adopted NPC candidate for the 1956 elections. On Yahaya deciding to resign voluntarily from the Government—in a letter to the Premier dated 11th October 1956, the latter wrote 11/10/56 to the OAG withdrawing his former letter. See *Nigerian Citizen*, 13th October 1956.

112. *Annual Report*, 1956, p. 50. Part of this 'aggressiveness' was letting out the contracts for selling water from the standpipes only to NPC supporters.

113. The ITP laid down the following conditions for the alliance: "(1) that ITP will retain its identity in all matters affecting its political status; (2) that in all matters of elections to local councils in Ilorin division, the union reserves the right to nominate its own candidates; (3) that any matter affecting elections from Ilorin province to the House of Assembly or the House of Representatives will be determined in consultation with the NPC Headquarter's in Kaduna; (4) that the NPC as the party in power will support the legitimate demands of the ITP either local, regional or federal; (5) that the ITP retains the right to communicate direct with the NPC Headquarters at Kaduna without reference to the Ilorin branch of the NPC, and (6) that the Union shall support the policy of the NPC and be loyal and faithful to the Northern Party." The conditions were provisionally accepted at a meeting between the ITP and the Sardauna and four of his Ministers. A majority vote of the NPC Executive later ratified it at the end of December 1956. In March 1957, however, the ITP abrogated the alliance because the NPC violated "the first condition of the alliance". See *Nigerian Citizen*, 1st and 29th December 1955 and 11th April 1956.

114. But it is significant that only 35% of the registered electorate voted the ITP polling 21% to the NPC's 14%.

115. See *Statement of the Government of the Northern Region of Nigeria on the Report of the Committees of Inquiry appointed to investigate allegations about the Ilorin N.A.*, Kaduna, 1958.

116. See e.g. M. Asad, *The Principles of State and Government in Islam*, California U.P., pp. 39, 69.

117. See *Provincial Annual Report*, 1958 p. 53. Effective power in the Caretaker Council rested with its 'Caretaker' and 'Establishment' Committees, the composition of which is shown in the Debates of the Northern House of Assembly 5th August 1958, cols. 787–88.

118. *Annual Report*, 1958, p. 53.

119. On the AG Crisis, see J. Mackintosh, 'Politics in Nigeria; the AG Crisis', *Political Studies*, vol. II, no. 2, June 1963.

120. See S. Greer and P. Orleans, 'Mass Society and Para-political Structure', *American Sociological Review*, vol. 27, no. 5, 1962. The 'level of urbanization' in the North, East and Western Regions are 9%, 25·5% and 43% respectively taking centres with 5,000 people and over. See Population Census of Northern Nigeria, p. 11, East p. 21 and West p. 10. On urbanization in general, see W. Bascom, 'Urbanism as a Traditional African Pattern', *The Sociological Review*, vol. 7, no. 1, 1959. Bascom made the point that the Fulani raids led to considerable depopulation in the North, op. cit., p. 36. On the correlation between societalization and urbanism, see K. Little, 'The role of Voluntary Associations in West African Urbanism', *American Anthropologist*, vol. 59.

121. K. W. J. Post, op. cit., pp. 103–10.

122. Quotations are from the texts of the "alliances" in NEPU Headquarter's Files 0127.

123. See Debates of the Northern House of Assembly 12th March 1957, p. 883 and 17th September 1957, pp. 1144–47.

IV

The NPC: "One North, One People..."

Less than a year after the Northern Peoples' Congress was declared a political party, it was written of it that "it is far from being a political party and is at best a reunion platform for old boys of the Katsina College—through which most members of the Northern Peoples Congress and the Assemblymen passed".[1] Twelve years later, a not dissimilar judgment was made when it was asserted that "The Northern Peoples Congress is not a political party as we know it in the South (i.e. of Nigeria)"; "it is merely a political expression for an existing system of administration dyed in religion and innate traditions".[2] Both statements, though obviously exaggerated, point in different ways to certain characteristics of the Northern Peoples Congress; for instance, its structural diffuseness, the relationship between the party and the traditional social and political structure of the North, the relationship between the leaders and the mass-membership of the party. All of these are closely related. Thus, the relative lack of a tightly knit structure can be explained in terms of the traditional structure of Northern society which makes it possible for the Northern Peoples Congress to rely for its support principally on the village and district heads, Native Authority functionaries, and the chiefs, without bothering over-much with the development of mass party organs as a means of gaining widespread acceptance. And by relying mainly on these groups—the traditional leaders in the North—relationships between the leaders and the party rank-and-file get defined not in terms of stated rules but in terms of traditional obligations. For as a Northerner put it: "the rank-and-file would then have to assume their usual attitude in dealing with their senior native authority officials—a discipline not partisan but administrative and based only on acquiescence since they could not argue or reason out anything with their seniors".[3] To see this with greater clarity necessitates a description of the structure and organization of the Northern Peoples Congress. It is party organization which, as Duverger rightly noted, characterizes modern political parties more than any other factor.[4] Though in 1952 the Northern Peoples

Congress sent out a two-man delegation with the expressed aims of 'reorganizing' the party, membership drive and fund collection, very little organization in any sense existed. The *Report on the Kano Disturbances* noted that Northern political parties were yet in an "embryonic stage organizationally", adding that "so far as the great majority of the population (were) concerned, party names and political catchwords (held) no meaning".[5] The *Annual Reports* of this period also contained references to the relative absence of a party organization.[6] Whatever 'organization' there is, is thus something which has been slowly evolved. A party 'constitution' was drawn up and adopted in 1954 but this provides only a rough guide to the organization of the Northern Peoples Congress. Besides, as will be subsequently shown, there is no clear correlation between the specifications of the Constitution and actual party practice. A realistic account of Northern Peoples Congress party organization must therefore differentiate between 'fact' and fiction. The constitution, which is hardly more than a statement of intentions, pertains rather to the latter.

Some consideration must first be given to the concept of 'membership' before any description of the party organization is attempted. This is particularly relevant as the connotation of the expression 'party member' is far from being clear. Thus, the *Report of the Kano Disturbances* noted that "In a Western European community, the number of membership cards issued by an organization could be expected to give reasonable evidence as to the number of party adherents. In the Northern Region, however, this can be only regarded as a haphazard and unreliable guide. Experience has shown that on the conclusion of a political meeting, members of the Northern public without political leanings are always prepared to purchase cards, possibly for no other reason than not to appear discourteous, possibly in some sense in payment for their entertainment. They just as readily purchase membership cards of the opposing political organisation should it hold a meeting a day or two later."[7]

The party Constitution stipulates the following conditions for membership: the payment of an enrolment fee of 2s., purchase of a membership card costing 6d. and an annual subscription of 12s. (25% of which goes to the National Headquarters). Yet in 1953 when membership was supposed to be about 100,000, the *Financial Statement* of the party for the period 3rd July 1952 to 24th July 1953 showed only £60 3s. 8d. for party subscriptions received at party Headquarters. The *Statement* showed only £16 3s. 6d. for the sale of membership cards during the same period, though not less than 30,000 were supposed to have been enrolled as new members.

Similarly in 1957, the party headquarters budget showed that the party only expected to realize £800 from membership contributions out of an estimated £1,500 per year. On the other hand, they expected to realize the full amount from the sale of party cards to new members. On this basis, one could therefore differentiate two categories of members—those who pay their dues regularly and those who purchase a party card and who only sporadically pay the monthly levies.

However, following Duverger, it might be more realistic to differentiate the different categories of 'membership' in terms of the individuals' degree of involvement in party activities. On this basis, Duverger distinguishes three categories of 'militants', 'members' and 'supporters'. The supporters of the party are those who are not directly committed but who nevertheless would vote for the party in an election. 'Members' are those who have committed themselves only to the extent that they carry a party card and periodically pay their dues. The 'militants' are those who have not only committed themselves in the sense of being 'members' but also are directly involved in carrying out different activities for the party. This last category usually are the officials of the various branches who at election periods tend to act as 'nominators' of party candidates. An indication of the social composition of this class for selected provinces, taking as an index the occupation of those who acted as nominators during the 1959 Federal election, is shown in the table on page 119. What emerges most clearly from the table is how well the Northern Peoples Congress is welded into the social structure of the North. Thus, about 68% of its militants are drawn from Native Authority employees, district and village heads and traders—the highest status-ranks in the North. NEPU, on the other hand draws only 20% of its militants from these groups, and even then, these are almost exclusively traders, who would not normally be classed as wealthy merchants (Attajirai). In contrast to the Northern Peoples Congress, NEPU's party activists (approximately 80%) come mainly from the class of small farmers, tailors, butchers, dyers and tanners, etc. The corresponding figure for the NPC is about 32%.

On the whole, then, the NPC is less broadly based than the Nigerian Elements Progressive Union which tends to derive both its leadership and its party activists from the lower strata of the society.

I. PARTY ORGANIZATION

Structurally, the organization of the Northern Peoples Congress follows the political divisions of Northern Nigeria. The region is

TABLE 3

Social Composition of Party Militants

Occupations	Sokoto		Kano		Bornu		Katsina		Zaria		Bauchi		Plateau		Niger		Ilorin		Benue	
	NPC	NE	NPC	NE	NPC	NE	NPC	NE	NPC	NE	NPC	NE	NPC	NE	NPC	NE	NPC	NE	NPC	NE
N.A. Employees	10	—	37	—	6	—	17	—	8	—	13	—	8	—	6	—	7	—	15	2
Dist. and Village Heads	5	—	7	—	3	—	6	—	—	—	2	—	—	—	—	—	—	—	—	—
Traders	11	5	7	10	9	5	3	3	3	1	2	5	2	3	6	2	2	—	3	4
Farmers	12	8	3	24	6	—	3	7	3	7	6	9	3	6	2	7	1	—	6	5
Teachers/clerks/ Koranic Mallams	5	2	12	—	3	1	1	2	2	—	2	—	2	—	1	—	2	—	2	2
Tailors	1	1	2	17	1	2	—	2	—	2	1	4	1	2	1	1	—	—	—	—
Artisans/skilled workers (a)	2	2	1	5	—	1	—	—	—	—	1	4	—	1	—	2	—	—	1	1
Others (b)	—	2	1	14	—	1	—	10	—	—	1	4	2	—	—	—	—	—	1	—
TOTAL	56	20	70	70	28	10	32	28	16	10	28	26	18	12	16	12	12	—	28	14
Seats contested	28	10	35	35	14	5	16	14	8	5	14	13	9	6	8	6	6	—	14	7

(a) Includes motor mechanics and drivers, builders and masons, shoemakers, contractors, watch-repairers and blacksmiths.
(b) Includes butchers, dyers and tanners, newspaper vendors, washermen, mat-makers, bicycle hirers, daily paid labourers and unemployed men.

NE = NEPU

divided politically into thirteen provinces, each province being sub-divided into divisions or Emirates as the case may be, these again being made up of a number of districts. The number of divisions, Emirates and districts making up a province varies between the thirteen provinces. Sokoto province, for instance, comprises Sokoto, Argungu, Gwandu and Yauri Emirates, each of which is made up of 47, 7, 15 and 5 districts respectively. On the other hand, Zaria has only two divisions, Zaria Emirate and Jama'a Federation, the former composed of sixteen and the latter of nine, districts respectively. Each district includes a number of villages or village areas.

The Branch

The basic organizational unit of the party is the branch, which is coterminous with the village, or in the main towns with the wards of the town. (There are only eight towns in Northern Nigeria with populations exceeding 40,000.) Members of the party within the branch constitute the branch unit which elects its own officers. Article 46 of the Party Constitution provides that these shall be the President, and Vice-President, Secretary and Assistant, Treasurer and Financial Secretary, Publicity Secretary "and any other local officers that may be considered necessary".[8] Besides the constitutional provision that the branch and its executive shall hold a meeting once every month, no functions are prescribed for branches. But a circular letter from the party national headquarters later enjoined on the branches the primary task of "winning more people to this party" stating that "the building of a party is just like building a house—both require firm and permanent foundations. When you build your house you hope that it will stand the years to the extent that it will be used by your sons, grandsons and grand-grand-sons. Thus if you will build the NPC on firm foundations, surely it will come to benefit your sons and grandsons onwards."[9]

The impression of militancy which this statement supports is almost completely foreign to the normal run of branch activities. Discussion at branch meetings is invariably in terms of local, topical questions, mainly administrative and economic. Thus, a report by the Administrative Secretary[10] of the Northern Peoples Congress to the National Headquarters in September 1960 on a meeting of the Dass branch complained that it dealt "with very local and narrow problems such as loans to farmers, repairs of market stalls and so on". What emerges very clearly from reports from branch meetings is that members make no distinction between party political activity and that of the Native Authority—or the Regional Government. Put differently, this is to say that members, whether in the towns or in the villages identify the party with the Native Authority and the Government. Meetings therefore provide a forum in which demands are made on these authorities, demands which range from the suggestions by the Wase branch that the party should request the Chief of Wase to "snatch away the post of buying cotton in this area from Ibos . . . and give it to a true Northerner"; that "a senior Primary School be built in Wase" to those from the Kaduna branch demanding that "a special place (be) kept for the mad people who spoil the market at night"; "the issue of land to Southerners to be minimized here in Kaduna Town" and "married women seeking divorce to be given a special place to sit before they see an Alkali". Complaints equally feature prominently such as those about taxation in Nguru, or that "elected members show no sign of gratitude to the people who have elected them". Periodically, however, larger issues crop up, for instance a debate by the Potiskum branch (according to another report by the Administrative Secretary) on the "position of the Native Authorities when Independence has been achieved". The Report added that the members "perceive (that) more powers will be vested to them (the Native Authorities), but are liable to be much more dependent upon the Government".[11]

The concentration on primarily local administrative and economic problems to the almost complete exclusion of policy issues, can be seen as pointing to several interesting factors. In the first place, it can be taken as indicative of the absence of that "comprehensive societalization" which, as Weber has pointed out, political parties presuppose.[12] Secondly, it is a reflection of the minimal place which the branch occupies in the party structure. In a status-differentiated society, it is sufficient, for most purposes, if the traditional leaders in the society support the party which capitalizes on such differentiations. That this is achieved at the branch level is seen from the fact that the branch militants are drawn from the village heads and native authority functionaries of the village. This, however, points to a problem for the Northern Peoples Congress. Given Weber's 'societalization' or what would now be regarded as 'modernization', the involment of members on party activities could encourage a spirit of partisanship rather than administrative subservience and thus lead to a questioning of the ground on which traditional obligations are based with probable effects on the social structuring of the society, the traditional leadership and the stability of the party.[13]

The District and Provincial Organizations

The several branch executives within a district together form the second level in the organization hierarchy of the party. This is the

District Conference, about which the party Constitution is silent and whose main functions are to co-ordinate branch activities, decide on what policy lines the district should pursue at the Provincial Conference and finally to act as a communicating link between the latter and the branches. District Conferences elect the District Executive and these in addition to the President and Secretary of the individual branches, collectively form the Provincial Conference—the third level of the party organization.

The Provincial Conference elects both the Provincial Executive, which is supposedly the governing organ for the whole province, and the Divisional Executives. In provinces with mixed ethnic groups, however, the Divisional Executive tends to be more important than the provincial counterpart. Though the Provincial Executive is constitutionally the policy-making organ, in practice, this role is performed by the parliamentary members of the province (or division), who form a caucus within the Executive. All field secretaries within the province are responsible to, and are paid by, the Provincial Executive.

Article 58 of the party Constitution sets out in some detail, the main functions of the Executive, which inter-alia, includes the establishment of new branches, the recruitment of new members and acting as the communicating link between the branch (and district) organizations, the National Headquarters and the National Executive Committee of the party.[14] These functions are in practice responsibilities of the Provincial Secretariat which is made up of the field secretaries and a few other paid officials of the party. The Secretariat in turn, is responsible to the Provincial Executive.

Membership of the Provincial Executive is a much sought after, and therefore highly contested office. It is an avenue to a wide variety of other opportunities and offices, such as seats in the Provincial Loans Boards, the boards of the various public corporations, both regional and federal, the possibility of being adopted as a candidate for local and parliamentary elections and membership of the National Executive Committee of the party. For some, it provides necessary contacts through which governmental and native authority contracts could be obtained. It also provides opportunities of being in a position to hand out, or influence the distribution of, minor forms of partonage—obtaining loans from the co-operative schemes, providing both jobs and promotions in the Native Authority.

During election periods, the Provincial Executive or a sub-group of it, meets to consider the selection of candidates for elections. Since in this process its role varies between the different areas of the

North, it is useful to distinguish, for analytical purposes, two stages in the process of nomination, 'certification' and 'selection'. The former includes the social screening and political channelling that results in eligibility for candidacy. The latter involves the actual choice of candidates to represent parties in the general election.[15] In the far North, that is in the Emirates proper, the Provincial Executive is involved only in the 'certification' process, while in the lower North, in Plateau, Southern Zaria, Niger and Benue provinces for instance, the Executives carry out both 'certification' and 'selection'.

Since it is from the Provincial Conference that the Executive is elected, the strategic position of the latter makes it the main focus of the power struggle in the Northern Peoples Congress. It is thus at the level of the Provincial Conference that the competing interests and groups within the party are most clearly shown—interests such as those of the various districts and divisions, the parliamentary versus the non-parliamentary interests, the upper Native Authority ranks as against the lower, the Native Authority versus the non-Native Authority interests, the district and village heads as against the party rank and file, the 'progressive' versus the 'conservatives', and urban as against rural interests. The conflicts which arose over the election of the Kano Provincial President illustrate some of the issues.

The Election of the Kano Provincial President 1959–60

The background of the conflict was the resignation of Maikano Dutse, the Provincial President, late in 1957, on his being appointed Northern Minister of Local Government. At the 1958 Provincial Conference, three candidates were put up to contest the office: Alhaji Abdulkadir Koguna, the Native Authority Supervisor of Rural Water Installations, Mallam Baba Daradara, a Native Authority Assistant Treasurer and Rilwanu Abdullahi, a scribe in the Native Authority Legal Department. Both the first and the third candidates were known to be canvassing their candidacy for the federal elections of 1959, but while Rilwanu seems to have been more acceptable to the Kano Parliamentary group and the Native Authority hierarchy,[16] Koguna, more populist in outlook and temperament and certainly much more 'generous', had the support of the party rank and file. Mallam Baba Daradara on the other hand was reputed to have been favoured by the trading and other commercial interests. Rilwanu, backed by his supporters, won the election. Koguna, the runner-up, became the Vice-President, while Baba Daradara was elected the Treasurer.

By 1959, however, opposition had mounted, amongst the rank and file, against Rilwanu. He had not only tried to halt the attempts being made to streamline the party,[17] but had also suspended some of the paid field secretaries whom he accused of plotting against him. A threatened split in the party was only averted through the intervention of the central Working Committee which suspended the Executive and appointed in its place a 'Caretaker Committee', with Rilwanu as its Chairman. This was resented and interpreted, possibly rightly, as a move to side-track popular demand.

Continued opposition to this 'Committee' led to the summoning of a Provincial Conference in February 1959. Here, a motion by the Chairman of the Conference, Alhaji Inuwa Wada, that the 'Committee' be allowed to continue in existence was ruled out by a majority vote. At this stage in the proceedings, other interests became evident when the Emir's (now the Ex-Emir) chauffeur, backed by the Parliamentary Secretary to the Regional Minister of Lands and Survey introduced a motion of 'no confidence' in the Regional Minister of Local Government—Alhaji Maikano Dutse.[18] (The people of Dutse District subsequently met and rejected this 'motion' on the grounds that they were not represented at the Conference.) With the rejection of the 'Caretaker Committee', a move was made to have elections for the Provincial Executive. As other likely candidates declined to stand and Rilwanu withdrew his nomination, Koguna, the only candidate remaining, who had been nominated by the rank and file, was declared elected. But curiously, the Chairman announced his office as being that of a Divisional President. (Kano Province comprises four divisions: Kano, Hadeija, Gumel and Kazaure.) Dissatisfaction with this announcement was such that the conference 'fizzled' out soon after. Subsequent pressure from the branches, in the form of letters to the Provincial Secretariat, led to Kogonu being recognized *de facto* as the President when another Provincial Conference met in July 1959.

In December 1959 Koguna was adopted as one of the party's candidates for the Federal Elections. As a result of his election, it was argued by the Native Authority faction at the 'Conference' of the party that, as he had to be away in Lagos, Koguna could not continue in office as the Provincial President. They then nominated Maikano Dutse, who in the meantime had resigned his Ministerial office, for the Presidentship. Significantly, at this meeting, the upper echelons of the Native Authority were heavily represented (the Madaki of Kano was the Chairman of the opening session and read out a message from the Emir) and most of the district heads were present. Koguna (the only other candidate) who, it was alleged, had been pressured into not contesting, then publicly withdrew his candidature, whereupon Maikano Dutse became the President. Soon afterwards Koguna was appointed Nigerian Ambassador to Pakistan.

This suggests some of the conflicts of interest within the Northern Peoples Congress, between in this instance, elected representatives and top native authority officials on the one hand, and the party rank and file on the other, and between one district (Dutse) and the other districts. It also points to the dominating role of the Native Authority officials (and these include the large bulk of the elected representatives) in party affairs.

Similar accounts can be given for the other divisions and provinces, all of which illustrate the determination of the top Native Authority officials and parliamentarians to retain the Northern Peoples Congress in a system of closed politics, or more specifically, to preserve a style of politics which has been characterized by C. P. Snow as 'Court politics'.[19] Professor Miller has suggested that "it may be possible to modify the extent of . . . court politics by enforcing further popular control" but adds that "the attempt may well prove vain".[20] The failure of a number of such attempts to enforce popular control has led, in the Northern Peoples Congress, to the formation of splinter groups, for instance, the Northern Youths' Movement in Kano in 1961[21] and the Reform Committee in Adamawa in 1959. So far, none of these have had any significant impact on the politics of the North. However, they all have long-run implications for the internal stability of the party.[22]

The Regional and National Organization

The various branches of the Northern Peoples Congress meet in a common forum in the Regional and National Conventions of the Party. Both form the 'mass' organs of the party. Though in practice the composition of both is identical, analytically they should be differentiated. At the Regional Convention, which seldom meets, the Regional President of the Northern Peoples Congress—since 1952 Alhaji Musa Gashash, the North Regional Minister of Lands and Survey—presides, while the National President, Alhaji Sir Ahmadu Bello, presides over the National (usually, but misleadingly, referred to as the annual) Conventions. The Regional Convention is not even mentioned in the party Constitution, and in the history of the party it has only met once.[23]

In contrast to its silence on the place of the Regional Conference the party Constitution sets out in great detail the functions of the Annual Conventions. Article 14 states that "the Supreme Authority of the Congress (i.e. the Northern Peoples Congress) shall be vested in the Annual Convention which shall have absolute power to decide major policies of the party and to consider matters referred to it by the Executive Committee". Decisions taken at the Annual (or Emergency) Conventions are regarded as "final and conclusive" and "binding upon all the branches as the voice of the whole members of the Congress".[24] As against the Annual Conventions which are supposedly constitutionally mandatory, special or Emergency conventions may be convened by the President-General of the party, the Executive Committee, or on the request of not less than a third of the branches of the Congress.[25] So far, in the fourteen years' history of the party, three emergency conventions have been held—the Kaduna Conventions in 1952 and 1956 respectively and the third in Zaria in 1957. All three were summoned by the President. No convention has yet been convened on request of the branches.

The Party Constitution provides that Annual or Emergency Conventions "shall have power to:

(a) Amend the Constitution;
(b) Remove from office any officer of the Congress;
(c) Elect any officer provided in the Constitution;
(d) Impose any levy on the branches;
(e) Make any negotiations or decrees and initiate any policy in the interest of the Congress;
(f) Appoint any sub-committees as may be deemed necessary or advisable to carry out duties assigned to them;
(g) Govern the Executive Committee."[26]

An obvious implication of the powers of the Convention would seem to be that the political theory under-pinning the Northern Peoples Congress is populist. Public statements by party leaders tend to enhance and further this theory. Thus, when it was proposed, or rather suggested, that the North might consider the establishment of Ministries over which Northern Ministers would be in control, the Sardauna rejected the suggestion, on the grounds that the Northern Peoples Congress "had no mandate from the people".[27] Precisely the same argument was used by the Sardauna to reject the motion demanding Independence for Nigeria in 1956.[28]

To accept this at its face value, however, would be seriously to misrepresent the facts, for as so often is the case in African political parties (for example, party systems in Ghana and Ivory Coast) there is a gulf between stated rules and principles and actual practice.[29] This can be shown more clearly by examining the role of the Annual Convention in the election of 'officers' of the Northern Peoples Congress, a role reserved solely to the Convention.[30]

The Emergency Convention which met in Kaduna in July 1952 was confronted with a serious problem of leadership. No convention was held in 1951 with the result that the party Executive was made up of members elected in 1950.[31] By 1952 the Northern Peoples Congress found itself in a position such that its leaders in the Northern House of Assembly were not members of the party executive and therefore had no influence on the formulation of party policy.[32] Such a situation would be anomalous in any system which claimed to be based on a parliamentary form of government. It was in an attempt to correct this that the 1952 Emergency Convention met to elect a new party Executive, the first such election since the NPC became a political party. It was at this Convention that the Sardauna became the Vice-President of the party, Alhaji Musa Gashash was elected the Regional President and Mr. Michael Audu Buba, the Regional Secretary. Both the latter have since retained the same offices (though no elections for these offices have been held since 1952). Besides M. Mohammadu, the then Wali of Bornu who was elected the legal adviser on Muslim Law, none of the other parliamentary leaders of the party, Abubakar Tafawa Balewa, then Federal Minister of Works, the late Mohammadu, then Federal Minister of Natural Resources, Shettima Kashim (now Sir Kashim Ibrahim), Federal Minister of Social Services, Mallam Bello Kano, M. Aliyu, Makaman Bida, Yahaya Ilorin and Peter Achimugu, Regional Ministers of Community Development; Education and Social Welfare; Health, and Local Industries, respectively, held any party office. The President of the Party was still (1951–54) Alhaji Sanda, who was neither literate nor a member of any of the legislative Assemblies in the country. The 1952 constitutional crisis in the Eastern Region demonstrated the problems inherent in a situation in which the parliamentary leadership and the party leadership were more or less dichotomous.[33] With this as a pointer, and the pressing need to make the Northern Peoples Congress more acceptable to the Emirs and Chiefs, a reorganization of the party leadership became even more necessary,[34] and at the Jos Conference of the party in 1954, an election of party officers was made the prime issue of the Convention. The Sardauna now became the President, with Balewa and Ribadu as first and second vice-presidents respectively, while Shettima Kashim and Abba Habib became joint auditors. Inuwa Wada, who was then Parliamentary Secretary to the Sardauna, was elected the Secretary. Other offices were then left to the new President to fill. But having secured control of the party leadership, the Parliamentary leadership has since 1954 stultified every attempt to alter the composition of the party executive.[35] Not only has no election of a new executive been held since 1954, but alterations to the composition of the Executive have since become a responsibility of the President.

With this has grown the practice of concentrating all offices of any significance in the hands of members of the Northern House.[36]

If the Conventions of the Northern Peoples Congress now play no part in the election of the officers of the party, they have equally had no control over the formulation of the broad outlines of policy. Hardly any discussion and criticism of party organization is permitted. Plans for reorganization of the party drawn up by the Secretariat Staff and submitted to the Kano Convention were rejected by the Party Officers[37] without any discussion being allowed. When the 1958 Convention was told by the General Secretary that the party was short of funds, a member called for the Financial Secretary's Report only to be ruled out of order on the grounds that the Convention was not competent to debate the financial position of the party.[38] In the same spirit, when delegates criticized the inefficiency of the headquarters staff of the party, they were overruled by the President who argued that no reference to the staff of the Secretatiat was made in his Presidential address, the theory then being that only items contained in the speech could be proper subjects for debate.

Far from being involved in any of the functions normally expected of the 'mass' organ of a political party,[39] and contrary to whatever is stipulated by the party's constitution, the Conventions of the Northern Peoples Congress have been subjected to systematic control and become atrophied, a phenomenon which has led one Northern commentator to write as early as 1956:

"Personally, I am not so much concerned with the deliberations of the Convention for I knew right from the start that the delegates would be spoonfed and must adopt what their masters had approved."[40] It only needs to be added that no Convention of the party has been summoned since that held in 1958.[41]

The National Executive Committee and the Central Working Committee

The National Executive Committee (NEC) was, until 1957, the policy-making organ of the Northern Peoples Congress. Since that date, it has gradually been superseded in this role by the Central Working Committee (CWC), formally constituted in 1956. According to the party Constitution, the composition of the NEC "shall be all officers of the Congress and the President and Secretary to every branch".[42] (For 'branch' one should more properly read provincial or divisional organization.)

In practice, the composition has varied. Until about 1958, the membership varied between sixty-eight and seventy-four, of which close to a third were not Members of Parliament. In more recent times, the total membership has fallen, and it has come to be drawn almost exclusively from the Northern House of Assembly as the following table shows:

TABLE 4

Unofficial Members[43] of the NEC (NPC)

Year	Northern House of Assembly	House of Representatives	Others	Total
1960	44	5	9	58
1962	30	5	7	43
1964	28	6	8	42

According to the Party Constitution, the National Executive Committee is "responsible for the general administration of the Congress in the intervals between Annual Conventions".[44] It administers "the business and offices of the Congress", its decisions or orders being "binding on all members and branches", and not to "be questioned, reversed, controlled or suspended except by way of an appeal to the Annual Convention".[45]

With a cross-membership between the National Executive Committee and the CWC and the provision that six members of the National Executive Committee shall form a quorum, it becomes impracticable to distinguish meetings of the National Executive Committee from those of the CWC. The most recent occasion when the National Executive Committee met as a body was in December 1963 when it was summoned to discuss issues arising from the population census of the country. Before this, the last known occasion when the National Executive Committee met was in September 1959. Very little is known of the internal working of the National Executive Committee, but a member, Mr. Abdul Razaq, has commented that "up till 1959, the procedure of the Executive was fairly democratic with open and free discussions before decisions were taken. But even at this period, the Bornu block tended to assert their influence and in some cases they have been given way to for fear of their breaking away from the North.[46] But from 1959, decisions have invariably been taken on the Sardauna's initiative and rubber-stamped by the Central Working Committee—a body chosen by the Sardauna himself." While the National Executive Committee as a formal party organ may be used periodically to mobilize party opinion, it has in fact been superseded by the CWC as the policy

K

making organ of the party.[47] The CWC is more or less coterminous with the Executive Council of the North. Besides its Chairman, Alhaji Ahmadu Bello, who is the President-General of the party and Premier of the North, of its present (1964) membership of thirty-two, thirteen are Northern Cabinet Ministers, eleven are parliamentary Secretaries, and five are Provincial Commissioners (these have Ministerial status and are members of the Northern House of Assembly). The remaining three members are the Party Manager, Raji Abdallah, the Principal Organizing Secretary Mohamadu King and the former Minister of Establishments and Training, Mustapha Mongono (now known as Mustafa Ismail). None of the NPC members of the Federal Legislature are members of the Working Committee.

This exclusion has been rationalized by the argument that since it is often necessary for the CWC to meet at very short notice attendance at CWC meetings by Northern Peoples Congress members of the Federal Legislature would be difficult, if not impossible.

Though, unlike most other Nigerian political parties, the Northern Peoples Congress has consistently maintained a united front, the exclusion of members of the Federal legislature from the governing organ of the party has on occasion led to divergent policies being pursued by the regional and federal parliamentary bodies of the party, as for instance, over the negotiation for economic aid from Israel by the federal government in 1960.[48] Such instances, however, are few and far between.

Given, then, the composition of the CWC, and the fact that it is the final decision-making body in the Northern Peoples Congress, it would follow that party political power is vested in the Northern Parliamentary Executive. This conclusion is diametrically opposed to that reached by Dr. Sklar who writes that: "The parliamentary wings of the major parties are strictly subservient to the Executive bodies of their mass organizations. This is inevitably the case since each major party has at least two parliamentary wings in different legislative chambers in the Federation and confusion would result if the Executive Committees were not supreme."[49] The National Executive Committee, which is what Sklar refers to as the 'Executive Committee', had fallen into dissuetude. It is not logically necessary that the NEC should be supreme, nor is there any empirical evidence requiring us to believe this to be so.

The National Secretariat

The reliance of the Northern Peoples Congress leadership on the network of Native Authority Officials, village and district heads,

Chiefs and Emirs, to propagate and disseminate its ideals and appeals and to co-ordinate the activity of its various branches largely explains why the party only hesitatingly developed a central secretariat staff. Even in 1965 this remained rudimentary when compared to the Secretarial organization of either the old Action Group or the NCNC. Before 1954 the headquarters Secretariat organization rested on two men—an unpaid Principal Organizing Secretary, M. Nuhu Bamali and a paid administrative Secretary (on a salary of £48 per annum)— Mallam Garba Abuja. A single rented room in the Tudun Wada area of Zaria served as office for both. This "office" was transferred to Kaduna in 1954 when the Vice-President of the Party, the newly elected President, the Sardauna of Sokoto, welcomed the move to Kaduna on the grounds that it would now be possible for the Secretariat to be "under the supervision of the Party's Ministers". The significant move towards the establishment of a Central Secretariat came with the appointment, in May 1954, of a paid full-time organizing secretary aided by four field-secretaries. These had become necessary with the impending federal elections of that year. (An earlier suggestion to make such appointments was rejected in 1952 because the costs were yet to be worked out.) After the 1956 regional elections, D. A. Rafih, the founder of the JMA, was appointed a paid party manager, and was assisted by a full-time principal organizing secretary—M. Raji Abdallah, who had been an NCNC organizing secretary for Kabba Province until March 1955.

Under these two men, the Secretariat was reorganized in May 1957 into three departments: a Department of Administration, under the immediate supervision of the party manager (Rafih died in 1960 and was succeeded by Abdallah) and responsible for the general administration of the Party; a Department of Organization, dealing with the co-ordination of party activities and in charge of the chief organizing secretary (since 1960 Alhaji Mohammadu King); and finally, a publicity department, responsible for party publications, press announcenemts, advertisement and propaganda,[50] and headed by Yesuf Dantsoho, a former NEPU member. When the Secretariat moved to its present buildings in 1961 further sub-departments and sections were created: research, local government, and Youth's Wing.

It is not easy to determine the actual role of the staff of the party's national headquarters, as even their own conception of this evinces some ambiguity. Thus while on the one hand, they regard themselves as "the hunting dogs of the party",[51] a subservient role, on the other they see themselves as "the guardians protecting the interests of the party and the North".[52] It was in the latter role that they issued a public release in April 1957 (broadcast over the Regional Broadcasting Service) that "the present set-up and policy implementation of the Northern Peoples Congress is nothing short of a menace—the present policy-making body of the party caters only for the opportunists, and privileged few—the leaders have deviated from the party's policy which we believe to be the best suited for the North".[53] Similarly, after the regional elections of 1956, they criticized the appointment of Mr. George Ohikere, as a Regional Minister of Health and demanded "that Ministerial appointments should be a matter within the party's rank and file", adding that "Ministers serve the whole region and not a single province and therefore provincial consideration should not be given".[54]

However, the mere fact that the headquarters officials play no part in the formulation of party policy (the two of them in the CWC only act as Secretaries to the CWC), subjectively rank themselves as being next in status to the elected representatives of the party whom they greet in the formal language of deference "Ranka ya Dade", and could be removed from office at any time by the CWC,[55] all point to the 'hunting dog' description as a more accurate assessment of their role and status. The Northern Peoples Congress's legal adviser, M. Abdul Razaq (in a conversation with the writer), summed up their position when he stated that "In party affairs, both at local, regional and national levels, there is increasing dominance by parliamentary members, especially the Ministerial class. Paid party officials, and other party leaders just carry out decisions with little chance of influencing these decisions". But it is obvious that controlling the administrative nerve centre as they do, party officials are in a strategic position to influence the fortunes of the party. Thus, given the present ambiguity of their position, in the event of any internal reform movement in the Northern Peoples Congress, the stand of the party officials will be crucial.

Ancillary Wings of the NPC—The Youth's and Women's Organizations

Parallel to and patterned on, the parent Northern Peoples Congress are the youth's and women's organizations. Both are separately represented at the party's provincial and annual conventions where they (and especially the youth organization), form an increasingly significant group.[56]

Leaders of the Youth organization regard it as the "militant and radical wing" of the Northern Peoples Congress. But their 'radicalism' should not be construed in any ideological sense. So far, their main efforts have been concentrated into attempts to liberalize the

Native Authorities through elective councils, and pressing for more and systematic northernization both of the local and regional bureaucracies and its extension to include the staffs of foreign commercial concerns. In other words, the radicalism of the youth wing has been directed at the creation of more opportunities of employment, not altogether surprisingly since most of its members are drawn from the class of petty traders, kola-nut sellers and the lower ranks of the Native Authority, mainly clerks and messengers. Thus of the forty-six Executive members of the Gusau branch, which is not untypical, nine are Native Authority employees, thirty-two traders, three bicycle repairers, a butcher and one washerman.

The youth organization had its origins in the *Jam'iyyar Mahaukata* which was formed in 1953.[57] The following year the Mahaukata (or society of madmen) was converted into the Alheri Youth Association (AYA) and was accepted for affiliation by the Northern Peoples Congress. It was the AYA which later in the same year became the Northern Peoples Congress Youth Organization.

Because women are as yet without a franchise and are classed as legal minors, they have not played any significant role in the party. In fact, most Northern Peoples Congress women members are unmarried (a status quite often equated with being a prostitute), but their presence in the party is regarded, as the President of the Gusau Youth branch put it, "as glorious, because they influently (sic) attract more and more members into the party".[58]

This brief account is not intended to be a detailed description of the organization of the Northern Peoples Congress. To do this would necessitate the examination of the party organization in the thirteen provinces individually. Variations both in practice and theory exist, but the account serves to provide a general picture of the party, emphasizing mainly the salient features. The account can therefore be regarded as a generalized model of the NPC's organization.

II. THE DYNAMICS OF LEADERSHIP

It has already been shown that at the local, regional and national levels, parliamentary members dominate party affairs, and to say that they dominate the party is to imply that they constitute the leadership of the party. To examine the basis on which this leadership relation depends, it will be necessary analytically to distinguish, at least, three senses in which the term 'leader' is used: in the sense first, of 'leader' among equals; secondly, of one to whom others defer because of the status he occupies, and lastly, of one who emits stimuli that are "responded to integratively by the members of a group" in such a fashion as to forward the performance of whatever activities are characteristic of that group.[59]

In Chapter II it was suggested that leadership in the far North was primarily a function of one's status in the society, which is determined largely by birth and wealth. These two variables confer the highest political and social status which are accorded to the lineages of the ruling families and members of the top-ranks of the native administration. An examination of the social origins of Northern Peoples Congress parliamentary members shows that they are drawn mainly from the ranks of those with high status in the society. Thus of the ninety members 'elected' in 1951 to the Northern House of Assembly, 18·7% were sons, brothers, cousins and nephews of ruling Emirs, 30% were district heads, 26% were District Alkalis (District Judges), 6% were Chief Alkalis and 69% were Native Authority functionaries with high rank. Similar figures for the House elected in 1956 show that 11·2% were of the lineages of the Emirs, 28·5% District Heads, 2·7% District and Chief Alkalis while 32% were Native Authority top officials.[60] And in the Federal House of Representatives, of the 134 NPC members elected in 1959, 19% were sons of ruling Emirs, 10·4% district heads and 74% Native Authority councillors and officials.[61] These figures demonstrate not only a significant correspondence between party leadership and high status in the society but also the extent to which the NPC is interwoven into the framework of the social structure and the administrative system.

It would follow from the above that some with the Sardauna's status—a great-grandson of Uthman Dan Fodio, and who is besides related to some of the most august Emirs[62] in the North, an educator and administrator—would be an obvious choice for the national leadership. It was thus no surprise that he was expected to lead the parliamentary Northern Peoples Congress in 1952 and was preferred to the present Prime Minister for the national party leadership in 1954.[63]

But since assuming the party leadership, the Sardauna has gradually built around himself a mystique of leadership which in many respects approximates to Weber's conception of charisma.[64] Part of this image is perhaps best shown by taking a representative selection of speeches in the Houses of Assembly and the Chiefs respectively. Thus, he has been referred to as "our divine leader (who) is in a way a reincarnation of Shehu Othman Dan Fodio";[65] a man who "has got the second world in his right hand and this world in his left".[66] In the same spirit, he has been seen as a forerunner of the Madhi[67] and was accorded the title of Bayajidda II—symbolic

N.P.C. PARTY ORGANIZATION

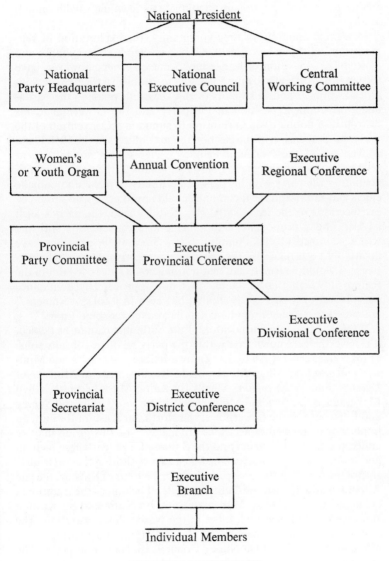

NPC PARTY ORGANIZATION

of the Bayajidda who, in Hausa mythology, founded the seven Hausa States, the Hausa Bokwoi.[68] And as if to provide legitimacy for this image, the Sardauna has in his autobiography 'traced' his ancestry to the Prophet Mohammed,[69] and has now made the traditional Islamic pilgrimage an annual (some would say bi-annual) affair.[70]

In a predominantly Islamic community, the exploitation of religious symbolism and sentiment can be expected both to enhance and to stabilize a position of leadership. Some observers, however, have seen in this an attempt by the Sardauna to establish a form of 'personal leadership',[71] and in support of this thesis, to point to the Sardauna's pre-eminent position in the party and the Government, his disregard of popular will in refusing to summon a Convention of the party, his suspension of the election of party officers at the 1958 Kano convention of the Northern Peoples Congress, his not infrequent references to his colleagues as "my Lieutenants", the popular identification of the party with his person, his ability to make and unmake chiefs and Emirs and the fact that he could now dictate who should be his successor to the leadership. Mr. Abdul Razaq, the party's legal adviser, and a proponent of this theme in a conversation with the writer, summed up the situation thus: "Since 1959, decisions have invariably been taken on the Sardauna's initiative. Expressed negatively, it would be true to say that nothing could be carried out in the region of which the Sardauna does not approve. His dominance extends not only over party affairs, but even in local government." He added that "the Sardauna could be swayed by some Emirs".

While the pre-eminent position of the Sardauna cannot be denied, it is nevertheless known that within the party he often consults some of his colleagues, Sir Abubakar Tafawa Balewa, Federal Prime Minister and the late Alhaji Mohammadu Ribadu, Federal Minister of Defence, and in the region, Alhajis Isa Kaita, Musa Gashash, Aliyu Makamau Bida, regional Ministers of Education, Lands and Survey and Finance, and the Governor of the North, Sir Kashim Ibrahim on important issues before decisions are made.[72] To this group may be added the Emir of Katsina and the Sultan of Sokoto. These men, in addition to the Sardauna, can be taken as constituting the top leadership of the party. Of this group, the Sultan, the Emir of Katsina, the late Alhaji Ribadu and the Sardauna himself, all belong to the traditional ruling aristocracy. Aliyu Makaman Bida, Isa Katia and Sir Kashim Ibrahim have all held high office in the Native Administration. The first, Aliyu Bida, is a member of the Bida (Nupe) aristocracy, and also a member of the Etsu Nupe's Council; Isa Kaita is at present the Wazirin (Prime Minister) of Katsina; and Sir Kashim formerly held a similar office in Bornu before being appointed Governor. Isa Kaita and Aliyu Bida are Financial Secretary and Treasurer respectively of the Northern Peoples Congress. Only the Prime Minister and Musa Gashash may be said to have come from the non-aristocratic ruling families of the North. Neither belongs to the groups which traditionally held political power, but while the Prime Minister through his own efforts rose to high office in the Native Administration (N.A. Education Officer and member, Bauchi Native Authority Council), Musa Gashash, as a wealthy merchant, an Attajirai (the only man not connected with the native administration), may be said to belong to the top-most class in the three-class stratification system in the Fulani North.[73] Most of these men, for example, the Sardauna, Isa Kaita, Tafawa Balewa and the Makaman Bida, received their formal education at the Katsina Higher College and in a sense were all contemporaries.

However, while individual experiences derived from a common educational institution, the Native Authority, Islam and a not too dissimilar social background have contributed to maintaining the cohesiveness of the top leadership of the Northern Peoples Congress, some of the party leaders are of the opinion that the party is now confronted with a problem of leadership (in the first sense distinguished above) which it will at some time have to resolve. There are, it seems, two aspects to the problem. In the first place, it is felt that while it was necessary in the initial stages for someone with the social background of the Sardauna to lead the party if it was to gain acceptance with the Emirs, too close an association of the party with the chiefly class would create an unfavourable image and in the long run handicap the party should it wish, as it now does, to project a mass image of itself. Thus, to change the image of the party, it would be necessary not only to dissociate the party from the chiefly class but also to place the party over and above the Chieftains and Emirs, and this, it is argued, would not be readily acceptable to one with the Sardauna's background.[74]

This argument obviously brings into question the basis on which the claim to leadership should rest, the challenge being one from those not connected with the traditional political ruling groups. But this poses a dilemma, one which in fact confronted the party in its early history. Given the seeming esteem in which the people, either because of historical reasons or religion, hold the Emirs and Chiefs, to what extent could the party rely on mass support if its leadership were dissociated from the Chieftain class?[75]

The second aspect of the problem is the dissatisfaction with the concentration of party political power in the hands of members who are wholly resident in the North and also members of the Northern governmental Executive. Resenting this concentration, Northern Peoples Congress federal parliamentarians argue that with the growing importance of the Federal Government the overall leadership of the party should be in the federal centre and not in the region. Neither of these two issues, it is generally accepted, can be resolved with the Sardauna as the leader of the party. But on their resolution depends the continued existence and stability of the party as it is known at present.

III. IDEOLOGY AND PARTY SUPPORT

It can be stated as a general proposition that given leadership attitudes and the organizational form of any political party its stability will to a large degree be a function of the extent of the party's mass support and its ideological appeals. In determining the extent of the Northern Peoples Congress's support, it should be remembered that women as yet do not vote in the North. While no definite prediction can be made about their reaction when enfranchised it is not improbable in view of the subordinate status of women in northern society, that their voting patterns will follow that of their men folk. Another factor, to be noted is the apathy of northern voters observable from the results of the two direct elections in the North, the 1959 Federal elections and the 1961 regional elections.[76] Comparing the results of both elections the percentage of the total votes cast to the the registered vote fell by 27·3%. Here again, no specific judgment can be made about the behaviour of this large group of non-voters should they decide to vote.

However, with these two limitations, the electoral support for the Northern Peoples Congress and its representativeness in terms of the distribution of the seats won for the two elections (1959 and 1961) is shown in the tables on pages 139 and 140.

From the tables it can be seen that though the percentage of non-voting was fairly high, the Northern Peoples Congress's share of the total votes cast rose in all the provinces shown except in Kano where the figure remained constant. Its share of total votes cast went up considerably in Plateau, Zaria, Benue, Sardauna and Adamawa provinces where in 1959 it had least support, and but for Benue province where it shared the total seats equally with the UMBC, the NPC is not only equally represented in all the provinces, it dominates each and every province.

The overwhelming control and predominance of the party is also

TABLE 5

NPC Electoral Support 1959 and 1961

Province	Actual Vote as % of Registered Vote		Increase or Decrease	Actual Vote as % of Total Vote Cast		Increase or Decrease
	1959	1961		1959	1961	
Bauchi	48·2	36·2	−12·0	56·5	59·1	+2·6
Bornu	90·6	71·2	−19·4	84·2	86·2	+ 2·0
Ilorin	51·4	38·5	−12·9	60·1	66·5	+ 6·4
Katsina	56·2	56·8	+ 0·6	61·4	70·5	+ 9·1
Niger	59·9	46·6	−13·3	67·8	72·2	+ 4·4
Plateau	33·4	34·9	+ 1·5	37·4	54·0	+16·6
Zaria	33·4	49·3	+15·9	36·7	67·2	+30·5
Benue	24·5	29·1	+ 4·6	26·5	40·6	+14·1
Adamawa	45·3	40·4	− 4·9	52·1	70·2	+18·1
Sardauna	33·5	35·9	+ 2·4	42·8	70·5	+27·7
Kano	70·9	53·6	−17·3	77·0	77·0	—
North as a whole	54·4	41·0	−13·4	61·2	66·6	+ 5·4

evident at the local level as shown by the following table giving party composition of the elected town and district councils for the provinces shown.[77] (Table 7, p. 141).

No single generalization can be made to explain the apparently overwhelming support which the Northern Peoples Congress has. Some of the complex factors which contribute to this may be noted.[78] In the first place there is the indentfication of the party with the whole administrative framework of the Native Authority. The party is, in fact, the Native Authority and whatever are its deficiencies, the Native Authority is nevertherless the central institutional reference point of social action for most, if not all, northerners. Socially habituated and psychologically conditioned to thinking in terms of the Native Authority as represented by the Emirs, district and village heads, Councillors and Alkalis, it is but normal to expect that the majority of the populace will support the party identified with it.

It follows that opposition to the Northern Peoples Congress becomes opposition to the Native Authority. Psychologically, oppositional activity is then regarded as deviant behaviour which stands in need of correction and the network of Native Authority

TABLE 6

Constituencies Contested: All Parties

Province	Contested								Seats Won					
	NPC		NCNC/NEPU		UMBC/AG		IND/Others		NPC		NCNC/NEPU		UMBC/AG	
	1959	1961	1959	1961	1959	1961	1959	1961	1959	1961	1959	1961	1959	1961
Bauchi	14	14	14	13	14	14	8	2	13	13	—	—	1	1
Bornu	14	14	9	5	14	14	6	—	13	14	—	—	1	—
Ilorin	6	6	5	—	6	6	1	1	5	6	—	—	1	—
Katsina	15	16	15	13	15	16	1	2	14	16	1	—	—	—
Niger	8	8	8	6	8	7	3	1	7	8	—	1	5	1
Plateau	9	9	9	7	9	9	2	2	3	7	1	—	4	7
Zaria	3	8	8	6	8	8	3	—	2	8	2	—	9	7
Benue	14	14	14	7	14	13	9	5	5	7	—	—	1	—
Adamawa	8	8	8	3	8	8	4	1	6	8	1	—	4	—
Sardauna	7	7	7	4	7	6	3	4	3	7	—	—	—	—
Kano	35	36	35	30	35	12	2	1	33	36	1	—	—	—
Kabba	3	3	7	—	7	7	6	6	2	2	—	—	—	—
Sokoto	28	28	28	11	28	13	2	—	26	28	2	—	—	—
Kaduna C.T.	1	1	1	1	1	—	1	—	—	1	1	—	—	—

NOTES: One seat each was won by an Independent Candidate in 1959 in Niger and Kano respectively. The Northern Peoples Congress contested all seats in 1959 and 1961 except in Kabba where apart from three seats, it left the field to its parliamentary allies, the Igala Union and the Igala Divisional Union.

Province	No. of T.C.s	Year estab.	NPC	NCNC/ NEPU	UMBC/ AG	Others	No. of D.C.s	Year estab.	NPC	NCNC/ NEPU	UMBC/ AG	Others
Bornu	7	1963	95	4	—	—	37	1963	1,060	—	—	8
Sokoto (a)	6	1961	82	3	—	—	74	1960	825	21	—	17
Benue (b)	9	1964	95	1	—	—	38	1964	623	5	2	—
Ilorin	1	—	21	—	13	—	46	—	308	—	13	37
Bauchi (c)	4	60, 63 and 64	51	13	—	1	40	60/1	792	29	16	3
Katsina	4	60, 62 and 63	59	5	—	—	26	60/1	455	13	—	—
Kano (d)	3	—	—	—	—	—	43	—	—	—	—	—
Adamawa	4	1963	62	1	—	—	32	61/3	685	4	49	1
Plateau	3	1963	35	19	2	—	54	as for T.C.	734	4	16	4
Sardauna	1	1960	24	4	—	—	18(e)	1960	292	3	18	—

NOTES: (a) Does not include figures for Argungu T.C. All members of the Council are, however, NPC.
(b) Does not include figures for Oturkpo T.C. Keffi Councils were dissolved in February 1964.
(c) Does not include figures for Jema'are T.C. All its members are NPC.
(d) Figures not available, but the life of all T.C.s have been extended indefinitely. All but one of these are Caretaker Committees appointed by the Government and all are NPC.
(e) Five of these in the United Hills Native Authority Area and two in the Cashaka/Mambilla N.A. Area are non-party Councils.

T.C.s and D.C.s include nominated and ex-officio members and the ratio of these (who are all NPC) to elected members varies between 1:2 and 1:3. Thus, e.g. Wukari sub-N.A., a D.C., has 28 members of which 16 are elected. Similarly Ibi T.C. with a membership of 11 has 6 elected. Takum T.C. on the other hand has 5 of 18 members nominated. Some T.C.s, but not D.C.s, are wholly and directly elected. There are, on the whole, 6,988 elected members of Town and District Councils, 1,701 nominated members, 921 Presidents and 978 ex-officio members, a total of 10,588, of the total of 940 N.A. Councillors, 518 are elected, 400 nominated and 32 ex-officio. All of these 940 are NPC.
SOURCE: NHA Debates, 25th August 1962, p. 617.

police and courts are readily available for such corrective action.[79] It would follow from this, that failure to check or prevent tendencies towards deviance is equally 'reprehensible'. It was, thus, hardly a coincidence, that all but one of the district heads of areas where opposition parties won seats in the 1959 federal elections were relieved of their appointments.[80]

Secondly, there are decided economic advantages in supporting the 'party in power'. Besides the possibilities of appointments to various Board memberships, there are the opportunities of obtaining loans from the many development agencies. Thus of the total membership of 144 of the Provincial Loans Boards existing in 1958 in the twelve provinces of the North, 8% were Emirs and Chiefs, 17·5% were district and village heads, 37·6% were Native Authority Councillors and officials, 15% Legislators, 14% traders and 8% were auctioneers, pastors and 'others'. And of the 20 people who at one time or the other were members of the Northern Region Production and Development Board (1950–55) 40% were Emirs, 55% legislators of which 25% were district heads, and 5% employees of the Native Authority. Similarly, of the 23 people who in one year or the other formed the Board of the Northern Region Development Corporation (Loans) (1950–58), 26% were Emirs, 69.5% were legislators of which 17% were district heads and only 4·5% traders.[81] The association between Board membership and the obtaining of loans is shown in the following extract from the debates in the Northern House of Assembly.

Ibrahim Imam (former Leader of Opposition, quoting from Statement of the Acting Permanent Secretary Ministry of Social Welfare and Co-operatives to the Public Accounts Committee, verbatim Report of Meeting held in June 1960, pp. 75–77): "It was found that the principal culprits (i.e. those who failed to repay loans from Co-operatives Loans Boards) were the District and Village Heads and Alkalis, so it is not very easy to do something about it. The Emir (of Katsina) has sent out instructions to all District Heads, Village Heads and Alkalis not to accept any loans in future. But the Assistant Registrar has reported that he finds difficulty because he believes that District and Village Heads and Alkalis are now putting forward their nominees to accept money on their behalf."

Speaker: "Members should have the opinion that the District and village heads referred to in the Report, referred specifically to members of this House personally."

Ibrahim Imam: "Some of them may be involved, but I do not know."[82]

Since the composition of the loans Boards reflects the structure of the Native Authority which has at its disposal and control, the only effective system of social communication, these Boards are in a position to discriminate between those entitled to receive loans, and those who get them are, more often than not, those known to support the party. Thus, in a predominantly rural, under-developed economy such as that of Northern Nigeria, the control of loanable funds is an effective instrument of ensuring party support.[83] A problem here, however, is that the disbursement of funds, such as the co-operative loans schemes, has in practice tended to favour the more successful farmers and middle-man buyers than the small peasant farmer.

Thirdly, there are the personality of the Sardauna and the bonds of Islam. The charismatic leadership of the Sardauna has already been noted. Islamic influence in winning mass support can hardly be underestimated. The identification of the party and its leaders (the patron of the Northern Peoples Congress is the Sultan of Sokoto, the Sarkin Muslummi) with the religion of Islam is such as to suggest that the party represents the consensus of the society—*Ijma'*—and not to accept the consensus of society is to be heretical—*Bid'a*— a rebel from the community, but as the Prophet said: "The hand of God is upon the community (*al-jama'ah*); and he who sets himself apart from it will be set apart in Hell-fire. He who departs from the community by a handspan ceases to be a Muslim";[84] a sufficient restriction in a society 65% of whose members are Moslems.

This notion of a 'community' leads on to the final point—the ideological basis of the party.[85] To have defined or drawn the boundaries of the community in terms principally of religion, and Islam at that, would have alienated the sizeable minority of non-Moslems in the North. Hence, the ideology of the party is centred around its motto: "One North, One people, irrespective of Religion, Rank or Tribe." Thus while it is useful to appeal to religious sentiments in particular circumstances, the Northern Peoples Congress maintains an essentially pragmatic attitude which emphasizes unity while allowing for diversity, and at the same time has a 'political style' which is flexible enough to be changed when circumstances alter. For example, it readily permitted a membership open to all though it had earlier stated that membership was restricted to people of Northern origin.[86] Similarly, when the support of the Emirs was thought necessary, the party modified its original eight-point programme to make it more acceptable to the dominant ruling groups.[87] Again, though it had earlier maintained a policy of 'Western' alignment as its stand in foreign affairs, it readily changed this to one of 'non-alignment' on forming a coalition federal government with the NCNC after the 1959 federal elections. It follows then that the ideology of the Northern Peoples Congress is essentially conservative, but it is a conservatism in the tradition of Burke and Bradley of which, perhaps, Professor Oakshott is the best living representative. Thus the Northern Peoples Congress would subscribe to Oakshott's statement that "in politics, the only concrete manner of activity detectable is one in which empiricism and the ends to be pursued are recognized as dependent alike for their existence and their operation, upon a traditional manner of behaviour". Political activity thus "springs neither from instant desires, nor from general principles . . . and the form it takes, because it can take no other, is the amendment of existing arrangements by exploring and pursuing what is intimated in them".[88]

But there can be divergences of opinion[89] as to how the 'existing arrangements' are to be amended, a divergence often taken to mark off, within the framework of any given tradition, the radicals from the reactionaries, the 'progressives' from the 'conservatives', the 'left' from the 'right'. This is no less true of the NPC and the distinctions noted are nowhere better brought out than in the attitudes of party leaders to the native authority system. Thus, the conservatives, represented by the Sardauna, would like to retain the existing system with only minor alterations. On the other hand, there are the radicals, who feel that "it is high time in the development of local government systems in this region that obsolete and undemocratic ways of appointing Emirs' Councils should close".[90] In between these two groups, the 'Centre', are progressives like the Prime Minister, who while not prepared to abolish the system, would rather see the authorities more responsible to the mass of the people and some measure of control vested in the latter. This has meant in practice that in domestic affairs the Northern Peoples Congress has been content largely to maintain the *status quo*, allowing only minor modifications as the need for these arises. It has thus been extremely cautious in its attitude to local government reform. And economically, it has been opposed to any measure of nationalization, preferring instead government participation in local enterprise wherever this has been deemed advisable.

As the 'conservatives' and 'moderate progressives' monopolized the top leadership of the party, their views have predominated, but with the 'dilemma of leadership' already noted, it is not unlikely that the 'radicals' will become increasingly important in the not too distant future.[91] One might add, however, that the terms 'conservative', 'radical', and 'moderate progressive' are not to be construed as designating fixed groups within the party, but are to be interpreted relatively to given policy issues or lines of action.[92]

IV. PARTY AND NOMINATION SYSTEM

Possibly no single fact brings out the general character of a party more than its procedure for the nomination of candidates to contest elections, and an analysis of the process adopted in the Northern Peoples Congress reveals only too clearly how closely interrelated the party is to the social structure. As has already been suggested, it is useful for analytical purpose to distinguish the two stages of 'certification and 'selection' in the nomination procedure.

Various factors have to be taken into consideration in the social screening which leads to eligibility for candidacy. Foremost of these is to be an incumbent seeking renomination. Of those elected to the House of Representatives in 1954 72·5% were renominated in 1959, while 25% had sat in the House since 1952. In the Northern House of Assembly, 38·8% of those elected in 1951 were re-elected in 1956, and of those elected in the latter year, 1956, 63·5% were again re-elected in 1961. Only 16% had, however, maintained a continuous membership of the House since 1952. In considering the seemingly low figure of 16%, it should be remembered that the membership of the House was increased from 90 to 130 in 1956 and again to 177 in 1961.

The table below gives a rough picture of renominations for selected provinces. It shows also the degree of circulation amongst what one might call the 'élite' of the party, with maximum circulation between 1952 and 1961, in provinces such as Benue, Kabba, Zaria, Bauchi, Adamawa, Ilorin and Sokoto in descending order. Conversely, provinces such as Katsina, Niger, Plateau, Bornu and Kano, in that order, have maintained the greatest degree of permanence among their leadership.[93]

Probably equally important is being associated with the Native Authority either as a Councillor, a district or village head, an Alkali or head of a department in the Native Administration. Thus these groups made up about 96% of the total members elected to the federal parliament in 1959, just under 4% being made up of traders, contractors, employees of commercial firms and so on. The position in the Northern House of Assembly is hardly any different.[94]

Besides the above, Emirate or divisional balance and dynastic or lineage interests have also to be taken into consideration. In Niger province, for instance, divisional interests led early to apportioning candidates almost equally between the three main Emirates of Nupe (Bida, under which were subsumed the minor emirates of Lapai and Agaie), Abuja and Kontgora. In some cases where this factor has

L

TABLE 8

Re-nominations to the Northern House of Assembly 1952 to 1961

	Adamawa	Bauchi	Benue	Bornu	Ilorin	Kabba	Kano	Katsina	Niger	Plateau	Sokoto	Zaria
(i) % of 1951 re-elected in 1956	75·0	16·6	—	33·3	33·3	25·0	50·0	100·0	75·0	33 3	28·4	—
(ii) % re-elected in 1961	50·0	44·4	30·0	50·0	33·3	16·6	57·7	90·0	83·0	50·0	56·4	42·6
(iii) % continuous membership	12·5	7·1	—	21·3	16·6	—	21.0	43·1	37·5	25·0	10·5	—

been ignored, dissatisfaction has led to prospective candidates standing as 'Independents'. This is particularly important with dynastic competition, or even competition amongst different segments of the same dynastyc. Thus, in the 1959 federal election the Wakilin Gona Daura decided to contest Daura as an Independent against M. Saidu Daura, the official Northern Peoples Congress candidate. Both men belong to the ruling Duara dynasty, but whereas the official candidate is the grandson of the present Emir, the father of the other is out of office. The official candidate, however, already has an elder brother in the Regional Assembly and as such, M. Mai Daura, the Wakilin Gona, felt his segment ought to have provided a candidate for the federal elections.

The actual process of screening is an exercise performed by the Provincial Executive Committees or the parliamentary caucus of the latter.[95] The procedure for selection, however, varies from one province to the other. In the lower North, in provinces such as Benue, Kabba, Ilorin, Niger and Plateau, this is done by the Provincial Executive. Not infrequently disagreements occur between a constituency and the Provincial Executive over particular candidates. In such cases the dispute is referred to the Central Working Committees for resolution, and wherever possible the CWC attempts to ensure that the constituency's wishes are respected.[96] In the far North, that is in Kano, Katsina, Sokoto, Bornu and Zaria provinces, the situation is more complicated. Katsina and Kano may be taken as representing the two poles in the selection process. In Katsina the Emir exercises only a negative control over selection: he can disallow the candidature of any nominee. In Kano, on the other hand, under the ex-Emir Sanusi, not only did he negative the choice of any candidate, he also selected his own nominees over and above the party. A similar situation obtained in Bornu while the present governor of the North, Sir Kashim Ibrahim, was the Waziri.[97] But whether the influence exercised was negative or positive, the Emir, or, as in Bornu, the Waziri, was the final authority over the selection of candidates. It can then be stated as a general proposition that "in the far North, the degree of independent action open to provincial leaders (in the 'selection' process) varies inversely with the commitment of the Emir in party affairs".[98]

At this point, one might note that the preponderance of Native Authority functionaries amongst party nominees has not gone unquestioned by the rank-and-file of the party. At the Sokoto provincial Conference of 1957, for instance, a member asked how it was possible for a party leader who was also a parliamentarian, a district head and a Councillor to combine these different roles effectively while performing each with any semblance of efficiency. It is probably this question of effectiveness and efficiency which another had in mind when he asked: "What qualifications enable a member of the Northern Peoples Congress to be ranked high or to be a suitable candidate for election? Is it his affinity to royalty, age, stature (sic), popularity or aptitude to political science?"[99] So long as the system of nomination is dominated by the parliamentarians and Native Authority functionaries themselves, it is not possible to see what change can be expected. On the other hand the present whispers of protest could gather momentum and become an explosive force. It would thus be paradoxical if the social development which the leaders must pursue should eventually lead to their decline.[100]

V. PARTY DISCIPLINE

Because status-based parties—or élite parties in Hodgkin's terminology—tend to reflect the social structure, it has been suggested that they need not take seriously the question of discipline, in contrast, for instance, to 'mass parties'. Unlike the latter, the former rely on the ties of traditional loyalties and obligations to maintain discipline and whilst mass parties tend to disintegrate with defection, 'status' parties are only weakened by it. Proponents of arguments such as these[101] have carefully avoided stating whether their arguments are (a) to be taken as hypothesis for subsequent verification; (b) generalizations arrived at through observation, or (c) purely definitional and therefore tautological. If the last, then the thesis would be simply formal while if the second, it would empirically be false as the Action Group crisis of 1962 and several crises in NEPU demonstrate.[102] If the first, then it would seem, from what has just been said that either or both of the conclusions postulated is possible and the hypothesis incapable of verification. It would follow then that possibly the much more humble exercise of examining the methods and techniques of maintaining discipline is a more profitable line of enquiry.

In the Northern Peoples Congress there do not seem to be any specific rules regulating discipline. A case study may however illustrate the general mode whereby discipline and coherence is maintained. As a result of a vacancy in the Federal Parliament caused by the death of the NPC member for Zaria Central in 1957, the Provincial Executive met and nominated a M. Sa'adu Zango[103] to contest the seat. In nominating the candidate, however, the Executive had resolved that only people indigenous to Zaria were to contest elections in the province. Abdul Razaq, the party's legal adviser, then decided to challenge this decision when he came to know of it on the grounds that the decision contravened the motto of the party, was contrary to precedent elsewhere and finally that it introduced "an unnecessary element of parochialism and 'tribalism' into the party".[104] The Kano Convention of 1958 had, however, resolved that any party member standing against the party's official candidate was to be expelled for life.[105] Razaq went ahead to contest and lost the election. He was then expelled by the Zaria Provincial Executive. On appeal to the CWC, the decision of the local executive was rescinded and Razaq was 'suspended' from the party for five months, his stipend as legal adviser being withheld during that period.[106]

Most cases of discipline within the party are in practice not dissimilar. In all such cases, there is the possibility of appeal to the CWC, whose decision is final. In no case can it be said that the party was weakened by disciplinary action, even when such action has led to defection from the party, as for instance, the expulsion of the Plateau Provincial President, Alhaji Audu Gobe-zan-tashi, in 1961. Neither can it be maintained that the party does not take the question of discipline seriously. So long as the disadvantages of defection tend to outweigh its advantages, as would be so wherever no distinction is made between party and government, arguments such as that with which this section started would be purely academic.

VI. PARTY FINANCE

The sources of a party's funds are often a good index of the levers of control within the party. But like the Conservative party in Britain and unlike some of the other Nigerian parties, the NPC has attempted to maintain a shroud of secrecy about the sources of its finance. However, the table on page 150 abstracted from 'The Annual Budget of the National Headquarters Secretariat' for 1957 provides a rough guide to the primary known sources of the party's funds.[107]

It would seem, then, that besides the sale of party publications, including party membership cards, constitution and other pamphlets the proceeds from 'social events' and donations, the main known source of the party's funds come from the contributions from the legislators who in fact control and direct the party. The suggestion that M.P.s should contribute a percentage of their salaries to party funds was first put forward at the 1952 Kaduna Convention of the party. Since that year, however, the suggestion has become a 'rule' though the actual percentage has varied. Normally, M.P.s contribute 5% of their salaries, though this is often increased during election

TABLE 9

Annual Revenue of the National Secretariat 1957

Source of Revenue	Estimated Amount	Amount to be Realized at Least
	£	£
1. Dues from Regional Members, £40 per member 106 all NPC	4,240	3,000
2. Dues from Federal Members, £40 per member 82 all NPC	3,280	2,000
3. Twenty Board Members other than Legislators, £10 per member	200	150
4. Annual revenue from all branches in Nigeria	1,500	800
5. Sale of party publications	1,500	1,500
6. Donations voluntary	5,000	3,000
7. Proceeds from lectures and other social events	5,000	3,000

NOTE: While it is indubitable that the actual figures will have risen over the years, it is highly improbable that the relative proportions will have have changed significantly since 1957.

years. Thus in 1959 and 1961 the figure was raised to 10%. Members of public corporations other than the chairman and those who are legislators are normally expected to contribute about 2·5% of their salaries to the party, which suggests that only party members can expect to be appointed to the boards of the public corporations.

The table also suggests that only a negligible percentage of party funds come from the regular monthly contributions of members. Members are expected to make a monthly payment of one shilling, one third of which is remitted to the National headquarters. If one then takes the Northern Peoples Congress's declared membership of 500,000 in August 1956, as a basis of calculation, and taking the estimated revenue of £1,500, it would be seen that only about 2% of the total members can be classed as regular financial members of the party, and at the most optimistic calculation, the figure would rarely exceed 5%. It would follow from this that only the most rudimentary form of organization can be maintained at the primary-branch, district and provincial-levels of the party. With the system of indirect elections which obtained in the North prior to 1959,[108] this would not necessarily be a handicap. But since the introduction in that year of direct elections based on the single member constituency and the single, non-transferable vote, properly organized local party units will become increasingly essential. In 1959 the party headquarters for the first time subsidized provincial organs by providing campaign vehicles. Also the payment of the salaries of provincial organizing secretaries was taken up by the central organization. It is, however, doubtful for how long this procedure can continue given the fact that revenue from legislators is by its nature highly inelastic. Obviously primary units will have to exploit local sources of revenue and here the most promising would be membership dues. But it is hardly conceivable that if more party members make regular contributions they will not demand an increasing share of control over party affairs: for instance, over nominations. This cannot but alter, in the long run, the present tendency for Native Administration functionaries to dominate the party and the legislatures.

Similarly, and reinforcing the above argument, it is only to be expected that the private individuals and interest groups who now contribute, it is reported, the main bulk of the 'Voluntary Donations'[109] will demand a share in the control and direction of the party. Wealthy merchants like Ibrahim Musa Gashash, Regional Minister of Lands and Survey, Chairman of the Kano Citizens Trading Company and a prominent motor transport magnate, already wield a lot of influence in the party. Others, such as Alhaji Ibrahim Ringim, trader, transport owner and member of the Kano Provincial Loans Board, Alhaji Aminu Dantata, member Kano Provincial Loans Board, a director of the well-known trading company of Alhassan Dantata and Son, to name a few from Kano alone, have been given seats in the Northern House of Assembly. These attajirai (wealthy merchants) who traditionally had no share in the political control of the Hausa–Fulani State, are now, under the modern party system, gradually being assimilated into the old ruling class of the North. Interest groups, such as the Northern Middlemen's Trading Association, the Northern Association of Motor Transport Owners, have also begun to exert noticeable pressure[110] on the party and the government. Being still small in numbers, the Attajirais have found it politically advantageous to support the old ruling class. With widening economic opportunities brought about by a steady, though slow growth of the economy, it would be naive not to expect that these men will want a greater share than they now have in the political direction of the affairs of the Region.

The combination of a politically and socially mobilized electorate and an assertive commercial class may well constitute a tremendous force of social change in the North. How well the existing régime can stand against such changed circumstances will depend on its ability to conciliate the new forces of change, for as Livingston succinctly put it, "the internal stability of a régime can be measured by the ratio between the number of social forces that it controls or conciliates, in a word, represents, and the number and strength of the social forces it fails to represent and has against it."[111] However, until much more is known, no prediction can be made one way or the other.

Summarily, the NPC can be said to be a weakly articulated, organizationally diffuse but highly centralized political party. The degree of centralization in any political party can be expressed as a function of two main variables—the extent to which the mass organs of the party actively participate in the formulation of the broad policies by which the party is governed and the extent of the responsibility of the leadership to the mass organization. It will thus vary inversely with the articulation of these two variables. In the NPC, it has been shown that these variables have very low articulation, certainly much lower than in the other Nigerian parties. It would follow that the NPC is more highly centralized than any of the other major Nigerian political parties.[112]

The party rests on the time-sanctioned system of Native Administration, which provides it with its system of communication, co-ordination and control. The party is thus a political extension of the Native Authority system and the almost one-to-one relation between the two makes the Northern Peoples Congress essentially a 'regional' party. The 'regional' nature of the party, together with the concentration of political power in the 'Northern' members is reflected in the refusal of the leadership to change the name of the party to 'Nigerian Peoples' Congress.[113] It also reinforces the party's policy of 'Northernization', and in the last analysis has significant implications for the over-all balance of political power in the country. These, however, are themes to be taken up in subsequent chapters.

NOTES

1. *West Africa*, 9th February 1952.
2. *Daily Times*, (Lagos), 14th December 1963.
3. M. Howeidy, 'Northern Nigeria's Parties', *West Africa*, 2nd January 1952, p. 1228.
4. M. Duverger, op. cit., p. xv: "Modern parties are characterized primarily by their anatomy." As against Duverger's structural definition, parties can also be defined in functional terms, e.g. as by Weber in Gerth and Mills, op. cit., pp. 194–95. The broadest pragmatic definition given for West African conditions is by T. Hodgkin who writes that "all political organizations which regard themselves as parties and are generally so regarded will be referred to as 'parties' "; 'A Note on West African Political Parties' in *What are the Problems of Parliamentary Government in West Africa*, Hansard Society, 1958, p. 51. Under the latter definitions of Weber and Hodgkin, there could be no denying that the Northern Peoples Congress is a political party.
5. Op. cit., p. 3. para 10.
6. *Annual Reports*, 1952, p. 25; 1954, pp. 15, 59, 63; 1956, p. 131.
7. Op. cit., p. 3, para. 11.
8. *N.P.C. Constitution and Rules*, no date. Text in English and Hausa, p. 10.
9. N.P.C. H.Q. Files No. 190/11 dated 6th February 1956 and signed by Abba Habid, the NPC General Secretary.
10. Report by M. Garba Abuja, Administrative Secretary of the NPC. M. Abuja has since left the NPC for the Action Group.
11. Quotations are from the text of branch reports to the National Headquarters of the Party. These are in Hausa, but the author had English translations. Though most reports are dated, file references are rarely given for branch reports.
12. Max Weber, *Essays in Sociology*, p. 195. A statement by Sir Ahmadu Bello is illustrative in this context. Replying to a motion by an NPC member of the Regional Assembly requesting that membership of the House be made a full time employment, the Premier said: "I remember that I met a group of Native Authorities and discussed the question of self-government with them. What they asked me was: 'Do you mean to say that you have no more slaves and you want to start a war again and that is why you want the British to go?' I told them 'No', and I gave them a full explanation." Debates, 7th August 1956, p. 24.
13. This concentration on local issues may also be due to the influence of the leadership of the branch. As this is usually the village head and his scribe, and as traditionally they had only executive powers, they would discourage discussion which is geared to wider issues of policy. On this see Smith, *Government in Zazzau*, pp. 89–91, 267 and his *Economy of Hausa Communities in Zaria*, pp. 6, 10.
14. The functions of the Provincial Committee as set out in the Constitution seems to be a systematization of the points contained in a letter by Ibrahim Imam (then General Secretary of the NPC) to M. Inua Wada, Secretary of the Kano NPC (now Federal Minister of Works), dated 2nd November 1953. Imam, it is reported, took a large hand in drawing up the Party Constitution. In terms of the development and tactics of the NPC, it is interesting to note that in the letter referred to, Imam had written that "Special attention be paid to the Jam'iyyar Mahaukata (Society of Mad Men, a 'terrorist' group which grew up in Kano and which set out to destroy NEPU). It is very essential that in order to get the whole party coming to our side, we start by first getting the support of its leaders."

He also added: "Whenever it is heard that 'our friends' (i.e. NEPU) are becoming strong, constant talk should be held until they are crushed completely."

15. Lester G. Seligman, 'Political Recruitment and Party Structure', *The American Political Science Review*, vol. 55, no. 1, March 1961, pp. 77–86.

16. His candidacy for the Presidentship was being sponsored by Inuwa Wada, a federal Minister, the Madaki of Kano, the Deputy Speaker of the Northern Assembly, M. Shehu Ahmed, Madawakin Kano, the Regional Minister of Lands and Survey, Alhaji Musa Gashash and his Parliamentary Secretary, Alhaji Sule Gaya (later Minister of Local Government).

17. No formal provincial organization existed in Kano before this date.

18. On the issues involved, see my 'The Nomination of Parliamentary Candidates in Northern Nigeria', op. cit., and also Debates, N.H.A., 18th February 1959, cols. 79, 90.

19. C. P. Snow, *Science and Government*, Mentor, 1962, p. 57, and J. D. B. Miller, *The Nature of Politics*, Duckworth, 1962, pp. 119–22.

20. Miller, op. cit., p. 122.

21. See Chapter III, p. 87.

22. A case that closely parallels the 'Koguna case' developed in Katsina in 1960. In an interview with Alhaji Ladan Baki (Acting Provincial President Katsina, N.A. Councillor of Works, Provincial Commissioner of Zaria and a nephew of the Emir of Katsina), he informed the writer that the rank-and-file members, whom he called "hooligans", "threatened to kill Musa Yar'Aduwa (the popular Provincial President, later Federal Minister of Lagos Affairs) rather than have him step down". In this instance, the district head of Munsawa, an elder brother of the Emir of Katsina, had attempted to replace Yar'Aduwa with his son (i.e. son of the D.H. of Munsawa) as Provincial President. With Yar'Aduwa, a Minister in Lagos, a compromise solution was found when Ladan Baki was made Acting Provincial President.

23. From 13th to 14th February 1960. The circular summoning the members (Ref. NPC(NH.NR) 9/1960/1 dated 23rd January 1960) specified that matters "likely to be discussed are as follows: (*a*) Provincial Organization, (*b*) NPC Party Vehicles, (*c*) Future elections, (*d*) Other matters," Nothing of significance issued from the meeting. The Secretary of the Regional Wing is Mr. Michael Audu Buba, Wazirin Shendam and Regional Minister of Trade and Industry.

24. Article 20.

25. Article 19.

26. Article 17.

27. House of Representatives, Debates, 30th March 1953, pp. 975–76.

28. Ibid., 31st March 1953, p. 992.

29. That this is far from being accepted by the NPC leaders is in fact shown by the Sardauna's statement on the demand by the AG during the 1953 Constitutional talks that the question of Lagos be referred to the electorate of the Western Region. On that occasion his comment was: "And to whom would they refer it? After all, the bulk of their leaders, and of the Western Government itself was present in London at the time." Ahmadu Bello, *My Life*, p. 157. Several other instances from the Sardauna's autobiography can be cited to the same effect. For the example of Ghana, D. Austin, *Politics in Ghana 1946–60*, Oxford University Press, 1964, p. 363 *et seq*; and Ivory Coast, A. R. Zolberg, *One Party Government in Ivory Coast*, Princeton, 1964, p. 261 *et seq*.

30. The Constitution only allows the Party Executive to fill "any vacancy that may occur later in any of the offices . . . for the period unexpired". Article 26.

31. With the one change that with the conversion of the NPC into a political

party in 1951, Dr. Dikko, the General President, had resigned his office being a civil servant and Alhaji Sanda, his Deputy, had become the President. By 1952, the NPC found itself in a position such that its leaders in the Northern House of Assembly were not members of the party executive and therefore had no influence on the formulation of party policy.

32. Of the thirty-man Executive of the Party elected in 1950, only four of these became members of the Northern House of Assembly and none of these four held any Parliamentary office.

33. On this issue, see Debates of the Eastern House of Assembly, vol. I, 30th January—11th February 1953; Okoi Orikpo, 'On being a Minister', *West Africa*, 24th and 31st July, 7th and 14th August 1956; and A. Aloba's articles in the 17th January 1953 and 14th February 1953 issues of the same journal.

34. Alhaji Nuhu Bamali, NPC Federal Minister of State in the Ministry of External Affairs expressed this point in a personal interview as follows: "In the early days of the party it was imperative that the leadership must be in the hands of a person of a very high birth." Bamali, himself a key figure in the NPC, and then Zaria Provincial President, belongs to one of the ruling houses in Zaria.

35. One of the methods used by the leadership to achieve this is the summoning of 'Emergency Conventions' as against 'Annual Conventions'. No elections are held during Emergency Conventions. See *Nigerian Citizen*, 11th August 1956. At the Maiduguri Convention in 1955 the election of party Officers was suspended by the President when it became apparent that the radical' elements of the party were determined on ousting some of the Sardauna's stalwart supporters from office. In the confusion following attempts to elect a new Executive, Sule Katagum, the Secretary of the Katagum branch, moved a readoption of the existing Executive. See *Nigerian Citizen*, 4th August 1955. A similar practice occurred at the 1958 Kano convention of the Party. In the latter case the decision not to elect new party officers was based on a resolution, supposedly taken in Maiduguri to suspend such elections for a period of five years. No evidence, however, has been found by the writer to substantiate this resolution. On the Maiduguri Convention, see *West Africa*, 9th July 1955; *Nigerian Citizen* 16th and 23rd June 1955; and *Nigerian Citizen* 15th January 1958. See *Daily Times*, 27th January 1958 for the Kano Convention.

36. On becoming members of the House of Representatives in 1954, Inuwa Wada and Mohammadu Sanusi the General Secretary and Treasurer of the NPC respectively were replaced by Abba Habib and Alhaji Aliyu, Makama Bida, the latter two being members of the Northern House. When the North became Independent in 1959, Abba Habib, was replaced by Alhaji Pategi, Regional Minister of Health as Acting General Secretary. Abba Habib comes from Dikwa, which in 1959 was part of the former Northern Cameroons. In the U.N. plebiscite of 1961 the Northern Cameroons voted for integration with Northern Nigeria and became known as Sardauna Province. In 1962 Dikwa Emirate was excised from Sardauna Province to become part of Bornu Province.

37. The officers of the Party are given by the Party Constitution (Article 25) as the "General President, General Secretary, Asst. General Secretary, Financial Secretary, Two Auditors, Education Advisor, Economic and Welfare Officer, Legal Advisor, Treasurer and Asst. Treasurer". No education officer or an Economic and Welfare Officer has ever been appointed or elected by the NPC.

38. Both the Treasurer and Financial Secretary submitted 'Annual Reports' to Party Conventions up until 1954. After that date, the practice ceased. Strictly therefore the Chairman, Alhaji Abubakar Tafawa Balewa, could not have had legitimate grounds for disallowing debate on this issue. Dr. Sklar's statement

that finance is a matter exclusively reserved for the Executive and not discussed at Annual Conventions cannot therefore be strictly accurate.

39. On this, see e.g. J. K. Pollock, 'The British Party Conference', *The American Political Science Review*, vol. 32, 1938, pp. 525–35; R. T. Mackenzic, *British Political Parties*, passim.

40. Mustapha Dambatta, political correspondent of the *Nigerian Citizen*, in ibid., 11th August 1956. Dambatta, who became a member of the NPC after resigning from NEPU in 1954, was given a scholarship by the Northern Government to read journalism for one year in the United States. He returned to Nigeria in 1962 and for a time assumed the editorship of the *Nigerian Citizen*.

41. In a recent statement, an NPC member of the Northern House of Assembly, Bature Dangyand (Jos South) has said that there was no need for the NPC to hold a Convention because "its members had no complaints". Annual Conventions of political parties, he added, were only necessary when such parties were facing a rift or losing their supporters. See *Daily Express* (Lagos), 31st October 1963.

42. Article 36.

43. The "official members" are the officers of the party: The President General, Sir Ahmadu Bello, Premier of the North and First and Second Vice-Presidents, Sir Abubakar Tafawa Balewa, Federal Prime Minister and Mohammed Ribadu, Federal Minister of Defence, respectively, the Acting General Secretary, Ahman Pategi, Regional Minister of Information, the National Treasurer, Aliyu Maka- man Bida Regional Minister of Finance and the Financial Secretary, Isa Kaita, Regional Minister of Education. The table is drawn from names given in the Nigeria Year Books of 1960, 62 and 64 at pp. 79, 105 and 10 respectively.

44. Article 36.

45. Article 40.

46. Mr. Razaq explained that "Bornu was never conquered by the Fulanis and has remained fairly distinct from the North. The Kanuri man in fact is contemptu- ous of the Hausa-Fulani."

47. Article 62 of the Party Constitution provides that "the Committee shall if so desired be given power to discharge *all* functions of the Congress on behalf of the Central Organization or the Executive Committee".

48. On this issue, see *Nigerian Citizen*, 18th June 1960, *Daily Times*, 16th June 1960, and *Sunday Times* (Lagos), 26th June 1960. Alhaji Nuhu Bamali, NPC Senator and Minister of State in the Ministry of Internal Affairs, in an interview, admitted that the failure of the Prime Minister in not disallowing the Federal Government's action may have been due to his being unaware of the CWC decision in 1959 that the NPC should have no dealings with Israel. It is significant, however, that once the Northern Government came out against any economic agreements by the Federal Government with Israel, this was immediately dropped.

49. Sklar, op. cit., p. 613. Even the AG does not bear out Sklar's thesis. Allegedly the best organized political party in Nigeria, the AG suffered a split when the Executive Committee wanted to make the parliamentary body sub- servient to it. On the AG crisis, see J. Mackintosh, 'Politics in Nigeria: The Action Group Crisis of 1962', *Political Studies*, vol. 11, no. 2, 1963.

50. NPC, Department of Organization: Proposed Programme of Reorganiza- tion No. 2, dated 1st May 1957. This became effective as "Office Organization and Order" dated 25th July 1957. The programme was part of a whole party reorganization plan. The CWC only accepted the sections relating to the Secreta- riat reorganizations, and that the salaries of the Party Manager, Publicity Sec- retary and principal organizing secretary should be £30, £17 and £25 respec-

tively. Other secretaries were to be paid £15 and the manager/storekeeper £10 per month.

51. The expression was used by the NHQ staff in a petition dated 17th October 1955 submitted to the NPC President-General and Executive Council. The petition was for increased cost of living and similar "allowances, Gorsuch, etc." The reference to Gorsuch is the *Report of the Commission on the Public Services of the Governments in the Federation of Nigeria 1954–55*, Lagos, 1955 by L. H. Gorsuch. The report put forward suggestions for increases in the salaries of civil servants based on a cost of living index. The principle was subsequently adopted and applied by the private sector of the economy.

52. In an interview with Raji Abdallah, NPC Party Manager.

53. Release dated 10th April 1967 and signed by Garba Abuja, Yesuf Dantsoho, Abubakar Tugga, Abba-El-Ansari, Mohammadu King, Wada Kushariki, Moh. Maiganga and Mansur Buhari. The broadcast version (broadcast on the 11th April) differs in many aspects from the original text. In the broadcast version, it was stated, e.g. that they suggested that the party should be reorganized "by overhauling the party from the Executive right down to the local branches to ensure that leaders realize that it is the Ministers that belong to the party; and not the party to the Ministers". After the April release, a junior Whip, M. Abubakar Balewa (no relation of the Prime Minister), in a letter to the signatories of the release dated 12th April 1954 wrote *inter alia*: "Moreover, you should remember that you are an NPC official and as such you *cannot* criticize her. I am expecting your reply before 14th April."

54. Letter to the Premier Ref. NPC(NH)299/5 dated 6th December 1956. The objection to Ohikere was that he was "only a friend and supporter of the NPC whenever he steps into Kaduna but the greatest enemy of the NPC and its policy at his home town". Mr. Ohikere was the leader of the Igbirra Tribal Union, which contested the elections against the NPC to which it was allied at the Parliamentary level. Tribal Associations, such as the ITU, the Igalla Union, Igalla Division Union use these tactics as a bargaining weapon against the NPC. In the 1961 Regional Elections, Ohikere contested as an NPC candidate and was defeated by the ITU candidate. After his defeat, he was appointed Chairman of the Nigerian Ports Authority.

55. In a petition ("Humble Submission and Supplication by the Secretariat Staff") to the CWC dated 25th September 1957, the Staff added significantly "If, however, you find this (request for increases in salary) impossible, then we humbly request that you use your good offices to find us appointments elsewhere with a view to relieving us of our present posts . . ." It was signed by the Party Manager (Rafih) Principal Organizing Secretary (Raji Abdallah), Administrative Secretary (Garba Abuja), Publicity Secretary (Yesufu Dantsoho), and others.

56. See above page 125 and footnote 22 for example.

57. For the immediate cause of the formation of the Mahaukata, see *Provincial Annual Reports* 1953 and 1954. The society was founded by Mamman Nagending Waya, Ado Dan Kakau and Sarkin Akusa—praise-singers and hangers-on at the Ex-Emir Sanussi of Kano's palace. They all wore red head-bands embossed with a curved sword, and went about the city terrorizing political opponents, mainly NEPU. The movement quickly spread to Bida and Sokoto. After about four months of continued lawlessness, the Resident invited NPC, NEPU and the Mahaukata leaders and some Mallams (Nasiru, Haido and Fege) to a meeting to see if the prevalent hooliganism could not be stopped. This meeting may have been responsible for Dr. Sklar writing that some of the Mallamai helped in organizing the Mahaukata, a view which in the light of the above is untenable.

58. In a written document NPC-Y/3/G1 dated 30th December 1961, for which I am indebted to Mr. Post. One important function the women perform is helping to raise funds for the local parent organization. This they do through performing exhibition dances for which they charge entry fees of about two or three shillings. This practice was copied from NEPU which first exploited the use of women in this way.

59. A. Ranney and W. Kendall, *Democracy and the American Party System*, Harcourt Brace, 1956, pp. 244–49. Also, A. W. Gouldner, (ed.), *Studies in Leadership*, Harper, 1950.

60. The figures are taken from Tables I and II in B. J. Dudley, op. cit., p. 50.

61. Based on date abstracted from *Guide to the Parliament of the Federation*, Lagos, 1961. The percentage for D.H.'s is based on a figure of fourteen. This differs from the figure of eight given by J. P. Mackintosh in his 'The Nigerian Federal Parliament', *Public Law*, autumn 1963, p. 336. With this difference, I can only claim that my figure is accurate.

62. The *Nigerian Citizen* 19th June 1952 political correspondent, writing of the proposed Kaduna Convention of the NPC (held 5th and 6th July 1952) noted that "leadership of the Parliamentary party is not in doubt—the Sardauna is the only choice but the Presidency of the Congress may still be retained by Alhaji Sanda". For instance, the Sardauna is related by marriage to the ex-Emir of Kano.

63. The election for the National President of the party was held on 4th April 1954. Two days earlier both the Administrative Secretary—Garba Abuja and the Principal Organizing Secretary, Mallam Nuhu Bamali (now a Senator and Federal Minister of State) were approached by Alhaji Aminu, D. H. of Sabon-Gari Zaria (now Emir of Zaria, he had helped the Sardauna financially in 1944/45 when the latter appealed against a sentence passed on him by the Sultan's Court for misappropriation of funds) and the Chief Alkali of Zaria, M. Yahaya, and held that it would be in the interests of the party if the Sardauna was elected the President. Preliminary canvassing by these two party officials had shown that Balewa was the popular candidate. They next met Balewa on the 3rd April and urged him not to insist on formalities during the election. It had been impressed on him that the Emirs desired that Ahmadu Bello should lead the party. At the election on the 4th, contrary to previous procedure, it was decided that the election should be by a show of hands (paper balloting had been adopted in the past). Three candidates were nominated, (1) Balewa, (2) Ahmadu Bello, (3) Alhaji Sanda, almost it seemed in order of preference. With Alh. Bello Dandago (now NPC Government Chief Whip in the Federal Parliament) in the Chair, Sanda's election was first taken. He scored 75 votes. Balewa, the next man, scored 239 votes, while the Sardauna, the last man, secured 373 votes. Those whom I interviewed have suggested that the counts for Balewa and the Sardauna were 'engineered' in favour of the Sardauna.

64. Girth and Mills: From Max Weber, *Essays in Sociology*, pp. 245–52 and 262–64.

65. Alhaji Ladan Baki, Provincial Commissioner, Zaria, nephew of the Emir of Katsina, in the House of Assembly. Debates 8th March 1963, p. 73.

66. Emir of Nassarawa Eggon. House of Chiefs, Debates 28th March 1963, p. 38.

67. Emir of Keffi—"We have learnt from our grandfathers that in the Dynasty of Shehu Usman dan Fodio there would be someone who would rise to greatness and lead his people to the appearance of the Mahdi. Now the time has come and we saw Sir Ahmadu leading his people and we believe that this is the man

we have heard of." House of Chiefs, Debates, 29th March 1963, p. 60. On the Mahdi, see Chapter I p. 20 and references given in the footnotes.

68. *Daily Times*, 26th November 1960. On the 'myth' of Bayajidda, see Chapter I p. 2.

69. Sir Ahmadu Bello, op. cit., p. 239. Mr. El' Masri, lecturer in Islamic Studies at the University of Ibadan, and engaged in a study of Uthman Dan Fodio, informs me that in one of his writings Shehu Uthman declaimed any descent from the Prophet.

70. Not to mention the annual 'pilgrimages' to the tomb of Uthman dan Fodio at which the Sardauna is often accompanied by the Sultan, some of the Emirs and Ministers and civil servants of the Regional Government.

71. S. Neumann in 'Towards a Comparative study of Political Parties' in S. Neumann (ed.), *Modern Political Parties*, University of Chicago Press, 1956, pp. 406–07 makes a distinction between 'Personal' and 'Institutional' leadership. Of the former, he writes "he is responsible to no man but to God and the Nation (who are conveniently removed from any direct interference)—he is revered by the emotional, rootless and amorphous masses seeking mystery, devotion and the miraculous", p. 407. Cf. some of the Sardauna's own statements in '*My Life*', e.g. at p. 238.

72. Though the Sardauna is alleged often to have taken decisions without consulting any of his colleagues—for instance in his appointment of the Ex-Emir Sanusi of Kano as Acting Governor of the North—it is also said that over some issues his hand has sometimes been forced. Thus it is reported that over the decision to exile Sanusi of Kano, while the Sardauna, the Sultan of Sokoto, and the Emir of Katsina were for some form of disciplinary action, Sir Kashim Ibrahim, Musa Gashash, Isa Kaita, and the Makaman Bida were bent on the exile of the Emir, Kashim Ibrahim, threatening, it was reported, to resign his governorship if this was not done. Interviewees, who would rather remain anonymous, pointed out that only after the order of exile was signed by the Governor were the NPC leaders informed of the decision, though some had earlier been asked their views.

73. See Chapter II, p. 48.

74. The Sardauna has often expressed the wish to become the next Sultan, and though he has been critical of the Emir, he has publicly in various statements announced that he would not be party to any derogation from the authority of traditional rulers. But see note 62, p. 158 above.

75. Note 34, p. 155 above. Nuhu Bamali, NPC, saw this as one of the reasons for the concentration of power in the North. As he put it "we would like to convert the NPC to a real mass party—our future lies in this, but we just can't see how to do this. The Emirs are still very powerful. This is the main danger for the NPC."

76. Turnout in the Federal Election of 1959 and the Regional Election of 1961 were respectively 88·9% and 61·6%. NPC members explain the 'apathy' or indifference as being due to the one election being federal and the other regional. They argue that there is only apparent apathy for in NPC marginal areas in the Middle Belt their vote increased. Most people, however, argue that the NPC would in any case win and it was therefore 'pointless' voting. They add that to vote against the NPC often leads to some reprisal or the other.

77. Table based on data supplied by the Provincial Secretaries for areas shown. To these men I am greatly indebted.

78. Complex in that belief (which to some people may be totally unreasonable and nonsensical) to the extent that they are behaviourally significant have to be

taken into consideration. Thus, for instance, it is popularly held that agents of the NPC have suprasensible means whereby they can determine the individual's voting behaviour and that party "mallams" can, even against one's will, through prayers, compel one to vote the party ticket. If one's will can be so influenced, it would seem pointless not to support the party from the start. See e.g. the author's 'Elections in Sardauna Province', *West Africa*, 9th December 1961.

79. On the attitude of mind here suggested see, for example, the speech by Alhaji Maiwada in the Northern Assembly, Debates, 11th August 1956, p. 179–80. On the role of the N.A. as a "corrective" agency, see Debates, N.H.A. 2nd March 1957, p. 464; 12th March 1957, pp. 847–848; 7th April 1960, cols. 38–39, 41, 57, 59, 68; 8th April 1960, col. 71 and 9th April 1960 col. 95. Also Debates, House of Representatives, 19th April 1960, vol. I, col. 1366 ffg; 12th April 1960, vol. I, col. 1133. Opposition party estimates of people arbitrarily imprisoned by the N.A. should be taken with caution. Thus, while there have been estimates of 7,000 and 10,000 (1960) imprisoned, the total number of prisoners in Northern Nigeria as at 30th June 1959, 1960 and 1961 were 8,976, 8,545, and 7,309 respectively. Figures given in reply to questions in Northern House of Assembly. Debates, 25th August 1962, p. 625. It is hardly credible that almost if not all, prisoners are opposition party members.

80. The exception was the D. H. of Gusau who is a distant relation of the Sardauna. The Sardauna once held the district headship of Gusau.

81. Data compiled from Annual Reports of the Northern Region Development Corporation; Northern Region Production and Development Corporation and Provincial Loans Boards. All these no longer show the unofficial composition of the Boards. The NRPDB has been merged into the NRDC since 1960.

82. Debates, 14th March 1963, p. 341. The occasion was the debate on the Bill to sanction the pledging of Government credit for the sum of £2·5 million to enable Co-operative Societies to finance cultivation and marketing of crops.

83. See N.H.A. Debates, 8th August 1955, p. 42; 1st August 1958, cols. 702 and 706. Where loans are granted to opposition members, the threat of recalling such loans in between 'seasons' is often a strong weapon for effecting a change of party allegiance.

84. Quoted from M. Asad, *The Principles of State and Government in Islam*, p. 69. On the concepts of Ijima and Bid'a, see H. A. R. Gibb, *Mohammedanism*, Oxford University Press, p. 99; Gandefroy-Demombynes, *Muslim Political Institutions*, p. 61 *et seq*; M. Watt, *Islam and the Integration of Society*, pp. 141–80 and 238–51. On the influence of Islam in the North, J. Schact, 'Islam in Northern Nigeria', *Studia Islamica*, vol. 8, 1957, pp. 123–46.

85. Ideology should here be understood in the sense in which it is defined by Lasswell and Kaplan: "the ideology is the political myth functioning to preserve the social structure . . .", op. cit., p. 123. Also L. Dion, 'Political Ideology as a tool of Functional Analysis in Socio-political Dynamics, An hypothesis', *Canadian Journal of Economic and Political Science*, vol. 25, no. 1, 1959, pp. 47–59.

86. The restriction of membership only to those of northern descent is provided by the party Constitution, Article 10, and reaffirmed in a resolution by the Executive in January 1955, *Nigerian Citizen*, 13th January 1955. Yet, three years later Alhaji Inuwa Wada, justified a change of policy in a speech to the 1958 Convention by saying that "in order to remain in power in the federation and also to have our own man as the leader of the federal government, we must open our hands of co-operation to all parties and all individuals interested in our ideology". *Nigerian Citizen*, 15th January 1958. The decision to change the policy on

membership was taken by the CWC at a meeting in December 1957, *Nigerian Citizen*, 4th December 1957. Thus it can be argued that the CWC did alter the Party Constitution though theoretically it had no power to do so.

87. Expressions in italics show the measure of change in the two versions which is here quoted from the *Nigerian Citizen* 18th September 1952. Amended Version: (i) Regional autonomy within *one* Nigeria; (ii) Local government reform within a progressive Emirate system based on tradition and custom; (iii) The voice of the people to be heard in all Councils of the North; (iv) Drive for education through the whole of the North, laying due emphasis on the improvement of social, economic and cultural life of the people; (v) Eliminate bribery and corruption in every sphere of Northern life; (vi) Eventual self-government for Nigeria with Dominion Status within the British Commonwealth; (vii) *Membership of the NPC is open to all people of Northern descent whether as individuals or as a Union or as a political party*; (viii) Industrial and economic development of the Northern Region; (ix) One North, one people, irrespective of religion rank or tribe.

Original Version: (i) Regional autonomy within a united Nigeria; (ii) Local government reform within a progressive Emirate system; (iii) The voice of the people to be held in all Councils of the North; (iv) *Retain the traditional system of appointing Emirs with a wider representation on the Electoral Committee;* (v) Drive throughout the whole North for education while retaining and increasing cultural influence; (vi) Eliminate bribery and corruption in every sphere of Northern life; (vii) Eventual self-government for Nigeria with Dominion Status within the British Commonwealth; (viii) One North, one people, irrespective of religion, tribe or rank.

88. M. Oakshott, *Rationalism in Politics*, Methuen, 1962, pp. 123–24.

89. Cf. Lasswell and Kaplam, op. cit., p. 123, "In a society with a stable social structure, the ideology is a matter of consensus, not of opinion".

90. Speech by Abdul Mummuni (NPC) in the debate on the N.A. (Amendment) Law 1955. Debates 10th March 1955, p. 2.

91. Compare, e.g. the demand by the NPC Federal Minister of Economic Planning and Development for the Nationalization of Banking, Insurance, Retail and Wholesale trade, etc. Demands such as this are increasingly becoming popular and cannot but influence the public which already look on these enterprises as evidence of the shackling effects of neo-colonialism and Imperialism. For the Minister's speech, *Daily Times*, 9th April 1964.

92. R. Aron, The Opium of the Intellectuals, Secker and Warburg, 1957, pp. 7–16. Cf. also Michels, op. cit., (Dover Books end.) footnote 4, pp. 3–4.

93. The higher level of circulation amongst the party élite in the lower North is a reflection of the egalitarianism of the social structures of these areas (see chapter 2). What is interesting is Sokoto. An explanation which has been suggested to account for this deviation from the pattern of 'permanence' for the far North is the determination of the Sardauna not to have any competitor who might eventually attempt to exploit the 'mystique of Sokoto'.

94. See Section 2 for statistical data on the relationship between the N.A. and parliamentary membership.

95. In Katsina, for instance, the 'caucus' is composed of Alhaji Musa Liman—D. H. of Mussawa and Government Chief Whip in the Regional Assembly; Alhaji Isa Kaita, Regional Minister of Education and Musa Yar'Adua-Federal Minister for Lagos Affairs. In Kano it is made up of the Madaki of Kano, Alhaji Bello Dandogo, D. H. of Gwazo and Government Chief Whip in the Federal Parliament, the Dan Iya, Ado Sanusi, son of the Ex-Emir of Kano,

M

Inuwa Wada, Federal Minister of Works and Surveys, Musa Gashash, Regional Minister of Lands and Surveys and Maikano Dutse, D. H. of Dutse.

96. In the 1959 Federal Elections, Ibrahim Waziri, the popular choice was eventually nominated, after CWC pressure, to contest Konduga in Bornu Province. Similarly with Olarewanju Afoloyan in Ilorin South in the 1961 regional Elections.

97. For instances, see B. J. Dudley, op. cit., pp. 51–55.

98. Ibid., p. 54.

99. Quoted from *Nigerian Citizens*, 31st July 1957. For similar complaints from Zaria and Plateau respectively, *Nigerian Citizen*, 7th August 1957 and *Nigerian Citizen*, 9th September 1957, to cite a few cases.

100. Cf. Gaetano Mosca, *The Ruling Class* (translated by H. D. Kahn and edited by A. Livingston), McGraw-Hill, 1939, pp. 65-66. "Ruling Classes decline inevitably when they cease to find scope for the capacities through which they rose to power . . . or when their talents and the services they render lose in importance in the social environment in which they live."

101. E.g. Ruth Schacter, 'Single Party Systems in West Africa', *The American Political Science Review*, vol. 55, no. 2, June 1961, p. 295; T. Hodgkin, *African Political Parties*, passim.

102. On NEPU see the next chapter. The AG, an 'élite' party, disintegrated after the 1962 crisis. On this, J. Mackintosh, op. cit. The 1953 crisis in the NCNC a 'mass party', neither weakened it nor led to its disintegration. On this R. Sklar, op. cit., passim.

103. M. Zango was a scribe in the Iyan Garis Office (the present Emir of Zaria). Most people regard him a poor choice as against Razaq and his nomination by the party temporarily split the Zaria Executive.

104. Mr. Razaq is an Ilorin Yoruba who before his appointment as the Nigerian Ambassador to Ivory Coast lived and had a law practice in Zaria.

105. There was in fact a dispute as to whether such a resolution was actually passed. See *Nigerian Citizen*, 15th January 1958 and 9th July 1958.

106. In an interview, subsequently confirmed through other sources, I was informed by Razaq that the CWC split into two factions when his case came before it. The majority were for his explusion. While the minority included the Sardauna, Abubakar Tafawa Balewa and the Alhaji Aliyu, Taraki Zazzau, a Minister of State upheld his stand. His suspension was thus a compromise between the two groups.

107. Budget dated 1st May 1957 and signed by D. A. Rafih, party manager, showed 'Expenditure' of the party as follows:

Personal Emoluments

Title	Salary per annum	Total
	£	£
1. Party Manager	840	660
2. Principal Organizing Secretary	660	480
3. Publicity Secretary	360	360
4. Administrative Secretary	300	300
5. Six Organizing Secretaries at £240 p.a.	1,440	1,440
6. Clerk Typist	148	148
7. Messenger	84	84
TOTAL	£3,732	£3,472

Personal Emoluments—continued

General	£	£
1. Office Maintenance	300	300
2. Publicity	500	500
3. Vehicle Maintenance allowances	2,000	2,000
4. Other Emergency costs	50	50
TOTAL	£2,850	£2,850

In view of the Proceedings of the Foster-Sutton Tribunal of Enquiry (Lagos, 1957), 2 vols., which enquired into allegations of improper conduct by the Premier of the Eastern Region, Dr. Azikiwe, and the Report of the Coker Commission of Enquiry (Lagos, 1962), 4 vols., into six public corporations in Western Nigeria, the qualification should be emphasized.

108. There were direct elections in nineteen urban constituencies in the regional elections of 1956.

109. Some of these come from 'expatriate' communities, e.g. the Lebanese, in the North. Compare the revealing statement of the General Secretary in the Assembly when NEPU members accused the NPC of being partly financed by these communities: "The reason why these traders are to be singled out and discredited for their business is, as I understand, because they did not give *generously* to the NEPU during the election campaign", Debates, 23rd February 1957, p. 170.

110. The Middlemen's Association were able to pressure the Government into instituting a Commission of Enquiry into retail trade in Northern Nigeria. As a result of this, there was a noticeable move for expatriate Commercial firms moving out of retailing. Similar shift was observed after a call by the Northern Nigeria Contractor Union for no Government or N.A. contracts to be awarded to non-Northerners.

111. In the Introduction, p. xix, of Mosca's *The Ruling Class.*

112. This conclusion contrasts sharply with that reached by Dr. Sklar who writes that "effective centralization varies with the Action Group, National Council of Nigerian Citizens and the Northern People's Congress in descending order", op. cit., p. 801. Dr. Sklar, however, nowhere explains what he means by 'effective centralization". The usage here is not dissimilar to that of Michel, who wrote that "effective power is . . . in inverse ratio to the number of those who exercise it", op. cit., p. 52. Compare also the usage in 'Towards a More Responsible Two-Party System', *The American Political Science Review*, vol. 44 September 1950, Supplement.

113. See for instance *Nigerian* Citizen, 15th January 1958 and Morning Post, Lagos, 14th July 1962.

V

The Opposition: The Nigerian Elements Progressive Union and the United Middle belt Congress

The Nigerian Elements Progressive Union (formerly the Northern Elements Progressive Union, NEPU) and the United Middle Belt Congress (UMBC) together form the only significant opposition to the dominant NPC in Northern Nigeria. NEPU, though formed before the NPC has, however, never won enough seats in any election to constitute an opposition in a parliamentary sense. It was not represented in the Northern Assembly between 1952 and 1956. In 1956 it won seven seats, its ally, the BYM, winning two more, in a House of 131 elected members. It was represented in the Federal Parliament for the first time in 1959 when it won eight of the 174 seats from the North. In the 1961 regional elections, its representation fell from seven to one, and even that was won by the NCNC to which NEPU was allied. The UMBC, unlike NEPU, is localized in the areas known as the 'Middle Belt' of the North. In the 1956 regional elections, its two rival wings together won eleven seats. And in the 1959 federal elections, the UMBC with its allies, the AG and the ITP, secured twenty-five seats. During the 1961 regional elections, the UMBC, now essentially a Tiv protest movement, won only nine seats, seven of which were in the Tiv Division of Benue Province, the other two coming from the Tangale-Waja Constituency in Bauchi Province and Jos North West Constituency of Plateau province respectively. Thus, in the Regional Assembly of 177 members elected in 1961, the opposition is represented by only ten members.[1]

Though barely represented in the Region's legislature, both NEPU and the UMBC parties represent a not insignificant proportion of the electorate who have found themselves unwilling to accept the values for which the NPC, as the governing party of the North, stands. This is clearly illustrated by the table on page 166 which shows the comparative distribution of votes for both parties in the federal election of 1959 and the regional election of 1961.

Whilst in 1959 it polled over a third of the votes in only 6·6% of the constituencies it contested, in 1961, the latter figure rose to just over 25%. Although the performance of the UMBC in areas where it had 'marginal' support did not improve, its position, in areas where it had its main strength barely changed from one election to the other.

At a press conference held by Sir Ahmadu Bello, the Sardauna of Sokoto in May 1961, immediately before the North regional elections, he had referred to NEPU members as "prodigal children who have temporarily strayed from the fold of the NPC" but who sooner or later would return to the fold. But the evidence of the 1959 and 1961 elections hardly seemed to bear out this contention, the votes for the party in both elections being relatively stable. This is shown in Table 10, for selected provinces in the North.

Despite the fewer constituencies which it contested, NEPU increased its percentage of the votes cast in Bauchi and Kano Provinces. The significant point, however, is that irrespective of the various limitations and handicaps under which both parties operated, their electoral support remained fairly stable, and it can be argued with some plausibility that supporters of both parties have been much more consistent in their support than those of the NPC, for whereas NEPU's and UMBC's share of the total registered vote fell in the 1959 and 1961 elections by only 5·6% and 2·6% respectively, that of the NPC fell by 13·4%.[2] It is obvious therefore that the parliamentary representation of the opposition bears no relation whatsoever to their electoral strength and that both NEPU and the UMBC still represent a significant element of discontent in Northern society.

I. IDEOLOGICAL EXPRESSION OF THE OPPOSITION

Most observers of the African political scene have remarked on how little there is to distinguish the 'Government' from the 'Opposition' either in terms of ideology or policy. With a fluid, changing social structure, independence meant scarcely more than the transfer of power from the Colonial Administration to an emergent 'middle class' composed of the educated professional élite of doctors, lawyers and teachers which constituted the leadership of the political parties that had developed in the pre-independence era. This class, faced with the dual problem of how to increase rapidly the living standards of the people while at the same time remaining in control had little to distinguish or divide it with the result that whatever

TABLE 10

Distribution of Votes, NEPU and UMBC 1959 and 1961 Elections

Election	Party	0–9.9%	10.0–19.9%	20.0–29.9%	30.0–39.9%	40.0–49.9%	50.0–59.9%	60.0–69.9%	70.0–79.9%	80.0–89.9%	90.0–99.9%	Total
1959	NEPU (a)	65	49	28	11	9	3	1	—	—	—	166
1959	UMBC (b)	100	29	9	12 (won 3)	6 (won 4)	6	7	—	3	2	174
1961	NEPU (a)	22	32	24	25	5 (won 1)	—	—	—	—	—	108
1961	UMBC (b)	64	34	15	9 (won 2)	4	—	1	1	3	2	133

NOTE: (*a*) read NEPU-NCNC; (*b*) read UMBC-AG.

TABLE 11

NEPU Electoral Support 1959 and 1961

Province	No. of Constituencies Contested		Actual Vote as % of Registered Vote		Increase or Decrease	Actual Vote as % of Total Vote Lost		Increase or Decrease
	1959	1961	1959	1961		1959	1961	
Bauchi	14	13	18·2	16·2	−2·0	21·4	27·0	+5·6
Bornu	9	5	8·0	4·2	−3·8	8·9	5·9	−3·0
Katsina	15	13	22·6	15·9	−6·7	24·8	19·8	−5·0
Niger	8	6	14·4	8·2	−6·2	16·3	12·7	−3·6
Plateau	9	7	14·4	6·9	−7·5	16·2	10·6	−5·6
Zaria	8	6	27·7	6·6	−21·1	30·5	18·0	−12·5
Kano	35	30	16·1	14·1	−2·0	17·50	20·2	+2·7
Region	166	108	14·3	8·7	−5·6	16·1	14·1	−2·0

TABLE 12

UMBC/AG Electoral Support 1959 and 1961: Selected Provinces

Province	No. of Constituencies Contested		Actual Vote as % of Registered Vote		Increase or Decrease	Actual Vote as % of Total Vote Lost		Increase or Decrease
	1959	1961	1959	1961		1959	1961	
Bauchi	14	14	11·8	6·9	−4·9	13·8	11·3	−2·5
Ilorin	6	6	30·9	16·0	−13·9	36·2	27·6	−8·6
Niger	8	7	7·7	4·5	−3·2	8·7	6·9	−1·8
Benue	14	13	55·1	38·3	−16·8	59·7	53·1	−6·6
Plateau	9	9	39·2	21·1	−18·1	43·9	32·6	−11·3
Adamawa	8	8	22·5	12·3	−10·2	25·9	21·5	−4·4
Region	174	133	15·2	9·0	−6·2	17·2	14·6	−2·6

difference there was between the Government and the opposition, this meant no more than one between the 'ins' and the 'outs'. Election programmes thus tended to be similar and directed to the peasant masses. Not infrequently, therefore, a transition was soon made to a one party state.[3]

In Northern Nigeria this pattern was not followed. Not only was the society more hierarchically stratified than most, but the colonial impact for the most part served to preserve the *status quo ante* and with the transition to independence, the transfer of power was, with a few exceptions, not to a 'middle-class', but to the traditional ruling oligarchy.[4] This provided the 'middle-class' led opposition[5] with a radical, revolutionary ideology which drew its inspiration from Marxian concepts.[6] Thus against the conception of society as an on-going organic entity with mutually interdependent interests held by the NPC, the NEPU opposition projected the image of Northern Society as one of irreconcilable interests. This "antagonism of interests" manifests "itself as a class struggle between the members of that vicious circle of the Native Administrations on the one hand and the ordinary 'Talakawa' on the other" and as "all political parties are but the expression of class interests", NEPU "being the only political party of the Talakawa" has its interests diametrically opposed to those of the NPC "Family Compact" oligarchy which it is "determined to reduce to nonentity". Towards this end, the Talakawa must work with the party as a necessary condition of their emancipation.[7]

It can of course be argued that the idea of a society divided into two classes whose interests are opposed is an over-simplified notion of Northern Nigerian society; that the development of a growing indigenous regional bureaucracy where recruitment and advancement are based on achievement criteria makes even the notion of a two class society redundant. As against this view, the objection can be made that NEPU's class conflict ideology is only a crude restatement of the basic distinction made of far Northern society between the Fulanis and the Habes; in other words, a reassertion of the ethnic division of the society, a view not without importance when it is realized that most supporters of NEPU tend in fact to be Habes or Hausas.[8] Put in this form, NEPU's ideology then becomes a demand for the restructuring of Northern society to allow for more and wider political and economic opportunities to the "oppressed". This entails, for NEPU, the building up of the economy on "socialist" lines, which the party interprets to mean the "conversion of villages into co-operatives and the gradual nationalization of some assets, the final and total elimination of poverty" which would help to lay the "foundation of a new society whose middle class is prosperous and whose peasantry is contented".[9] Associated with this restructuring, is the drastic reform of political and juridical institutions through direct elections, based on "universal franchise" of "all local authorities whether village, district, city or executive".

In its simplest terms then, whereas the governing NPC has been content to reflect the structure of society as it is, NEPU's ideological orientation aims at imposing a new type of structure upon the society.[10] In this process it has, however, not concerned itself with the Northern Region alone. Thus, as early as 1961 the party had advocated republicanism for Nigeria at a time when this was not a debated issue in Nigeria politics, the type suggested being "one with an executive Cabinet with a Prime Minister and a President as the head of State, as in the case of India".[11] On the other hand, it has vacilated as to what form the eventual structure of government in Nigeria should take. This vacilation has led it not to see the inconsistency in supporting the demand by the UMBC for the creation of a Middle Belt state with the same constitutional status as the existing regional governments while at the same time advocating a unitary form of government for the country as a whole.[12]

Unlike NEPU which at least aims at being a region-wide party, the UMBC the other main opposition party, has restricted itself to the peoples of the 'riverian' or 'middle-belt' areas of the North. With one or two exceptions[13] these were not subjected to the Fulani rule which followed the nineteenth century Jihad. Similarly, they have as yet not accepted Islam, though Islam is gradually gaining ground in their areas.[14] Moreover, the individualism which underlines these societies is not compatible with an hierarchical social order which the Hausa–Fulani societies represent. Attempts to foster the latter amongst the Tivs led to rioting;[15] while among the Igbiras and Biroms it has resulted in instability at the level of local government.[16] The combination of these factors led to a determination to resist what the leader of the UMBC has termed the "aristocratic feudalism" represented by the NPC, the UMBC thus being the political expression of this resistance. Its rationale is the creation of a separate state which will incorporate the peoples of the riverain areas. But such is the paradox of Nigerian politics that of the seventy representatives elected from these areas at the 1959 Federal elections, approximately 80% were elected on the platform of the NPC or its parliamentary allies, though the NPC is committed to resist any attempts at the creation of a separate state in the North.[17]

Summarily then, both NEPU and the UMBC, represent 'the dispossessed' group of the North, but like most such groups they have lacked effective means of articulating their grievances. Several factors contributed to this weakness, for instance, the lack of a proper organization; ineffective leadership and other political and legal restrictions and limitations.[18] These will be examined in turn.

II. PARTY ORGANIZATION—NEPU

One of the shortcomings of NEPU as a political party is that it has lacked, until very recently, a formal organization. And for a mass party based largely on individual membership, this cannot but be a serious handicap. Equally interesting perhaps, is the fact that it has never had a constitution. Whatever organization it had, was therefore largely *ad hoc*.

The first attempt at organization was announced in March 1952 at the party's Third Convention held in Maiduguri. Here the party decided on the introduction of a 'school of politics' and the formation of a committee to plan a structure for the party. The latter did not meet and no plan was ever produced. The former became the nucleus of a four-months course, run by unpaid party officials at the party's headquarters in Kano, for members on how to organize party branches and publicize party political slogans. None of the twenty-five members who began in October 1952 completed the course which came abruptly to an end after two weeks.[19] Defection within the leadership, in fact, made any attempt at organizing the party problematic. In 1954 the relegation of the party's President to the status of a Vice-President (which followed the election of Mallam, now Alhaji-Aminu Kano as President) and the formal decision to ally the party to the NCNC, led to a split within the leadership, the new Vice-President, M. Abba Maikwaru, breaking away from the party. With him went some of the members of the newly elected executive. As the party had so little prospect to offer, most of the better educated members similarly broke away to join the NPC.[20]

Denuded of talent, NEPU hardly existed as a party between 1952 and 1959 outside the main towns of the North where there were branches of the party. The records of the Organization Department shows for instance that by 1958, there were only 14 branches in Bornu Province, 13 in Katsina, 11 in Kano, 10 in Benue, 4 in Niger, 2 each in Plateau and Kabba and 1 each in Sokoto and Zaria.[21] In the rural areas NEPU represented no more than a resentment, on the part of the peasants, of the NPC and the native administration authorities. NEPU was thus more of a 'movement' or 'congress', in Hodgkin's terminology, than a political party.[22] What co-ordination there was, was effected largely through the Executive elected annually by 'branch' representatives who met at the party's conventions.

The 1959 Federal elections, however, forced the party to consider seriously the question of organization. But the reaction consisted only in the hurried and temporary institution of constituency election committees formed from the leading personalities of the 'branches' within the constituencies, and provincial election committees to co-ordinate the activities of the constituency committees. Provincial, divisional and district organizers were appointed to provide liaison with the party headquarters,[23] while the North as a whole was divided into four zones each of which was placed under the charge of a party leader.[24] These arrangements were retained for the regional elections of 1961. But by this time the unsatisfactoriness of this mode of operation had already become apparent. Conflicts developed between the provincial organizers and the local branches. Not infrequently, the presence of the provincial organizers who were appointed from the headquarters was resented.[25] In some cases, these men did not even reside in the areas they were supposed to administer, for example, the Katsina organizer lived in Kano and was in Katsina only during the period of the elections.

As a result of this chaotic state and the performance of the party in the federal elections, the January 1961 Convention of the party finally appointed a commission of six men to draw up a Constitution[26] for the party which was to lay down the details of what should be the party's organization. In the meantime the Life President of the Party, Alhaji Aminu Kano, in his presidential address to the Convention suggested an outline which the Commission subsequently followed.

The new dispensation began in late 1961—after the regional election—with a 'census' of the party's 'branches' and membership. To be recognized, the local units were requested to re-register, and a new fee of 21s. was imposed to replace the existing charge of 5s. 6d. Only such registered branches were to be allowed to send delegates to the party's annual conventions which elected the National Executive Committee of the party, and which was to be composed on a 'provincial' basis. It should be noted, however, that the word 'province' does not refer strictly to the administrative province. Thus, the NEC elected in 1962 was drawn up as follows: Adamawa, Bauchi, Benue, Bornu, Kano, Katsina, Niger, Sokoto, Plateau, Zaria administrative provinces were represented by four elected members each. Ilorin, Kabba, Kano City, Kaduna, Sardauna province, the Eastern region, the Youths' Wing, Women's Wing, Ex-Servicemen's Union[27] were regarded as 'provinces' but each of these was entitled to only two representatives; Kano Waje and 'Labour', as provinces, had one representative each; the Western Region had three while the President General, who was also taken as a 'province' nominated seven members. (The President General is entitled to nominate, in his capacity as a 'province', not less than seven and not more than twelve members.)

The NEC meets at least once a year, immediately preceding the meeting of the Annual Convention. The latter is theoretically the final authority on all policy issues affecting the party. In practice, however, it has tended to ratify most decisions previously taken by the NEC. Between meetings of the NEC, the Central Working Committee (or Central Committee) acts on behalf of the party. The CWC is a body chosen exclusively by the President-General from amongst the members of the NEC, and is made up of the national officers and five others. Those amongst the national officers with 'departmental' responsibilities constituted, in conjuction with the President-General, the Strategic Committee which now became the main policy making organ of the party. Decision-making thus lies with the principal officials who man the party's secretariat headquarters. As the party is barely represented in any of the Legislative Assemblies of the federation this was only to be expected.

The secretariat itself was reorganized into seven 'departments': organization, local government, legal, information and publicity, finance, administration[28] and education. The 'heads' of these departments come under the Secretary-General. Under this new scheme 'departmental heads' each have a 'vote' and employ their own subordinates but they no longer receive monthly stipends, rather they receive allowances which "will be attractive".[29]

At the local level, 'branches' were organized around the various constituencies from which the constituency electoral committee is constituted. Constituencies within a province elect a Provincial Electoral Committee. For election purposes, nominations proceed from the constituencies to the Provincial Electoral Committee which has the right of veto subject to ratification by the NEC. To be qualified to be a candidate, a nominee must have been a financial member of two years standing, and for federal but not regional elections, must be able to read, write and speak the English language. Other requirements included (a) the payment of a fee, £21 for federal elections and £25 for regional elections, and (b) the signing of a contract which obliged the nominee to pay to the party a sum of £1,000 in the event of his defecting from the party.[30]

Whilst in the past NEPU had tended to rely on the petty traders, kola-nut sellers and primary school teachers for the communication of its ideas, these were to be supplemented with a number of provincial, divisional, field and sept organizing secretaries who were to form the main link between the constituency organizations and the party headquarters. Paid from central party funds, these organizing secretaries are ultimately responsible to the national organizer who heads the Department of Organization of the party's Central Secretariat.

Fundamental to these proposals obviously is the attempt at organizational centralization, greater control being vested in the officials of the party's headquarters. It was in pursuit of this policy that the party Executive ordered that the various youth organizations be merged into one single body.[31] The state of these groups was symptomatic of the general chaos in the party. The first youth organization to be formed was the Askiansit Movement which had amongst its objectives the ending of colonialism, "the ending of the oppression of old persons without family support who die of hunger in the market for lack of support" and the establishment of a school "so that people may understand their condition and demand justice which is their due from those in authority over them". Ostensibly a 'social' rather than a 'political' organization, the Askianist Movement rapidly grew into a militant youth wing of NEPU, and was recognized as such when, in 1954, it was given the new name *Runduna Samarin Sawaba* (RSS).[32] But so successful was the RSS experiment that some of its leaders[33] were encouraged to branch out in an attempt to recruit youths under the age of sixteen years and as a result formed a 'young pioneers' group with the title *Zaharal Hak* (Truth will out), which rapidly extended to most provinces where there was strong NEPU support. However, the revulsion against young persons taking part in politics led to the dissolution of Zaharal Hak, when, by the Northern Region Children and Young Persons Law 1958, it became illegal to induce those under the age of sixteen to engage in political activities.[34]

Meanwhile, internal disputes within the leadership of the RSS was such that it was already in the process of disintegration. In 1956 two illiterate traders broke off from the RSS to form the 'Followers of the Truth'—*Tabiunal Hak* which was soon duplicated with the formation of 'Stars of the Era'—*Nujumun Zaman*. While the former functioned largely in Kano, Funtua in Katsina Province and Jos, the latter was restricted to Kano. Thus by 1957, besides the parent RSS there were three other youth organizations existing, each more or less autonomous. Though both the TH and the NZ were formed without the party's approval, they were represented separately in the party's Executive. Collectively, these organs formed an important pressure group within the party and they were used as such by various individuals in the incessant leadership struggles which have characterized the history of NEPU. It was after one of these struggles, when first the Publicity Secretary, Mallam Tanko Yakasai, and next the Deputy General Secretary, M. Yahaya Abdullahi, were respectively expelled from the party's Executive Committee and suspended as members, but as a result of pressure from the youths, later received into the Executive[35] that the Executive ordered the merging of the various youth organizations into a single body which is still to be known as the Runduna Samarin Sawaba (Sawaba or NEPU Youth Association).

How effective these measures at party organization will be, will obviously depend on the availability of able leaders and funds, but these are items of which NEPU is very much in short supply.

III. THE DILEMMA OF LEADERSHIP

In a report on the 1961 North regional elections, Mr. R. B. K. Okafor, NCNC Federal Parliamentary Secretary to the Minister of Justice, noted that "the constant failures (of NEPU) lie in the fact that it has not got many important figures like M. Aminu Kano. Even if it has some of those figures, the position will not change."[36] In different ways, Mr. Okafor's statements point to some interesting facts about NEPU and the place of the Opposition in Northern Nigeria.

The lack of 'important figures' in NEPU is in itself not difficult to explain. Michels, writing in 1951, demonstrated the psychological and technical needs for leadership in any formal organization including 'mass' parties. But he also showed that the indifference of the rank-and-file of 'mass' parties to political involvement and action; the relative poverty of such organizations which makes it difficult for them to employ, on a full time basis, capable men to direct the affairs of the party; the need for intelligent direction and co-ordination of policy if the energies of the mass are to be properly chanelled, have contributed to mass organizations drawing their leaders from outside the class from which the general run of the rank-and-file member derive.[37] This was no less true of NEPU in its early years when most, if not all, of its leaders came from the class of native authority functionaries, school teachers, the Koranic Mallams —in a sense, the 'middle-class' of the North.[38] But the emergence of the NPC as the dominant political party in Northern Nigeria, the identification of that party with the Emirs and Chiefs, and therefore the Native Authority itself made the continuing membership of NEPU of the middle-class problematic. Koranic Mallams, for instance, who continued their association openly with NEPU had their students withdrawn by parents on the instructions, or rather, orders, of the Emirs and Chiefs. Given the traditional respect of the masses—peasant farmers, craftsmen—for the Chieftain class, it was hardly to be expected that they could have acted differently by disobeying the instructions presumed to have been issued by the Emirs. Besides, the whole authority of the Emirs, exercised through arbitrary taxation,[39] arrests by the Yan Doka, Native Authority police, on the flimsiest of excuses, arbitrary imprisonment by the Alkali Courts, the confiscation of land, was sufficient to ensure compliance. As most Koranic Mallams relied on the "voluntary contributions"[40] of their students for their livelihood, they were faced with the alternatives of either dissociating themselves from the opposition or starving.

Similarly, Native Authority officials had to choose between continued membership of NEPU and dismissal or at best stagnation in their careers. All schools, besides the few 'Government Colleges' and 'voluntary agency' schools, are run by the Native Authority, and school teachers were faced with equally effective pressure. Another related aspect is that fees in all secondary schools controlled by the Native Authority, are subsidized by the Native Authorities on the basis of a 'means test'.[41] This makes them particularly attractive to Northerners with comparatively low incomes. But since it was known that children of NEPU members, most of whom belonged to the low income group, would either not be admitted into these schools,[42] or if admitted would not have their fees subsidized, this was often a sufficiently strong incentive preventing members of the 'middle-class' from openly identifying themselves with the party.

The Native Authorities have provided most of the political leadership in Northern Nigeria and as this source is more or less closed to NEPU, little remains from which NEPU can draw. Civil servants are by law forbidden to take part in active politics. Wealthy merchants, businessmen and contractors[43] have found it in their own interests to work with the NPC rather than against it, while the expatriate commercial firms have not encouraged senior members of their staff to take part in politics, especially when such participation takes the form of involvement in opposition political activity. Finally, there are the public corporations, but for members of the opposition conditions in these are little different from those in the Native Authorities.[44]

Hence the dilemma of the opposition. To get the necessary leadership which it requires to give it active direction, the opposition must perforce draw its leaders from the sectors enumerated. Even where these areas are not closed to the opposition, conditions are such that leaders cannot long continue being associated with the party. A necessary corollary is the drain even on the existing leadership of the opposition, an ever continuous movement from the opposition to the governing party, the NPC. The decline in the social status of leadership which these restrictions entail is shown in the following tables.

TABLE 13

Occupations of the Members of the NEC (NEPU)
1954–62

	1954		1958		1962	
		%		%		%
Civil servants (a)	3	16·6 ⎤	4	6 ⎤	1	1·5 ⎤
N.A. employees (b)	3	16·6	3	5	3	5·5
Commercial firms employees	2	11·0 ⎬66·0	6	9 ⎬26·0	—	— ⎬13.0
Lawyers (c)	—		2	3·0	2	3·0
Teachers	4	22 ⎦	2	3·0 ⎦	2	3·0 ⎦
Businessmen (d)	3	16·6	11	17·0	2	3·0
Petty traders	2	11·0	23	36·0	36	54·0
Artisans (e)	—	—	6	9·0	10	15·0
Farmers	1	5·5	2	3·0	5	7·5
Others	—	—	5	8·0	5	7·5
TOTALS	18	99·3	64	99·0	66	100·0

NOTES: (a) Junior civil servants, i.e. clerks, messengers.
   (b) Composed as for (a).
   (c) The two lawyers are in fact NCNC members who were co-opted into the Executive.
   (d) Made up largely of small contractors, produce buyers, etc.
   (e) Tailors, washermen, dyers, etc.

N

TABLE 14

Educational Qualification of Members of the NEC (NEPU)
1954–62

	1954		1958		1962	
		%		%		%
University trained	1	5·5⎫	3(c)	5·0⎫	3(c)	4·5⎫
Secondary school	2	11 ⎬55·5	1	2·0 ⎬15·0	1	1·5 ⎬9·0
Middle IV (a)	7	39 ⎭	5	8·0⎭	2	3·0⎭
Primary school	4	22	12	19·0	9	14·0
Illiterates (b)	4	22	43	65·0	51	77·0
TOTALS	18	99·5	64	99·0	66	100

NOTES: (a) Roughly equivalent to two years post primary education.
   (b) I.e. not literate in English. Some of these, a very small number,
       certainly not more than 5%, are literate in Arabic.
   (c) Includes the two lawyers in note (c) Table 13. The third univer-
       sity trained man is Alhaji Aminu Kano.

The low quality of NEPU's top leadership is also reflected at the lower levels of the party's hierarchy. This should be evident given the fact that it is the most prominent members in the various 'provinces' who get elected to the party's National Executive. The nature of the leadership also explains Alhaji Aminu Kano's status in the party. He is the only man with some sort of a university education in the whole of the party. In 1954 he was made the President of the party, and in 1959 he was elected the Life President. He nominates the party's Working and Strategic Committees. Before being elected to the House of Representatives in 1959 and thereafter becoming Deputy Chief Whip in the coalition federal Government, he dominated the party and its policy-making organs.[45] Since 1959, however, as a result of his having to be in Lagos most of the year (that is, when he was not out of the country) day-to-day direction which he formerly exercised has tended to pass to the Strategic Committee of the party, over which he now only exercises minimal control. This has led to some interesting results, such as misappropriation of party funds. A report of an enquiry in October 1960 into the personal accounts of some of the members of the party's executive stated that three of these, the Publicity Secretary, M. Tanko Yakasai, the Chairman of the Finance Committee, Mallam Shehu Satatima, and the then Deputy Secretary-General, had embezzled party funds. The last named for instance was found to have misappropriated the sum of over £6,000.[46] Curiously but understandably, no disciplinary action was taken against the culprits: to have done so would be to alienate the three most educated, apart from Aminu Kano, of the party's Executive with obvious implications for the administrative apparatus of the party.[47]

Weber in his essay on 'Politics as a Vocation' distinguished between those who live *for* politics and those who live *off* politics. Taking the latter in its narrow construction,[48] it can, as a broad generalization, be shown that most of NEPU's leaders have increasingly tended to fall into the category of those who live *off* politics. In 1959 for instance, it was reported that the party 'borrowed' the sum £225,000 from the African Continental Bank through the NCNC. This was to be used in financing the electoral expenses of the party's candidates, in the federal election of that year, each candidate being given £350. A party report, however, noted that only the candidates from Kano province received the money and they were in fact given £900 each, instead of the proposed £350. In the final result of the election in Kano province, NEPU won only one seat. In the constituency of Mallam Aminu Kano alone £3,000 was spent.[49] Yet no accounting was ever made to show how the bulk of the money was spent.

For a party which claims to represent the poor, the Talakawa, NEPU presents a paradoxical image of its leadership. Thus a member noting that some of the party leaders were using "the party's money to buy houses and vehicles for commercial uses, and (have) employed old women at six pounds a month to carry their children in carriages like European children" while "the supporters were suffering severe hardship . . . not even sure of their daily meals" asked: "is this really the ideology which NEPU wishes to pursue?" He added, "what kind of trade were these people engaged in? Had they any independent source of income except through the party since they had no independent occupation".

This image of NEPU's leadership has certain consequences while also raising some questions. In the first place, it has had the effect of alienating from the party the present generation of secondary school and university students, from whom the next generation of leaders both political and administrative will in all probability emerge. Should the party ever be elected to power, the comparatively low quality of its leadership, they argue, would preclude its providing the leadership in government which the North needs, a view they claim to be confirmed by the open evidence of corruption within the party leadership Secondly, such an image of the party leadership raises the question of the continued support which NEPU still commands amongst a not insignificant section of the community. This would seem to be because NEPU remains the symbol of opposition to 'class' privilege which the NPC is presumed to represent; it remains the organ of protest against Fulani conquest and domination.[50] One notable consequence of NEPU's alienation of the middle-class, however, is that it has tended to lend some plausibility to the party's ideology of class conflict. Far from reinforcing the party this merely underlines its signal failure.

IV. THE PROBLEM OF PARTY FINANCE

Besides the dilemma of leadership which confronts NEPU, the party seems to be involved, in its financial administration, in a vicious circle. Because of the lack of a sound organization, it was impossible, prior to the 'party census' already referred to, to determine party membership, and because of this, the collection of party dues was difficult which in turn affected the organization. And unlike the NPC, the party has no wealthy patrons—businessmen, contractors, board members, Emirs and chiefs, parliamentarians and Ministers who make 'voluntary donations' to the party's coffers. Neither has it an alternative institution similar to the Native Authority network to provide it with a means of communication as does the NPC. But yet the party has not only to compete with the government party organizationally and electorally, it has to provide some of the services which the NPC renders to its members, such as the payment of fines imposed on party members by the Courts and wherever possible, the provision of legal defence for those arrested.[51]

It is hardly surprising then to find that the party has lacked any formal organization and has found it extremely difficult to employ able people as full-time party officials. For the federal elections of 1959 for instance, the party employed about 130 full-time officials but was forced to dismiss sixty of these immediately after the elections. As a result of the 'reorganization' of the party, the number of full-time officials was in 1961 increased to 110, excluding those party officers who head the various departments of the party's Central Secretariat. The monthly wage bill for the full-time paid staff of the party and the cost of maintaining the Secretariat is about £2,000.[52] On the other hand, the annual revenue is just about four times the figure of the monthly expenditure. Party revenue derives mainly from membership dues which varies between 1s. and 12s. a year per member, of which at least 1s. per member goes to the party headquarters; the sale of membership cards, badges and other literature; registration dues; fees to conventions, and other moneys from sources such as dances and lectures. Not infrequently, party dues are paid in kind, a small quantity of groundnuts or cotton, which when finally sold may fetch more than the expected contribution.[53]

With much of party revenue taken up in the payment of party officials and running the party headquarters, there is literally nothing from which to organize the party. This becomes particularly crucial during election periods when burdens have to be incurred. For the 1961 regional elections, over 21,000 polling agents had to be hired at a daily cost of 5s. per agent. The party had also to pay the deposits (£75)[54] for most of its candidates. With such limited resources the party has been forced to rely on its ally the NCNC. The latter helped out in the 1959 elections by enabling NEPU to 'borrow' from the African Continental Bank. In 1961, however, as a result of the mismanagement in 1959, the NCNC insisted on paying directly the deposits of the eighty two candidates whose nomination it had approved while also helping to defray the cost of hiring the 16,000 polling agents employed in the eighty two constituencies.

But NEPU's relationship with the NCNC has not been without its problems. Most of the early leaders of NEPU were not uninfluenced by the NCNC in the immediate post-war period. When NEPU was formed it seemed natural that it should maintain some relations with the NCNC. In 1954 a formal alliance was entered into by both parties. From that year NEPU became increasingly dependent financially on the NCNC, a factor which has tended to strengthen the relationship between the two. This relationship, however, has also been the source of embarrassment to NEPU. For instance, the North regional administration was before 1956 dominated largely by officials of southern origin. This proved a useful ploy for the NPC in its attempt to win mass support. As Alhaji Ladan Baki, Provincial Commissioner, Zaria, put it, he said "we had to teach the people to hate Southerners; to look on them as people depriving them of their rights in order to win them over".[55] Thus, by associating with the NCNC, NEPU became 'traitors', a point well put by Alhaji Maiwada, an NPC parliamentarian in a speech in the Northern Assembly: ". . . what I see of treachery is that a certain political party in the North linked itself with a political party in the South and seeing this, the Northern people disagreed with them . . . it is like a man looking after somebody else's house without looking after his own . . . how

can I be confident of that sort of person ?"[56] A NEPU publicity secretary expressed the same point when he said: "It is because of this
alliance that the NPC has been describing us to the electors as 'the
Ibos of the North'. This has given the NPC a great advantage over us
and has done irreparable damage to our party image."

The NCNC-NEPU alliance became of doubtful value to NEPU
after the 1959 federal elections. Immediately before the elections
NEPU issued a public statement in which the party stated it was
never going to become partner to any coalition government of which
the NPC was a member. Yet after the elections, with the formation of
the NCNC-NPC coalition, NEPU became a partner in the federal
Government, thereby creating the anomalous position of co-opera-
ting with the NPC to which it was opposed in the North, and under
which, as NEPU claims, "a large number of (its) supporters have
been imprisoned and have been suffering from all sorts of victimization. (NEPU's Alhaji Aminu Kano even became the Deputy Government Chief Whip.) It is a sufficient testimony to Aminu Kano's hold
over the party that he was able to avert the threat to his leadership
which followed, by arguing that he decided to join the coalition
government because not to have done so would have been to play
into the hands of the Imperialist British Government which wanted
to delay Nigeria's Independence by inciting the North against the
South. The Governor-General, Sir James Robertson, he argued, had
invited Alhaji Sir Abubakar Tafawa Balewa to form a government
even before the full results of the elections were known and when it
was not certain that the NPC would have a majority over all the
other parties combined. But persuasive as he was, he was unable to
prevent a split in his Executive, a minority of which broke away to
form the Northern Elements Freedom Organization, thereby not
only immediately weakening the Executive but also the party, which
lost some of its supporters to the new organization,[57] The leadership
was further weakened after the 1961 regional elections when a section
of the Executive questioned the propriety of the NCNC nominating
candidates for the elections contrary to the 1954 terms of agreement
between the two parties. (This stipulated that in return for support of
the NCNC, the NCNC would undertake to help NEPU financially
while refraining from putting forward any candidates of its own to
contest elections in the North.) A meeting of the Executive in Jos in
June 1961 then sought a re-guarantee of the 1954 agreements failing
which the party would be forced to reconsider the alliance between
the two parties.[58] In the absence of any such guarantee, a faction of
the NEC critical of the party leader broke off from the party to join
the NPC.[59]

Summarily then, the poverty of the party is found to influence party organization, the looseness of which in itself accounts in part for the lack of funds. And it is hardly conceivable that any mass political party could maintain an efficient organization with grossly inadequate resources. It would therefore seem that NEPU is condemned to an ineffective role in its attempt to represent the talakawa of the North. The attempt to break this circle which has led NEPU into a partnership with the NCNC has tended in practice to be more of a hindrance and a handicap. That the alliance has continued is due largely, if not exclusively, to Aminu Kano, but it is also this which constitutes one of the main threats to his leadership. How long he can continue to retain his role as the party leader with growing discontent, as evidenced by the 1959 and 1961 crisis in the party NEC, is open to question. Similarly, that NEPU has been content to work within the existing framework of law in the Northern region is also, in all likelihood, due to his leadership. But should the challenge to his authority succeed, the probabilities are that the party, as a party, would disintegrate or it would resort to more radical, possibly illegal methods in its campaigns against the ruling order, for which it would not be without precedent from the NPC.[60]

V. THE UNITED MIDDLE BELT CONGRESS

Much of what is written above about NEPU applies to the UMBC. From its inception in 1955 to about the early part of 1958, the UMBC in fact was hardly more than the summation of the various ethnic associations, such as, the Tiv Progressive Union, the Idoma Hope Rising Union, the Habe Peoples' Party, the Birom Tribal Party, of which it was composed. By the latter date, most of these had either contracted out and formally joined the NPC or had broken off to stand independently though maintaining some relations with the Northern Peoples' Congress.

Formal party organization thus did not begin until late in 1958 when the party was already in alliance with the AG and it was possible for the latter to provide the UMBC with financial aid.[61] But the imminence of the 1959 federal elections meant that very little could be done besides the employment of an army of canvassers, 'organizing secretaries' and polling agents. Not until March 1960 therefore was any real attempt made at establishing a party organization with the institution of divisional and provincial party organs and below this, the constituency organizations. At the primary level of the branch, party organization was centred around

the lineage segments of the various ethnic groups. But this immediately poses problems of control and co-ordination, which is best
illustrated by considering the organization of the party in Benue
Province. Here, though theoretically there was supposed to be one
provincial organizing secretary responsible for the whole province
(Mr. Peter Acka, a Tiv, held this office in 1960–61 before he left the
party), in practice, the need to make allowances for ethnic differences
meant that another provincial organizer had to be found and one
was chosen from the Idoma, the other main group in Benue Province
(a Mr. Ela Abogonye was appointed). Not only this, to supervise
these men there were the 'Provincial Leaders', again, balanced by a
Tiv (a Mr. Vincent Orjime who has since joined the NPC), and
another (a Mr. Ahmadu Angulu) to represent the Aragos and
Gwaris of Lafia, Nasarawa and Keffi districts.

This 'countervailing' technique was applied in the other provinces
of the Middle Belt and had its culmination in the Executive of the
party in which the Idomas, Tivs, Biroms and others were evenly
balanced.[62] The logic of this technique of organization entailed that
the mechanism of control at the provincial level was never clearly
defined, which inevitably led to abuses with their obvious repercussions on the party. Thus, for instance, after the federal and regional
elections of 1959 and 1961 respectively, in Benue Province a number
of canvassers, polling agents and field secretaries complained that
they had never been paid the stipends promised them. Yet the
money for this had been drawn from the party treasury. With no
single identifiable leader to be held responsible, dissatisfaction, not
unnaturally, led to withdrawal of support and a switch of party
loyalties. But, paradoxically, it tended also to enhance the status of
the leader of the party. Given the propensity to sectional rivalry and
competitiveness inherent in the party structure, the party leader
must of necessity assume the role of an arbiter of disputes, a factor
which cannot but enhance his status.[63] The personal ascendancy of
J. S. Tarka, the party leader was demonstrated, for example, by his
control over the nomination of candidates for both the regional and
federal elections. In the latter elections he vetoed the nominations
of Dominic Andiir Tor for Kwande Constituency, Angwe Asen for
Gaav-Shangaev-Tiev, Tartsegha Aji for Iharev-Nongov and Peter
Acka for Ukum Shetire, even though the last named was one of the
first nominations to be announced in the country. In 1961 he vetoed
the local nomination of Mbakaa Tudiohwer for Jemgbar, to make
room for Ibrahim Imam, the BYM–AG leader who could not
contest, as a result of physical intimidation,[64] the elections in his home
province of Bornu and as the leader of the opposition in the Northern

Assembly had to have a safe seat found for him. Admittedly, all of these constituencies are in the Tiv division. But before the emergence of Tarka, such a procedure would have been inconceivable and it was only under him that a breach was made with the 'alternating principle' which characterized elections in the Tiv division before 1959.[65] On the larger UMBC scene, it was Tarka's opposition which largely prevented the absorption of the UMBC by the AG.[66]

In October 1962 the UMBC broke its alliance with the AG.[67] The latter had met all the financial obligations of the UMBC during the alliance, before which the UMBC was plagued by a chronic lack of funds, though it did receive help from some of the Christian missions, principally the Dutch Sudan United Mission.[68] But with the increasing regulation of missionary activities[69] by the Northern Government, most of these missions are now wary of any relationship, even covert relations, with opposition political parties. Hence the breach with the AG becomes particularly crucial for it raises the whole question of the continued existence of the UMBC as an opposition political party in the Middle Belt of the Northern region. It is very probably the realization of this fact which has impelled the UMBC and NEPU to pool their resources in the new Northern Progressive Front (NPF).

The NPF came into existence in October 1963 following a meeting between the leaders of the two parties. While both retained their separate organizations, the NPF, of which Alhaji Aminu Kano was elected President and J. S. Tarka General Secretary, was to be a co-ordinating agency with a Secretariat in Kaduna to plan a common electoral programme in the event of any election in the Northern Region. Part of its programme will be to ensure that opposition party candidates do not compete against each other and thereby split the opposition vote.[70] While such an attempt to channel into a single stream the efforts of the opposition parties might be of some advantage to them, it by no means solved the problems of the individual parties forming the Front.[71] In any event, its success will depend on the opportunities, or rather, restrictions, placed on the opposition parties.

VI. RESTRICTIONS ON THE OPPOSITION IN THE NORTH

The opportunities for legitimate political action open to any opposition party depend largely on the system of rules and the rule-enforcement agencies current in the society. A particular rule or law may in itself not be ostensibly discriminatory, yet its incidence may work hardship on specific groups. Similarly, though a rule may not be restrictive, its enforcement or non-enforcement may nevertheless be such as to confer advantages to some groups or parties while putting others at a disadvantage. Admittedly, any governing party expects to derive maximum advantage from the operation of any given system of rules, but it is part of the essence of democratic government that this must not be necessarily at the expense of the opposition. To fail to accept this as an operational principle will not only question the basis of constitutionalism, it will eventually threaten the continued existence of the opposition. This seems to be the plight of the opposition parties in the North, which has led to the North becoming virtually a one-party 'state'. To understand this process of transformation would necessitate examination of some of the handicaps under which opposition parties operate. And this, in effect, means the examination of the role of the Native Authority and its agencies in the political process.[72]

Though the over-all responsibility for 'law, order and good government' lies with the regional government which may by statute issue regulations and pass legislation for this purpose, the day-to-day maintenance of law and order is a duty of the Native Administration. This is the 'main *raison d'être* and obligation' of the N.A.s. The basic instrument governing the N.A.s is the Native Authority Law 1954,[73] which confers on the N.A.s the power to make rules and issue orders.[74] In the exercise of these powers, the N.A.s have not infrequently acted in such a way as to handicap seriously parties opposed to the ruling NPC. For instance, section 37, sub-section 44 of the 1954 Act, provides that N.A.s may make orders "prohibiting any act or conduct which in the opinion of the native authority might cause a riot or a disturbance or a breach of the peace". Under this rule N.A.s make orders regulating the holding of public meetings, processions and the like. Permission to hold a public meeting has to be obtained from the N.A. which requires that it should be given at least twenty-four hours' notice of any application. But while the NPC often manages to secure a permit in less than the stipulated period of notice given, opposition parties have often been refused a permit on the grounds that not enough notice was given, the N.A. claiming that twenty-four hours was insufficient for it to make necessary arrangements to maintain peace and order. Opposition parties in practice often have to give at least seven days' notice before they could ever hope to obtain a permit. Besides this, the N.A. may require the subjects or topics to be discussed at such meetings to be specified in the permit, a departure from which will then render sponsors and/or speakers at the meeting liable to arrest for infringement of the conditions laid down in the permit.[75] On being arrested, the individual may be detained in jail for a period not exceeding fourteen days before being brought to trial[76] and on conviction by the Alkali Courts[77] (judges of which are invariably members of the NPC), be liable to a fine not exceeding £25 or imprisonment for a period not in excess of three months.

In rural areas, the district head, acting as the Native Authority, may in addition give specific directions as to the venue of any meeting[78] and it is not uncommon to find opposition parties being given a permit, a couple of hours before the scheduled time, with directions that it be held at a village forty or even eighty miles away. The result, inevitably, is that the meeting is never held. Even where the venue of a meeting is easily accessible, the opposition may have to confront other problems. Thus, in rural areas where the population is widely dispersed, they may, and often are, prohibited the use of loudspeakers and other amplifying instruments.[79]

Various other methods may be applied, particularly in the rural and semi-rural areas, to harass or intimidate, individually, members of the opposition. They may be "directed to attend before . . . a native authority" at any time.[80] Innocent as this may seem, it often has disruptive effects. The farmer or craftsman-dyers, weavers, cap-makers, tailors (the class from which NEPU draws its main support and membership) who has to leave his business to 'attend' before the native authority now and again may start losing custom; or if a farmer, may find himself spending less time on his farm. Failure to 'attend' is a crime[81] which on conviction[82] could lead to a fine of as much as £100 or six months imprisonment or both.[83] The individual opposition member may also, if he is not a native of the district[84] be 'deported' from the province on the grounds that he is incapable of supporting himself.[85] Under the taxing powers[86] of the N.A. polling agents may be sufficiently induced to desist from their functions. During the 1961 regional elections, people canvassed by the NEPU candidate in the villages of Giwa, Birnin Gwari and Igabi in Zaria North-west Constituency were all over-assessed. It is hardly coincidental that soon after the elections a majority of these changed their allegiances to support the NPC.[87] Debtors, if they are known members of the opposition, may have their property confiscated.[88] Their houses could be declared insanitary and an order made for its demolition.[89] They may even be 'deposed' from offices such as those of heads of the various 'economic orders'.

There is, of course, provision for redress against wrongful or arbitrary actions by a Native Authority.[90] But a series of difficulties faces any prospective litigant. In the first place, Section 110 (2) provides that "no suit shall be commenced against a Native Authority until one month at least after written notice of intention to commence the same shall have been served upon the Native Authority by the intending plaintiff or his agent. Such notice shall state the cause of action, the name and place of abode of the intending plaintiff and the relief which he claims." During the interval between notification of intention and commencement of action, all sorts of pressures can be brought to bear on the intending plaintiff to make him reconsider his proposed action. Where such action is brought before the Alkali or Customary Courts, the plaintiff may not be sure of getting justice (the judges may even be the defendants). On the other hand the legal costs of an action in the magistrate courts are sufficiently prohibitive for most supporters of the opposition to rule them out as a possible source of redress. [91]

Besides the Native Authorities, the electoral system also works against the opposition. Jerrymandering could easily convert a safe seat to an unsafe one for the opposition. An example of this may be taken from Kano East Constituency, contested and won by Alhaji Aminu Kano in the 1959 federal elections. At the regional elections, this constituency which was made up of Fegge, Sabongari and the City, was split so that Kano City became one constituency while Fegge and Sabon-gari were merged with outlying districts. Sabon-gari, with a registered electorate of over 7,000, a NEPU stronghold (the area is inhabited almost exclusively by non-northerners who would vote NEPU) was merged with Ungogo and another village with a registered electorate of 15,000. At the 1961 elections in Kano City, NEPU only polled 9,000 votes of the total vote of over 22,000, while at Ungogo, an NPC stronghold, it polled 32·9% of the votes cast to the NPC's 67·1%. By an extension of the same principle, one safe NPC seat could be made to yield two safe constituencies, as was the case with Hadeija South which, with a registered electorate of 28,897, was split into two—Hadeija South and East while Hadeija North, with a larger registered electorate was left as a single constituency.

Other handicaps derive from the close relationship between the NPC and the social structure. Not unusually, the district head who is a candidate may find that his younger brother who is a village head, is the presiding officer, the district head's cousin who is the district scribe will be returning officer, while other cousins and nephews may be polling officers, counting agents, electoral and returning officers— the primary officials at any election. In rural areas especially, the polling station may be in the village head's compound and it is not unknown for ballot boxes to have been placed in the open courtyard without any screening whatsoever.[92] Even where screens are provided these are often constructed from *zanna* mats[93] through which the voter can be seen casting his ballot, with the Alkali, district head or their agents not far off observing the whole process.[94] Not least in importance, is the deposit which to most opposition candidates represents a fortune or the product of a life-time's savings, With a more than even chance of losing his deposit, an election may be too risky an investment for the candidate who does not have his party to pay for his electoral expenses.[95]

The organizational weakness of the opposition parties coupled with the legal and political handicaps they encounter are such as to suggest that they are condemned to electoral ineffectiveness. It is dubious whether any system of electoral reform will improve the situation, for where restrictive measures do not succeed, physical violence may be relied upon to repress and suppress disentient opinion.

VII. PARTIES AND VIOLENCE

The close relationship between the NPC and the traditional ruling groups in the North, the inordinate zeal of party activists and the intolerance of the Native Administration functionaries have together created deep-seated resentment which on several occasions has led to outbreaks of physical violence, a feature which has tended to mar the otherwise quiescent political scene of Northern Nigeria.

The first incidence of organized violence was the Kano riots of 1953 which subsequently led to the emergence of the Jam'iyyar Mahaukata, a fanatical group bent on the elimination of NEPU who could count on the support of the members of the extreme right in politics, that is, most of the Emirs, chiefs and top Native Authority officials and councillors. The Mauhakata rapidly spread to other provinces in the North from Kano and was to provide the prototype of organized opposition baiting which flared into open riots in Maiduguri in September 1958 and again in August 1960. It is not without interest that before the 1958 riots, an NPC supporter, Alhaji Mustapha Harunabe had sold pieces of green cloth to NPC men which they were later to wear as a mark of identification. And in the 1961 riots, it is curious that only BYM members were arrested including women with young children whose ages ranged from three days to two years.[96]

The basic cause of both the Kano and Maiduguri disturbances was that the NPC was not prepared to tolerate opposition. The same intolerance, this time complicated by religious factors, marked the disturbances in Gusau and North-east Sokoto in March 1957. The Tijaniyya groups, a Moslem brotherhood,[97] in these areas were known to be supporters of NEPU.[98] On the pretext that they were disrespectful to constituted authority, whereas Islam enjoins on its adherents absolute obedience to authority, and that they were not the real Tijanniya, the members were attacked, their property looted and in some cases their houses burnt down. A letter from the Sultan of Sokoto to the district heads authorized severe handling of Tijanniya members arrested.[99] Some were forced to smoke cigarettes while in prison contrary to their religious beliefs.[100] It is symptomatic of all these cases that retaliation to provocation was inevitably taken as proof of guilt to which the severest measures were applied. And inevitably such measures often had the effect of ensuring conformity.

In the Middle Belt it was also the desire to ensure conformity, the determination to break, particularly, Tiv opposition,[101] a group traditionally known for their individualism that led to the Tiv riots of 1960 and again in early 1964. The Tiv Native Authority, one of the few almost exclusively elected Councils in the North, was composed wholly of and controlled by the UMBC. But the wishes of the people were circumvented by the Government through the injection of 'traditional members' into the Council. These were made to understand that unless they supported the ruling NPC they would be removed from their offices of district and village headships. The outcome of this injection was that for most of the time, the Council was in deadlock, or alternatively, the elected members found their decisions being overridden by the nominated traditional members. Anti-NPC sentiments gradually crystallized around the deputy Tor Tiv, Mr. Bendega Ukpada, who shared the sentiment of the UMBC and it was the eruption of this sentiment, brought about by arbitrary taxation, the unwarranted closing down of markets which led to the March 1960 riots[102] and was to lead to the 1964 riots in which, according to the estimates by the Northern Ministry of Information, forty-seven people were killed, nineteen by the police who were called in to quell the riots.[103]

Organized violence may succeed in suppressing opposition parties, but may on the other hand force these groups underground. The former seems the more probable result, but to the extent that it succeeds, the North will become a monolithic one-party state with even fewer checks on the excesses of the ruling party. Whatever reform may be excepted in the North will thus have to come not from the opposition, but from within the NPC itself. A monolithic North may lead to further strengthening of the bipolar tendencies in Nigeria and thereby provide a built-in factor of instability in the system.

NOTES

1. Two of these UMBC/AG representatives have since crossed over to the Government, that is, the NPC.

2. If the votes cast for each of the three parties, NPC, NEPU and UMBC are expressed as precentages of the total registered votes in contested constituencies, the corresponding figures will be 10·2%, 4·9% and 5·5% respectively.

3. See e.g., G. M. Carter, editor, *African One Party States*, Cornell University Press, 1962; M. Kilson, 'Authoritarian and Single-Party Tendencies in African Politics', *World Politics*, vol. 15, January 1963, pp. 262–94; I. Wallerstein, *Africa: the Politics of Independence*, N. Y., Random House, 1961 and Fatma Mansur, *Process of Independence*, Routledge and Kegan Paul, 1962. It should be noted, however, that the statements made are generalizations to which there are exceptions but these only prove the rule.

4. See Chapter I pp. 16–17 and Chapter II pp. 51–52.

5. Compare the editorial in the quasi-government newspaper, *Nigerian Citizen*, in which NEPU was described as "a not very large group of dissatisfied and vociferous intelligentsia" *Nigerian Citizen*, 31st July 1952.

6. T. Hodgkin in his *A Note on the Language of African Nationalism*, St. Anthony's papers no. 10, Chatto and Windus, 1961, has pointed out that NEPU's 'language' was closer to James Mill than Marx. But it is highly improbable that any of the leaders of NEPU would have read Mill. In fact, in may interviews, none of them seems to have heard of James Mill.

7. *Sawaba Declaration of Principles*, Baseco Press, Jos, 1952.

8. Of the sixty-six members who formed the Central Working Committee and National Executive Committee of NEPU in 1962–63, 69% were Habes, 9% were Nupes, 15% were Fulanis and 7% were other Nigerian ethnic groups.

9. Presidential Address to the NEPU 1961 Annual Convention Holding in Zaria 1st-2nd January 1961. Mimeographed.

10. T. L. Hodgkin in his *African Political Parties* contends that, in the last analysis, this is the main criterion which distinguishes an 'elite' from a 'mass' party. Ibid., p. 69.

11. In a memorandum headed *NEPU Proposals for Republican Nigeria* (mimeographed, no date, text in Hausa), the party suggested that the President should be elected by both Houses of Parliament. An annotation, however, amended this to read "let the President be directly elected not as proposed by the two Federal Houses". The party also suggested that Education, Justice, Social Welfare, Economic Planning and Regional and Federal electoral regulations should be made a federal responsibility.

12. A similar vacilation is exhibited in NEPU's attitude to Pan-Africanism. While demanding a Union of African States, and the cessation of foreign aid because this "pollutes the international atmosphere and corrupts politicians of the so-called under-developed countries" it nevertheless would like to see more foreign aid in the respective Africa States. In 1965 NEPU started to advocate the creation of a Kano State.

13. Principally Ilorin and Nupe. The lesser emirates of Lafiagi-Pategi, can be discounted.

14. During a visit (March 1964) to Southern Zaria, the Sardauna was met by 125 new converts to Islam. After making cash presents to these, they were exhorted to carry out vigorous proselytizing.

15. For instance, the Tiv riots of 1960 and 1964. These arose largely from

attempts by the NPC appointed district heads to coerce the Tivs into supporting the NPC. For the Government account on the 1960 riots, see N.H.A. Debates, 19th April 1960, cols. 314–15. The report of Commission of Enquiry into the 1960 riots was never published by the Government. Another Commission of Enquiry was appointed after the 1964 riots. Its report was not publicly released.

16. On the Birom case, see K. W. J. Post, op. cit., pp. 81–82.

17. One reason given in an interview with Senator Abaagu (NPC) former leader of the UMBC and later the MBSP was as follows: "The NPC will still control the Middle Belt State. There is no need for it."

18. These were some of the reasons actually given by M. Yerima Balla, NEPU Vice-President in a letter dated 11th August 1961 to the General Secretary, NEPU Headquarters files 0042/53.

19. See *Nigerian Citizen*, 18th September 1952 where the course was announced. The cost per member to be borne by the branches was put at £8. This was never paid.

20. Of the seventeen members elected to the Executive in 1954, about 50% crossed over to the NPC before the end of the year. This does not include other NEPU-NCNC stalwarts, e.g. Zanna Bukar Dipcharima, Maitama Sule, Ibrahim Waziri—all of whom later became Federal Ministers, and others who had earlier left NEPU for the NPC.

21. Ibid., NEPU Headquarters File No. 0158.

22. T. Hodgkin, *Nationalism in Colonial Africa*, pp. 141–45, and *African Political Parties*, pp. 50–56.

23. There were in fact 1 national organizer, 13 provincial and divisional organizers respectively, 52 field secretaries and 32 sept organizers. NEPU H.Q. File 0138.

24. Zone A was made up of Kano, Katsina and Bornu and was under Lawan Danbazau; Zone B, Adamawa, Bauchi, Plateau, under Tanko Yakasai; Zone C, Ilorin, Niger, Sokoto, under Sani Darma; and Zone D, Benue, Kabba and Zaria, under Yahaya Abdullahi.

25. See, e.g. Report by Zonal Leader, Sani Darma, dated 16ht October 1960. File no. 0042/S4.

26. This 'Constitution', the first ever, is still in a draft stage (1964). It has as yet not been officially adopted by the party. The six-man Commission who drew it up were: (1) The Secretary-General, Alhaji Abubakar Zukogi, (2) the Vice-President, M. Yerima Balla—NHR, (3) The Publicity Secretary, M. Tanko Yakasai, (4) Assistant Secretary-General, M. Yahaya Sabo, (5) the National Organizer, M. Lamin Sanussi and (6) the President-General—Alhaji Aminu Kano who in fact attended the meetings of the Commission only once.

27. The Ex-Servicemen's Union (Northern Nigeria) or more appropriately the Nigerian Ex-Servicemen's Working Association has tended to play a dual role in the North. Thus, it is 'allied' to both the NPC and NEPU. One of its Secretaries, Garba Abuja, was until 1960 the Administrative Secretary of the NPC. In a letter dated 8th June 1960, Ref. NEC/NN/27, addressed to NEPU by NEWA, the latter demanded from the former £3,800, four vehicles, e.g. Jeeps and 150 bicycles in order to help campaign for NEPU. A similar letter was also sent to the NPC. But whereas NEPU agreed to meet, in part, these demands (letter from NEPU Secretary General, dated 24th August 1960, File 0133), the NPC replied to say they would give the request due consideration. It never finally gave NEWA any 'aid'.

28. The head of the Department of Administration, the Administrative Secretary, ceased under the new scheme to count as a national Officer. Besides

the Central Secretariat, the party also maintains a sub-secretariat in Jos, but this comes under the direction of the Secretary-General.

29. NEPU 1961 Annual Conference—Presidential Address, p. 9. Mimeographed.

30. See Chapter III, p. 105.

31. Handing over Notes and Instruction of Aminu Kano, dated 13th February 1961, File No. 0046.

32. The full aims and objectives of the Movement are quoted in the Report on the Kano Riots, pp. 45–46. Sections cited are from p. 46. The Movement, formed by Alhaji Mudi Spikin, Tanko Yakasai and Mustapha Dambatta, was to have been the NEPU wing of the Zikist Movement, or rather, a counterpart of the Zikist Movement. After the Kano riots in 1953, it was converted into the 'Positive Action Wing' (PAW) and it was this which on the suggestion of Mallam Sa'ad Zungur became the Runduna Samarin Sawaba.

33. Principally two illiterate traders—Mallams Nasidi Kofo Wohibai and Halilu Mokwala who became President and Secretary respectively.

34. N.R.L. No. 28 of 1958, especially ss. 33–35. Though 'officially' dissolved, Zaharal Hak in fact continued to exist separately until 1961.

35. Tanko Yakasai was expelled in 1959 and Yahaya Abdullahi in 1960. Both were readmitted in late 1960.

36. Paragraph 10, *Report on the Recent North Regional Elections* by Hon. R. B. K. Okafor, Parliamentary Secretary, NCNC. Confidential to F. S. McEwen N.A. National Secretary, NCNC. The Report is dated 6th May 1961.

37. Michels, op. cit., pp. 85–114.

38. See Chapter III, p. 78 and note 5 p. 191.

39. The N.A. is responsible for assessing, levying and collecting taxes from those with incomes of under £300 within its jurisdiction. The rate of taxation varies from one N.A. to the other (for a schedule of these see Local Government Year Book, 1963, prepared by the Department of Local Government, Institute of Administration, Zaria—pp. 40–42). In levying taxes, the N.A. can and does act arbitrarily. There is no appeal against a levy by the N.A.

40. This, since it is often inadequate, is usually supplemented by Mallams sending out their pupils periodically to beg for alms.

41. This also includes the 'Government Colleges'. Tables 13 and 14, pp. 79–84 of the *Local Government Year Book*, 1963 provide lists of Public and Voluntary Schools by N.A. and Province and Cost per student for Education to the N.A.

42. The author came across a number of instances where children of known NEPU parents have had to change their names in order to gain admission. In one case in Zaria when Gambo Sawaba, a NEPU leader requested the author to seek admission for his son into the Native Authority controlled Zaria Provincial Secondary School, the Principal asked the author for the *real* name of the parent of the student. The boy was never admitted.

43. See Chapter IV, p. 143. In paragraph 11 of his Report, Mr. Okafor noted that "many Southern contractors and big businessmen have taken NPC membership cards. Some complain that since they have no places in the South to work or obtain contracts, they must vote for the NPC in order to ensure their daily bread."

44. The use of Statutory Corporations as instruments of patronage is well shown in the 'Coker Report'. In fact recruitment into, and advancement in the Corporations depends largely on one's political 'credentials'. Some commercial firms want to establish party affiliations of job applicants. A firm in Kano

O

NICCO, with a naturalized Nigerian (formerly Sudanese) as manager, a Mr. Usman El Taibe, dismissed those in its employ who refused to join the NPC.

45. Sklar op. cit., passim, explains Aminu Kano's status by reference to Aminu's knowledge of Arabic and the Koran. But this can hardly be regarded as an adequate explanation as there are others in NEPU just as knowledgeable as Aminu Kano about the Koran and Arabic.

46. *Report of the Board of Auditors appointed by the NEC of NEPU* dated Kano 17th January 1961. Unpublished and confidential.

47. The same set of peole were reported in 1961 to have misappropriated £500 of the £5,000 given to NEPU by the NCNC to purchase a building in Kano for the party's headquarters. For similar reasons no action was taken.

48. Girth and Mills, op. cit., p. 84. The narrow construction here suggested is that in fact used by Weber, ibid., loc. cit.

49. "These are the reasons why I want the alliance between NEPU and the NCNC to be broken." A mimeographed document by M. Isiyaku Ibrahim, Publicity Secretary, NEPU, Ibadan, n.d. (c. 1961).

50. One of the factors in Aminu Kano's leadership is the fact that in spite of his Fulani and 'aristocratic' social origins, he was seen as symbolizing this protest and opposition.

51. Innumerable letters requesting aid of one type or another are to be found in the NPC's Headquarters Files; for instance, the letter Ref. NPC/ER/23/52 dated 26th August 1960, from members from Enugu asking for money to celebrate Independence because "The East Regional Government has entirely ignored us as participants of this unique occasion".

52. The actual figure given by the Deputy Secretary-General is £1,800.

53. Because of the geographical areas involved, officials estimate that costs of collection of 'fees' take up about one-quarter of the amount collected.

54. By the Electoral Law 1963, NNL No. 12 of 1963 Section 17 (1), this has been raised to £100.

55. In an interview.

56. N.H.A. Debates, 11th August 1956, pp. 179–80.

57. See Chapter III, p. 87.

58. 'Resolution presented to the National Secretary of the NCNC', dated 13th June 1961. NEPU H.Q. File no. 0178.

59. No guarantee was given because the Resolution (Note 58) never reached the NCNC. Though addressed to the National Secretary of the NCNC, it was to be presented through him to the NCNC President, Dr. Okpara, Premier of the Eastern Region. The latter, however, was away from the country then. As the letter was handed over to Aminu Kano, who was going to Lagos, he then 'received' the Resolutions, acting now in his capacity as 1st Vice President of the NCNC. When this was known, it led to further attacks on Aminu who, it was argued, had always broken the 'rule' of the party which forbade dual membership in any other party.

60. It is significant in this context that a section of NEPU's leadership, Mallams Tanko Yakasai, Shehu Sattatima, Adimola Uba Na Alkassim, who visited China in 1960–61 wanted to include the 'General Programme' of the Constitution of the CPC as the 'Preface' to NEPU's new Constitution. This proposal was only withdrawn through Aminu Kano's intervention. The 'General Programme' of the CPC is contained, pp. 9–16, in *The Constitution of the CPC: Report on the Revision of the CPC* by Teng Hsiao-Puig, Foreign Languages, Peking, 1956.

61. The AG, for instance, spent over £100,000 on behalf of the UMBC/AG

alliance in the 1961 regional elections, while its expenditure for the UMBC in 1961 was over £22,000. On the financial aid to the UMBC, see *Record of Appeal from the High Court of Lagos to the Federal Supreme Court* (the treason trial involving Chief Awolowo and twenty-six others), vol. 2, pp. 162, 165, 180; vol. 3, p. 50 et seq.

62. The list showing the composition of the 1961 Executive, Ref. UMBC/AG/BPS/16/1 UMBC H.Q. Files, showed that two each were Tiv, Idoma, and Birom respectively and one each for other ethnic groups. In early 1961, following proposals from Alhaji Ibrahim Imam (*Record of Appeal*, vol. 2, p. 165, exhibit 33), the AG organization in the North was divided into two zones, the Far North and the Lower North. The executive referred to is for the Lower North.

63. It is not, of course, being suggested that this is the sole factor in Tarka's ascendancy. Other factors have contributed, such as the financial backing he received from the AG, a party which accepts the idea of 'personal leadership'; his being a Tiv, the largest single ethnic group in the UMBC; his education (he was Senior Science Master at the Provincial Secondary School, Katsina Ala) and finally, the aura of political martyrdom surrounding him. His father, for instance, was dismissed from his office of a district head largely because of his son's politics, and in April 1961 Tarka himself was arrested and kept in jail for two months before being brought to trial for 'instigating and managing' the Tiv riots of the previous year. Though he was acquitted, it is hardly coincidental that his arrest took place immediately before the May 1961 regional elections and that he was not brought to trial until after the elections.

64. Imam fled from Bornu in 1958 after a clash between the NPC and the BYM. Five people, all BYM, were killed, though no one was ever brought to trial for this. On fleeing to Jos, he was advised by the police to move to an area with strong AG. support as they, the police, could not guarantee his safety. See his evidence at the 'Awolowo Treason Trial', *Record of Appeal*, vol. 2, p. 162. In 1962, the Northern Government promised to give Imam police protection should he want to visit his home town of Maiduguri.

65. On this, see J. W. Walace, 'The Tiv System of Election', *Journal of African Administration*, vol. 10, no. 2, 1958, pp. 63–70.

66. See *Record of Appeal*, vol. 3, p. 16, and the *Daily Mail* (Kano) 14th November 1961.

67. Imam gives the date as September 1962. *Record of Appeal*, vol. 2, p. 180. The date given is that by Patrick Dokotri, the UMBC General Secretary, ibid. vol. 2, pp. 20, 28. For Tarka's reasons for the breach, see *Daily Express* (Lagos) 23rd October 1962.

68. Interview with Hon. Vincent Orjime MHA (NPC, formerly UMBC) and Senator Abaagu (NPC, formerly UMBC and MBSP). It is interesting to note how many of the past and present leaders of the UMBC are Christians. Pastor David Lot (SUM), Jonah Asaadugu (SUM), Dokotri (Catholic), Tarka (Catholic), Achiga Abuul (CMS), Moses Rwang (CMS), and Abaagu (Catholic).

69. E.g., over education and medical activities, avenues through which the missions have carried out their proselytization.

70. On the NPF, see *Daily Times*, 24th October 1963, *Daily Express*, 20th November 1963 and 21st November 1963, *Morning Post* (Lagos Federal Government Newspaper) 22nd November 1963. At a meeting held in Kaduna 13th–15th July 1964, the parties forming the NPF agreed to a common list of candidates, for elections, a uniform electoral manifesto and a single symbol—a white eight-pointed star on a black background. *Daily Times*, 17th July 1964. See also Appendix V.

71. It should be pointed out that the NPF is not the first attempt at forming a united opposition in the North. From 1960, several attempts to unify NEPU, UMBC, Sawaba Party of Nigeria, a breakaway NEPU group led by Tanko Yakasai, NEFO, led by former NEPU leaders in Zaria, Ibrahim Imam's BYM, and a Jos NPC breakaway faction led by Audu Gobe-san Tashi, were made. But none of these came to anything. The poverty of the parties, struggle for leadership, the greed of the leaders themselves prevented any concrete decision being reached. In most cases, these attempts failed when the question of whether they should ally with the AG or unite without any alliance came up.

72. The general policy governing the relationship of N.A. staffs to Local politics is laid down in a circular letter issued by the Ministry of Local Government Ref. MLG.412/9 dated 7th June 1955 which stated, inter alia, that "N.A. Staff should for the present be permitted in local government activities, with the exception of official members of N.A. Councils, and heads of N.A. departments—and employees shall not without the premission of the N.A. take part in local political controversy; and the public expression of opinion contrary to the policy of the N.A. may be regarded as an offence against discipline." N.A. councillors, departmental heads, Alkalis, may contest elections to the Regional and Federal Legislatures but may not contest elections to district, provincial and town councils. For the categories of those so permitted or disallowed, see the reply of Alhaji Usman Sulaiman, Parliamentary Secretary to Minister of Local Government in N.H.A. Debates, 13th March 1963, p. 275.

73. NRL no. 4 of 1954 as amended by NRL No. 4 of 1957, No. 5 of 1958, No. 37 of 1960 and No. 23 of 1961. References, however, except where otherwise shown will be to the original 1954 Act.

74. NRL no. 4 of 1954, Sections 37, 41 and 43. N.A.s also exercise powers conferred on them by other laws and ordinances or imposed on them by Native Law or Custom.

75. A five-point complaint (with suggestions for reform) on these lines was presented to the Emir of Zaria and his Council by NEPU in 1960. See *Nigerian Citizen*, 9th July 1960. The files at NEPU headquarters contain endless letters and protests to Emirs and Residents on these issues.

76. Section 133, NRL. no. 4 of 1954.

77. Members of the opposition so arrested could previously get out of conviction by asking that their case be tried before the magistrate courts—which apply 'English Law'—on the grounds that they are not Moslems. But by the Criminal Code (Amendment) Act 1962, this is no longer possible. The Act provides for anyone resident in the North to be subject to the jurisdiction of the local Moslem Courts irrespective of religious persuasion.

78. In pursuance of Sections 37 (45) and 43 (5).

79. Section 43 (4).

80. Section 104 (1).

81. Of disobedience of an 'executive order' *Kin Umurci*. On this see M. G. Smith, *Government in Zazzau*, pp. 89, 267, and *Economy of the Hausa Communities in Zaria*, pp. 6, 10. Smith writes, "the chief is the executive authority in the community, whose control is sanctioned by law, and whose orders, general or particular, lawful or otherwise, are obeyed by his subjects". Ibid. p. 10. Cf. Section 103, NRL no. 4, 1954, which enjoins on the individual the duty to assist the Native Authority.

82. Section 108 (2) provides that where there is no time or where it is impracticable an arrest can be made without a warrant and the individual tried by the court having jurisdiction over him.

83. Section 105 (1) as amended by NRL no. 4 of 1957.

84. A 'native' of Kano for instance will be regarded as a "non-native' in Zaria.

85. Section 47. There is a right of appeal to a magistrate's court, but on the problem here see text. Besides, the onus of proof lies with the plaintiff. Mallams Ahmadu Mairami, Ibrahim Kabullu, Adamu Mairami, Madu Kai, were all expelled from the village of Fowame in Bornu Province by the Village Head of Jawullam, Lawan Awami in July 1961.

86. Section 77 substituted for and amended by NRL No. 37 of 1960.

87. Series of letters in the *Nigerian Citizen*, e.g. that by Usman Mohammed (an NPC!) in ibid., 26th July 1958.

88. The pathetic case of one Kachalla Koribe, BYM Provincial Organizing Secretary is instructive. In May 1959 he bought a lorry for £250 from one Ahmed Nassir, a Shuwa Arab, for which he made an initial payment of £50. But unfortunately, on one pretext or another, he was arrested and imprisoned and while in prison, Nassir sued for recovery of the sum owed to him. Kachalla Koribe was brought from jail and tried as a debtor. The lorry was not only confiscated and sold, his house was also sold, a house estimated as worth over £1,000 being sold for £180 to an NPC supporter under the authority of the Chief Alkali, M. Talba, the Sarkin Hausawa, Zanna Gaddawa, and the N.A. Registrar, M. Baba Gana.

89. Three NEPU members in Zaria had their houses so destroyed in 1959 on the orders of the N.A. Superintendent of Health, Alhaji Ismaila Ahmed. See also NRL no. 14 of Section 37 (63c).

90. Section 102 for a list of 'offences' for which an N.A. may be made liable.

91. To help meet these costs, both the AG and the NCNC maintained party lawyers to take up cases for members of the UMBC and NEPU respectively.

92. Contra Sections 29 (a), 36 (4) of NRL no. 12 of 1963. This act largely consolidated previous Acts.

93. Mats made from a local type of grass.

94. The author reported observed cases in 'Elections in Sardauna Province', *West Africa*, 9th December 1961. Other practices included NPC canvassers being permitted with in a distance of less than 200 yards of the polling booths—contra Section 85 of NRL no. 12 of 1963; the use of Native Authority vehicles to transport voters to polling stations (contra Section 85), though the Electoral Commission may in some cases permit this (Section 158) and even then their use is discriminatory. Instances of ballot boxes being removed to an Emir's palace rather than to the counting station contrary to the Electoral regulations; of illegal ballot papers having been used by the NPC, are not unknown. See for cases during the 1961 elections—evidence by Patrick Dokotri—*Record of Appeal* (Awolowo Treason Trial) vol. 3, pp. 48, 52, 54; vol. 2, p. 166. Reports of illegal practices to the N.A. police are hardly likely to receive sympathetic hearing, while there are too few lawyers and the costs prohibitive to make a petition to the Courts a practicable proposition.

95. Deposits were raised from £25 in 1954 to £75 in 1961 and has by NRL no. 12 of 1963 Section 17 been raised to £100. During the debates on this law, NEPU and UMBC members claimed that the bill was aimed at them—see N.H.A. Debates, 14th March 1963 pp. 347–353. It is interesting to note that Britain with a *per capita* income of £532 requires £100. The Federation, with a *per capita* income of £27·6. requires £25—the same amount for elections in the East and West with comparable incomes of £25·9 and £36·2 respectively. All income figures quoted are from *The Industrial Potentialities of Northern Nigeria*, Kaduna, Ministry of Trade and Industry 1963, p. Table 6.

96. Affidavit sworn by M. F. A. Thanni, an AG lawyer, before the High Court

Registry, Kano. In all, 132 were arrested, some of whom were later released. Three were sentenced to death, two to seven years imprisonment and others to varying terms of imprisomnent.

97. On the Tijaniyya, see *Encyclopedia of Islam*, Luzac and Co., 1934 edition, vol. 4, pp. 745–747. The predominant Islamic tradition in Northern Nigeria is the Kadiriyya, on which see ibid. (1927 edition) vol. 2, pp. 608–11. Tijanniya while being more puritanical in religious observances is more liberal in politics, unlike Kadiriyya which is more liberal in religion but sanctions authoritarian politics. On this, see T. Hodgkin, Islam in West Africa, *West Africa*, especially 22nd September 1956, p. 727, 13th October, p. 797 and 20th October p. 823.

98. NEPU represented the Yan Tijaniyya of Gusau at the Minorities Commission. The Tijanniya Memorandum to the Commission dated 16th October 1957, is in NEPU H.Q. File 00221. With Tijaniyya's egalitarianism and radical liberal political ideology, one would have expected the Brotherhood to be more formally associated with NEPU sharing as it does with the latter some characteristics of a protest movement. Several factors make such an association problematic. Firstly, one of Tijaniyya's main doctrines is obedience to the government (see A. S. Tritton, *Islam*, Hutchinson's University Library, 5th imp. 1966, p. 99). Secondly, most of the Brotherhood's leadership are NPC. The head of the Brotherhood in the North (appointed by Shaikh Ibrahim Nayas in 1956) is the ex-Emir Sanussi of Kano. In Kano itself, the main centre of the brotherhood, the leading Tijaniyya mallams, such as Alhaji M. Tijani, M. Shehu Maihula Gadaranci, M. Ibrahim, Alhaji Atiku and Alhaji Sani Kajunga are all NPC. An adequate explanation which will cover the history of the brotherhood, its doctrinal position and distribution of membership etc. is beyond the scope of this study. A study on these lines is being undertaken by Mr. John Padden at Harvard.

99. The Sultan's letter is reprinted in N.H.A. Debates, 12th March 1957, pp. 855–56.

100. N.H.A. Debates, 12th March 1957, pp. 847–48.

101. Compare for instance, the statement by Alhaji Muazu Lamido, Minister of Animal and Natural Resources when faced with demands for improvements in the Tiv Division: "It is up to the Tiv people to realize their mistakes and stop electing people belonging to irresponsible political parties in the future". N.H.A. Debates, 11th March 1963, p. 178.

102. For the Government account of incidents leading to the riots, see N.H.A. Debates, 19th April 1960, cols. 314–15.

103. *Sunday Times* (Lagos), 19th July 1964. Unofficial estimates put the number killed at about 4,000.

VI

Parties and the Political Process

The induced attrition and gradual elimination of the opposition[1] discussed in the previous chapter has meant that the NPC remains in
practice the main political party in the North. But as V.O. Key has
pointed out[2] there is a duality of character in any political party. On
the one hand, the party has its organization outside the Government
to nominate candidates and to campaign for their election. On the
other, the party members occupying legislative and executive posts
have responsibility for conduct of the Government. As Key put it,
"the party group within the representative body has its own organization and its own identity quite independent of the party outside the
government".[3] Concretely, a 'government' is a system of complex and
inter-relating institutions, institutions which influence and condition
party performance in the conduct of public policy and in the process
reflect the political forces operative at any given moment. It is this
interactive pattern between party (that is the NPC) and government
which is examined in this chapter.

I. PARTY AND THE LEGISLATURE

The constitution of Northern Nigeria[4] prescribes a bicameral legislature, an Upper House, the House of Chiefs, and a lower House, the
House of Assembly, the composition of which is 230[5] while that of
the House of Chiefs is 110 (including an adviser on Moslem Law),
and is made up of first and second class chiefs and other 'nominated'
chiefs.[6]

1. *The House of Assembly*

The general conduct of the House of Assembly follows closely on
that of the Federal House of Representatives,[7] but there are some
differences between the two. Unlike the Federal Parliament, both
English and Hausa are recognized as official languages. Again, unlike

the House of Representatives, the Northern Assembly has no Business Committee, to regulate together with the Leader of the House the number of days to be allotted the second and third reading and Committee stages of the Appropriation Bill, the order in which private members motions will be taken or the sequence in and rate at which business of the House is to be conducted. This is usually determined by the respective Ministers with the consent of the Speaker of the House. The House also meets for much fewer days in the year, averaging for the eleven years between 1952 and 1962, twenty-one days, the highest number being twenty-nine days in 1958, 1960 and 1961 and the lowest, fourteen days in 1952. But, although the standing orders of the Assembly provide for three standing Committees, as in the Federal House all bills are taken in Committee of the whole House. And as in the Federal Parliament, a Committee of Selection (on which the opposition is represented by only one member) appoints the Standing Orders Committee, the Public Petitions Committee, the House Committee, the Public Accounts Committee and the Joint Standing Committee on Finance. The last named was abolished in 1959 and in 1962, the PAC became the Public Accounts Joint Committee (on which, like the Committee of Selection, only one member represents the opposition).[8]

Though the NPC has formed the Government since 1952,[9] it is characteristic that the first Ministers of the NPC were elected by the House. Most members were elected either as individuals or as representatives of their respective Native Authorities and only become party representatives after being members of the House. The debates of this early period reflect the absence of any parliamentary organization. They reveal a considerable division of interests. This is illustrated, for instance, in the debate in 1953 on a motion introduced by the Minister of Education and Social Welfare, Alhaji Aliyu Makaman Bida, which sought to amend the electoral regulations to provide for representation on a divisional rather than on a provincial basis, with direct representation for the major towns. The conflict of viewpoints showed not only individual, but also divisional and provincial bias. Thus, while the Bauchi contingent wanted the electoral regulations to remain as they were and objected to any form of direct representation, Isa Kaita, the spokesman for the Katsina bloc, thought that divisional interests could be catered for by the House of Chiefs and therefore representation should be on a provincial basis. To this, the Kano contingent objected on the grounds that since the Emirate (which is what a member of the House of Chiefs represents) is not coterminous with the division, representation on the basis of the latter was the more logical.[10]

Similar division of interests can also be seen from the debates on the Potts-Maddox Report on the Local Government[11] and on the Native Authority Bill of 1954. In the latter case, the then General Secretary of the NPC Alhaji Ibrahim Imam, criticized the bill (which was introduced by the Minister of Local Government, Alhaji Ahmadu Bello, President General of the NPC) because it entrenched the position of the Emirs whom he thought were already an anachronism. To this criticism, Alhaji Abubaker Tafawa Balawa[12] was able to reply that: "As for the views of the General Secretary, I am afraid to say . . . that that view was the personal view of the General Secretary as an individual . . . the General Secretary was so strong in his views that it was right and proper that he should be allowed to voice them."[13] The open criticism of the Government in members' speeches contrasts rather sharply with the policy statement by the then Minister of Natural Resources, Alhaji Mohammadu, Walin Bornu, to the effect that while members were free to express their opinion, this should not extend to party policy as formulated by the Executive.[14] It is not improbable, however, that the tolerance shown by party leaders was due not only to the lack of a party parliamentary organization, but also to the fact that the Government was then regarded as being 'expatriate' since they (the expatriates) controlled the important 'departments' of finance, justice (through the Attorney-General) and internal affairs (represented by the Civil Secretary the effective head of the whole administration).

In 1954, the Sardauna of Sokoto became the Premier of the North and with the change in his status, came the beginnings of party-government. As Premier the Sardauna became effectively responsible for the appointment of Ministers (in effect, the Governor appoints on the advice of the Premier) over whom he exercises full control as can be seen from the table on the following page which shows the turnover of Ministers in the various Ministries.

Thus, excluding the Premier, the mean number of years during which an individual has held one Ministry is just under 2·5 years. It is also interesting to note, taking into consideration the previous discussion of leadership in the NPC, that those ranking next to the Sardauna, Alhajis Isa Kaita, Minister of Education, Makaman Bida, Minister of Finance, Musa Gashash, Minister of Lands and Survey, Ahman Pategi Minister of Health (since 1964, Minister of Agriculture) are also those who have held their Ministries for the longest period of time.

While the Premier can exert his influence and authority in at least one respect by altering his Cabinet, his choice of colleagues can be seen to be limited by considerations of geography and population.

TABLE 15

Ministerial Turnover in Northern Nigeria 1952–62

		No. of Ministers in One Ministry for						
	Year Estab- lished	1 yr.	2 yrs.	3 yrs.	4 yrs.	5 yrs.	6 yrs.	7 yrs.
1. Premier's Office	1954	—	—	—	—	—	—	1
2. Ministry of Works	1962	6	3	—	—	—	—	—
3. Ministry of Local Government	1953	1	1	2	—	—	—	—
4. Ministry of Land and Survey	1956	2	—	—	—	—	1	—
5. Social Welfare and Co-operatives (a)	1952	2	1	1	1	—	—	—
6. Education	1956	2	—	—	—	—	1	—
7. Natural Resources ⎫ (b)	1952	1	1	—	—	—	—	—
8. Animal Health and ⎬ Forest Resources ⎭	1957	1	1	1	—	—	—	—
9. Trade and Industry ⎫ (c)	1953	4	3	—	—	—	—	—
10. Agriculture ⎭	1958	2	—	—	1	—	—	—
11. Internal Affairs	1958	—	1	1	—	—	—	—
12. Health	1953	1	1	—	—	—	1	—
13. Establishment and Training	1961	—	1	—	—	—	—	—
14. Economic Planning	1961	—	1	—	—	—	—	—
15. Finance	1957	—	—	—	—	—	1	—
16. Information	1960	—	—	1	—	—	—	—
17. Justice	1962	1	—	—	—	—	—	—

NOTE: (a) Was first Community Development before being converted into Social Welfare in 1956.

(b) 8 was part of 7 before being created into a separate Ministry.

(c) Similarly with 10 and 9. A Ministry not shown—the Ministry of Cameroons affairs was created in 1955 and was merged under the Ministry of Works until 1957 when it was then placed under the Ministry of Animal Health and Forest Resources. The Ministry of Cameroons Affairs was abolished in 1961 after the United Nations Plebiscite.

Thus of the sixty-five people who have been Ministers, Ministers of State, Ministers without Portfolio and Parliamentary Secretaries between 1952 and 1963, seven each were appointed from Bornu, Katsina and Sokoto (not including the Premier himself), five each from Niger Kabba and Ilorin, four each from Adamawa and Benue and three from Zaria, Plateau and Bauchi respectively. Kano alone provided eleven of the total.[15] This is not to say that there is any limitation on his choice of one individual rather than the other from any given province. In 1960 when Alhaji Maikano Dutse, Minister of Local Government 'resigned', he was replaced by Alhaji Sule Gaya, Maikano Dutse's Parliamentary Secretary. Both men are from Kano. In general terms, the choice of candidates for Ministerial offices will depend on the individual's lineage affiliations, his status within the Emirate, Native Authority and provincial party hierarchy and his preparedness to accord implicit obedience to the Sardauna. By extension, the same influences which determine the choice of candidates for Ministerial appointment can also influence his removal from office. Thus, in the case of Alhaji Maikano Dutse, Minister of Local Government from 1957 to 1960, local opposition by the Kano party bosses, supposedly engineered by the ex-Emir Sanussi, was enough to ensure the demand for his resignation. Finally, whereas in the past, appointments were made from ordinary members of the Assembly, it is now becoming the practice for potential office-holders to serve a year or two of apprenticeship as Parliamentary Secretaries before being given a Ministerial appointment. As Parliamentary Secretaries, potential office-holders learn how to handle questions during question time and in general help to 'protect' the interest of their respective political superiors.[16]

A concomittant of party-government has been the near total control of back-bench opinion. During the debate on the Native Authority (Amendment) Law of 1955, Abdulmumuni, District Head, Galadima of Katsina and a member for Katsina province observed that since it was party policy that the bill should be passed, he could not criticize the bill though he had "a lot to disagree with in principle"[17]. And in the Committee stage on the bills to establish a Development Corporation and Provincial Loans Boards for the North, amendments which had been tabled in the names of Alhajis Sa'ad Alanamu (now Agent-General of the North in the Nigerian High Commission in the United Kingdom) and Abdulmaliki (now Nigerian High Commissioner in Britain) were withdrawn "after assurances and discussions from outside the House". When a member of the opposition suggested that this might have been due to pressure from the Party Whip, Alhaji Abdulmaliki replied: "Not from any pressure but only from our democratic and parliamentary discipline upon which we members of the NPC are being run."[18]

Lapses do occur as when, for instance, a motion by an NPC back-bencher, Mallam Umaru Audi, member for Niger Province, that membership of the House should be a full time occupation was allowed to reach the floor of the House. The motion had hardly been called when a member for Kano Province, Alhaji Uba Ringim countered that "if he (Mallam Audi) has got anything to say, as he is a member of the NPC, he should have proposed it to his party".[19] The Motion was withdrawn. Such lapses of 'discipline' become increasingly rare and from about 1959 have totally ceased. As a result, debates in the House have become routinized with back-bench opinion tending to take the form of pleas and reminders to Ministers of what specific services and benefits are needed in the members' constituencies. All negotiations therefore take place outside the House which has become merely a rubber-stamp for executive decisions.

The machinery for negotiations is the Parliamentary Committee first instituted in 1955.[20] This is made up of one representative from each of the thirteen provinces. Members from a province meet before a session of the House and here matters coming before the House are discussed and debated. Provincial opinion is then relayed by the provincial spokesman to the Parliamentary Committee which in turn meets the respective Ministers to iron out contentious issues. The result of negotiations between the Parliamentary Committee and the relevant Minister is finally conveyed to the Members together with whatever orders, assurances and instructions were also given. Ministers can rely on the total compliance of members firstly, because recalcitrance can be punished by dropping the member at the next elections, a sufficient threat when it is remembered that few members earn an income larger than that of an M.P. Since social considerations require that a member must maintain a large retinue of dependants (besides having a not inconsiderable household of relatives) the number of people affected by an M.P.'s loss of income is quite large. Secondly, as most members are also Native Authority employees, independence on the part of an Assemblyman can be immediately dealt with by means of administrative action at the Native Authority level.

The district or village head may thus find himself removed from office, the Councillor from the Emir's Council or the departmental head may be transferred to a less 'lucrative' department or one that carries less patronage. Where the M.P. is a businessman, and these form less than ten per cent of the House at any time, he may lose profitable contracts with the Native Authority, or have his trading licence withdrawn, or other restrictions, sufficient to hamper if not actually to cripple his business, imposed on him.

If the NPC back-bencher has abdicated his function of acting as a check on the Executive, no matter how minimal this may be, the opposition is in no position to remedy the deficiency. Besides the debates on government business such as that on the 'Speech from the Throne'—the address by the Governor when a session of the House is convened—and the debates on the Appropriation Bill, the only other ways by which the opposition can criticize the Government are through private members' motions, questions in the House and debates on the adjournment.

The length of time needed to get a question accepted by the Clerk of the House, the fact that most questions, whether from the opposition or not tend to be concerned with specific, local constituency issues, the tendency for most Ministers and Parliamentary Secretaries to refuse to accept 'supplementaries' have all tended to diminish the significance of question time as a means of 'venting grievance' or of scoring political points. Besides, few members ever come to know their constituents or encourage their constituents to bring forward their problems or grievances.[22]

The practice of most Ministers of leaving the Assembly[23] before the adjournment has in effect deprived the opposition of using this opportunity to raise important issues and in fact, no motion on the adjournment has been raised by the opposition since 1957. Another opportunity open to the opposition is private members' motions. But the opposition has not made much of this advantage. One severe limitation here is the heterogenous character of the opposition itself. For some time opposition members were unable to agree on a common leader. They were also divided on specific issues. Thus while those of the UMBC/AG were interested in the creation of a middle-belt state, and succeeded in tabling two separate motions to this effect,[24] NEPU members, because of their ideological stand, were not particularly committed to the idea of such a state. However, the introduction of the system of balloting for time for private motions—"to conform with the procedure in the British House of Commons"[25] has in effect limited severely the chances of the opposition. Given the number of the opposition from 1957 to the end of 1963—eight in an Assembly of 177—their chance was one in twenty-two, with the result that they only succeeded in getting two motions on to the order paper.[26]

The main opportunity for the opposition to put forward its point of view is therefore during the debates on government business. Even here, the peculiar circumstances of politics in the North provide built-in restrictions on the opposition: for instance, Standing Order 24 (8) of the House precludes "the conduct of judges or the performance of judicial functions by other persons" from criticism except on a substantive motion. In a society where judges or those carrying out quasi-judicial functions are not openly identified as actively participating in party politics and are not permitted by the electoral regulations to contest elections, in other words, in societies where the 'impartiality' of the judges is not only proclaimed but seen to be maintained, this may be a suitable and a desirable rule to protect judicial office-holders from undue criticism. This is not the case in the North, where Alkalis are very much 'in' politics. Obviously then, the rule is simply a case of the Executive wanting to have their cake and eat it.[23] Since this is palpably possible, the opposition is placed in the worst of possible worlds.

Besides the built-in restrictions, there is the obvious partiality of the Speaker of the House which found classic expression, during the debates on the Appropriation Bill of 1963, when he said: "I think the opposition should just clear so that *we* can finish"[28]—a statement which succinctly epitomizes the general attitude to the opposition.

In the gradual transition from Colonial to Independent status in Nigeria, it was not unreasonable to expect those who shaped the political fortunes of the country to want to model the institutions on the 'Westminster Model',[29] but the evolution of party-government is now such as to make any comparison or reference to the 'model' otiose, for the British House of Commons, if it is nothing else, is still a 'Debating Chamber' where members can at least, as Laski put it, ventilate grievance, extract information, criticize the administrative process and discuss "large principles which test the movement of public opinion".[30] Only the naïve would claim that any of such possibilities exist in the Northern House of Assembly. A few cases will suffice to substantiate this proposition.

The total number of days in the year in which the House meets in effect rules out any possibility of constructive debate. In the 1962 session, the House met for a total of eighteen days and during the budget meeting in April, debated and passed in addition to the Appropriation Bill for the year, twenty-five bills including two Supplementary Appropriation Bills for the years 1960–61 and 1961–62. Not only has over-expenditure gone unquestioned,[31] money is not infrequently expended without prior parliamentary sanction, for instance, the authorization by the Premier of expenditure on the State House which received parliamentary sanction two years later in 1959.[32] Similarly, the Annual Report of the Regional Public Corporations, the Regional Marketing Board and the Northern

Region Development Corporation, laid before the Assembly, are accepted with scant debate. The unquestioning acceptance of Executive decisions is perhaps nowhere better exemplified than in the meetings of the Public Accounts Joint Committee. When, for instance, the Accountant-General informed the 1962–63 Session of the PAC that the NRDC had requested that the sum of £1·3m which it owed the Government should be written off, the members thought no comments were needed or necessary when asked by the Chairman for their opinion.[33]

The same unquestioning spirit also permits maladministration to pass by default. Thus, the accounts for the years 1958–59 and 1959–1960 were only certified by the Director of Audit in February 1962 but could not be laid before the House because it was not clear who should lay them—the Ministry of Finance or the Ministry of Local Government. No questions were thought necessary by the PAC, neither did they comment on the fact that the Director of Audit was unable to certify the accounts of 1961–62 because of "the delay of information from the Ministry of Local Government".[34] On the other hand, despite the constitutional guarantee of independence from political control of the office of the Director of Audit, a Minister of State in the Premier's Office, Mr. S. A. Ajayi, saw no impropriety in publicly denouncing the auditor for reporting an alleged loss of £13,000 from Kabba Native Authority treasury—the Minister's home province.[35]

Despite the structure of authority in the North which has in part contributed to this loss of independence of M.P.s their abdication of their role is also related in part to the structure of public opinion and the media of mass communication in the region. Given the general level of literacy in the North and the fact that almost all forms of communication are controlled by the Government,[36] the Member of Parliament can rest assured, absolved from all responsibility, in the full knowledge that he cannot be held accountable for his performance by his constituents who, in any case, will be unaware of the proceedings of the House. By controlling mass-communication media, radio, television and the press, the Government makes sure that the public acquire information only of those issues about which it wants them to be informed. In other words, it is the Government which determines what should be a public issue, and not unreasonably, the Government has thought it a safer policy to maintain a 'conspiracy of silence' on all but those issues which are most favourable to the government. Thus, when in 1961 the Government felt that it was being given 'unwanted publicity' by the news division of the Nigerian Broadcasting Corporation, Northern Region, it quickly requested the dismissal of the head of that division,[37] and not infrequently (as if to protect their own deficiencies) Government back-benchers have called for the banning of the few opposition newspapers in the North[38] with the result that, short of having their licences revoked, these newspapers have found it more prudent to pursue a middle-course in their criticisms of Government policy. In the absence of a forum of public debate and thus, a socially mobilized public opinion in the North, the preparedness of the Assemblyman to bow to the Executive becomes more readily understandable. As a corollary to Duverger's 'mathematical type of formula' that "the influence of parties on candidatures varies in direct relation to the size of the constituencies"[39] we might add that with any system of party government, other things being equal, the independence of the back-bench member is inversely proportionate to the Government's control of the media of communication.

In the Federal Parliament, Ministerial control of back-bench opinion amongst the NPC is hardly any different from what obtains in the North. Similar processes of 'negotiations' between back-benchers and Government, through the Parliamentary Committee also take place. Co-ordination of party attitudes amongst members of the two legislatures, however, takes place at three different levels. First, there is the meeting of all provincial M.P.s, both in the regional and federal Houses, before each session of the particular legislature. Here matters of policy affecting the province are discussed. Secondly, there is the occasional meeting of all members of both legislatures in Kaduna. This may be either before the budget session or as occasion demands, for instance when there is need for a definite policy on specific issues such as the census. Lastly, there are the not infrequent consultations between individual members, or groups of members of the federal executive and the Northern Cabinet or members thereof. In general, the final decision on any issue rests with members of the Northern Executive, federal M.P.s being expected faithfully to carry out such policy decisions. This is not to say that there may not be difference of opinion between the two. Thus, for instance, when the Federal Prime Minister expressed his desire for a National Government after the 1964 federal elections, the Northern Premier suggested that the NPC might break its agreement with the NCNC, its partner in the federal coalition Government. But whatever the difference, the freedom of action open to NPC federal leaders will depend on the ability of federal members to convince their 'Northern' counterparts on the advisability of such action. When in May 1963, the Northern Executive opposed the idea of a National government, the Prime Minister had to plead unpreparedness, even though he had publicly expressed the need for such a government. A similar back-pedalling occurred with the Nigerian-Israeli negotiations on economic aid in 1960. As one commentator on that occasion put it: "When the Northern Regional government talks, even against the provisions of the Constitution, the Federal government must say *Salaam*."[40] In the last analysis, the Sardauna is still the leader of his party.

Chiefs and the Upper Chamber

Unlike the other regions of Nigeria the North's second chamber ante-dates the regional Assembly, its history dating back to 1932 when a conference of Emirs and Chiefs was first summoned. Thus, next to the colonial Legislative Council it is the oldest 'legislative' assembly in the country.[41] This early start had one practical consequence. It helped in constituting the Chiefs of the North into the only effectively organized interest group in the region, which, with an intuitive grasp, saw in the emergent political parties a possible source of challenge to its collective interest. Since, however, the chiefs could not oppose the parties, the formation and organization of which had become inevitable with the introduction of the franchise and the institution of an electoral system, they were faced with the choice of supporting, howbeit grudgingly, one or the other of the two northern parties—the NPC or NEPU. And given the Declaration of Principles of both parties, the NPC seemed the only possible party they could support. This is important in order to understand the attitude of the members of the House of Chiefs in the early period of the North's constitutional development. For whereas in the South the second chambers were in a sense creations of the nationalist politicians with whom the chiefs did not seek to compete, in the North this was not the case. Between the chiefs and the elected representatives there was an element of rivalry which the respect, traditionally owed to the former, only alleviated without eliminating. In such a situation, it was to be expected that the chiefs would watch the proceeding of the Assembly with suspicion and distrust.

This became apparent soon after the first meeting of the Assembly in 1952 when the Sultan of Sokoto and the Emir of Zaria were both appointed to the Executive Council. The Emir of Kano demanded to know on which side these two men would vote in the event of a disagreement between the chiefs and the Government. But the chiefs were immediately assured by the Lieutenant Governor (who was then the President of the House) that "it has always been our way of doing things to decide policy after consultation".[42] The possibility

P

of disagreement, he pointed out, was entirely hypothetical and he could not conceive of such situations arising.

When, however, the Government suggested in 1953 the creation of a Ministry of Local Government with an indigenous Northerner as Minister, the Chiefs came out in open opposition, and it is significant that the proposal was shelved. The machinery of consultation apparently was not sufficiently effective in disabusing the Chiefs of their fears. Further reassurance was needed in the form of a policy statement a year later by the Civil Secretary in the Chamber before the Chiefs were reconciled to the proposal. The reassurance was to the effect that an indigenous Minister of Local Government would not (a) be expected to give orders to the Native Authorities; (b) concern himself with the appointment and removal of native authority office holders, still less Chiefs; (c) interfere with the day-to-day administration of the N.A.s at any level and (d) concern himself with complaints against N.A.s or their office-holders. The Minister's functions would be simply to tour the N.A. areas, carry suggestions of the Lieutenant-Governor to individual Native Authorities, encourage and advise the N.A.s and publicize their progress.[43] The point of opposition was stated by the Emir of Gwandu, Alhaji Yahaya when he said: "In the first place we were too frightened when this proposal was first presented to us. We did not oppose a Minister of Local Government who would tour around and inspect the progress of various local administrations; what we opposed was that the Minister would be above the Chiefs." Though reconciled to the proposal, the Emir added that "We would like an undertaking from the Lieutenant-Governor that the statements explained would remain, and nothing would change. If there would be any changes in the powers, I argue that the Chiefs would be consulted before such a move . . . what we do not like is to reduce the dignity and authority of the Chiefs and that the Minister should be above them."[44]

If members of the North's second chamber were suspicious of the Assembly, the elected representatives were themselves cautious in their dealings with the chiefs.[45] Thus they were prudent enough to submit the proposals they intended to put forward at the 1956 Constitutional Conference to the Chiefs for their approval[46] and in the White Paper on the Hudson Report were careful to state that "the government agrees that Native Authorities will in no sense be subordinate to Provincial administrations".[47] Though power was gradually tending to shift to the lower house, as it gained confidence, the elected members were unprepared to defy the Chiefs for "you can take a horse to water but you cannot make it drink" as the Mai Bedde, Alhaji Umar Suleiman reminded the Premier in the debate on the Hudson Report. When therefore the Mai added that though the Chiefs supported the introduction of Provincial Authorities in principle "things that are suitable in Sokoto would hardly be so in Bornu"[48] the Government thought it wiser to drop the whole question.

It is hardly to be expected, however, that an elected House would for long tolerate a second chamber which insisted on obstructing policies which it finds unpalatable. Traditionalist Northern Nigeria was not prepared to be an exception. In fact, though the chiefs were scarcely fully conscious of it, their position was already changing. The Native Authority Law of 1954 had in effect placed the N.A.s under the regional Government—a change emphasized by successive amendments to the original statute.[49] The control of the region's purse-strings exercised by the lower House meant that they could now call the tune as the Sardauna was quick to point out to the chiefs in the debate on the 1955 Appropriation Bill when he said "I will begin by expressing my pleasure at the Chief of Kagoro's saying that if the tune is changed, the dance also follow suit. I would say no more than this—a word is sufficient for the wise."[50]

Constitutionally, the second chamber in the North could hold the Government to ransom. While it may not amend the budget but only delay its passing for thirty days, it could veto all other legislation by the Government. In the event of a disagreement between the two Houses, the constitution provides for a joint meeting of an equal number of members chosen from the members of both Houses over which the President of the Upper House presides.[51] Differences of opinion are to be resolved by a simple majority vote, but in the case of an even division of votes the Chairman has a casting vote. In effect, this gives the House of Chiefs a final veto power over the Assembly. This power has not yet been formally exercised since the lower House has in most cases been prepared to withdraw those measures disapproved of by the Chiefs before these got to the stage of being embodied in a government bill. One fact which has so far worked in favour of this procedure is the Chiefs involvement in the 'selection' of candidates for parliamentary elections. Theoretically, therefore, elected members conceive of themselves as in part 'agents' of the chiefs who also look on the elected member as such. Besides this power of veto the approval of the chiefs, in a joint meeting of both Houses, is required for appointments to the Senate.[52]

As against the chiefs veto power, the Government on the other hand, has the power to appoint, to depose and to determine the place of residence of any Emir,[53] a power which the Government has not hesitated to use against "obstructionist" chiefs, for instance, the

Lamido of Adamawa, the Chief of Bunu, the Emir of Argungu, and more recently, the Ex-Emir Sanusi of Kano. Others, such as the Shehu of Dikwa, the Emirs of Bauchi, Kaiama, Lafia and the chief of Jos, were merely warned.

In 1958 the Government created a "Council of Chiefs" to advise on all questions affecting the status and welfare of Chiefs. The Council is comprised of (a) the Premier (who is Chairman), (b) those ministers of the Government who have been appointed from among members of the House of Chiefs and (c) four other chiefs co-opted by the Premier.[54] The Council's role is strictly advisory. The ultimate decision on all matters affecting the Chiefs therefore still rests with the Government and therefore in practice, with the Premier. However, to appreciate the changing position of the Chiefs, it will be necessary to examine in some more detail, the contrasting cases of the ex-Emir of Kano and the Emir of Zaria, Alhaji Aminu.

Kano and Zaria: A Case Study in the Changing Status of Chiefs

Sanusi and Aminu became Emirs of Kano and Zaria in 1954 and 1959 respectively. As district heads both men helped the Sardauna when he appealed against his conviction by the Sultan's court for alleged embezzlement of funds; both played significant parts in establishing the NPC as a political party in their respective provinces. While Aminu played a part in the lobby to elect the Sardauna President of the party in 1954, Sanusi between 1952 and 1954 was an NPC member for Kano in the House of Assembly. Between the Sardauna and Sanusi there are lineage ties. The Sardauna's grandmother comes from a segment of the Kano ruling family;[55] the Sardauna is also, in a sense brother-in-law to Sanusi's son—Ado Bayero, as the latter married a sister to the Sardauna's wife, a daughter of the Emir of Gwandu, the other wing of the Sokoto 'empire' of Shehu Uthman-dan-Fodio. On succeeding his father in 1954 the Sardauna, now Premier of the North, appointed Sanusi to his Cabinet as a Minister without Portfolio (an office which Sanusi held from 1954 to 1963 before his forced resignation and subsequent exile to Azare in Bauchi province) and in 1961, he was appointed to act for the Governor, Sir Gawain Bell, as Acting Governor of the North. Next to the Sultan of Sokoto, Alhaji Sir Mohammadu Sanusi was deservedly the most august and important native ruler in the North and it has been suggested that he was deliberately being 'built-up' by the Sardauna (Sanusi is the official head of the Tijaniyya brotherhood in the North) to counter the traditional influence of the Sarkin Muslumi, the Sultan of Sokoto (leader of the Kadiriyyas).[56]

Besides being politically the more significant in terms of being a

Regional Minister and member of the North's Executive Council, Sanusi wielded an influence which far surpassed that of Aminu of Zaria. Kano is monodynastic with one royal lineage, though with two segments. In effect, this meant that the Emir's authority over the Native Administration, within the limits of the law, was almost total. With no competing royal interest group, he dominated his Council, members of which were either his own children or his appointees. Not only did he control the most prosperous native authority,[57] Kano members of the Assembly form the largest single provincial interest group in the lower House, and most, if not all of these, owed their electoral success to the Emir.

Unlike Kano, Zaria Emirate is multi-dynastic, with four royal lineages, the Bornawa, Katsinawa, Suleibawa and the Mallawa. For seventy-three years the Emirship was held by the Bornawa dynasty when, as the 'Report of the Commission of Enquiry on Zaria'[58] put it, "Nepotism, inefficiency and dishonesty went unchecked. The Council was essentially a Monarch's court, with heavy Yan Sarki (hereditary title holders of the royal lineages) representation, mostly of the Emir's dynasty". When therefore Aminu became the Emir in September 1959, he 'inherited' a Council dominated by the Bornawa dynasty. (Aminu comes from the Katsinawa lineage.) In the Council of eighteen members, seven thus belonged to the 'Yan Sarki group of whom five were Bornawa, while of the outer Council nomination of six, three were controlled by seven district Heads who were of the Bornawa lineage. Not less than eight members therefore belonged to a rival dynasty to that of the new Emir, the remaining ten being shared between the other three lineages in different proportions. The 'constant intrigue' between the various lineages meant that in practice the new Emir's authority was essentially limited not only within the administration itself but also in the local party politics of Zaria.

Whereas then, in Kano, the Emir held full sway over the administration, in Zaria, as the 'Report' put it, the operative principle was one of 'live and let live' between the Emir and his dynastic rivals. In both areas, however, corruption, inefficiency and maladministration went unchecked. Inevitably, this led to a financial crisis in both Native Authorities. In Zaria, though the budget on the 1st April 1960 showed an estimated surplus of £181,000, by the end of the financial year in March 1961, it had become necessary for the government to guarantee a bank overdraft of £100,000 to the N.A. to enable it pay its staff salaries and meet other financial commitments.[59] In Kano by the beginning of the 1962 financial year, the crisis was such that the N.A. was in need of an overdraft of not less than £750,000. The N.A.s portfolio investments were worth approximately half-a-million pounds and the government was forced to give the N.A. an interest-free loan of £260,000 to enable salaries to be paid and "the Native Authority system not brought into disrepute".[60]

In a circular letter in June 1960[61] the Premier had warned all Native Authorities that the Government was no longer prepared to allow "any degeneration in the standard of administration'.' Earlier, in November 1959 when he met the new Emir of Zaria and his council, he had instructed them to "put their house in order". Similar suggestions were also made to the Kano N.A. With the too obvious evidence of continued maladministration, the least the Government could do was to order an enquiry into the affairs of the two Native Administrations, first, into the Zaria N.A. in September 1961, and then the Kano N.A. in December 1962. Both enquiries found evidence of fraud and "financial irresponsibility" throughout, as the *Government Statement* on the Kano enquiry put it, "the whole fabric of the Native Authority". Both enquiries put forward suggestions for overhauling the Native Administration and the Native Authority Council. Here the similarities end. In Zaria, the Emir remained to head a reconstituted Council which had its Yan Sarki or royal representation cut down to one member per dynasty with instructions that this was not to be altered except with the specific approval of the Premier. The elimination of the Bornawa dominance in the Council meant that the authority of the Emir Aminu was automatically enhanced. (It should be noted that the Emir was not included in the dynastic re-allocation. This in fact gave the Katsinawa, the Emir's dynasty, two representatives, and it was hoped that "the Emir would be impartial". As there was no 'suitable candidate' from the Suleibawa dynasty, they were not represented. Provision was therefore made for the inclusion of a Suleibawa when such a 'suitable candidate' became available.) In Kano, on the other hand, the Emir was induced to tender his resignation to the Governor "to make way for reforms to be carried out". Sanusi went to Kaduna to hand in his 'resignation', and was exiled to Azare, a remote village in Bauchi.

It would be facile to attribute the difference in the treatment of these two men to their different statuses within the complex structure of their respective Native Authorities. Admittedly, the Emir of Kano occupied a more pre-eminent position, but as the individual enquiries pointed out (and the Government accepted), "the whole fabric of the N.A." was involved in the financial abuses that were revealed. Besides it seemed odd that the Emir should have been removed whilst the Madaki, the head of the N.A. Department of Finance was permitted to continue in office. The underlying reasons for the removal of the Emir must be sought elsewhere.

By 1961, it was generally felt that there was need for better and more effective liaison between the regional bureaucracy in Kaduna and the N.A.s. Independence had rendered the advisory role of the Residents superfluous and even in that role, they had been largely ignored by the Emirs and Chiefs. The obvious solution would have been to vest the Residents with executive powers, but this was regarded as unsuitable. Members of the Regional Assembly had earlier complained that the powers possessed by administrative officers were so excessive as to make "proper progress (of the N.As) impossible and that they must be curtailed".[62] Moreover, the regional elections of 1961 had resulted in an increase in the number of parliamentarians. The number of Ministers and Parliamentary Secretaries that could be appointed from this increased House was necessarily limited by the number of existing Ministries and there were obvious candidates for Ministerial appointments and areas to be conciliated with Executive appointments. An obvious solution was to appoint Provincial Commissioners who would have Ministerial status from amongst the members.[63] As Provincial Commissioners were expected to reside in the respective provincial headquarters, this immediately raised the question of the definition of status of the Commissioner *vis-à-vis* that of the Emir. Three possibilities presented themselves. The first alternative was patently unacceptable. To make the Commissioner subordinate to the Emir in terms of official precedence would not only be against protocol but would also stultify whatever purpose the Commissioners were supposed to serve. Equivalence of status was by the same argument ruled out, besides the fact that this would sooner or later lead to conflicts. The third possibility, subordinating the Emir to the Commissioner was one not acceptable to some of the Emirs. But while most acquiesced in the knowledge that the "tune had changed", the Emir of Kano did not, and thereupon began to lobby his fellow Emirs in opposition to the proposed Provincial Administration Law[64] which was to institute the system of Provincial Commissioners. Without much success in this direction, the Emir then instructed the Kano Assemblymen to oppose the measure and if possible ensure that it was not presented to the House.

It is instructive to note some of the grounds for the Emir's opposition. These are essentially two-fold. In the first place, he is said to have argued that the proposed Bill was an attempt to re-introduce aspects of the 'Hudson Report' which the Government had previously withdrawn under pressure from the Emirs. Secondly, not only was the proposal an unwarranted interference with the Native Authority, and therefore derogatory to the authority of the Emirs, the Emir himself was a Minister. As a member of the Regional Executive Council, it would be against protocol to subordinate himself to a Commissioner who though a Minister, had no seat on the Executive Council.[65]

Because of the significant role of the Emir in the process of 'selection' of parliamentary candidates and in the actual elections, it is not unlikely that they should wish to influence party policies through the elected members themselves. The extent to which such moves might be expected to succeed would obviously depend on the degree of unanimity between the Emir, his M.P.s and other top-party men in the province. In Kano, by 1962, the relationships between the Emir and most of these men was far from being cordial. For instance, such a key personality in the party and the Native Administration as the Madaki, a personal friend of the Sardauna, could hardly be expected to support the Emir who had only recently taken over some of the Madaki's functions and devolved them on the Sarkin Fada, Maiunguwa Mutawali, one of his favourites. Nor was the Madaki pleased when, though official head of the Administration, he was made to give precedence in the N.A. Council to both the Emir's son Ado Sanusi and the Emir's son-in-law, the Maiunguwa Mundubawa (who moreover was not a native of Kano Emirate but the son of the Emir of Kazaure). The Madaki, Alhaji Shehu Ahmed, is not only a member of the Assembly, but also Deputy Speaker.

Then there was Maikano Wudil, NPC district President and a member for Wudil in the Regional Assembly who was not allowed by the Emir to succeed his late father, Makama Isa, as district head of Wudil, the Emir instead appointed someone from a different lineage—Alhaji Bello Danbarau Yola, member of the Regional Electoral Commission, and also the Emir's son-in-law. Again Alhaji Musa Gashash, Minister of Lands and Survey and Regional President of the NPC was ordered by the Emir to desist from erecting a building (to be let to the Kano branch of the Central Bank of Nigeria) on a piece of land he had recently acquired and about which some of the previous owners had protested to the Emir.[66] In this instance, the Minister, to circumvent the Emir, introduced a Bill, the Land Tenure Law[67] the effect of which was to vest the control of all land in the Minister. Not surprisingly, the Emir instructed the other Kano M.P.s to oppose this bill.

Finally, the relationship between the Emir and the Sardauna had become strained. To conciliate latent Bornu separatism, the Premier had had to choose Shettima Kashim (now Sir Kashim Ibrahim) as Governor of the North in 1962 in place of the Emir who acted in that capacity the previous year. In turn the Emir had let it be known that Kano might demand a separate state for itself. On a more personal level, as if in support of his father, the Emir's son, Ado Sanusi divorced his wife—the Sardauna's sister-in-law, a pointer to Kano's rejection of Sokoto.

With these underlying personal relationships, the Emir's attempt to get Kano M.P.s to oppose the Government policies in land tenure and provincial administration reforms was construed to mean a challenge to the Government's, and particularly the Premier's, authority. It was therefore hardly surprising that the Government should use the Kano enquiry as a legitimate excuse for the Emir's removal.

The forced resignation and exile of Sanusi of Kano demonstrated beyond any doubt that it would be unwise for any Emir to oppose the Government. It showed, in the Mai Bedde's analogy, that not only could the horse be taken to the water, it could be made to drink. The Premier emphasized this in a ministerial statement to the House of Chiefs in 1962 when he said: "Let me make it quite clear that this government intends to rule and intends that its policies and lawful directives shall be carried out. The govermnent has the power and will not have to seek it from anywhere."[68]

This is quite a significant change from the early 1950s when the Government had to pander to the Chiefs, who collectively formed, in a sense, some sort of an opposition. With the changing 'fortunes' of the Emirs, however, they have had to learn, as the Premier again told the House of Chiefs in 1958, that in the House "there are no opposition members".[69] In effect this has turned the second-chamber into a charade where the debates are little more than humble reminders to the Government of the particular needs of the various Emirates, Thus, when the chiefs were called upon to sanction the pledging of Government credit of £2.5 million to the Region's Cooperative Societies, scarcely a member bothered to ask where the money was coming from, what had been done to recover past Government credits[70] or whether alternative forms of help could be given to farmers' co-operatives other than cash.[71] The routine nature of debates has made the House, like the back-bench M.P.s, no more than a mechanical rubber-stamp for Government decisions. It would seem therefore that Professor S. A. de Smith's assessment of the House would need to be seriously modified. In his *The New Commonwealth and Its Constitutions*, he asserted that: "If the upper houses in the East and Western Regions may be criticized as partly artificial creations, this cannot be said of the Northern House of Chiefs, which wields an influence commensurate with the difference traditionally paid to its members in their capacities as customary rulers."[72] This would now have to be rephrased: The influence of the

House of Chiefs is only commensurate with the support the Emirs give the Government. For as the Emir of Borgu, Alhaji Mohammadu Sani, humorously exhorted the House, "It is better to keep standing than sitting for anything pushed while standing will move faster than one pushed while sitting". It was necessary to stand because the Governor (Sir Kashim) "in the past . . . was my servant, but now he is my master". He added: "And it is essential that a servant praises his master."[73] In many senses, the North's second chamber is no more than a place where praises are sung. Changing the metaphor, one moves faster that way.

II. PARTY AND THE BUREAUCRACY

A parliamentary form of government presupposes that the governing party, through its Ministers, must control the administrative apparatus if it is to impress on the latter the party's conception of the public interest. The bureaucracy not only originates proposals for legislation but could also influence the direction of new policy and it is of the essence of party government that in neither case should these drives run counter to the dominant inclinations of the party in power. The party can meet the requirements of accountability only if it can bring under control those actions which are likely to touch party policy or to produce party embarrassment. In this aspect however, the bureaucracy confronted the party in power with two problems. The first was largely structural. The second dealt mainly with the personnel of the administration.

Between 1952 and 1957, the administrative apparatus consisted largely of a heterogenous, unco-ordinated collection of 'ministries' and departments each headed by a Director who more often than not was a specialist.[74] When party politicians were appointed Ministers in 1952, these exercised no control over, nor were they able to influence the directions of, policy. A change from this situation occurred in 1954 when the new Constitution provided for Permanent Secretaries who were to be administrative heads of Ministries and were to be responsible to the Minister who became formally charged with responsibility for matters under the provenance of his Ministry. But curiously, the Governor as the head of the Executive resisted any attempt at reorganization of the bureaucracy to conform with the constitutional changes. The Secretaries (Permanent Secretaries) who were appointed in 1952 remained as liaison officers between Ministers and the Directors who continued to retain administrative control, and policy, in their respective departments. But unlike the

Eastern and Western regions of Nigeria, most Northern Ministers were already familiar with the realities of administration, long experience of which they had acquired in the Native Administration. Political power without the ability to translate this into administrative actuality they found meaningless. Dissatisfaction thus mounted particularly between the years 1955 and 1957, and led to schemes being proposed for the integration of departments into Ministries. After the regional elections of 1956, the Governor, Sir Brian Sharwood-Smith, who held the key to administrative change was induced to enforce integration which began in 1957. The North thus laid the pattern which first the East, then the West and the Federation (finally Ghana) was to follow.

Integration raised the problem of the relation of the Directors of departments to the new Permanent Secretaries. The solution adopted was the abolition of the office of Directors and their conversion into 'Advisers' with limited functions. This preserved the promotional pyramid while allowing for the self-liquidation of the Advisers themselves. Though a short-term measure, the new arrangement was administratively unsatisfactory. The conversion rested on a misconception which confused policy—what one might term 'policy-making' ministries, for instance, the Ministry of Finance, with Ministries which are largely 'executive agencies' such as the Ministry of Works and Transport. By retaining the former Directors as Advisors, the problem of 'adjustment' of specialists to being subordinated to 'non-professional' administrators was left unsolved. Specialists can admittedly provide the authoritative knowledge needed for the resolution of differences of technical opinion. With integration adjustment was achieved gradually with the absorption of these specialists into the technical and professional classes and in some cases their becoming administrative heads of Ministries. From 1957, integration proceeded rapidly and Ministries were organized into individual effectively self-contained units. This solved the structural problem and provided the framework for party control of the administrative apparatus.

Nevertheless, integration left the question of personnel untouched. While the neutrality of members of the Civil Service was not questioned, party politicians wished to have as administrators those who, they felt, were committed to the ideals commonly held by the society. In other words, men who would more readily appreciate party policies and therefore be loyal to the party in power. Yet by 1955 there was hardly a single Northerner in the administrative class of the public service. The party accordingly promulgated the policy of 'Northernization'. Late in that year, five Northerners were appointed to the administrative grades as Assistant District Officers. By mid-1958, the position had slightly improved as shown in the following table:

TABLE 16

Indigenization of the Higher Levels of the Northern Civil Service
1st June 1958

	Northern Nigerians	Southern Nigerians	'Ex-patriates'
Superscale	5	—	195 + 17
Administrative and Professional	69	23 + 3	612 + 400
Executive and Higher Technical	237 + 8	261 + 7	124 + 341

NOTE: The numerals after the additive symbol signifies the numbers whose employment were on contract terms.
SOURCE:[1] N.H.A. Debates, 4th August 1958, cols. 731–32.

'Northernization' was defined by the Regional Public Service Commission as a system wherein "if a qualified Northerner is available, he is given priority in recruitment; if no Northerner is available, an expatriate may be recruited or a non-Northerner on contract terms".[76] In 1958 it was interpreted by the Premier and NPC President, Sir Ahmadu Bello, as a policy which aimed to have "Northerners gain control of everything in this country".[77] Its practical implementation thus extended beyond the public services to include all aspects of economic life,[78] but only the public services will concern us. Here, the definition given to the term by the NPSC showed clearly the categories of persons involved and their relative order of importance. 'Non-Northerners' would normally have included 'expatriates', but by making the latter a separate category, the term referred exclusively to Southern Nigerians. In effect, so far as the public service were concerned, Northernization became a policy which aimed at excluding all Southern Nigerians from the regional bureaucracy.

By 1957, with the integration of 'departments' into Ministries and the vesting of practical control of the administrative machinery in the Ministers, northernization became a paramount party and governmental policy in pursuance of which Southerners in the public services were 'encouraged' to seek employment in their respective regions while the promotion prospects of those who remained were frozen. By October 1959 there was but one Southern Nigerian left in the Northern public service. So rapid was the pace of northernization that though in 1955 the precentage of Northerners in the civil service was negligible, by mid-1961, the figure had exceeded the 50% mark. The following table gives an indication of the pace of Northernization.

TABLE 17

Northerners in the Northern Civil Service 1961 to 1963

	1961	1962	1963
Superscale	62	65	69
Scales A & B (professional and Administrative)	225	290	404
Scale C (executive and Higher Technical)	733	815	929
Clerical and other junior grades	(a)	7,729	7,817

NOTE: (a) non-available.
SOURCES: Figures for 1961 from Report of the PSC for the period 1st January to December 1961, Kaduna 1962. Those for 1962 and 1963, ibid., for the period 1st January to 31st December 1963, Kaduna, 1964.

By 1961 of the thirty-seven combined posts of Permanent Secretaries, Residents and heads of departments, fourteen were held by Northerners, the remaining twenty-three by 'expatriates', eight of whom were about to retire. And whereas by 1959 all thirteen Permanent Secretaries were expatriates, in 1963 the figure had dwindled to four though there were now sixteen Permanent Secretaries. In the same year eleven of the thirteen provinces had Northerners as Provincial Secretaries—the former Residents.

Besides indigenizing the bureaucracy, Northernization has political and administrative implications. Taking the political implications, in the first place, it has meant, in a narrower sense, party political domination of the civil service. Of the twelve Permanent Secretaries in 1963, four were at one time or the other active party men.[79] Two of these, Ibrahim Dasuki, in local government and Ibrahim Argungu in Establishments and Training were once NPC members of the regional Assembly. The other two, Ali Akilu, Secretary to the Premier and official head of the Civil Service was an early member of the JMA and a convener of the Second Convention of the party in 1950, whilst Dr. Dikko was a founder member of the JMA and for three years its president. Similarly, most of the Provincial Secretaries were at one time or the other active in the party and one of these, Yahaya Gusau (once an Acting Permanent Secretary) was for a period, a member of the regional legislature. In addition, both the Chairman and the Permanent Commissioner of the region's Public Service Commission, Abubakar Imam and Dan Buram Jada respectively, were also at one time members of the Regional Assembly, the latter having been a Regional Minister.

Secondly, Northernization has resulted in the region's top bureaucrats being drawn from the same socio-political group as the parliamentarians and Ministers. In effect this means the concentration of political and administrative power in the hands of the narrow class of top Native Authority officials who were part and parcel of the traditional ruling oligarchy.

TABLE 18

Characteristics of 40 Northerners in the Superscale Grade of the Northern Public Service (compiled from Northern Region Disposition List, August 1963)

	Total	% N.A	% Far North	% Sokoto and Bornu	% Lower North
Superscale total	40	62·5	62·5	40·0	37·5
Permanent secretaries	12	63·0	72·0	54·0	27·0
Provincial secretaries	11	81·0	45·0	45·0	54·0

The fairly high proportion of the top-level offices going to the far North and particularly to Sokoto and Bornu has led some critics to describe the process of Northernization as 'Sokotonization'.[80] Whilst Sokoto influence may have been expected (both the Premier and Akilu are from Sokoto) 'Bornu-ization' can be explained only by reference to latent Bornu separatism which would make of 'Northernization' merely another form of political patronage.[81]

Lastly, the conversion of the bureaucracy into an avenue of party patronage raises the question of the impartiality or rather neutrality of the civil service. Party political considerations in Civil Service appointments were brought out, by implication, in the statement of the Accountant General to the Public Accounts Joint Committee meeting (Session 1962/63): "Mr. Chairman, where a vacancy occurs, it is the responsibility of the head of a division of the Ministry to indent for a replacement. This has been done regularly by myself since I came to the position to do so, and over the past two years, we have had up to eleven vacancies out of an overall establishment of thirty-two senior staff. Several of these vacancies have been filled without any reference to myself. Had they been referred to me, I would have had to refuse the officers so recruited."[82]

While it is understandable that the NPC would wish to have known and trusted party men in the Civil Service, this however, makes the neutrality of the bureaucracy suspect, at least to non-party men and the opposition. Thus, for example, electoral administration in the North has been criticized by the opposition on the grounds that the civil servants cannot be relied upon to act impartially. Similarly, most opposition members believe that it is in practice, impossible to expect any sense of 'fair play' or redress against administrative injustice, from a service which they regard as politically biased against them. Whatever may be the merits of the criticisms of the opposition, it cannot be denied that the politicization of the Civil Service by the NPC will raise serious difficulties in the highly improbable, though not impossible, event of the opposition coming to power in the North.

There are other problems raised by Northernization. There is first, the factor of educational differentiation. Only 16·6% or two of the twelve Permanent Secretaries are graduates. Most, if not all, of the top civil servants with a Native Administration background have no post-secondary grammar school educational qualification. The educational experience of the general class from which all of these men derive is not dissimilar from that shown in the following table of a not unrepresentative sample of N.A. Councillors and departmental heads.

TABLE 19

Educational qualifications of N.A. Functionaries in Selected Emirates[83]

Emirate	Province	Illi-terate	Pri-mary	Secon-dary			1 yr. or under UK training	Av. No. of yrs. NA Ex-perience	Av. Age	Total
				2	4	6				
Sokoto	Sokoto	–	–	–	5	1	2	21·5	45	8
Ilorin	Ilorin	–	–	–	4	1	3	18·0	41	8
Zaria	Zaria	3	1	–	8	1	–	16·0	43	13
Katsina	Katsina	4	3	2	12	2	3	24·0	44	22
Igbirra	Kabba	–	2	9	5	–	–	14·0	37	16
Fika	Bornu	5	6	6	4	2	–	17·0	45	23

Given the limited education of most of these men (which may or may not have been supplemented with a further nine months training at the Institute of Administration, Zaria) and the fact that they now hold the top offices, it would be unreasonable not to expect that they would be resented by the crop of graduates whom the North now seek to recruit into its administrative grade.[84] These not unnaturally tend to look on the N.A.-type as unqualified for the office he holds and therefore constituting an unjustified impediment to their progress in the service.[85]

A second factor derives from the high likelihood of provincial or sectorial differences. While the 'far North' have so far tended to predominate in the top-ranks, the new crop of administrative grade civil servants are more likely to come from the 'lower North'. Thus of the thirty-nine students who entered Ahmadu Bello University in 1962 to read for degrees in Administration and Law respectively—and most of these would make the Civil Service their career—66·6% are from the lower North. The percentage intake from this area in 1963 is higher, this being 84·0%.[86] In other words, Northernization is creating a situation in which the upper reaches of the administrative class are dominated by N.A.-type men largely from the far North with relatively poor education but long administrative experience, while the bottom ranks of that class may soon be filled by younger graduates from lower North. The position is made no less easier by being complicated by what one might very loosely term 'class' divisions in that while those from the far North tend to be associated with the families of the traditional ruling oligarchy, Chiefs, district heads and so on, those from the lower North have more humble social antecedents being sons of farmers, traders and artisans of varying skills. An analysis of the social origins of students undertaking the administrative Service Training Course at the Institute of Administration is very suggestive in this respect.[87] Most of the students from the lower North had parents in Group C with a few in Group B, while those from far North fell largely into the Group A category, again with some in the B class. Those from the far North with Group B antecedents tended to have parents who are N.A. employees.

Thus far, the aim has been to trace the influence of party politics on the bureaucracy and the relation between the two. Most observers would hardly deny that civil servants have been fairly reticent in seizing the obvious opportunities open to them to influence political decision making.[88] But as the volume of government business continues to increase, as it must, it is apparent that civil servants will have to show greater initiative if bottlenecks in the decision making process are to be prevented. The historical experience of the 'developed' nations certainly suggests this. Such initiative, however, presupposes

TABLE 20

Social Origins of Administrative Cadres—Institute of Administration Zaria
(in %)

Father's Occupation	1957	1958	1959	1960	1961
GROUP A					
Chief	—	—	4·0	4·0	—
Traditional title holder	6·0	22·0	18·0	32·0	36·0
Alkali/Koranic Mallams	19·0	18·0	11·0	4·0	4·0
GROUP B					
Government Employee	6·0	—	—	—	—
N.A. Employee	19·0	15·0	8.0	15·0	8·0
Commercial/corporation employee	6·0	—	—	—	—
GROUP C					
Farmer	37·0	37·0	41·0	31·0	36·0
Trader	—	4·0	11·0	7·0	8·0
Evangelist	—	—	—	4·0	4·0
Tailor/carpenter/messenger/ labourer	6·0	4·0	7·0	7·0	4·0

reasonably efficient bureaucratic machinery. But the burden of Northernization on the other hand, has been to create, it is argued, situations which are likely to be dysfunctional for an effective, smoothly operating bureaucracy. The feed-back effect of this is not unlikely to retard the process of political development with a consequent realignment of political forces. But it is difficult to predict precisely what form a realignment of political forces will take. It should be emphasized at this point that the intention has not been to question the desirability or otherwise of Northernization. The concern has been mainly and strictly diagnostic, not prescriptive.

It only needs be added to the foregoing (though there is no adequate supporting data) that Northernization has tended to engender an ethnocentric outlook in the North. As a Northerner put it (Alhaji Abdul Razaq), "Northernization, in its psychological effects, is turning the North and northerners into introverts such that nothing is good for the North which is not Northern".[89] This would entail a denial that there could be claims which override Northern interests and therefore constitute a stumbling block to the over-all progress of the federation. For instance, the refusal of the North to permit the exploitation of iron ore located in that region were the ore-using industry not to be sited in the North. The proposed steel industry was so held up for three years while discussions continued in the National Economic Council.[90] Though the consensus of opinion seems to have been that the most economic location was somewhere around Port Harcourt in the Eastern Region, Northern intransigence finally led to the decision to have two plants, one in the East, the other in the North.[91] The unhealthy competition which such an attitude creates was best symbolized by the 'Census Crisis' of 1962 and constitutes a threat to the stability of the federation. Some aspects of this competition will be examined later.

For the present, the results of the analysis may be summarized. This has shown that party organization in the legislature has led not only to the domination of the legislature by the Government but also to the suppression of the parliamentary opposition and the abandonment by back-benchers of their parliamentary role. The same process has resulted in a curtailment of the powers of the traditional Chiefs who must now support, of necessity, the Government. In consequence, the traditional class of native authority functionaries have emerged as the dominant political class, who as a result of Northernization have also succeeded in extending their control into and over the regional bureaucracy, power being vested largely in the hands of the former Native Authority functionaries from the Far North. Even within this group, the influence of Sokoto and Bornu seems to have greater predominance. But this influence has not been without its cost—these being, specifically within the bureaucracy, a lowering of standards of efficiency and a polarisation into far North and lower North sectors—of the public service itself. Since this is likely to retard political development the continued authority of the present ruling oligarchy must necessarily depend on how effectively it can ensure communication between the sectors and upward mobility to those from the lower North.

NOTES

1. This of course is hardly what Bryce meant by his aphoristic statement describing the party system as "the best instrument for the suppression of dissident minorities that democracy has yet devised". Lord Bryce, *Modern Democracies*, 2 vols., London 1921, vol. 2, p. 44.

2. V. O. Key, *Politics, Parties and Pressure Groups*, N. Y., 4th edition 1961, p. 702–3.

3. Ibid., p. 703.

4. N.N.L. number 33 of 1963.

5. Membership of the Assembly was increased from 91 in 1952 to 131 in 1956 and from that to 177 in 1961 and 230 in 1965. For 'attributes' of the members from 1952 to 1956, see Coleman, *Nigeria, Background to Nationalism*, pp. 380–383, and B. J. Dudley, op. cit., p. 50.

6. Like the Assembly, the composition of the House of Chiefs has also varied. In 1952, this was 49, 1956, 78, 1960, 76 and 1964, 85. Besides the most august Emirs, such as those of Sokoto, Gwandu, Bornu, Kano, Bauchi Katsina, Zaria and a few others, the designation of a chief is determined by the Governor-in-Council. The membership of the House was increased to 110 in 1965.

7. See J. P. Mackintosh, 'The Nigerian Federal Parliament', *Public Law*, autumn 1963, pp. 333–61.

8. No member of the opposition is at the time of writing (August 1964) included in this committee, the opposition member having crossed over to the NPC.

9. This was denied by the Expatriate Acting Civil Secretary in 1953—after this statement, the Secretary was made to resign from the Government of the North.

10. N.H.A. Debates, 25th November 1953, pp. 53–58.

11. Ibid., Government Printer, Kaduna, 1951. See *Nigerian Citizen*, 10th July 1952. Action on the Report was shelved, partly because of this opposition of members, and partly because of opposition from the Emirs and Chiefs. The report was resuscitated in 1954 and became the groundwork of the Native Authority Law 1954.

12. Between 1952 and 1954, members of the Federal Legislature were also members of their respective regional legislatures from which they were chosen.

13. N.H.A. Debates, 20th February 1954, p. 244. Balewa himself criticized the Report saying ". . . in this House I am a floor member, and I am at liberty, like any other member to criticize the Regional government". Ibid., p. 242.

14. In a broadcast talk on 'The Duties of Regional Ministers', 19th June 1952.

15. The present (1964) Ministers are drawn from the various Provinces in the following order—two each from Kano, Bornu and Sokoto (excluding the Premier), three from Katsina, one each from Niger, Bauchi, Plateau, Adamawa and Zaria. None from Benue. The population factor refers to the population size of the various provinces.

16. Alhaji Pategi, then Parliamentary Secretary to the Minister of Education, expressed the relationship between the Minister and his Parliamentary Secretary thus: ". . . and so in the Parliamentary policy, the Parliamentary Secretaries are the Ministers' bodyguards"—the analogical reference being the Emir and his bodyguards—a servile relationship. N.H.A. Debates, 22nd February 1957, p. 109.

17. N.H.A. Debates, 10th March 1955, p. 2.

18. N.H.A. Debates, 10th August 1955, p. 127. The bill was passed with only a minor amendment from the Premier, the Sardauna of Sokoto.

19. N.H.A. Debates, 7th August 1956, p. 125.

20. A similar Committee was introduced into the Federal Assembly at the same time. See *Nigerian Citizen*, 20th January 1955. A 'Parliamentary Committee' was in fact proposed as early as 1952 (*Nigerian Citizen*, 19th June 1952) but no action was taken.

21. In some instances, however, members merely do not follow up questions and accept Ministerial answers as final. Thus, when a member asked why there were no Tivs in the Civil Service or any given a regional scholarship, he was told that no scholarship had been given to the Tivs because there were none suitably qualified. Debates, 7th March 1957, p. 666 and 9th March 1957, p. 770. In neither

instance did the member think it worth while asking what was being done to remedy this situation.

22. Constituents have always complained of the lack of interest shown in their affairs by their elected representatives. Letters of protest in the newspapers (even as early as 1952, *Nigerian Citizen*, 21st and 28th February 1952; 6th and 20th March; 3rd, 10th, 15th and 24th April; 29th May; 19th June 1952 for a representative selection—the list can be extended for any year) have had no effect whatsoever in changing attitudes. Most people now accept the fact that a member only revisits his constituents when seeking re-election or re-nomination.

23. This includes even the back-benchers themselves. In 1957, the President (later Speaker) had to warn members "to resist the temptation of packing their bags before the business is over", adding that "I would also remind Honourable members that it is not correct to rush out of the Chamber before the President has left his seat after the adjournment". Debates, 23rd February 1957, pp. 175–76.

24. Debates, 6th March 1956, cols. 179–222 and 26th February 1957, cols. 250–94.

25. Debates, 8th March 1957, p. 717. The decision to introduce a system of balloting was in fact taken by the President after criticism by government back-benchers that too much time was being given to the opposition.

26. Motion for the Abolition of Corporal Punishment—Debates 4th March 1958, pp. 470 ff., and Motion for a Commission to Probe Lawlessness in Tiv Division, Debates 19th April 1960 pp. 314 ff. The Motion for the Protection of Minorities debated 12th March 1957, pp. 836 ff. got on the Order Paper before the system of balloting was to be introduced. It was actually one of the points of complaint by back-benchers—see previous note.

27. The present Standing Orders of the House were formulated by a Committee of the House in 1956. It was based largely on the Standing Orders of the House of Commons and thus provides a good example of an uncritical copying which does not take local conditions sufficiently into consideration.

28. N.H.A. Debates, 12th March 1963, p. 234.

29. That members of the Assembly look to the British Commons as a 'model' and source of inspiration is shown by the Debates, e.g. 25th February 1957, p. 179; 12th March 1957, p. 838.

30. H. Laski, *Parliamentary Government in England*, Allen & Unwin, 5th imp. 1952, p. 166.

31. The lack of control of public expenditure is shown in the following tables of cases of over-expenditure in recent years:

Year	No. of Excesses	Amount of Excesses
1960–1961	172	£404,776
1961–1962	142	£276,804
1962–1963	104	£255,968

Excess expenditure for 1960/61 received parliamentary sanction by the Third Supplementary Estimates NNL no. 4 of 1962—*Report of the Director of Audit on the Accounts of the Government of Northern Nigeria for the year ended 31st March 1963*, Government Printer, Kaduna, 1964, p. 146.

32. The expatriate editor of the *Nigerian Citizen* (and general manager of the Gaskiya Corporation, publishers of the *Nigerian Citizen*) who criticized this in an editorial was obliged to resign after this attack on the Government.

33. Public Accounts Joint Committee Session 1962–63: Minutes of Evidence—ordered to be printed 6th March 1963, Government Printer, Kaduna, p. 152.

34. Ibid., p. 23.

35. *Daily Express* (Lagos), 4th August 1964.

36. Besides radio and television, the main newspapers (in 1961) are all controlled by the Government, either directly or indirectly. These are the *Nigerian Citizen* (bi-weekly newspaper, circulation c. 22,000), the *Gaskiya Tafi Kwabo* (Hausa language bi-weekly, circulation c. 23,000); both newspapers are published and printed by the Gaskiya Corporation. *The Northern News* is a Ministry of Information daily release while the *Daily Mail*, a Kano daily begun in 1961, is an NPC party news organ. Other Government-sponsored vernacular newspapers (published fortnightly) are: *Saruma* (Hausa, 12,000); *Gamzaki* (Hausa, 15,000); *Himma, Bazzaga* (both in Hausa, each 7,000); *Zummita* (Hausa 3,000); *Durosi Oto* (Tiv 3,500); *Nnanyitsu* (Nupe 2,500); *Oko-Ane-Igala, Imole* (Igala, 3,500 and 2,500 respectively); *Oka K'Idoma* (Idoma, 3,500); *Igbirra Boro* (Igbirra, 2,500); *Haske* (Hausa, 3,500). All of these were sponsored by the Northern Literature Agency (NORLA) which was wound up by the Government in 1960. Most of these newspapers were then discontinued. The *Comet* (daily 3,500), the *Middle-Belt Herald* (4,000 daily) and *The Northern Star* (daily 3,500) are opposition (NCNC/NEPU and AG) newspapers, on which see text.

37. The NBC maintains regional stations in three of the four regions. Since it is a Federal Public Corporation, the Northern Government has no control over the Kaduna NBC station, and in the case referred to, the Head of the News Division was immediately removed from the North.

38. See, for example, N.H.A. Debates, 8th April 1960, pp. 68–71; House of Chiefs Debates, 28th March 1963, pp. 30 and 34.

39. M. Duverger, op. cit., p. 357.

40. Ebenezer Williams (Abiodun Aloba), 'Where does power lie?', in *Daily Times*, 26th June 1960.

41. See K. Ezera, *Constitutional Development in Nigeria*, Cambridge, 1960, and O. Odumosu, *The Nigerian Constitution: Its History and Development*, Sweet & Maxwell, 1963.

42. Northern House of Chiefs, Debates, 25th February 1952, p. 14.

43. N.H.C. Debates, 14th February 1953, p. 76.

44. Ibid., pp. 78–79.

45. In 1952, despite pressure for the appointment of a Northerner as Minister of Local Government, the Sardauna who thought such a move was inopportune was reported to have said "who would take it?" *Nigerian Citizen*, 14th April 1952.

46. As a result, the Sultan of Sokoto summoned all Chiefs in the North to an informal meeting at Lugard Hall to discuss the party proposals. The main issue was in fact whether it would be necessary to have the Status of Chiefs constitutionally defined. *Nigerian Citizen*, 20th June 1956.

47. N.H.C. Debates, 26th March 1957, col. 156.

48. Ibid., col. 160.

49. E.g. N.A. (Amendment) Law of 1955 which made the prior approval by the Minister of Local Government a prerequisite for the appointment of any District Head whose salary was over £350 per annum.

50. N.H.C. Debates, 24th March 1955, p. 11.

51. It should be clear that the President of the House of Chiefs is an additional member to those chosen by that House.

52. Elections (Senate) (Northern Region) Regulations 1959, NRLN No. 121 of 1959. The Northern Region is entitled to a total of twelve Senators in the Federal Senate.

53. Appointment and Deposition of Chiefs Ordinance—Cap. 12 of the Laws of Nigeria 1948. This Ordinance vested in the Governor the power to appoint

and depose Chiefs on his own initiative, but since 1954, the power became exercisable in practice by the Government.

54. N.R. Notice No. 347, Gazette No. 22 vol. 7, 24th April 1958, p. 183, for the formation of the Council. The composition is given in N.N.L. No. 33 of 1963, section 75 (1) and (2).

55. In his autobiography, the Sardauna writes that "my grandmother was a daughter of Dabo, Emir of Kano, and my mother was a Sokoto woman". Ahmadu Bello, *My Life*, p. 5.

56. See for instance, The Bug in Sir A's (Ahmadu's) Turban, *Sunday Express*, 1st July 1962. Sir Ahmadu has not made secret his ambition to succeed to the Sultanate of Sokoto. He need not relinquish his office as Premier either, as the Constitution of Northern Nigeria provides that the Premier could be appointed from either House of the regional legislature. There is, however, little chance of his achieving his ambition, short of the sudden death of the Sultan or his removal by the Government, which most people would doubt. The difference in age between the two men is merely eight years. As a result of the Sardauna's ambition, some observers have suggested that the relations between the two men are far from being cordial. It has also been suggested that as the Sardauna may not be able to succeed the present Sultan, he has attempted instead to usurp some of the traditional functions of the Sultan as leader of the Moslems. For instance, one outcome of the Commission appointed by the Premier to enquire into Islamic Religious Observances (Taron Kwamitin Bada Shawara Kan Al'Amuran Musulunci, N.A. Press, Kano, 1963) is the new practice for the Sardauna to announce over the Northern wireless network the beginning and end of the Moslem Ramaddan, a function traditionally performed by the Sultan, (Incidentally, the colonial government suggested doing precisely this in 1942, but the suggestion was negatived by the Sultan. See Report of the Conference of Chiefs and Emirs of the Northern Provinces, 1942.) Part of this projection of himself as a Moslem leader is the Sardauna's successful attempt in getting himself elected as the Vice-President of the World Muslim Congress.

57. In terms of income, the five largest Native Authorities are Kano, Bornu, Sokoto, Katsina and Zaria. Their revenues and expenditures for 1961–62 and 1962–63 are as follows:

	Expenditure approved Estimate 1961/62	Expenditure Estimate 1962/63	Revenue Revised Estimate 1961/62	Revenue Revised Estimate 1962/63
Kano	£2,152,462	2,396,154	2,125,705	2,280,105
Bornu	1,041,361	1,033,241	1,032,840	1,112,815
Sokoto	1,049,960	1,089,812	1,107,942	1,082,825
Katsina	890,464	948,752	943,234	991,935
Zaria	463,309	478,784	480,594	505,993

SOURCE: *Local Government Year Book 1963*, pp. 44–46.

58. The 'Report', which is confidential, was never published. However, Mr. J. P. Mackintosh succeeded in seeing the Report, I am indebted to him for allowing me to see the comprehensive notes he made from it.

59. 'Speech by the Premier of Northern Nigeria Hon. Alhaji Sir Ahmadu

Bello, K.B.E. The Sardauna of Sokoto to Zaria N.A. Council, 3rd August 1961,'
Kaduna, Government Printer, n.d., p. 2.

60. *Provincial Annual Reports, Northern Nigeria,* 1962, Kaduna Government
Printer, 1963, p. 68.

61. Circular letter No. PM138/98 dated 11th June 1960.

62. Speech of the Premier . . . etc. page 5.

63. The Eastern Nigeria Government, controlled by the NCNC, was the first
to make use of the Provincial Commissioners as a means of "providing jobs for
the boys" but with no system of Chieftaincy comparable to that of the North, it
did not face the same problems discussed in the text.

64. NNL No. 2 of 1962.

65. The law nowhere spells out the relationship between the Commissioner
and the Emirs. This is shown in *"Administrative Instructions to Provincial
Commissioners and Provincial Secretaries"*, Kaduna, Government Printer, n.d.
where it is stated that: ". . . the Provincial Commissioner will take precedence
over all others in that province except Ministers of the Executive Council with
portfolios and members of the Council of Ministers when they are on tour in
their official capacity. In this province, he will be senior to Ministers without
portfolio. He will be senior to a Chief in his Chiefdom", op. cit. pt. 2, paragraph 2,
p. 3, see also paragraphs 6 and 7, p. 4, and pt. 3, paragraph 2, o. 5. The motives
indicated in the text were obtained from interviews with relatives of the ex-Emir.

66. These are not the only people who had a grievance against the Emir. The
list could be extended but this would add nothing to the principle being established.

67. NNL No. 25 of 1962 as amended by NNL No. 19 of 1963.

68. N.H.C. Debates, 11th April 1962, col. 124.

69. N.H.C. Debates, 12th August 1958, dol. 156.

70. Figures for 1961–62 and 1962–63 are £1·7m and £2·0m respectively.

71. See N.H.C. Debates, 2nd April 1963, pp. 116–25. The only dissentient
voice was the Etsu Nupe's, Alhaji Usman Sarki. However, the Ochi'Idoma, Mr.
Ajene Ukpabi, felt he ought to apologize on the Etsu's behalf "because he has
been away from the Region for some time and does not seem to have the idea of
what is going on", ibid., p. 121. The Etsu was from 1959 to 1963 NPC Federal
Minister of Internal Affairs in Lagos.

72. S. A. de Smith, *The New Commonwealth and its Constitutions,* Stevens &
Son, 1964, p. 125. Also pp. 128 and 157.

73. N.H.C. Debates, 28th March 1963, p. 39.

74. The term 'specialist' is here used in much the same sense as Bosanquet's
when he made the distinction between 'specialists' and experts, "the former
denoting members of the 'professional' class, the latter those in the 'administrative' class". See G. C. Field, *Political Theory,* Methuen, 1963 edition, pp. 108–9.

75. Sklar, op. cit., footnote 5, pp. 582–83 quoting a report from a Nigerian
newspaper wrote that only 24 Southerners remained in the Northern Public
Service and that 2,148 had been dismissed between 1954 and 1958. The correct
figures then were 2,148 Southerners on the permanent establishment, 57 dismissed and 20 terminated. Obviously the figures were both reversed and inaccurate. See N.H.A. Debates, 4th August 1958, cols. 731–32.

76. *Report of the Northern Public Service Commission, 1954–57,* Kaduna, 1958.

77. N.H.C. Debates, 18th March 1958, col. 36.

78. For the details of the party's proposals for Northernization see *Nigerian
Citizen,* 15th September 1955. With the publication of the proposals, a plethora
of various commercial pressure groups came into existence—e.g. The Northern
Transporters and Contractors Company, the Northern Nigerian Contractors

Association, the Northern Transport Owners Union and the Northern Amalgamated Merchants Union. All are affiliates of the NPC. Pressure from these groups led to the reassessment of the procedure for awarding Contracts by the Provincial Tenders Boards (see Ministry of Finance Notice published in the *Nigerian Citizen* 8th and 15th November 1958). In response to further pressure, the Government instituted a Commission of Enquiry into Retail Trade in the North 1960. Though its report was never published, it was noticeable immediately afterwards that most retail trade companies found it was inconvenient not to have Northerners in their employment. By 1963, besides the Lebanese, most expatriate retail firms had given up their retail trade.

79. Mr. R. B. K. Oakafor in his *Report of the Recent* (*1961*) *North Regional Elections* wrote, for example, that before the elections there was an instruction from heads of Ministries to Sectional heads ordering them to impress on those under them the necessity to vote the NPC ticket. Kaduna which had previously been an opposition 'stronghold' was lost to the NPC. And in a letter from the NPC Administrative Secretary to the Administrator of Kaduna Capital Territory (Kaduna became a Native Authority in 1962) dated 18th November 1960, the Administrative Secretary requested that on instructions from Party National Secretary, all leases of land in Kaduna should be first referred to the party.

80. The opposition made this one of their campaign issues at the 1961 regional elections. See the writer's, 'The North's Quiet Election', *West Africa*, 6th May 1961.

81. 'Bornu-ization' cannot be explained in terms of relative literacy figures. According to the 1952 census figures, next to Kano Bornu had the lowest literacy percentage of the provinces of the North, this being 0·9%. In the 'sample' of the 40 superscale men, 22·5% are from Bornu with 25% for Permanent Secretaries and 27% for Provincial Secretaries.

82. Public Accounts Joint Committee Meeting Session 1962–63: Minutes of Evidence, Kaduna, n.d., p. 37.

83. The table is compiled from *Selected characteristics of Key N.A. officials* by G. W. Fairholm, Institute of Administration Zaria, mimeographed, November 1963.

84. The Governor of the North announced in late 1962 that as from 1963 the North would only recruit graduates into the Administrative class of the Civil Service. In their *Staffing and Development of the Public Service of Northern Nigeria*, mimeographed, January 1961, Dr. Kingsley and Sir Arthur N. Rucker estimated that the North would then need about 105 graduates to 'Northernise' fully. This figure would obviously need to be revised upwards in the light of the six-year Development Plan.

85. There is little hope of the N.A. type retiring early enough to make room for the 'new generation'. The age structure of the forty superscale men already noted is as follows:

Age Range	% Total	N.A. %	63 Law and Admin. Undergraduates at Ahmadu Bello University, Zaria —1st and 2nd Year
20–29	10·0	8·0	94·0
30–39	62·5	56·0	6·0
40–49	17·5	24·0	—
50 +	10·0	12·0	—

86. It is interesting to note that a number of these students already have no illusions about their prospects in the Civil Service. Information supplied by A. H. M. Kirk-Greene.

87. Data owed to Mr. A. H. M. Kirk-Greene, who is, however, not responsible for the interpretation given here.

88. In part, this can be accounted for in terms of the paramountcy of politics over all else in developing nations, in part, to the nature of the bureaucracy itself.

89. When in the debate on the 'Address' in 1955, the Government announced that in pursuance of its 'Northernization' policy, the decision had been made to import 238 officers from the Sudan, the opposition criticized this on the grounds of the expense involved and suggested recruitment from the South. The Sardauna's reply was: "What is the South? We face the East . . ." N.H.A. Debates 4th March 1955, p. 15. Obviously religious differences play some part in the North's ethnocentricism.

90. The NEC was set up after the International Bank for Reconstruction and Development *Report on the Economic Development of Nigeria* recommended it. The NEC has an advisory role and exists to co-ordinate regional and federal economic planning.

91. See *Daily Times* (Lagos), 13th May 1964. Rather than one plant with a ½m. tons capacity, the decision in effect means two plants each with half that capacity and therefore less economic to run.

VII

Aspects of Grass Roots Politics

The last chapter dealt with some of the facets of regional politics, or, adapting the terminology of the economists, what may be regarded as macro-politics. Here, an attempt will be made to bring out some of the aspects of politics at the local or micro-level. In some respects, we shall be concerned with forms of community power structure.[1] Though insights into this have already been given in previous chapters, the intention is here to draw together the main issues in order to put these into better perspective. Some repetitiveness may thus be unavoidable. But first, some distinctions are necessary, in particular that between areas with concentrations of heterogeneous ethnic groups and those with a fairly homogeneous population. Homogeneity and its converse heterogeneity are here defined largely in terms of historico-cultural patterns. Thus, while the Hausa–Fulani–Kanuri are regarded as constituting a homogeneous group, the combination of Birom, Hausa, Ibo and Yoruba is regarded as heterogeneous. In such a perspective, the Jos area of Plateau province would be the main area with a heterogeneous mixed population, and all other areas would be largely homogeneous. Jos district in fact has the peculiarity of being the only area in the North where the indigenous inhabitants are more than outnumbered by the non-indigenes, and in the division as a whole, it is the only area where non-indigenes constitute more than half the total population. Table 20 contrasts Jos with some other areas.

The Biroms are indigenous to the Jos district as the Hausa–Fulani are to the Sokoto–Kano–Zaria areas. In crude terms then, the distinction being made can be stated in terms of an indigene—'settler' basis. Unlike the areas contrasted with it, the Jos district has been fairly recently settled, and it might be thought that the distinction being made is not dissimilar to Southall's suggestion of the "broad contrast between old established, slowly growing towns and new populations of mushroom growth".[2] This would, however, be misleading. In the first place, Southall's distinction was drawn with a sociological orientation, not political. Secondly, the term town

TABLE 21

Ethnic Composition of Selected Areas in Northern Nigeria

Area	Total Population	Fulani	Hausa	Ibo	Yoru-ba	Birom
Jos Division	246,406	20,238	45,299	19,283	8,274	114,003
Jos District	31,582	914	13,183	8,889	5,061	279
Jos Township	6,945	164	436	3,794	835	125
Bukuru Town	8,450	307	2,477	3,516	1,109	107
Kano Division	2,822,414	836,730	1,813,340	12,225	7,498	—
Kano City District	127,204	12,119	88,715	11,135	5,783	—
Sokoto Division	2,020,340	316,972	1,423,103	3,059	2,764	—
Gusau District	86,601	19,915	61,658	1,440	975	—
Zaria Division	795,922	82,287	360,443	17,997	9,531	—
Zaria City District	59,389	11,216	44,125	614	525	—
Zaria Sabongari District	30,538	2,706	14,881	6,282	3,711	—

NOTE: The figures are based on the 1952 Census. Kano City district, Gusau district and Zaria City and Sabongari districts, have been chosen as contrasts because like Jos, they are important commercial centres.

(township), has no single clear meaning in the North. Administratively, 'township' would refer only to the Government Reservation Area (GRA) and the commercial areas inhabited by non-Nigerians. There are only three townships, Kano, Jos and Zaria, in this sense, in the whole of the North. On the other hand, politically, 'town' may refer to those areas which elect representatives to a Town Council. Thus Zaria Town Council contains elected members from Zaria City, Tudun Wada (traditionally inhabited by non-Zaria Hausas, but no longer exclusively so), Sabon-gari and the 'Township'. Lastly, the distinction between the 'new' and the 'old' is by no means clear cut.

The same 'town' may contain both a 'new' and an 'old', for instance, Jos town itself and between any two towns, e.g. Makurdi in Benue Province and Gusau in Sokoto Province, it may be impossible to say which is new or which old, or whether both are new or old. In view of these objections, the distinction which Southall seeks to make should not be confused with that suggested above.

I. POLITICAL COMPETITION IN AREAS WITH
HETEROGENOUS POPULATIONS

In these areas, political activity centres around ethnic competition for political and economic power. Nowhere is this perhaps better exemplified than in the Jos District.

Until about the 1920's the Jos district was little more than scattered villages.[3] The discovery and exploitation of tin casseterite during this period provided the main impetus to the development and settlement of the area. The paucity of labourers and medium skilled workers resulted in an artificially inflated wage rate—which in 1927 rose as high as 6s. 7d. per day, roughly 300% higher than the average wage elsewhere in the country. The high wages attracted a host of workers most of whom were Hausa. As, however, these lacked skill and tended to leave the mines after working for a couple of weeks, Southerners, mainly Ibo, were recruited to provide the base of stable workers for the expanding mining industry.[4] An urban concentration rapidly developed and with it a further influx of Southerners—Ibo and Yoruba—to provide secondary and tertiary services.

With the development of a Native Authority in the Jos district, it was inevitable that control over the native population should be vested in the Hausas amongst whom had emerged a local leader, the Sarkin Hausawa. Both the economy and the local administrative machinery were thus in the hands of non-indigenous settlers whilst the indigenous Biroms remained 'subject', landless peasants as more and more of the fertile alluvial plains were handed over by concessionary leases to the mining companies.

The reaction to this situation was the formation of the Birom Progressive Union already noted in Chapter III. Subsequently agitation led to the appointment in 1947 of a Birom, Mallam Rwang Pam, as the Chief of Jos and head of the Native Authority. Confronted by the Birom Progressive Union, the Hausa formed the Hausa Tribal Party as an affiliate to the NPC. To retain whatever political advantage they succeeded in acquiring under the leadership of the Chief of Jos, most Biroms have turned NPC. Nevertheless Hausa–Birom competition has remained the dominant issue in local Native Authority politics. It was central to the dispute within the NPC in 1958 when the party split into two as a result of the attempt by the Native Authority to remove Hausas employed by the Native Authority and to replace them by Biroms. One faction, led by the Hausa President of the Jos Branch, Alhaji Audu Gobe-zan-tashi, contended that the Chief of Jos should be removed in favour of a

Hausa Chief. As Rwang Pam, as Chief of Jos, was also President of the Jos Town Council, besides being head of the Native Authority Council, they also proposed that the President of the Town Council should be elected from amongst its elected members. The other faction led by the Provincial President, Alhaji Isa Haruna, a Hausa, wanted the Birom Chief of Jos to continue in office. A section of the Regional Government led by the Party Secretary-General, Abba Habib, a regional Minister, supported the vocal yet influential minority faction led by Gobe-zan-tashi in opposition to the majority faction led by Haruna.[5] Haruna, unlike Gobe-zan-tashi, was more interested in having Hausa men as chairmen of the committees of the Native Authority Council since in the last analysis it is these men who would control the Council. The dispute was only partially resolved by the intervention of the Premier, the Sardauna of Sokoto, but largely through the realization that the Biroms in the meantime had succeeded in getting most of their men elected to the fifteen district councils from which would be elected members to the Native Authority Council.

Ethnic competition between the Birom and the Hausa is, in effect, competition to control sources of patronage and economic profit. Since the Native Authority Council is the main policy making organ for the area, the chairmen of the Council's important Committees have fairly wide discretionary powers. Hence, ethnic rivalry becomes competition to control those committees, such as the General Purposes Committee, the Financial Committee and the Establishments Committee. It was the Chairmanship of the Establishments Committee by a Birom, Bitrus Rwang Pam, the son of the Chief of Jos, which enabled the Committee in 1958 to initiate the move to terminate the appointments of Hausas in the employ of the Native Authority. Similarly the rivalry which flared up again in 1961 can be traced to the dispute between Bitrus Pam, newly elected member of the Jos Divisional Council and Chairman of the Native Authority Lands Committee and Alhaji Ali Kazaure, NPC Divisional President, President of the Town Council and Chairman of the Native Authority Plots Allocation Advisory Committee (PAAC). Bitrus had wanted the functions of the Plots Allocation Committee transferred to his Lands Committee because Kazaure and his supporters were deriving 'benefits' from being members of the PAAC. The PAAC. which controlled the distribution of lands in the Jos area discriminated against the Biroms.[6] Local politics thus becomes the politics of the American 'spoils system' irrespective of party labels since the contestants were all NPC.

A consequence of the 'spoils system' has been inefficiency and was alluded to in the *Provincial Annual Report* for 1962 which noted that "the standard of efficiency of many of its departments . . . is woefully low, in most cases due to the poor example set by some Heads of Departments. As a result of the Committee system through which Jos Native Authority now functions there is no 'executive Council' and no councillors with portfolio and the Native Authority is finding it difficult to discipline and supervise the work of its inefficient Heads of Departments."[7] Corruption and graft thus go unquestioned for as the same Report also pointed out "goods and services continued to be bought from local shops and stalls far in excess of their recognized local purchase price".[8]

Inevitably such a situation creates a problem for the regional government. Should the government interfere in the activities of the Council, it would be accused of being autocratic or of supporting one faction or the other, the Biroms against the Hausas or vice-versa, yet the ultimate cost of mismanagement has to be borne, in the long run, by the regional government. In April 1964 for instance, the Minister of Local Government was compelled to set aside the recommendations of the Council in respect of the appointments of the President and the Chairmen of Committees and appointed other persons instead. He also ordered, against the wishes of a majority of the Councillors who are Biroms, that Bitrus Pam, Jos Divisional Secretary of the NPC should cease to be a member of the Council, though Pam was elected. The reaction to this was a 'walk-out' by sixty-two members of the seventy-man Council.[9] Bitrus Pam on the other hand interpreted the act of the Minister as directed specifically against the Biroms and in protest against 'Hausa domination' resigned from the NPC and rejoined the opposition UMBC. While the 'walk-out' may be taken as a show of resentment, more significant however is the Minister's action in placing the day-to-day administration under the direction of the provincial authorities—the provincial arm of the regional bureaucracy. The Jos case is by no means an isolated one. It merely conforms to recent trends,[10] and it raises the important question as to whether the Native Authority system can still be regarded as *local government* in the general connotation of that expression. Present trends may be only a transitional phase in the movement from the traditional Native Authority system towards a more rational form of local administration and any attempt to answer the question posed may therefore be premature.

The Native Authority may be regarded as the central institution around which the main political struggles revolve but no account of local politics in the Jos division will be complete which does not take into consideration the politics of the mining unions—the principal interest groups in the area. Here, as in the Native Authority, ethnic interests are paramount.

Though there are some fifty-three registered mining companies operating in the Jos area, the industry itself is dominated largely by four of these; the Amalgamated Tin Mines of Nigeria which is the largest and employs some 34% of the total labour force, Bisichi Tin Company, the Ex-lands Nigeria Limited and the Gold and Base Metal Mines of Nigeria, which combined, employ another 20% of the labour force.[11] Labour on the mines, which provide the mainstay of the economy of the division, is roughly divided into two grades, the skilled workers, largely of Southern origin and mostly Ibo,[12] and the unskilled labourers made up of Ibo, Birom and Hausa with the latter predominating.

The first trade union ever to have been formed by the mine workers was the Nigeria African Mineworkers' Union (NAMU) which was registered in January 1949. NAMU's main strength came from the skilled workers who in late 1949 led a strike for higher wages for the mineworkers. But in the final negotiations to end the strike, the skilled workers came up with a better bargain than the general mass of labourers, and since the former were mainly Southerners, the Hausa treasurer of NAMU, Isa Haruna, immediately criticized the union on the ground that it was Southern, or rather, Ibo, dominated and resigned. The strike was then interpreted as an attempt by the Ibos to obtain better working conditions for themselves. NAMU attempted to include all of the mineworkers, but like many of Nigeria's trade unions, it had scarcely started to function before it was confronted with problems of leadership. The competition came mainly from the ATMN workers who, as the largest single group amongst the workers, broke off to form, in April 1952, the ATMN—African Workers' Union. Both unions thus existing side by side. Both were led by non-Northerners.

Politically, the mineworkers form the main, effectively mobilized social group in the Jos Division. How they voted largely determined any election in the division, and since the two unions were led by non-Northerners, their members were encouraged to vote the non-NPC ticket. Jos Central, in particular has been a stronghold of the opposition NEPU, the northern ally of the NCNC. In such a situation it was to be expected that the few educated Hausa leaders of the mineworkers should accuse the skilled Ibo leaders of the unions of using these organizations for political purposes. Thus to the ethnic division which corresponded roughly to the division between the skilled and the unskilled workers was added a party political division which the NPC, already slowly growing in significance in the area, did not hesitate to exploit by encouraging, with funds, the Hausa former treasurer of the NAMU, Isa Haruna, to form a new union for Northerners only. Haruna, aided by another Hausa Northerner, Audu Dan Ladi therefore inaugurated the Northern Mineworkers' Union in August 1954. The ethnic nature of the NMU is clearly shown by the fact that in 1956, the composition was 75% Hausa, 14% Birom, the remaining 11% being made up of other northern tribes. By 1960 the percentage of Hausas had increased to 95%.[13] In 1957 the NMU opposed any attempt to amalgamate the existing unions into a single body.[14] Since the NMU is affiliated to the NPC, this had led to the NPC-controlled Northern Government being accused of attempting to destroy trade unionism in the North.[15] Whatever the merits of this charge, the fact remains that by restricting membership of the NMU only to Northerners, the union is contravening the labour code governing the formation and registration of trade unions but the 'protection' given the Union by the Northern Government has prevented any attempt to break the union's restrictive membership.[16]

As the existing unions tended more and more to be divided along ethnic lines—NAMN and ATMNAWU being Ibo or rather, non-Northern, NMU Hausa, each apparently orientated towards securing better working conditions and prospects for its supporters, the Biroms were prevailed upon by the AG/UMBC to break off from the NMU, and in 1958 they formed the Birom Mineworkers' Union, which, a year later, was converted into the Middle-Belt Mineworkers' Union.[17] Confronted by the Birom M-BMU and the Hausa NMU, the non-Northerners quickly realized the futility of maintaining two separate Unions. In April 1959, attempts were then made by a Mr. M. K. Iloh to amalgamate both the Nigerian African Mineworkers' Union and the ATMN African Mineworkers' Union,[18] but with their long established loyalties, it was not until 1961 that both could be united into a new Nigerian Mineworkers' Union. Thus by 1961, the three main unions were divided almost exclusively on ethnic lines, the Northern Mineworkers' Union claiming the support of roughly 65% of the workers, the Middle-Belt Mineworkers' Union some 5% while the Nigerian Mineworkers' Union asserted it had the support of at least 30% of the miners. The percentages in fact reflect pretty accurately the ethnic composition of the main groups employed on the mines.

The ethnic competition which has characterized the splintering and formation of trade unions in the mines is by no means peculiar to the mineworkers. It can be said to obtain in all the trade unions in the North with a mixed ethnic composition, but basically the main dividing line has been between Northerners and non-Northerners. Thus, for instance, the attempt to reconcile the three factions of the Nigerian (Northern) Electricity Supply Corporation African Workers' Union in a meeting summoned at Bukuru in January 1959 broke down over the demands by the Hausa–Fulani led faction that: (a) the General President and Secretary of the Union should be Northerners; (b) that in any negotiations between workers and employers, northerners should outnumber non-northerners by a ratio of 2:1; (c) that all correspondence between union and management should be translated into Hausa; (d) that Hausa should be the official language of the union, and finally (e) that at least one of the union's trustees must be a Northerner.[19] With the breakdown of negotiations under these conditions, the union resolved itself once more into its three factions. Hausa, Middle-Belt and Southern, and corresponding roughly to these three factions are divisions between the three political parties—NPC, UMBC/AG and NCNC/NEPU—which each faction supports.

Few, if any, areas in the North show as great a heterogeneity as Jos Division, but wherever heterogeneity is considerable, the basis of political competition and thus of party loyalties tends to be ethnic, as for instance in the Lafia division of Benue province. Here the main ethnic groups are the Kamberis (traditionally supposed to have migrated from Bornu) Aragos and Gwaris, though the competition is largely between the Kamberis (the ruling group) and the Aragos (the subject ethnic group). While the latter tend to be UMBC and/or NEPU, the former remain consistently NPC. In areas, however, with homogeneous populations, the basis of competition tends to centre around the Native Authority though the variables which enter into this competition differ from place to place. To this aspect of grass roots politics, we shall now turn.

II. AREAS WITH HOMOGENOUS POPULATIONS

Basically, there are three types of Native Authorities which are designated as Chief-in-Council, Chief-and-Council and Council.[20] All have the same powers and exercise the same functions, but under the original Native Authority Law of 1954 (as amended) only the Premier can constitute a Native Authority into a Chief-in-Council or Chief-and-Council while the designation of an N.A. as a 'Council' is for the Minister of Local Government. The division of jurisdiction between the Premier and the Minister of Local Government derives historically from the fact that the Premier previously held the portfolio of

R

Local Government. When the Premier gave up the portfolio, he retained control over these two types of Native Authorities.

The distinction between the N.A. with a Chief-in-Council and that with a Chief-and-Council lies in the status of the Chief within the Council. In the former, the Chief can override decisions of his Council should there be a divergence of opinion between himself and the rest of the Councillors. But in such cases the Chief is required to report his decision together with the reasons for his veto to the Provincial Commissioner who in turn forwards this either to the Premier or the Minister of Local Government. In other words, the Chief can act on his own initiative without the approval of his Council. He can also dispense with consultation with his full Council in matters which, in his opinion, are too unimportant to require the advice of the Council; or, in those which, in his judgment, are so urgent that it would be detrimental to delay action until a Council meeting can be summoned. However, in such circumstances, the Chief is required to consult at least two of his Councillors. Thirty-nine of the 70 N.A.s at present in existence are of this type, and they are mainly to be found in areas with long-established traditions of Chieftaincy. Most, though not all, are thus in the far North.

In N.A.s constituted as Chief-and-Council, less power is given to the Chief to act on his own initiative. He cannot, for instance, act contrary to the wishes of the Council nor can he dispense with the consultation of the full Council. He is in fact no more than the Chairman of the Council. There are eleven such Chiefs-and-Council, all of them in the lower North—where in the past, there were no definite traditions of Chieftaincy.

There are no specific provisions in the N.A. Law pertaining to the 'Council' type of Native Authority. In practice, they are federations of several small Native Authorities which have decided to come together in order to remain economically viable local administrative units. Thus as against the Council, the federating units become known as subordinate Native Authorities, the relationship between the sub-Native Authorities and the Council being dependent on the extent of the powers given up by the sub-units to the Council. These sub-N.A.s may in themselves be N.A.s of the Chief-in-Council, Chief-and-Council or 'Council' types; for example, Tangale-Waja a 'Council' type N.A. in Bauchi province is made up of Cham sub-N.A., a 'council', Dadiya sub-N.A., a Chief-and-Council, Kaltungo sub-N.A., Waja sub.-N.A. and West Tangale sub-N.A.—the last three being Chief-in-Council types. In the sub-N.A. the relationship between the Chief and the Council is exactly parallel to similar relationships in the main Native Authorities. The chairmanship or presidentship of the Council type N.A. varies. He may be designated by name or title where for instance one of the Chiefs of the sub-N.A.s is generally and popularly accepted as the 'senior' chief, or, be elected by members of the Council for a given period of time. The office, finally, may be held in rotation, with terms of office varying from one month to one year. There are only eighteen Native Authorities of the Council type.

Native Authorities vary not only in their type but also in their composition and procedure. Thus the N.A. may be composed of (a) wholly elected members of which there is at present only one; (b) a Chief, traditional and nominated members, and an elected majority (thirty-six of these); (c) a chief, traditional and nominated members with an equal number of elected representatives (only one such); and (d) Chief, traditional and nominated members with an elected minority, of which there are thirty. The present tendency is towards Councils with elective majorities though as will be argued later, it would be premature, if not inaccurate, to judge from this trend that N.A. Councils are being gradually democratised.[21] Traditional members are those who are ex-officio members of the Council by virtue of being holders of office in the traditional hierarchy, e.g. the Sarkin Fada, Chief official of the Royal Household, or the Wakilin Ayyuka, Chief of Public Works, etc. Nominated members are those appointed by the Minister or Premier to represent special interests. Of the 1,680 Native Authority Councillors in 1963, 399 were ex-officio members, while 427 were nominated. Approximately 51 % were therefore elected and only in 20 % of the Councils are the members directly elected. Most Councils have indirectly elected members with the sub-N.A.s, District, Village and Town Councils serving as electoral areas. Though elections are usually 'secret', in Dass Native Authority in Bauchi province, elections to the Council are open or non-secret.

Procedurally N.A.s may operate in one of two principal ways— they may work either on a 'portfolio system' or on a 'committee system'. In Councils where the portfolio system operates, traditional members and only these are given portfolios or responsibility for one or more of the 'departments' of the Native Authority. The Portfolio Councillor deals with over-all policy affecting his department, the day-to-day running of which is under a Head of Department, a paid employee of the Native Authority. The relationship between the Councillor and his head of department is not unlike that between the Minister and his Permanent Secretary. The 'Committee System' is usually followed by wholly elected Councils or Councils with an elected majority. The Council is divided up into various committees each of which is then responsible for specific departments or service, with the Chairman of the committee, the key figure, acting as the liaison between the Committee and the head of a department.[22]

N.A. Councils can by instrument (which can be revoked at will) set up subordinate councils such as District, Village and Town Councils to which they may delegate certain functions with or without appropriate fiscal sources.[23] Besides these subordinate Authorities, there may be an Outer Council (with indirectly elected members) serving in an advisory capacity all the Native Authorities within any given province. However, with the passing of the Provincial Administration Law in 1962, the Outer Councils, where they existed, are now being replaced by Provincial Councils.

The foregoing description of the structure of the Native Authority and its system of Councils can be shown diagrammatically—see below. It is apparent from this that the Native Authority Council is the hub of the Native Authority.[24] Everything else revolves around the Council. It is the main focus of competition between varying political interest. The forms which such competition takes and the consequent tensions that arise therefrom, can now be analysed.

STRUCTURE OF THE NATIVE AUTHORITY AND ITS COUNCILS

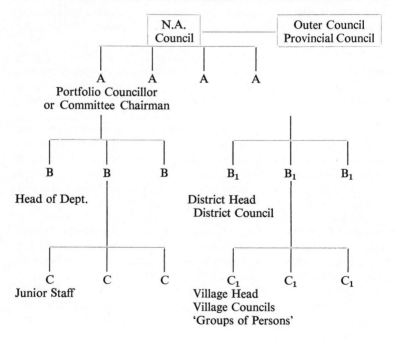

The first form of competition, and the most significant, is that between 'traditionalism' and 'modernity'. It is basic to, and characterizes, much of the politics of the Middle-Belt or lower North provinces. It should be noted that the two terms—traditionalism and modernity—are not used in any rigid, absolute sense. They refer mainly to attitudes which change not only over time but also vary with issues. However, as illustrative examples of this type of competition, one might consider local politics in Igala and Igbira divisions in Kabba province and Idoma in Benue.

The Igalas, like the Jukuns, are one of the few peoples of the lower North with a tradition of priestly-kings, but under British administration the Atta Igala gradually combined in his person both priestly and secular roles, the latter tending to supersede the former. By the time of the 1952 local government reforms, the Atta, Umaru Ameh Oboni had become an autocratic ruler who insisted on the observance of the traditional religious rites associated with his 'divine' office. Since it was alleged that this included human sacrifice, a reaction rapidly developed amongst the younger educated Moslems and Christians. In 1954 these combined to form the Igala Divisional Union to oppose the Atta's administration. Supporters of the Atta, the traditional priests and office holders who controlled the Igala Native Authority Council then formed the Igala Progressive Union which, as the *status-quo* party, was allied to the NPC. By late 1954 the people of Igala were divided into two camps, a major faction of the younger emergent middle-class, teachers, traders, lower echelon Native Authority officials and others, led by Mr. Daniel Ogbadu, a CMS-educated clerk of the Atta Igala's Appeal Court (the IDU), and the minority of traditionalists, the IPU allied to the NPC.

At the 1954 federal and 1956 regional elections, all IDU candidates were returned, but on being elected they decided to support the NPC.[25] At the 1955 elections to the Igala N.A. Council, the IDU won twenty-nine of the thirty-two seats and gained control of the Council. Thus, while locally opposed to the ruling 'oligarchy', the IPU/NPC, the IDU co-operated with it at the regional and federal levels.

The IDU's control, in terms of representation, of the N.A. Council led to a crisis in the Council. As a Chief-in-Council type Native Authority, the Atta and his traditional office holders could take decisions which ignored the sentiments of the majority in the Council. On the other hand, as the IDU was opposed to the Atta it was not prepared to co-operate with him or his henchmen who held the important portfolios in the Council. Dissatisfaction amongst the lower N.A. cadres caused bottlenecks and the level of administrative efficiency rapidly declined. To resolve the deadlock, in 1956 the IDU campaigned for the removal of the Atta, a demand which the NPC controlled regional government was reluctant to concede since it would then have been acting against its supporters. Opposition and pressure mounted and the Atta was finally prevailed upon to resign; soon after, he committed suicide.

On the resignation of Atta Ameh Oboni, the IDU sponsored M. Ali Ocheja Obaje, from the rival lineage to Oboni's for the Atta-ship. (The Igala divine kings were traditionally drawn from two lineages and in their opposition to Oboni, the IDU were naturally supported by the other lineage.) With the appointment of Obaje, the IDU, backed by the new Atta, immediately embarked on a programme of replacing with their own candidates the members of the Oboni lineage in the Native Administration. By 1957 the IDU members of the N.A. Council were already "converting themselves into *de facto* if not *de jure* employees of the Native Authority".[26] Nepotism in Native Authority appointments, the award of Native Authority contracts to loyal supporters, the use of the local police force against political opponents, corruption amongst the Councillors, the reduction of heads of departments to subordinate status thereby spoiling promotion prospects—all of these bred discontent which culminated in the resuscitation of the IPU in 1958, but this time as the Igala Union.[27]

Accusing the IDU of being responsible for the death of the late Atta Ameh Oboni, the Igala Union came out in open support of traditional mores, even including the use of the emblem of the late Atta on its party membership cards. But such was the opposition to the IDU's administration that at the Federal elections of 1959, the Igala Union won all of the four Igala seats and lost one to the IDU at the 1961 regional elections. One of its candidates defeated the IDU Minister of State, Daniel Ogbadu. At the 1960 elections to the Native Authority Council the Igala Union won all thirty-two seats to regain control of the Council, which in the interim period had converted to the Committee system from the original portfolio system. This change had the advantage of enabling the IDU to dominate the Executive Committee[28]—or All Purpose Committee—the day-to-day governing body of the Council, but in itself created a new disequilibrium. Since although the Igala Union now had an overwhelming majority in the Council, it was in no position to influence day-to-day policy. The uneasy situation continues with the regional government not disposed to interfere in support of the Igala Union—the local NPC—because of the poor educational standards of most of the Igala Union Councillors.

The IDU and the Igala Union both support the NPC at the level of regional and federal politics,[29] but are opposed to each other locally. Though the lines of opposition seem to be polarized around the two ruling lineages, this is rather a matter of convenience than of principle. Basically, the IDU draws its main support from the middle cadres of Igala society whilst the Igala Union's strength derives largely from traditional priestly caste and title-holders. The former represents a defence against a system of ascriptive statuses for which the latter seemingly stands, and it is this incompatibility of views and associated beliefs which distinguishes the one from the other. This is much more clearly brought out in the case of the Igbirras who, unlike the Igalas have no long-established tradition of chieftainship whether secular or divine.

The first Atta of Igbirra was appointed in 1946 to become the Sole Native Authority[30] in Igbirra. Under him and with the support of an advisory council of nominees, the local administration was rapidly centralized, the still clearly defined clan system being ignored in the process. Igniting the smouldering resentment of the Atta's administration, the 1951 elections led to a series of civil disturbances. The enquiry that followed showed that "the majority of the people containing a high proportion of literates and rapidly growing sophisticated class, no longer accepted the existing system of local government".[31] This sophisticated literate middle-class, led by George Ohikere, a teacher at the Roman Catholic School, Okene, and Raphael Braifor Ojeba, a Survey Assistant in the Native Authority, later formed the Igbirra Tribal Union. Opposition by the ITU resulted in 1952 in the conversion of the native administration to a Chief-and-Council type Native Authority composed of the Atta as Chairman, eight ex-officio and twenty-five indirectly elected members.

The N.A. reforms brought the tension between the ITU and the Atta to a head. The indirect elections of the councillors made it possible for pressure to be put on the district Councils—the electoral colleges for the election of the N.A. councillors—thereby ensuring that a good many of those elected were members of the Igbirra Progressive Union—a party formed by the elders and supporters of the Atta and allied to the NPC. Dissatisfaction resulted in a change to direct elections by secret ballot, and the Igbirra Native Authority Council became the first in the North to be so elected. In the 1954 local elections, the change enabled the ITU to gain control of the Council and to demand the removal of the Atta who was then forced to resign.

If the authoritarianism of the Atta made him unacceptable to the ITU, his successor, the Atta Ibrahima fared no better. By appointing his nominees to the important portfolios in the Native Authority and attempting thereby to replace officials of the N.A. with people of his own choice, the Atta created such antipathy towards himself that in 1956 he was deposed and replaced by M. Sani Omolurin, a former Chief Scribe in the N.A. Central office. Before his appointment Omolurin was an administrative assistant at the regional legislature. He was given the new title of Ohinoyi, an Igbirra term unlike the the word 'Atta' which was said to be of Igala origin.

Now in the ascendant, the ITU won both the regional elections of 1956 and the local N.A. elections of 1957. One of its candidates for the regional elections, Mr. Ohikere, was later appointed a Regional Minister of Works, though his party was opposed to the local NPC organization, members of which, with the aid of the N.A. police, the ITU then proceeded to intimidate. But firmly in the saddle, the ITU proved as inept and corrupt as the Atta Ibrahima's administration and its predecessor. In 1958 two of its Councillors had to be removed by the regional government for corrupt practices, and a struggle within the leadership led to a split into a pro-NPC faction ITU (1) led by Mr. Ohikere, and an anti-NPC faction ITU (2) led by a Mr. Kokori Abdul.

The orientation of the two groups provides the primary cause of the split. Whilst those of the ITU (1) wanted the local organization formally converted into a branch of the NPC, leaders of the other faction wanted to preserve the autonomy of the ITU, the argument being that by remaining autonomous, they would be independent of direction from the NPC central organization and therefore, in a better position to bargain with the NPC controlled regional government for various social amenities.[32] In the N.A. a majority of the Councillors took the position of ITU (2) in which they had the support of the Ohinoyi. ITU (2) then attempted to replace those native authority officials whose sympathies were with ITU (1), but having only a small majority was unable to do so without contravening the standing orders of the Council which prescribed a larger majority, for most decisions, than the ITU (2) had. With the Council sharply divided, decision-making became impossible. The morale of the N.A. employees deteriorated and the persecution of political opponents became accepted practice. Late in 1959, after a warning to the Ohinoyi from the regional authorities, the Council was dissolved and a District Officer appointed to act in place of the Council.

At the 1959 federal elections, ITU (2) proved its popular support when its candidates defeated the ITU (1) nominee. In the District Council elections in 1960 it won majorities in six of the eight districts. It repeated the same success at the 1961 regional elections by securing both seats in Igbirra division. In Igbirra South constituency, the party's leader, Kokori Abdul defeated the ITU (1)/NPC regional Minister of Works, George Ohikere, and was immediately appointed Parliamentary Secretary to the Minister of Information.[33] With this demonstration of popular support the regional government could no longer delay elections for a new Native Authority Council. Later in 1961 this was held, ITU (2) winning twelve seats to the ITU (1)'s eight.

With a comfortable majority in the Council, leaders of the ITU (2) went on to pursue their own advantage. Though committee membership is supposed to reflect that of the Council as a whole, Committees which carried the most patronage, such as those of Establishment, Contracts and Licensing, were taken over almost exclusively by the party's councillors. By the first half of 1962 the Annual Report for that year indicated that "the work and behaviour of the Igbirra Native Authority deteriorated to an alarming degree— Administrative ineptitude and victimization of political opponents and their sympathisers were the order of the day".[34] With the threat of another dissolution, ITU (2) leaders sought a way out in an alliance with the NPC which was concluded in December 1962.

The alliance ended the split in the ITU and entrenched the hegemony of the educated, 'middle-class' élite. With the hold of the 'elders' broken as far back as 1954 and in the absence of any other organized competing interest, 'politics' in Igbirra has tended to become 'administration' something Marx prophesied and Lenin hoped for.[35] If this 'reduction' was achieved in Igbirra through the effective political neutralization, or rather elimination of the 'traditionalists', in Idoma in Benue Province, a not dissimilar result was obtained by the partial assimilation of the 'modernists' by the traditional oligarchy.

The Idoma N.A. is of the 'Chief-in-Council' type and like the Tiv N.A. before its dissolution, it operated under a system of administrative Councillors—in other words, the N.A. Councillors were not only policy-makers, they also held executive offices as heads of departments. The administrative centralization which such a system entails and the nepotism which it permits, is best shown by the fact that, in 1956 for example, it was possible for the Och'Idoma, Ogiri Oko, to appoint a close friend of his, Omakwu Ogwiji, as district head of Akwaya and Councillor in charge of Establishment, his father-in-law a non-resident Councillor and district head of Oturkpo, and to make a son-in-law, Ajene Okpabi, district head of Ito, responsible for Licensing, and another relation, Aba Akor, a former N.A. Chief Scribe, head of the N.A. Tenders and Contracts Board. All these offices provide ample opportunities for graft, and corruption was rife.[36]

The opposition to the Och' Idoma, as in Igala and Igbirra, came from the educated lower echelon N.A. cadres and school teachers such as A. Echono, John E. Ede and others. These formed the Idoma Hope Rising Union which in fact was the old Idoma Divisional Union (formed in 1949) resuscitated and given a new name. Under constant criticism from this body, the Native Authority decided on reforms in 1958. The principal measure was the broadening of the Native Authority Council. Thus, in place of four administrative Councillors, there were now to be eight to be chosen by the elected representatives voting in four groups to select two Councillors to represent each group. Together with the Och' Idoma and four other Councillors (chosen by the twenty-nine elected Councillors from amongst themselves) these were to form the Executive Committee of the Council. With the proposed reforms, the IHRS and the Idoma State Union, the Och' Idoma's party (affiliated to the NPC) amalgamated. The dissolution of the Council in early 1959 and the elections in April of that year facilitated the introduction of the reform proposals and former IHRS leaders such as John O. Ede and E. Awe Odo (formerly N.A. Adult Education Officer) became Councillors for local Government and Works respectively. Relations further improved when, later in the year, the Ochi, Ogiri Oko, died and his son-in-law, Ajene Okpabi, was made the new chief.

Accounts of similar conflicts can be given for most other areas in the lower North.[37] The competition here described is central to the disturbances in Tiv division where the Native Authority has been suspended since 1960 and for varying periods before that. Admittedly in Tiv the situation is made complex not only by the opposition to the NPC of the party of the 'modernists', the UMBC, both locally and regionally, but also by the commitment of that party to the demand for a separate state in which the Tivs would be the largest single ethnic group. But this points to the logic of the relation of local to regional politics, which is that the regional leadership is only prepared to tolerate grass-roots political competition if the interests involved accept the basic orientation of the ruling party: "the North, one and indivisible". An ITU-controlled Igbirra Native Authority might not be unacceptable to the regional government, but the thought of a UMBC-dominated Tiv N.A. was an anathema. Hence the determination forcibly to convert the Tivs, the riots and the suspension of the Tiv N.A. Another example of this intolerance of local separatist sentiments was the Ilorin Talaka Parapo controlled Ilorin N.A. which the Government suspended in 1958, on the grounds that the N.A. arbitrarily dismissed some of the N.A. employees known to be supporters of the governing body.[38] The accounts of Igbirra and Igala show that such acts are not uncommon, unknown, and they are certainly not unexpected.[39] Unlike the ITP in Ilorin, however, neither the Igbirras nor the Igalas were committed to a union with the Yorubas of the Western Region. Repressive action in Ilorin succeeded in making the people "realize their mistakes and stop electing people belonging to (an) irresponsible party".[40] It has not as yet succeeded with the Tiv.

One variant of the theme of modernity versus traditionalism which should be noted is the conflict between the interests represented by the rural outlying districts and those of the 'metropolitan' or central administration. This often issues into a fissiparous movement, a demand for the creation of a separate Native Authority, distinct from the central organization for the division as a whole, as for example in the 'movement' by the people of Igbomina, Ekiti, Ibolo, Odo-Ogun and Offa, the southern and eastern areas of Ilorin, for a separate Native Authority. Here, the demand is basically a reaction on the part of the educated elements to 'economic discrimination', deriving from the concentration of welfare services and social amenities in districts to the North and in Ilorin town and to the comparative neglect in Native Authority employment of those from the south and east. With high localized unemployment[41] there has been a consequent migration of the educated elements to other areas, particularly Lagos and Ibadan. This in turn has engendered a divergence of outlook which on the part of the migrants is hostile to the Ilorin Native Authority.[42]

Under their influence various separatist movements such as the Egbe Igbomina Parapo (Association for the Unification of the Igbominas), the Offa Descendants Union and others emerged in 1954. As one would expect, the initial demand was for separation from the North but as the leadership gradually passed over to the local residents[43] such as Mr. Moses Olarewaju, NPC Federal Minister of State for Police Affairs,[44] Olarewaju Afolayan, member for Ilorin South in the regional assembly, A. F. N. Thomas, General Secretary of the Odo-Ogun branch of the NPC and others, the tune was altered to its present form. Though the regional Minister of Local Government has announced that "the Government . . . will ensure that all the people of the Ilorin Emirate irrespective of where they live, will receive equal treatment from the Native Authority"[45] one effect of the demand for separation has been a real decentraliza- tion of responsibility and financial resources to the districts and proposals to reform the basis of electoral representation of the Ilorin Native Authority.[46] (As an additional measure, one might note the encouragement given by the regional government to private investors to locate industrial enterprises, such as Unilever's Kwarra Tobacco Company, a cigarette-manufacturing concern, in Ilorin division to meet the problem of localized unemployment.)

The lower North areas provide a striking contrast to the far North. Unlike the former, where competition is 'open', in the latter it is 'closed', the main social basis of political activity being dynastic, though not exclusively so. The tradition-sanctioned, hierarchically differentiated centralized political system with its clearly defined modes of recruitment typical of the far North makes political activity an essentially in-group affair, its distinguishing characteristics being those of a 'face-to-face' society.[47] If in the lower North one can conceptualize politics as taking place between two parallel organized interests, in the far North the conceptual equivalent would be interests organized in concentric circles with the Emir and his immediate relations—either by blood or marriage—forming the innermost ring. The relationship between members within successive circles may be either one of co-operation or conflict, open or latent. The crisis which led to the expulsion of the Emir of Kano brings this out clearly. Kano therefore can be taken as an illustrative example.

Of the five traditional, thirteen nominated and five elected members which made up the Kano Native Authority Council (that is, not counting the Emir himself), by the time of the Muffett Commission of Enquiry, it was already clear that the real holders of power were a small group centred around the Emir and made up of the Emir's son, Ado Sanusi,[48] the Emir's two sons-in-law, the Makama, Bello Dambarau Yola and the Sarkin Fada (Chief of the Royal Household) Alhaji Ibrahim Zimit,[49] the Emir's brother-in-law, Alhaji Rufai Daura, Councillor for Education and the Emir's trusted lieutenant, the Mutawalin Kano, Alhaji Mohamed-Munir, Councillor for Finance, Works and N.A. Commercial undertakings.[50] They and a few of the heads of departments of the N.A. constituted the inner circle, 'the Kings Men', who attended the 'talata' (lit. Tuesday) meetings "at which" in the words of the Government statement on the Muffett Report, "major N.A. policy decisions were irregularly taken".[51]

Next to the 'Kings Men' came the 'Courtiers', (the middle circle) prominent amonst whom were people such as the Madaki, Shehu Ahmed (Senior District Administrator, married to the Ex-Emir's half-sister),[52] the Sarkin Shanu, in charge of Kano city administration (also married to the Ex-Emir's half-sister), Tafida Ringin, son of late Emir Usman of Kano,[53] two 'king-makers'—Ahaji Bello Dandogo, Sarkin Dawaki Maituta (Federal Government Chief Whip) and Alhaji Muhtari, Sarkin Bai (NPC Chief Whip in the

Federal Parliament, District Head of Dambatta) and others. Though members of the Council, they formed the second ring of influence.

Whilst the 'Kings Men' retained effective control of the Native Authority the 'Courtiers' were in no position to challenge their authority, since the need to court the good graces of the 'Kings Men' kept them relatively disunited. Between the two groups political relationship, were governed by a tenuous 'live and let live' policy,[54] which made room for "maladministration and financial irresponsibility, gross misuse of the allocation of plots (building land), . . . "irregularities connected with the inheritance of properties left by parents", and "the award of contracts at excessive rates and goods required by the departments and undertakings purchased at greatly inflated prices".[55]

When, however, the Commission of Inquiry to investigate the affairs of the Native Authority was appointed by the regional government (and it became clear that the position of the Emir and the 'Kings Men' might be at stake) the latent opposition between the 'Courtiers' and the 'Kings Men' became apparent. For, now that their status[56] had become precarious the 'Courtiers' encouraged the 'social climbers'[57]—the business men and wealthy traders, the third circle of influence—to appear before the sole Commissioner to give evidence.[58] Unlike the 'Courtiers', the 'social climbers', such as Alhaji Uba Ringim (NPC transporter, trader and member of the House of Assembly), Haruna Kassim (trader, pilgrimage agent, MHA) Baba Danbafa (trader, pilgrimage agent, NHR), Alhaji Abdullahi Nabegu (trader, member, NPC Provincial Executive) and others, had nothing to lose. As transporters, traders in primary products—groundnuts, cotton, and hides and skins—and contractors, they depended more on the goodwill of the Government than on that of the Native Authority. None of them traditionally belonged to the political ruling class but with the development of party politics, most have achieved some political power as members of the legislature. Excluded from the Native Authority power structure, they were none the less highly successful and influential members of the local community. They were thus in a position to co-operate with the 'Courtiers' to produce part of the evidence on which the 'Kings Men' were subsequently removed from office.[59]   ..

The comparison of Kano with Zaria is interesting. In the latter because of the long reign of the Bornawa dynasty (seventy-three years) the Bornawas had come to dominate the administration.[60] When the present Emir took office in September 1959 he was, as a Katsinawa, faced with a Bornawa opposition and accordingly drew his 'Kings Men' from the Katsinawa and Mallawa dynasties.[61] But unlike Kano, the Bornawa, now the 'Courtiers', were sufficiently well represented in the Council to be able to prevent any comparable use of 'talata meetings' from excluding them from policy making. The logical outcome was a constant conflict between the two groups. In the end, for reasons already suggested in Chapter VI, and unlike Kano, it was the 'Courtiers' who lost the contest, for of the seven councillors removed after the Commission of Inquiry five were members of the Bornawa dynasty.[62] No member of either the Katsinawa or the Mallawa dynasty lost office, not even the Emir's son, Mallam Abubakar Gardu, the Wakilin Tsabta who was shown to be thoroughly incompetent.[63]

Both Zaria and Kano demonstrated sufficiently the 'in-group' nature of local political competition characteristic of the 'centralized' Emirates of the North.[64] The social basis of this pattern of behaviour has been given in Chapter II. In a community where the individual's status ranking is not only ascriptively determined but where also the ranking-order is a function of the political fortunes of his lineage or dynasty, it is only to be expected that his loyalty would be to the lineage—segment or dynasty. Socio-political groupings would therefore tend to be of a 'primary order'. From this, it would follow that the politically best placed primary group must necessarily strive to maximize returns to its constituent members through placing them in the most favoured positions while excluding rivals.

It is only too obvious that, in practical terms, the end product of such a system is hardly any different from the descriptions given above for the lower North areas despite the fact that the areas of the middle belt have radically different social structures. Basically, as far as the local bureaucracy, the Native Authority, is concerned, both areas would seem to operate on the principle that 'the winner takes all'. But this does not imply that there are no differences between the two areas. If party politics in the lower North have led to a uniformity of political behaviour, nevertheless in the far North the associative principles of group formation are exclusive and narrowly defined, while in the lower North, they are much more inclusive and broadly construed.

III. SOME ISSUES FOR ANALYSIS

The foregoing description of grass roots politics, provides a suitable framework within which some issues already raised can be examined. The two main questions to be considered are, first, the adaptability of particular types of traditional social structures to socio-political modernization, specifically, to bureaucratic institutions, and secondly, the supposed democratization of local structures of authority.

The 'problem' of the relative receptivity or adaptability of types of traditional social structures to modern bureaucratic systems was introduced in Chapter II.[65] Briefly, the issue was whether hierarchically structured, politically centralized, traditional societies were more readily susceptible to 'modernization' than 'segmental', laterally repetitive relation structured ones.[66] Societies of the far North typify the former whilst those of the lower north, in general, exemplify the latter, But as already suggested, the emphasis of the different proponents is misplaced. Concerned as they were with the formal characteristics, they have tended to regard bureaucratic organizations almost exclusively as functional systems and to ignore the disfunctions. In both instances examined here, Igbirra (non-centralized) and Zaria or Kano (centralized) N.A. officials have on the former view been removed from office arbitrarily as a consequence of changes in the compositiom of the N.A. Council, appointments to office have followed no system of rules and have been more on individual loyalties than on criteria of skill and experience, promotions have been made arbitrarily, and offices allocated indifferently—all negations of the formal characteristics of a bureaucracy.

If the whole question is not to turn out to be a 'pseudo problem', some criteria other than merely formal characteristics must be proposed. Concentrating on the disfunctions within the Native Administration, it is suggested that the only operational criterion is that of efficiency, and from the negative[67] evidence available, it would seem that the N.A.s of the lower North are much more efficient than those of the far North. Certainly there have been no 'crises' of maladministration, comparable to those of Zaria (1961), Kano (1962), Bornu (1955, 1956), Argungu (1958), Gwandu (1962) in the lower North.[68] But it is far from certain that this would justify the assumption that there is any correlation between social structure and bureaucratic efficiency. Such an assumption would require that other factors, such as the levels of literacy, were constant. This would scarcely be legitimate especially in the case of Northern Nigeria where, in the far North, only Zaria has a literacy rate higher than the regional average, whereas in the lower North all but Benue and Bauchi have higher figures, and besides Zaria, no far Northern province has a literacy rate as high as the minimum for the lower North.[69] (To account for the differential literacy rates, an historical explanation would be needed. This was provided in Chapter I.) Although no definite conclusion is here offered about the receptivity of types of social structures to overall modernization, more fruitful lines have, it is submitted, been suggested for further enquiry.

The second issue raised relates to the suggestion[70] that the gradual transition and conversion of the N.A.s from a sole Native Authority to a conciliar system entails that N.A.s are gradually being turned into democratic institutions. On this view, 'democracy' is construed simply as government by elected representatives, and more than half of the N.A. Councils now have a majority of elected representatives.[71]

But this is extremely misleading. In the first place, it ignores the fact that all the Councils with elected majorities are in the lower North.[72] Secondly, it discounts the variations in the internal organization of the different Native Authority Councils. All the Councils of the far North operate under the portfolio system while only some of those in the lower North adopt the 'committee' form. Most Councils are thus of the 'portfolio' type and in almost all of these only traditional and nominated members can be portfolio Councillors.[73] Elected members are therefore excluded from responsibility. Besides, the procedure of taking major decisions in 'talata' meetings of the Council mean in effect that elected members play little or no part in the main deliberations of the Councils. Again the argument ignores the form of elections to the N.A. Councils. Of the seventy-one N.A. Councils in the North, only 21% have directly elected members. All of these are in the lower North. The remaining 79% have indirectly elected members, and of these approximately 19% or thirteen Councils, have no elected members.[74] And irrespective of whether the members are directly elected or not, it is always possible for the Emir or Chief and the 'Kings Men' to influence the elections. Either the Kings Men as District Heads can direct the course of the election or the Council can alter the basis of election by amending the electoral regulations so that any members of the District Council electoral colleges could stand for election as opposed to the elected members of the District Councils only. The result more often than not is to weight the elections in the favour of 'traditional members' who would give their support to the 'Kings Men'.[75]

Essentially, the point of these objections is thus to reject (at least for the far North or the traditional Emirates) the argument which seeks to suggest that the 'broadening' of the composition of the N.A. Councils implies that the Councils are being democratized. The restriction of responsibility for policy-making to the traditional and nominated members in effect means that the locus of authority has hardly altered and that power remains vested in the traditional oligarchy of the North. As has been shown in previous chapters, they also dominate both the regional legislature and the regional bureaucracy. The link between the local and the regional is provided by the party which gives the whole political system its essential monolithic character.[76]

The traditional structure of the N.A. created the framework for the emergence and predominance of the NPC through which present political leaders rose to prominence. Having achieved political power, it was to be expected that they would equally recreate at the regional level, institutions with which they are familiar while at the same time preserving the essence of the base. Thus, though the 'form' of the base may seem to be changing or have changed, the 'content' remains essentially unaltered. In the last analysis, the 'content' can be altered only if the nature of the party is changed.

NOTES

1. See e.g. Floyd Hunter, *Community Power Structure*, Chapel Hill, 1953; R. A. Dahl, 'A Critique of the Ruling Elite Model', *The American Political Science Review*, vol. 52, June 1958, and T. J. Anton, Power, Pluralism, and Local Politics', *Administrative Science Quarterly*, vol. 7, March 1963. It is not the intention here to enter into the debate on what Anton has called the 'reputational' and the 'pluralist' schools of community studies.

2. Aidan Southall, *Social Change in Modern Africa*, Oxford University Press, 1961, p. 6.

3. See Tanya M. Baker, op. cit.

4. In 1942 for instance, 10,000 labourers were recruited from all over the provinces of the North. But within six months, only 552 of these were left in the mines. See Bower, The Mining Industry, in M. Perham (ed.), *Mining, Commerce and Finance in Nigeria*, Faber, 1948.

5. See *Nigerian Citizen*, 12th and 15th March 1958, 5th April and 7th May 1958.

6. See *Middle Belt Herald* (Jos), 8th April 1961.

7. *Provincial Annual Reports 1962*, Kaduna, 1963, p. 149.

8. Ibid., p. 148.

9. *Sunday Express* (Lagos), 3rd May 1964.

10. See *Provincial Annual Reports 1962*, pp. 31–33, 78, 96–98, 199–200, for some further examples.

11. *Annual Report of the Mines Division of the Ministry of Mines and Power*, Lagos, 1961.

12. In 1958, the skilled workers employed at the ATMN Central Machine Shop by ethnic origin were as follows:

	Birom	*Hausa*	*Ibo*
Welders	3	2	18
Turners	4	—	12
Blacksmiths	1	—	4
Total	8	2	34

S

SOURCE: Letter from the Middle Belt Mineworkers' Union to the Labour Officer, Federal Ministry of Labour, dated 8th November 1958.

13. I am indebted for these figures to Mr. Len Plotnikov, an American research social anthropologist resident in Jos whom I met in May 1962. The Executive of the NMU at this date was made up of the following: (1) General President, Alhaji Isa Haruna (Hausa, NPC Provincial President), (2) General Secretary, Audu Dan Ladi (Fulani, NPC Provincial Secretary), (3) General Treasurer, Mama Yola (Fulani, member NPC Provincial Executive), (4) Vice President, M. Lawan Haske (Hausa, NPC Provincial Executive member), (5) Three District Presidents, (4) above, M. Wan Hamidu (Hausa) and Adama Ganawuri (Bauchi), (6) Two District Secretaries, Adama Yola (Fulani) and M. Abubakar (Hausa). All work at the ATMN except Isa Haruna and Audu Dan Ladi at Bisichi, the latter as a Welfare Officer, the former a Contractor for Bisichi.

14. *Daily Service* (Lagos), 5th October 1957.

15. Alhaji Ibrahim Imam in Debates N.H.A., 18th February 1959, col. 82. The answer by the Regional Minister of Trade and Industry was: "The AG has destroyed trade unions by presenting so many difficulties." Loc. cit.

16. A sidelight on how overt pressure can be brought to dissuade attempts to break NMU restrictionism is the letter from the Jos Assistant Superintendent of Police dated 17th February 1960 to the Regional Commissioner at Kaduna, alleging that the move being made by one M. Inuwa Gareji to get some of the mineworkers into a new organization, the Northern Tin Labour Organization, was directed at getting the workers to unite against the NPC dominated NMU. Gareji soon after lost his job with the mines.

17. Letter from the temporary Secretary to the Labour Officer, dated 29th May 1959. The MBMU was registered as a union on 28th April 1959.

18. Letter from M. K. Iloh to the Labour Officer, dated 7th April 1959.

19. See Labour Quarterly Returns, Quarter ending 31st March 1959.

20. Two other 'types' have been ignored—the sole N.A. and the 'Groups of Persons' types. None of the latter exist at present in the North. The former, which was the traditional 'prototype' also no longer exists. Whenever there is a 'sole N.A.' this is invariably an individual appointed to act by the Government on the dissolution of any of the existing types of N.A.'s. There are at present three such sole or 'caretaker' Native Authorities.

21. Contrast, e.g. the argument by Wraith in his *Local Government in West Africa*, Allen & Unwin, 1964, p. 129 and Campbell, op. cit., passim, where the udgment here being questioned is made.

22. In a wholly elected Council there is usually an Executive or All Purpose Committee the members of which are full-time paid Councillors dealing with the day-to-day problems of the Native Authority.

23. All but one (Ningi) of the Town Councils are directly elected. All District Councils except those in Borgu, Ilorin, Fika and Numan are directly elected. Elections to Lowland, East Yagba, Katagum and Wukari District Councils are non-secret or open.

24. In themselves the Native Authorities have been said to constitute "virtually *the* administration of the country". Wraith, op. cit., p. 127.

25. Mr. Daniel Ogbadu who was elected on the IDU platform was on joining the NPC parliamentary party appointed a Minister of State of the Regional Government.

26. *Provincial Annual Report 1957*, p. 71.

27. See *Nigerian Citizen*, 25th April 1959.

28. For instance, Ogbadu who was defeated in 1961 was immediately appointed a Councillor and made a member of the Council's Executive Committee.

29. The advantages are obvious. Not to do so would have been to deprive themselves of various social and economic benefits from the regional government. A good contrast here would be the Tivs who have been deprived of a good many amenities because of their opposition to the regional government.

30. For the connotation of this expression, see K. P. Maddocks and D. A. Pott, *Report on Local Government in the Northern Provinces of Nigeria*, Kaduna, Government Printer, 1951. There is a certain ambiguity in the use of the term 'Native Authority'. In some cases, it is used to refer to the totality of the local administrative machinery. It could also refer to the Emir or District Head etc. in which case the emphasis is on the exercise of authority. This ambiguity appears clearly in Section 2 (Interpretation) of the basic N.A. Law 1954 (NRLN No. 131 of 1954), in the definition of the term and the expression "member of a Native Authority". In most cases the context should make clear which is the correct referrent.

31. D. A. Pott, *Progress Report on Local Government in the Northern Region of Nigeria*, Kaduna, 1953, p. 17.

32. Dr. Sklar, op. cit., p. 550 and fn. 42 p. 594, suggested that the split was on religious lines, "the Muslim majority (ITU (2)) repudiating the Catholic leadership" which remained as ITU (1), but gives no reason for this. However, on a minor historical point, his account is inaccurate. He reported the split as occurring in 1957 whereas this took place in 1958. He is also misleading when he suggested that the NPC supported the Catholic ITU (1) in preference to the Muslim ITU (2) which "professes loyalty to the national and regional party leadership".

33. Mr. Ohikere was compensated on his defeat with the office of Chairman of the Nigerian Ports Authority, a demonstration of the place of patronage in Nigerian politics.

34. *Provincial Annual Reports 1962*, Kaduna, 1963, p. 78.

35. This does not imply a 'classless society'. It entails only the absence of competing interests which are necessary for 'politics'—see Bernard Crick, *In Defence of Politics*, Pelican, 1964.

36. See, e.g., *Nigerian Citizen*, 24th, 28th and 31st March 1956 and 9th May 1956.

37. A reading of the various Provincial Annual Reports shows this. See, e.g., *Provincial Annual Reports 1962*, pp. 16, 33, 64, 195.

38. See *Statement of the Government of the Northern Region of Nigeria on the Report of the Committee of Inquiry Appointed to investigate Allegations about the Ilorin Native Authority*, Kaduna, 1958.

39. In the Ilorin case, one of the first acts of the reconstituted N.A. was to remove all those known to have been sympathisers of the Talaka Parapo.

40. Alhaji Mu'azu Lamido, Minister of Animal Health and Natural Resources in the House of Assembly Debates, 11th March 1963, p. 178. For evidence of repression in Ilorin see Chapter 3, pp. 101–102.

41. In Ilorin province in 1962, 4,766 people registered with the Labour Exchange as unemployed. During the same year there were only sixty-two vacancies available. *Provincial Annual Reports 1962*, p. 72. It was also pointed out in the Report that "Unemployment is evident and this situation is inevitably bound to remain . . ." Loc. cit.

42. See *Nigerian Morning Post* (Lagos), 12th and 13th April 1962.

43. Mainly after the dissolution of the Ilorin N.A. Council in 1958. The leadership of these societies was from the start divided between those who thought the limited objective of a separate N.A. was the more feasible proposition (the residents), and those who wanted the area merged into the West (the emigrants).

44. The writer was informed that Mr. Olarewaju was made a Minister of State in order to induce him not to support the demand for a separate Native Authority. Formerly an N.A. Forest Ranger, he was actually one of the very few Igbominas employed in the Ilorin Native Authority.

45. *Morning Post*, 13th April 1962.

46. Though the NPC recorded clear wins in Ilorin East and South constituencies, the votes cast for the party in both constituencies in 1961 was considerably less than in the other two Ilorin constituencies—Ilorin North and Central. The actual figures were 58·4% and 57·1% for East and South and 70·7% and 66·5% for North and Central respectively.

Sectional competition based on socio-economic differentiation was also operative in the Birom districts to the north and west of Jos and explained why Jos north-west constituency consistently voted for the opposition since 1954.

47. On relations in face-to-face societies, see P. Laslett's essay with that title in P. Laslett (ed.), *Philosophy, Politics and Society:* First Series, Oxford, Basil Blackwell, 1957.

48. Ado Sanusi, the fourth son of the Emir, was before 1957 a medical clerk at Kaduna. In 1957 he was made District Head of Zakirai by his father and a few months later appointed a Councillor.

49. Alhaji Ibrahim Zimit is married to the Ex-Emir's granddaughter.

50. Alhaji Mohammadu-Munir was N.A. Superintendent of Works (1946–52) and Treasurer (1952–53). He worked closely with the Ex-Emir who before 1954 was Chiroma and head of the whole Native Administration machinery. On becoming Emir in 1954, the Ex-Emir appointed Mohammadu-Munir to his Council and placed him in charge of Finance, Works, etc.

51. *Nigerian Citizen*, 1st May 1963.

52. See Chapter 6, p. 216 on the Madaki.

53. The Tafida Ringim belongs to the other segment of the Kano royal lineage. He was one of the four people presented to the traditional electors after the deposition of the Emir. The other three were, the Dan Maji, District Head of Minjibru and son of the late Emir Aliyu of Kano; Ado Bayero, brother of the Ex-Emir and Mohammadu Inuwa, District Head of Dawakin Kudu, son of late Emir Abbas of Kano and a protege of Emir Abdullahi Bayero, father of the deposed Emir. Mohammadu Inuwa was elected Emir; he died after a reign of three months and was succeeded by Ado Bayero.

54. The phrase is from the Report of the Commission of Enquiry into the affairs of the Zaria Native Authority.

55. Government Statement on the Muffett Report—*Nigerian Citizen*, 1st May 1963.

56. Precarious, firstly, because it was not certain that the Emir would be removed (which would leave the 'Courtiers' open to the Emir's 'displeasure') and secondly, because they, the 'Courtiers', were as much involved in the general maladministration as were the 'Kingsmen'.

57. The expression is from Sir Lewis Namier, *The Structure of Politics at the Accession of George III*, London, Macmillan, 2nd Ed. 1961, p. 11. The impression the writer would like to convey by the expression is not dissimilar to that given by Sir Lewis.

58. For fear of subsequent reprisals, most people had at first hesitated to appear before the Commission, with the result that the Government had to issue a release promising to protect those who would agree to give evidence. The writer was reliably informed that a good many of those who finally went before the Commission were promised material protection by the 'social climbers'.

59. The co-operation between the Courtiers and the social climbers resulted in provision being made for three representatives of 'special interests' in the re-constituted Native Authority Council. These were essentially 'interests' of the business and trading community.

60. For Bornawa domination of the N.A. see M. G. Smith, *The Economy of the Hausa Communities of Zaria*, p. 84, and A. H. M. Kirk-Greene, *Traditional Authority and Leadership Cadres*, mimeographed, 1962, Figure II.

61. Both dynasties were in a minority as against the Bornawa. The fourth dynasty, the Suleibawa was scarcely represented in the Native Administration.

62. The five men are, Mallams, Nuhu Bayero, *Dan Iya*, Yahaya Pate, *Sarkin Yaki*, Suleimanu, *Katurka*, John Tafida, *Dan Galadima*, Alhaji Umaru, *Wali*. The remaining two are: Mallams Mohammadu Sani, *Alkalin Alkalai* (the Alkali families tend to be hereditary and specialize in legal matters) and P. I. Ibrahim, *Sarkin Ruwa*. M. Ibrahim owed his status and therefore loyalty to the Bornawa. *Italicised* expressions refer to traditional titles.

63. The Emir's son proved a failure at the Institute of Administration where he was sent to undergo a course in N.A. duties. He also later failed to obtain a Diploma in Local Government from the same institute. The then Resident finally suggested he should be sent to the U.K. under the sponsorship of the British Council. In the same category as the Emir's son is the Emir's brother-in-law who was appointed Wakilin Gona (Agriculture) by the Emir.

One noticeable feature of the case of Zaria was the absence of the class of 'social-climbers' amongst the political competing groups. This, however, can be accounted for in terms of the socio-economic differences between both societies. Whilst Kano is largely a commercial and business centre, Zaria on the other hand is very much the educational seat of the North.

64. In both cases, the reforms which have followed the Commissions of Inquiry have only served to preserve the in-group nature of political competition. In neither case have the reforms been such as to provide for direct election of members of the N.A. Council. Thus, in Kano, the reconstituted Council is com-posed of (i) the Emir; (ii) two members of the royal household; (iii) three tradi-tional members; (iv) four district and village heads; (v) seven members who are N.A. officials (including two ministers who are on leave of absence without pay); (vi) five elected members (indirectly elected) and (vii) three members representing special interests. The Zaria Council is similarly composed. One effect of the reforms, however, is that there is now greater control and direction of the N.A.s from the regional bureaucracy.

65. See pp. 63–64.

66. For the use here of the expression 'laterally repetitive' relations, see S. F. Nadel, *The Theory of Social Structure*, Cohen and West, 1957, p. 15.

67. The suspicion of the Northern Government and their hostility to research in current politics rules out the possibility of any other form of evidence.

68. One plausible reason for this may be in the different basis of group for-mation. The narrower construction of 'interest' characteristic of the far North certainly makes corruption and nepotism, and consequent inefficiency and malad-ministration, much more practicable given the limited resources of the individual Native Authority.

69. Population Census of the Northern Region of Nigeria, 1953, Bulletins 1–13.

70. See Note 1 p. 343 above.

71. It should be noted that part of the argument is the attempt to refute suggestions that the North is still 'feudal' in outlook. However, this aspect of the argument need not be discussed once it be shown that the argument about democracy is misleading.

72. For the composition of the N.A. Councils in the North, see Campbell, op. cit., pp. 66–68.

73. The only exception is Fika N.A. about which Mr. Fairholm writes as follows: "Elected councillors are in the minority and are ineffectual in operating areas of responsibility. Fika is unique in that it does have one elected portfolio Councillor. This man is the Emir's son, head of his political party (i.e. NPC) educated in England and a member of the Regional Legislature". Earlier Mr. Fairholm noted that "Fika takes its portfolio Councillors from nominated Councillors generally, as do most othe Emirates".

G. W. Fairholm, Summary of Survey of Fika Native Authority (16–19th June 1963), Institute of Administration, Zaria, mimeographed, November 1963.

74. The thirteen Councils are Biu and Bornu in Bornu Province, Kano, Hadeija, Kazaure and Gumel in Kano Province, Sokoto, Zaria and Wase, in Sokoto, Zaria, and Plateau Provinces respectively, Misau and Katagun in Bauchi and Katsina and Daura in Katsina Province. Since 1963, Kano and Zaria now have indirectly elected members.

75. Ilorin is a good example, see *Provincial Annual Reports 1961*, p. 49.

76. See M. Duverger, op. cit., Chapter III, Book II, on the relationship between party systems and political regimes.

VIII

The North and Nigerian Federalism:
The Balance of Political Power

In the previous chapters the analysis of the political scene of Northern Nigeria proceeded, in the main, by taking the North as a 'closed system', the analogy here being the 'analytically closed systems' of the economists. In this chapter that assumption is removed and an attempt is made to consider the place of the North in the over-all balance of forces in the federation. However before this is done, there is yet another sense in which the expression, 'a closed system' has been used which may briefly be noted, as it brings out some of the general features of the politics of the North. This second usage is that to which Max Weber first called attention.[1]

I. WEBER'S CONCEPTION OF A CLOSED SYSTEM AND THE NORTH

In Weber's terms, a political system (or society) is 'closed' "so far as, and to the extent that within the range of its subjective meaning and the validity of its authority, the participation of certain persons is excluded, limited or subject to conditions".[2] "Closure", Weber added may be "within" as well as against outsiders. The latter is the case where "monopolized advantages" are guaranteed to members of the system through their appropriation by individuals, sets of individuals or small groups on a more or less permanent basis, which advantages they come to regard, in time, as inalienable. Further, the closed character may depend on tradition or "affectual attitudes", or it may be "value-related" or based on pure expediency or on combinations of all of these. In the first case—closed systems or sub-systems characterized by tradition—membership and social relations are determined largely by family ties or lineage considerations. This may be reinforced by a "value-related" orientation where the members share a common religion, sets of beliefs, or widely and generally accepted norms.[3] Lastly, Weber pointed out that in such systems, phases of "expansion" and "exclusiveness" alternate with one another. Whilst in the latter case "the motivation is directed at improving the security of the power-position of the leaders", in the former, it is directed at protecting the value of their monopolistic control.[4]

The significance of Weber's conception of a "closed system' in appreciating the politics of the North should be apparent from the previous chapters. But for further elucidation the events surrounding the 1964 Federal elections can be examined from this point of view. The election, the first since Nigeria became an independent state in 1960, was a contest between two broad "alliances"—the Nigerian National Alliance (NNA) and the United Grand Progressive Alliance (UPGA)—a formation which lent the elections the aura of a contest between two parties.[5] In fact, each 'alliance' was a composite of various other parties: the NNA was made up of the NPC, NNDP, MDF and the NDC;[6] the UPGA, of the NCNC, AG and the NPF.[7] Essentially, the basis of the alliances was a North-South confrontation and the electorate, by and large, saw the electoral contest in these terms. In the North the contest was exclusively one between the NPC—the major partner in the NNA—and the NPF, UPGA's Northern ally, and the 'closed' character of the Northern political system can be seen from the attempts of the NPC-controlled Northern Government to limit, if not actually exclude, NPF participation in the electoral contest.

Despite the discouraging performance of the parties making up the NPF at the 1961 North Regional elections UPGA, perhaps a bit too optimistically, held fairly high hopes of their prospects at the 1964 elections, calculating to win between thirty and thirty-five seats in the North. On the assumption that they could win all but ten seats in the South, this would have given them a majority, howbeit small enough, to control the federal government[8] Much of this optimism stemmed from the belief that the NPF would not only win all the seats in the strife-torn Tiv division and a few others seats from the Middle Belt, but also a good many seats in Kano province where the party planned to exploit the dissatisfaction against the NPC caused by the exile of the ex-Emir, Sir Mohammadu Sanusi.[9] Reinforcing this belief was the fact that the opposition would on this occasion, unlike earlier elections, be presenting a united front, thereby consolidating its electoral strength.

The first disillusionment with these calculations came when the NPF found it extremely difficult to hold public meetings or campaign openly in the North. Applications for permits to hold meetings were either rejected or public meetings banned.[10] In one instance, the UPGA campaign team which left the South to aid their northern allies were forbidden by the Premier to enter the town of Gusau. Associated with these 'limitation' tactics was the continuous arrest and imprisonment of members of the opposition, in most cases on the flimsiest of excuses. An example of this was the arrest and subsequent imprisonment (without the option of a fine) of an UPGA lawyer on the grounds of holding an 'illegal' meeting and using 'insulting' language.[11] By late October conditions had deteriorated so much with incessant complaints by the opposition that a meeting of the leaders of all the major political parties had to be summoned to agree on the minimum conditions for free and fair electoral campaigning.[12]

Be this as it may, the closed character of the Northern political system was adequately demonstrated when the opposition ran into difficulties with the process of nomination of candidates. Some cases, taken from Kano province, may be cited as illustrative examples of the difficulties: (i) Abdullahi Adam, prospective NPF candidate for Dawakin Kudu constituency was arrested and jailed for one year on the day nominations opened for using 'insulting' language in references to the Premier, Alhaji Sir Ahmadu Bello; (ii) Lawan Maiturari, NPF prospective candidate for one of the two constituencies in Bici, suffered a similar fate; (iii) Bello Dawa, a school-master at Dambatta and prospective candidate for Gwaram was arrested, brought before the Emir and detained in jail for the period of the nomination; (iv) a not dissimilar situation confronted the prospective candidate, M. Ali Abdullahi, for Ungogo-Kumbotso. In all these cases, substitute candidates had subsequently to be found. In Gaya North, four sets of nominators of the prospective candidate—Adamu Gaya—were arrested and imprisoned. He finally succeeded in filing his nomination with a fifth set of sponsors. Mallam Maitama Sarkin Tafariki former head of the Kano Native Authority road overseers (expelled after the Kano enquiry) and nephew of the ex-Emir refused to be nominated for fear of victimization as he was now a contractor relying on the Native Authority. Then there was the case of M. Musa Sa'id Abubakar, NPF candidate for Sumaila. A school teacher at Kofar Kudu elementary school and son of the village head of Magani in Sumaila district, Mallam Sa'id was after his nomination jailed for four months for alleged 'incitement to violence'. On 19th December, while still in jail, he was reported to have been met by his father and a representative of the Emir, who jointly asked him to withdraw his nomination (in favour of the NPC candidate, Alhaji M. Inua Wada, a federal Cabinet Minister) failing which his father threatened to disinherit him. In complying, M. Said was released from jail and taken by the Yari, N.A. Head of Prisons, Alhaji Mohammadu Duse Injima to Wudil (a village some twenty-five miles from Kano) where he was lodged at a private house.[13] A fairly close parallel to this instance was that of M. Sabo Mohammed Dogorai who was made to withdraw his nomination in favour of the Sarkin Dalhatu in Gaya South constituency.

The difficulties encountered by the opposition were such that the Federal Electoral Commission (FEC) had to extend the closing date for nominations by an extra day[14] Dissatisfaction, however, continued. On 22nd December, three days after the closure of nominations, the chairman of the FEC, in a public broadcast, admitted that there were gross irregularities in many places and suggested a possible postponement of the elections in these areas. At this time, 68 or about 40% of the total number of constituencies in the North had returned NPC candidates unopposed.[15] The distribution of these constituencies is shown in the following table:

TABLE 22

Provinces Returning Unopposed Candidates 1964

	Adamawa	Bauchi	Benue	Bornu	Ilorin	Kabba	Kano	Katsina	Niger	Plateau	Sardauna	Sokoto	Zaria	Kaduna	Total
No. of Constituencies	8	14	15	17	7	8	31	14	7	7	5	25	8	1	167
No. Returned Unopposed	3	7	2	13	2	–	5	6	2	1	5	22	–	–	68
%	37·5	50	13·3	76·4	28·5	—	16·1	42·8	28·5	14·2	100	88	—	—	40·7

A few days later, the President of the Republic suggested a total cancellation of the elections and an invitation to the U.N. for experts to organize and run a fresh election. A day before the elections, disagreement amongst members of the FEC over the whole proceedings led to the resignation of two of its members, to be followed by a third on the day of the 'elections', at which point the UPGA decided to boycott the elections.[16] The effect of this boycott, which was ineffectively organized[17] on the voting patterns is shown in the table below, where the figures are contrasted with those of 1959.

TABLE 23

Northern Nigeria: Results of 1964 Federal Elections

Total Votes Cast		NNA/ NPC	UPCA/ NPF	NNA/ NPC	UPGA NPF	Total Seats
1959	3,258,520	1,944,045	1,085,453	141 (*b*)	33	174
1964	2,353,809 (a)	2,048,285	271,911	163 (*b*)	4	167
% Increase or Decrease −27·8%		+25·8%	−21·8%	+16·6%	−16·5%	−4·4%

NOTES: (*a*) No Contest in 68 Constituencies.
      (*b*) includes 7 Independents in 1959 and 1 in 1964.
      The % shown in columns (2) and (3) are differences in percentages of votes cast for a party (or seats won) as a percentage of total votes cast (or seats) at each election.

The boycott—which led to a constitutional crisis when the President refused to reappoint Sir Abubakar Tafawa Balewa as Prime Minister[18]—was thus a reaction to the NPC's monopolization of socio-political participation in the North. This monopoly not only guarantees to the NPC the over-all control of the North but also the domination of the federal government, a domination which it has sought to preserve through an 'expansionist' orientation in seeking parliamentary allies at the federal level[19] whilst retaining the North intact.

The domination of the centre, which the NPC's monopoly practices ensures, rests on the North's overall representational majority and it was the determined effort of the North to preserve this majority which caused the 'census crisis' of 1964. The crisis arose in the attempt by the NCNC controlled government of the Eastern region to have the 'census figures' rejected on the grounds that the figures for the North were grossly inflated. An earlier count in 1962 allegedly had shown that the figures for the North, East and West were 21·4m., 12·3m. and 10·8m. respectively.[20] These, in effect, would have given the East and the West an edge on the North, but in a speech in the Federal Parliament, the Minister charged with the census, Alhaji Ibrahim Waziri, Minister of Economic Development, accused the East of inflating its figures.[21] In the charge and counter-charge that followed, the decision was finally taken to have a recount. The recount in 1963—released the following year—showed that the

North's figure had risen to 29·7m., the East remained at 12·3m., the West (which in 1962 included the Mid-West) rose from approximately 8·0m. to 10·2m., whilst the Mid-West was 2·5m.; Lagos, the federal capital, remained the same at 0·6m.; the interesting fact emerging from these figures was that in the second count, the North curiously emerged with a figure which gave it the same percentage lead over the rest of the country as it had after the 1952 census, the ratios remaining at 53·4% to 46·6%. Faced with such a reversal, with opposition to the new figures coming from the East, the Mid-West,[22] the Lagos City Council, the Southern trade union organizations, the Eastern Government attempted to challenge the validity of the figures before the Courts. With the refusal of the Federal Supreme Court to entertain the suit by the East, the new figures were finally accepted, and the North assured of its built-in lead.[23] The drive by the NPC to control not only its region but also the Federal government can be readily appreciated and it is this question and the imbalance it creates which is now to be considered.

II. THE NORTH AND NIGERIAN FEDERALISM

The major constitutional changes that have taken place in Nigeria—from the first post-World War II change to the present, have all had the effect of whittling down the powers of the Central administration in favour of the regions.[24] The 'Richard's Constitution' which was put into practice in 1946 was essentially a 'unitary constitution'. Its successor, the 'MacPherson Constitution', while retaining over-all Central control, devolved greater political discretion to the regions. Its main characteristics were essentially unitary. The principal change towards federalism was therefore the 1954 Constitution which provided the central principles and legal framework on which the federation has been administered till the present. Under it, the bureaucracy, judiciary and the Central Marketing Board were regionalized, a process which continued with the administrative regionalization of the police in 1958. Thus between 1954 and 1958 when the proposals for the 'Independence Constitution' were finally formulated,[25] successive changes were merely amendments to the original constitution. The Republican Constitution equally provided no major departure from the basic 1954 constitutional structure.[26] Parallel with the process of political regionalization has been the increasing demand for financial autonomy by the regional governments and which has resulted in four separate Commissions on Revenue Allocation.[27] The Regions now not only control income tax, but also have the major part of all revenues from minerals, the export duties on primary products, duties on diesel and motor oil, wines and spirits, tobacco allocated to them. The significance of this demand for regional financial autonomy is shown in the following table quoting figures of current revenue of the regional government *vis-à-vis* the federal government.

Thus, whereas the federal government's current revenue increased for the time under consideration by just 74·4%, regional government revenues were just about trebled. Significantly, the West and the North, the two regions with higher magnitudes (the West with the highest precentage increase) were the chief architects of regionalism.

TABLE 24

Current Revenue Federal and Regional Government: 1953–60
in £000's

Year	Federal Govt.	R. Govts Total	North	East	West
1953	50,906	18,938	8,540	4,730	5,668
1954	59,256	18,993	6,338	5,348	7,307
1955	62,481	36,238	13,123	9,397	13,718
1956	59,950	38,150	13,748	9,008	14,381
1957	70,567	43,276	14,549	12,184	15,522
1958	70,945	44,475	14,319	13,380	15,709
1959	77,316	47,335	15,059	14,216	16,649
1960	88,824	53,323	16,608	14,875	19,681
% Change 1953/60	74·4	181·5	94·4	214·4	247·2

SOURCE: Federal Government Digest of Statistics

The demand for regionalism and the whittling down of the powers of the federal government can be easily understood. The fear of ethnic domination by one group or the other, North–South conflict over the question of independence, the expectation of rapid economic mobilization through autonomy, the regional nature of the major political parties—all of these were contributory factors.

But regionalism has not been without its attendant difficulties. The increased scope of regional government activities has led to a strain on regional finances enhanced in large part by falling commodity prices—the main source of regional revenues—in the world market. The changing structure of commodity prices is reflected in the following tables.

TABLE 25

Domestic Export Structure: £m

Year	Cocoa	Groundnuts	Palm Produce	Oil	Others	Total
1958	27	32	33	—	41	133
1959	38	32	40	3	48	161
1960	35	27	38	4	57	161
1961	34	37	32	11	56	170
1962	33	39	26	17	49	164

SOURCE: United Africa Co. Ltd.: *Statistical and Economic Review*, April 1964, p. 26.

TABLE 26

Export Value, Volume and Price Indices: 1954=100

	Year						% change
	1957	1958	1959	1960	1961	1962	1957–62
Value	85	91	109	110	116	112	+37·8
Volume	106	105	126	124	147	156	+47·2
Price	84	85	89	90	84	80	4·8

SOURCE: Ibid., p. 24.

So far revenues from personal income tax have not formed a significant part of total revenue. This is as should be expected, given that not only is per-capita income low, but the collection relatively inefficient. The proportion of revenue from income tax to total revenue is shown below.

TABLE 27

Revenues from Personal Income Tax as Percentage of Total Revenue 1959/60–1963/64

Government	1959/60	1960/61	1961/62	1962/63	1963/64
Fed. Govt.	4·0	4·2	4·5	2·8	3·0
North	7·3	8·4	6·3	9·2	10·0
West	2·0	1·3	6·2	9·4	10·5
East	17·0	18·0	18·0	11·0	17·0

SOURCE: Compiled from Official Estimates of the Federal and Regional Governments.

The significance of falling commodity prices—and therefore revenue and the increased volume of government undertakings brought about by regionalism can be easily seen in the volume of regional government surpluses or deficit on current account.

TABLE 28

Surpluses (+) or Deficits (−) of Governments on Current Account 1960–1964
£000

Year	Federal Government	North	West	East
1960	+7,075	+2,057	−2,471	+2,014
1961	+17,251	−798	−2,050	+1,602
1962	+5,241	−2,925	+2,121	+2,300
1963	+3,678	−1,181	−490	+2,158
1964 (a)	+138	+417	+565	+1,302

NOTE: (*a*) Estimates only.
SOURCE: Federal Government Digest of Statistics.

The relatively improved budgetary position of the East can be attributed in large part to the increasing contribution which oil makes to the economy of that region. But apart from the East, of the regional governments, both the North and the West have in successive years been faced with budget deficits, which they have had to make up by running down regional government reserves— accumulated in the main, in the period before 1957.

TABLE 29

Overseas Assets of Regional Governments and other Institutions
1959–63 £m.

	31st Dec. '59	31st Dec. '60	31st Dec. '61	31st Dec. '62	30th Sept.'63
Regional Government	31·6	23·3	19·5	18·5	6·5
Local Authorities	3·5	3·9	3·9	3·9	3·9
Regional Development Corporations	5·3	1·9	1·3	0·6	0·3
Regional Marketing Boards	35·2	19·2	−0·4	1·1	5·0

SOURCE: Federal Government Digest of Statistics.[28]

Taking the North alone, projected estimates of revenue and expenditure suggest that by 1968 the North will have had a budgetary deficit of some £16m. In fact, it was expected that budget surpluses should yield the North by that date some £7·5m. So that in effect, the actual size of the deficit would be of the order of some £23·6m.[29]

The burden of increasing regional governmental activities and relatively inelastic revenues has emphasized the role of the federal government on which the regions have now to rely for financial aid. Nigeria started out by uncritically accepting the Wheare 'model' of federalism[30] as the answer to its political problems. Economic factors, on the other hand, have gradually altered the working basis of the model by tending to subordinate the regions to the Centre which is now being called upon to give a necessary lead to the regions. Thus, under the 6-Year Development Plan (1962–68) the Federal government and its controlled agencies is expected to account for 61·0% of the total planned expenditure envisaged. This does not include aids, grants and loans to the regions; for instance, under the Plan, the Federal government is expected to provide £10m. towards regional agricultural expansion and another £15m. for recurrent costs. Besides the grant of £4m. to regional universities, it has recently decided to accept responsibility for 50% of total expenditure by these universities. A special grant of £3m. was also made to the North for the development of primary education.

Besides the economic lead expected of the federal government, the necessity to exercise general control over the price level, the balance of payments and the rate of growth[31] have led to the federal government taking over responsibility for the over-all direction of he economy. Thus since 1958 it has taken over the raising of all external loans over a year's duration[32] and since 1959 has been responsible for the floating of all internal loans. Under the Banking Amendment Act 1962 not only are regional governments and their agencies expected to deposit part of their reserves with the Central Bank, but the Act, by empowering the Bank to regulate the minimum interest rates charged by the commercial banks, to approve their interest rate structure, and to fix the liquidity ratio by determining which of their assets would be accepted in assessing the holdings of the banks, now places the federal government in a position to control the operations of the regional Marketing Boards and *eo ipso*, the financial policies of the regional governments.[33] Observedly too, federal co-ordinating agencies such as the Council on Establishments, the Council on Natural Resouces and the National Economic Council are gradually tending to assume a regulative, rather than their advisory role. The NEC, in this respect, it should be pointed out, has been the most successful.[34]

At this point, the rationale of the insistence of the NPC[35] on controlling the federal government, which its 'closed' politics makes possible, can now be examined. It need hardly be argued that the continued exercise of power by any political leadership depends on the legitimacy of its rule.[36] Legitimacy is a function not merely of the operative system of norms and beliefs but also of the extent to which the political leadership can satisfy the general economic aspirations of the people.

In the North, both history and religion have been used to 'legitimize' political domination by the NPC leadership. But to maintain this, the leadership still has to meet the rational expectations of the northern electorate. Here, however, lies the main problem confronting the party political leaders, a problem probably best illustrated by an examination of the experience of the North under its Development Plan. And the basic fact is simply one of failure.[37]

The record of the first year of the Plan shows, for example, underspending in the development sector and overspending in the administrative and social sectors. In effect, the economy is not growing at the expected rate. The differential rate of spending is shown summarily in the following table.[38]

TABLE 30

Northern Nigeria: 1962–68 Development Plan: First Progress Report

Sector	Plan 1962 –68%	Actual Expenditure 1962 – 63%	Estimated Expenditure 1963–64%
Development	57·0%	46·0 (−11·0%)	47·0 (−10·0%)
Social	42·0	47·0 (+5·0%)	50·0 (+8·0%)
Administration	1·0	7·0 (+6·0%)	3·0 (+2·0%)

A more detailed break-down gives the over-all situation as follows.[39]

Sub-Sectors	Plan Target		Actual Expenditure 1963–64		Estimated Expenditure 1963–64	
	£000	%	£000	%	£000	%
Agriculture	17,647	19·9	850	11·8 (−8·1)	1,726	15·9
Animal Resources	4,387	4·9	216	3·0 (−1·9)	1,065	9·8
Forestry	463	0·5	38	0·5 (—)	90	0·8
TOTAL	22,497	25·3	1,104	15·3 (−10·0)	2,881	26·5

T

Sub-Sectors	Plan Target		Actual Expenditure 1962–63		Estimated Expenditure 1963–64	
	£000		£000	%	£000	%
Trade and industry	2,157	2·4	177	2·4 (—)	557	5·1
Electricity	1,500	1·7	—	— (—)	14	0·1
Co-operatives	2,026	2·3	—	— (—)	12	0·1
Transport	19,484	21·9	1,432	19·8 (−2·1)	1,159	10·7
Public works	4,575	5·2	818	11·3 (+6·1)	823	7·6
Social welfare	2,735	4·9	512	7·1 (+2·2)	712	6·6
Information	90	0·1	139	1·9 (+1·8)	192	1·8
Admin. and Judicial (Buildings)	812	0·9	419	5·8 (+4·9)	270	2·5
Water supplies	7,674	8·6	906	12·6 (+4·0)	2,135	19·7
Education	17,637	19·9	1,258	17·4 (−2·5)	1,231	11·3
Health	4,392	4·9	512	7·1 (+2·2)	607	5·6
Land/Survey	3,021	3·4	37	0·5 (−2·9)	136	1·3
Staff training	61	0·1	8	0·1 (—)	46	0·4
Internal affairs	97	0·1	133	1·8 (+1·7)	81	0·7
TOTAL	88,755	100	7,228	100 —	10,856	100

Thus, besides the directly productive sector, under-spending has also taken place in other sub-sectors such as education and transport. Admittedly, the first-year experience of the Development Plan is not an adequate guide to the over-all prospects of the Plan fulfilment. But as against this, the Plan financing provides enough cause for extreme scepticism. Estimated expenditure for the year 1963/64, for instance, called for a sum about 150% higher than the 1962/63 expenditure. The original plan estimate was £21·5m., which allowing for 10% under-spending, should be £19·3m. However, estimated financial resources show only £8·99m., of which external aid in all forms amount to £1·6m. or 17·8% of the total. On the other hand, it is expected that actual capital expenditure will be about £8·2m., an approximate reduction in the Plan estimate of over 100%.

The prospects for the rest of the Plan are no better. Originally, estimated total expenditure was put at £98·9m. This has now been revised to £88·9m. (allowing for 10% underspending). Of this sum, total internal resources existing and new, are estimated at £15·3m., with matching foreign aid at an equal sum, thus leaving an uncovered gap of some £58·3m. or two-thirds of the total requirements. Even these gloomy calculations do not take into consideration, changing price-levels—an unrealistic situation when it is realized that more recent cost-estimates, for instance for urban water supplies, show that these have risen 3·75 times over and above the original cost.[40] The wage increases in 1964 have further pushed up costs.[41]

The problem here being posed can equally be illustrated from another standpoint, that of education. The 'Ashby Report' on post-school certificate and higher education in Nigeria[42] suggested that for Northern Nigeria, government policy should aim at raising the percentage of children of 6–13 age group in primary schools to 25% by 1968. The Northern government on the other hand raised this figure to 50%, which they later revised to 28% in the Development Plan. By 1964 the percentage of children in primary schools in the various provinces was as follows: Ilorin 45·5%, Kabba, 44·5%, Benue 27·8%, Plateau 26·5%, Zaria 21·5%, Niger 14·4%, Adamawa 13·5%, Bauchi 9·8%, Bornu 6·5%, Kano 5·8%, Katsina 5·4% and Sokoto 3·5%. The regional average in 1960 was 19·5% which by 1963 had risen to 21·0%. A projection of the rate of growth suggests that by 1968 the average will be approximately 24·0% or 3·2% short of the government's target. In view of the wide differential rates between the provinces, the government in 1963 imposed a ceiling on primary school expansion of 28·0%. In other words, no new school buildings will be sanctioned by the government in provinces where the 28·0% figure has been attained. Thus, in places like Ilorin, Kabba, Benue and Plateau, a halt has been called. In these provinces, therefore, enrolment can only be increased by cramming more pupils into the existing schools. But there is obviously a limit to this process. The 'fairness' of the government's rule may be subject to dispute. But be this as it may, it is hardly likely that the people of these provinces which interestingly enough are all in the Middle-Belt—will take kindly to a policy which must necessarily favour one set of people at the expense of the other. Not improbably, then, one might expect that should opposition be strong enough, this could lead to a resurgence of Middle-Belt separatism and thus, a direct challenge to the NPC leadership.[43]

Parenthetically, one might add that with the completion of new schools, hospitals, etc., recurrent expenditure will necessarily rise but already there is a stringent need to curtail this if there is to be any reasonable hope of the Plan fulfilment. As the authors of the North's First Progress Report noted, short of an economic breakdown, "fantastic economies" and increased efficiency of revenue collection are imperative in the region.[44] Paradoxically, despite this, the North, by the Constitution of Northern Nigeria Amendment Law 1965, has recently increased representation in the House of Assembly from 177 to 230, an increase of 30·0% and that of the House of Chiefs, from 110 to 125, a rise of approximately 14·0%, in order "to take into account the population increase" reported in the 1963 census.

Faced with rising recurrent expenditures, inelastic revenues and thus recurrent budgetary deficits, and depleted reserves—(the reserves of the Consolidated fund, which in 1964 were a mere £0·6m. are almost exhausted)—it is hardly surprising that the North's (that is the NPC's) main hope lies in the control of the federal government, the remaining principal source of finance. The extent of this reliance is shown in the expectations of the North of financial resources for development purposes.

TABLE 31

Development of Financial Resources (Expected not Actual) £m

Year	Earlier Resources	Recurrent Surpluses	Other Receipts	Federal Government Grants and Loans	Marketing Board Loans	Total 1–5	Foreign Aid %	£m.	Total
1962–63	1·1	2·6	0·6	3·0	—	7·3	11·0	0·9	8·2
1963–64	—	2·1	0·2	5·0	—	7·3	18·0	1·6	8·9
1964–65	0·5	1·5	0·6	5·0	2·0	9·6	23·0	2·9	12·5
1965–66	0·5	0·9	0·7	5·0	2·0	9·1	38·0	5·5	14·6
1966–67	0·5	0·4	0·8	5·0	2·0	8·7	45·0	7·0	15·7
1967–68	—	—	1·0	5·0	2·0	8·0	50·0	8·0	16·0
TOTAL	2·6	7·5	3·9	28·0	8·0	50·0	34·0	25·9	75·9

SOURCE: First Progress Report, p. 28
NOTE: The £75·9m. will represent a 25% shortfall as against planned under-spending of 10%. Besides, as the Report points out, if the Marketing Board does not realize the estimated £8m. (using percentage shown) total Plan estimates will be £62·5m. rather than £75·9m.

Clearly then, the North expects 56% of total 'internal' financial resources and approximately 37% of the over-all total from the federal government. In other words, a re-allocation of federal finances in favour of the North. The Report expressly recognizes this, for as the authors put it, "A re-allocation of revenues between the Federal and regional governments is imperative". It adds that such a redistribution "obviously does not add to total resources of Plan implementation, but will influence *each* (italics mine) of the separate plans which together form the National Plan."[45]

Already the North's control of the federal government has assured it particular privileges in the federal development plan. Thus, besides items connected with coastal waterways (the main items under Transport and Aviation £14·6m.), Lagos Affairs (£21·2m.), Information (£2·3m.), Communications (£30·0m.), a large proportion of development spending is being concentrated in the North. The Niger Dam (£68·1m.) centred in the North,[46] represents slightly more than 10% of the federal government's total spending. Almost all of the £29·7m. scheduled for defence is to be spent in the North and other than federal institutions such as the Ibadan and Lagos Universities (and teaching hospitals), a good proportion of the £39·2m. on health and education is to be directed to the North. Of the £10m. earmarked for regional agricultural expansion, the first £4m. disbursed in 1963/64 was distributed as follows: North £2·2m., East £1·1m. and West £0·7m., the North receiving more than 50% of the total. Again, besides the £12m. spent on the Bornu Railway Extension, much of the £35·3m. to be spent on roads is being spent in the North,[47] whilst the refusal of the Northern leaders to permit the exploitation of iron-ores located in the region for utilization elsewhere has led to the proposed iron and steel industry for utilization elsewhere has led to the proposed iron and steel industry (£30m.) being split into two or three separate plants, one in the North, the other in the East, with the probability of a third in the West.

Federal control also provides the North with ample opportunities for patronage and the placing of Northerners in high offices. In 1964, fourteen of the thirty-seven Nigerians employed as High Commissioners, Ambassadors and Chargé d'Affaires were Northerners; three of the eight board members of the Nigerian Coal Corporation, four of the eleven of the Nigerian Railway Corporation, were from the North. At the same period six of the sixteen federal ministries were headed by Northerners.

It is not being suggested that developmental spending should not go to the North, but given the fact that the South is more highly developed, it is possible that the concentration of resources in the North ignores not only the problems of the South, but also external economies of scale. The problems of the South are shown by the fact that already unemployment of pupils with school certificate and higher qualifications has reached (31st March 1962) the disturbing figure of 10·2%, with 89·8% for primary school leavers and below.[48] The average rate of urban unemployment in the South is more than twice the figure of the North, 28·9% as against 13·1%. The distribution in the South is even more disturbing, this being 38·4% in Lagos, 29·0% in the East and 19·5% in the West.[49] Then there is the significant point that with increasing balance of payments difficulties[50] caused in part by the development effort and in part by unfavourable terms of trade, the main stop-gap contribution will come from the oil production of the South, particularly the East and Mid-West (areas, other than Lagos, with the highest rates of unemployment). During the Development Plan period oil alone is expected to make a positive contribution to the balance of payments of over £100m.[51]

The economics of the location of federal political power in the NPC of the North has not unreasonably led to attempts to reassess the balance of political forces in the federation, a reassessment which was manifest in the form of party alliances before the 1964 federal elections. Underlying this reassessment is the basic proposition that the present system of representation which gives a majority of seats to the North, weights power in favour of the rural North against the urban more socially mobilized South. Put differently, this is to say that in educational terms, political power has been weighted in favour of the relatively uneducated as against the educated; in 'social' terms, in preference of the peasantry as against the industrial proletariat. These contrasts are shown statistically in the following tables on pages 279, 280 and 281.

However, as a prelude, the background to this reassessment can be briefly stated. The NPC–NCNC coalition federal government which resulted from the 1959 federal elections was a negotiated settlement between the top leaders of both parties, allegedly arrived at in the interests of independence and the unity of the country.[52] However, by 1961, faced with economic problems, the NCNC, primarily based in the Eastern Region,[53] was in the process of reconsidering its role in the federal government. The overtures made by that party to the AG of the West, in an attempt to form an alliance, fell through. Several factors contributed to this. In the first place, as a result of carpet-crossing, the NPC already had a majority of four in the federal Parliament. To have concluded an alliance with the AG would thus have meant the exclusion of the NCNC from the 'corridors of power'. Secondly, even the allegiance of some of the NCNC federal leaders was in doubt. Lastly, the AG itself was faced with an internal party crisis.

TABLE 32

Distribution of Teachers According to Regions 1963

Description	North	East	West	Lagos	Total South	Grand Total
Primary (all grades)	13,069 (13·9)	38,954	38,856	3,297	81,107 (86·1)	94,167
Secondary Grammar						
(a) Graduates	390 (17·1)	799	896	200	1,895 (82·9)	2,285
(b) Non-Graduates	200 (7·0)	1,272	1,171	243	2,686 (93·0)	2,866
Secondary Commercial						
(a) Graduates	— (—)	47	—	26	73 (100)	73
(b) Non-Graduates	— (—)	288	—	130	418 (100)	418
Teacher Training						
(a) Graduates	185 (34·5)	175	144	31	350 (65·5)	535
(b) Non-Graudates	307 (21·3)	504	591	41	1,136 (78·7)	1,443

TABLE 33

Employment of All Kinds 1952–1961

Area	Sept. 1957	1958	1959	1960	Dec. 1961
Lagos	103,500	95,600	94,900	94,500	84,000
West	86,300	96,300	96,300	133,000	119,800
East	94,400	98,100	100,100	128,000	103,400
Total	284,200 (64·7)	290,000 (65·7)	292,300 (67·4)	355,500 (71·2)	307,200 (72·6)
North	154,800 (35·3)	150,800 (34·3)	141,100 (32·6)	144,000 (28·8)	115,700 (27·4)
Grand Total	439,000 (100)	440,800 (100)	433,400 (100)	499,000 (100)	422,900 (100)

N.B. Percentages are of over-all total
SOURCE: *Annual Report of the Federal Ministry of Labour for the Year 1961/62*, Lagos, 1964. Table I, p. 9.

TABLE 34

Distribution of Factories by Size 31st March 1962

No. of Employees	Lagos	East	West	Total	North	Grand Total
10–24	83	113	96	292 (76·6)	89 (23·4)	381
25–49	60	146	71	277 (79·8)	70 (20·2)	347
50–99	46	33	49	128 (75·2)	42 (24·8)	170
100–199	32	27	31	90 (69·2)	40 (30·8)	130
200–399	13	6	16	35 (62·5)	21 (37·5)	56
400	11	6	4	21 (84·0)	4 (16·0)	25
% of Total	245	331	267	843 (76·1)	266 (23·9)	1,109
Average size per Factory	101	53	73	—	77	—

N.B. Percentages are of over-all total.
SOURCE: Ibid, Appendix 9, p. 56

One feature of the crisis which split the AG is significant for the present analysis. A central issue involved in the dispute was the basis on which political power was to be organized in the federation. A section led by Chief Awolowo, the AG federal President, dissatisfied with the regional base of party power which condemns the South to a prepetual minority at the federal level, wanted the existing parties to cut across regional boundaries. Under his leadership, the AG had attempted to break into the North and the East. At the 1959 federal elections the AG and its northern allies succeeded in winning a total of twenty-five seats in the North and fourteen in the East. The party, however, failed to win a majority of seats in the federation and was therefore forced into the opposition in the federal parliament. In this struggle for ascendancy, the party 'lost' over £4m., money of the Western Nigeria Marketing Board which had been diverted into the Party's purse through the National Investment and Properties Company.[54]

The other faction, led by Premier S. L. Akintola, Awolowo's second-in-command, saw in the Party's moves an attempt to betray the interests of the Western Region, preferring rather to accept the *status quo*. At least this had the advantage of guaranteeing the AG control of the West while promising the prospects of sharing in the

TABLE 35

A

Enrolment in Schools 1960–63
Primary Education (in thousands)

Year	North	East	West	Lagos
1960	282	1,430	1,124	74
1961	316	1,274	1,134	81
1962	359	1,266	1,108	98
1963	410	1,278	1,099	107

B

Teacher training 1960–63
(in thousands)

	North	East	West	Lagos
	4	12	11	·4
	4	11	11	·5
	6	11	12	·7
	7	10	12	·8

C

Secondary-General (in thousands)

Year	North	East	West	Lagos
1960	6	22	101	5
1961	6	25	128	7
1962	7	32	144	10
1963	9	39	150	11

D

Technical and Vocational (in thousands)

	North	East	West	Lagos
	2	8	·1	1
	2	1	·4	1
	2	1	·1	1
	2	1	·7	2

All educational data compiled from: Federal Ministry of Education, *Statistics of Education in Nigeria 1963*, Series No. 1, Vol. 3, Lagos, 1965.

booty which federal participation offers to those in the seats of power. Akintola's preference was therefore co-operation with the NPC and the North. The struggle between the two factions ended in an open fight in the Western House of Assembly in May 1962 (in which the NCNC supported the Akintola faction) and under the pretence that this constituted a threat to 'order and stability' in the Region, the NPC–NCNC coalition federal government declared a State of Emergency and suspended the regional government. Under the umbrella of the Emergency the Federal government completed the necessary arrangements and legislation that was to lead to the creation of Nigeria's fourth region in July 1963—the Mid-West region.

At the end of the Emergency, the Akintola faction was known as the United People's Party (UPP) and was reinstated in power with the aid of the federal government Akintola's theory of 'regional security' had suited the NPC which in the party dispute came out in open support of Akintola.[55] But the reinstatement was only possible through the collaboration of the NCNC: its parliamentary members joined the UPP to form an NCNC–UPP coalition government. If the NPC had its own motives in supporting Akintola, the NCNC saw in the AG split an opportunity to establish itself in control.[56] The UPP hardly existed outside the House of Assembly. In every respect it was scarcely a political party. Because the UPP had no mass base, the NCNC seized its opportunity in the Executive to dissolve local authority councils all over the region, replacing them with 'Caretaker Committees' composed almost exclusively of NCNC members.

The NPC, afraid that NCNC moves in the West might lead to an NCNC controlled Western Nigeria (which with the East and Mid-West would place it in a position to dominate the whole of the South), suggested the amalgamation of both 'parties' to champion the cause of the Yoruba West. Amongst the Yoruba members of the NCNC itself, there was dissatisfaction with the distribution of party patronage. A good many of the leaders felt that the interests of the Yorubas were being sacrificed to those of the Ibo in the distribution of federal public corporation membership and even in appointments and promotions in the universities.[57]

The 1963 census figures provided the catalyst uniting the NCNC West parliamentary party and the UPP into the Nigerian National Democratic Party (NNDP). The NCNC national Executive Committee had instructed the NCNC West parliamentary party to reject the figures. This they refused to do, noting at the same time that the NCNC federal Cabinet members were prevaricating in their stand on the census. With the NNDP now committed to support the NPC and the latter's influence extending into the Mid-West (in the form of the Mid-West Democratic Front; MDF) and the East (the Eastern Peoples Congress, the Niger Delta Congress, the Republic Party and the Dynamic Party), the NCNC was led into forming an alliance with the Action Group. In conjunction with the NPF, the new alliance emerged as UPGA to contest the federal elections. Thus, by the time of the elections, the alignment of parties had taken the form, in the main, of a North–South confrontation.

The 'boycott' and the constitutional crisis which followed—a crisis which all but destroyed the federation[58]—suggest that Nigeria has still to find a new basis for the distribution of power in the federation. The 'political settlement' which followed the resolution of the crisis emphasized this when the leaders agreed to a review of the Constitution in the search of a new formula for "Nigerian unity". That a formula has to be found few will dispute. With a census, which from being a statistical exercise turned into an exercise in political manoeuvrability, an "election that was never an election", it is hardly surprising that some have turned to the constitution as a way out of the socio-political imbalance.

III. THE DEBATE ON THE CONSTITUTION

Only once in its recent political history has the mass electorate of Nigeria been 'privileged' in shaping the constitutional structure of the country. This was the series of discussions and consultations which preceded the 1951 'MacPherson Constitution'. Since that date all forms of constitutional changes that have taken place have been decided upon by the party political leaders in one constitutional conference after the other. With this experience it is unlikely that the present exercise will involve anything like the debate of 1949 to 1950. However, the main lines on which reforms have been advocated seem reasonably clear. Most of these were canvassed in the electioneering campaigning prior to the 1964 elections. These have recently been supplemented by further suggestions from the President of the Republic, Dr. Nnamdi Azikiwe, in an article on 'Essentials for Nigeria's Survival'.[59] All of these suggested reforms fall broadly into two categories—structural and institutional.

1. *Structural Reform*

The principal reform of this kind currently discussed is the creation of more states. But such proposals are directed at the North from

which, it is suggested, at least two more states should be carved out—
a Middle-Belt State and a Kano State—demanded by NEPU and the
Kano Peoples' Party. This, it is argued, would have the effect of
breaking the monolithic character of the North and thereby permit
a greater degree of political competitiveness. The force of this
argument derives from what one might call Mill's law of instability
in federal systems of government, "that there should not be any one
State so much more powerful than the rest as to be capable of vying
in strength with many of them combined. If there be such a one,
and only one, it will insist on being master of the joint deliberations. . . ."[60]

A variant of this view is that which advocates a much more
centralized system of government based on the existing provinces.
In effect, this would be a return to the pre-1938 colonial system of
government in which the effective administrative unit was the
province headed by a Resident who was responsible, through a
Commissioner, to the central bureaucracy in Lagos. Both the
Commissioner and the Resident become then, mere agents of the
central government.

There is little likelihood of the latter proposal being seriously
entertained and whatever may be the merits of the former, there is
hardly any possibility of its proving acceptable to the Northern
leaders. In terms of practical politics, it can therefore be safely
ignored, a consideration which has led to the suggestion that since
the concrete problem is one of representation, this should be based on
the voting population and not on total population as at present.
The counter to this is that the female population in the North should
be enfranchised as elsewhere in Nigeria. The Secretary-General of
the NPC, on this question, has pointed out that "while many of us
might feel it only right to enfranchise the women of the North" to
do so might "offend the sentiments of the majority" and to insist on
female franchise is to throw away caution in "trying to force it on an
unwilling population".[61] He further noted that a committee of
Muslim experts was already studying the problem. The Northern
Premier has however, admitted that in the event of Nigeria having an
elected Executive President, women in the North might be called
upon to vote. It follows then that while the North is reticient about
enfranchising its female population, it would not hesitate to permit
this should the balance of political power be made to depend on the
women of the North being given the vote. The conclusion should be
obvious. It is hardly reasonable to expect that the North will accept
a representation weighted by its adult male population as this will
be to its disadvantage. On the other hand, given a tradition and a

religious system which subordinates the female to the male, it is improbable should the women be enfranchised that their voting patterns will be different from that of the 'superior' sex.

2. *Institutional Alterations*

If the proposed structural reforms are seen as being geared towards a readjustment of the balance of forces—between North and South, suggested institutional changes have largely been directed at checking the Executive and maintaining what can best be described as an 'open society'. The former includes alterations to the constitutional status of the federal second chamber—the Senate—and the office of the Head of State, the latter changes in the organization of the armed and security forces and the Courts.

To give a greater degree of independence to members of the Senate, it has been suggested that they, like the members of the House of Representatives, should be directly elected. Dr. Azikiwe has added further, that the Senate should have full concurrent powers with the lower chamber.[63] Under the present constitution, Senators are appointed by the Regional governments,[64] a procedure which not only makes the Senators subject to direction by the regional governments and their governing parties, but also provides those parties with a back-door entry into Parliament for those of their candidates who have failed to get elected in a federal election. In effect, this means that the Senate tends to reflect the power position in the lower chamber and as a check on an Executive manipulated House of Representatives is little less than useless.[65] On the other hand, it is difficult to see what practical difference the direct election of Senators would make under present circumstances. Since most parties literally dominate their regional base,[66] it is unlikely that the election of Senators would alter the party complexion of the second chamber. With such conditions, the suggestion that the Senate should be given full concurrent powers with the House of Representatives needs little comment. At the worst, such a change would only lead to general immobilism in the legislative process and thereby stifle political change when this is most needed.

UPGA made the conversion of the Head of State from a formal to an Executive President one of the main issues in its electoral manifesto. The President, Dr. Azikiwe, has himself stated that as a check on an "all-powerful Head of Government", Nigeria should either accept an elected executive Head of State and scrap the office of the Prime Minister or retain both, the former being vested with specific powers, the latter with the "plenary powers he exercises at present". The experience of most states, particularly in Africa, that have experimented with an executive Head of State has not, he contended, been encouraging in that such a system rapidly grew into an authoritarianism of the least desirable kind. Dr. Azikiwe's preference was thus for an Executive Head of State with specific powers. Like UPGA in their electoral manifesto, he advocated the transfer of control over the Federal Public Service Commission, Federal Audit, the Federal Electoral Commission and the Census Board to the President. As Dr. Azikiwe put it, "These are four explosive areas of politics and by placing them under the exclusive control of the Head of State, an impartial non-partisan, they can be insulated from being subverted for partisan ends".

The Republican Constitution provides for the election of the President at a joint meeting of the Houses of Parliament[67] and, except for the exercise of his discretionary powers relating to the dissolution of Parliament and the appointment of the Prime Minister,[68] the President is not expected to act except on the advice of the Prime Minister or the Council of Ministers as the case may be.[69] Whatever may be the deficiencies of having a formal Head of State—and these have nowhere been demonstrated in the debate—it is difficult to see why an Executive Presidency must necessarily be an improvement, this being the unspecified assumption of the proponents of change. In the first place, though in theory the President is expected to be above partisan politics, there is no guarantee that he will in practice be so. Secondly, there is no necessary reason to believe that a direct election of the President will result in the election of a non-Northerner, given the population majority of the North and the Sardauna's determination to have female suffrage should a directly elected President be insisted upon. (Another unspecified assumption of the protagonists of a directly elected President is that this will yield inevitably a non-Northern President.[70]) Lastly, in the hypothetical case of a non-Northerner being elected, since the Prime Minister, in the immediate future must needs be a Northerner, the possibility of a clash of personalities and policies cannot be ruled out with all the possible consequencies that this might have for the stability of the federation. Similar arguments can be brought against the transfer of the specific institutions advocated. Briefly, either the Constitution or the Statute setting up the Census Board, Federal Electoral Commission, Federal Audit and the Federal Public Service Commission provides for the independence of these institutions,[71] thereby, at least in theory, insulating them from "being subverted for partisan ends". There is thus little to be gained in subsuming them under the office of the Presidency and if their impartiality is being questioned, the difficulty must obviously lie—not in the locus of control, but in the personnel of these institutions and the lack of political consensus—the refusal to apply the 'rules of the game'—in the political system.

The proposals put forward to maintain an 'open society' lend emphasis to the point made above—the lack of a political consensus. The suggestions can therefore be briefly stated. With reference to the Courts,[72] these are: (a) the desirability of establishing a superior Court of review, over and above the Federal Supreme Court, to which appeals from the latter will lie and which will replace the appeal to the British Privy Council which was abolished by the Republican Constitution;[73] (b) the conversion of the existing regional High Courts to Federal Courts with rights of Appeal from these to the Supreme Court; (c) the reintroduction of a Judicial Service Commission, also abolished under the Republican Constitution, and (d) in the North, the recognition of the right of the individual to choose either to be tried by the customary and Islamic Courts or by Courts applying 'received Law'.[74] With regard to the police, the main point of dispute seems to be the Local Authority police forces, with proposals that these should either be abolished or be merged with the Nigeria Police Force.[75]

Of the suggestions relating to the Courts only (c) and (d) need be seriously entertained. The first of these is largely formal and pertains to improving the quality of people recruited to the judiciary. The latter, however, relates to wider issues such as the customs, traditions and religious belief systems of the people of the North. But while most people would not deny the right of the Northern political leaders to protect these, it seems hardly consistent to refuse the same privileges to those who do not share the outlook of the majority of the Northern populace. Besides, it is of the essence of 'fair hearing' guaranteed by the Constitution[76] that the individual should, within reason, be permitted to choose the court in which he is to be tried, particularly as non-Northerners and non-Moslems not infrequently hold the view that they do not expect to get justice if tried before the North's Islamic Courts.[77]

(One criticism of the Courts, specifically of the higher Courts, that has been made is that in their judgements the judges have tended to place too narrow a construction on the provisions of the Constitution and the statutes, with the result that the balance of opinion has been weighted more in favour of the Executive than the individual seeking redress from particular acts of the Executive.[78] Whatever may be the legitimate grounds for such criticisms, the problem, if such it is, is one which only time can change, this being a question of the 'ideological' biases and social backgrounds of the members of the Bench.)

Few people who observed the last general elections both in the North and the West would doubt that the local authority police forces[79] have become the private armies of the regional governments. Dissatisfaction with the role of these forces reached such proportions that in October 1964 political leaders were generally agreed that if the pretence of a free and fair election was to be maintained these 'private armies' should be merged with the Nigeria Police Force.[80] The merger which was supposed to come into effect as from the first day of November was scarcely put into practice, and throughout the elections there was sufficient evidence to suggest that the different forces were working at cross-purposes.[81] Thus, if the police, in general, are not to be brought into disrepute, some arrangement which will lead to the merging of the present local authority and Nigeria Police Forces would seem to be imperative.[82]

The conclusions to be drawn from the analysis may be obvious and possibly trite. But then the obvious is so often overlooked in the search for more profound and complicated answers which not infrequently themselves turn out to be empty. This is, for instance, indicated in the debate on the review of the constitution. No constitution, however consistent and laudable a document it is, can be made operable if there does not exist that willingness and co-operation, the determination to play according to the 'rule of the game', on which the political system itself rests. In the formative phase of federalism, as David Truman has pointed out, the main question is one of survival, but in time, this is invariably superseded by the question whether federalism "as structural fact rather than doctrine, must spawn an extra-constitutional system of party power which places limits upon the adaptability of the scheme as a whole and forces a choice between an inhibiting political veto and a drastic alteration to the whole pattern, perhaps through violent means".[83]

That the North holds a political veto[84] over the rest of the federation can hardly be questioned. This veto depends on the maintenance of the North as a 'closed political system' thereby giving the NPC a single-party monopoly of the North. But as V. O. Key has shown, a single-party monopoly based on the assertion or defence of a dominant sectional interest tends to inhibit the identification and expression of intersecting national issues.[85] Admittedly, the purely political advantages of a one-party monopoly are considerable and not to be surrendered without resistance. But because federalism rests on co-operation and compromise, what Dicey terms "the spirit of federalism" it can only succeed when open competition is permitted.

The 'imbalance' in the political system cannot be removed, it has been argued by implication, by juggling with the Constitution. The June 1964 general strike, which lasted for thirteen days, involved an estimated 800,000 workers and all but paralysed the economy, may indicate that the problems confronting the country are not so much political as economic.[86] But the economic problems[87] can hardly be adequately faced without the necessary leadership and political consensus. For the former to emerge, the latter must exist, and this is where the whole problem of free and fair elections, bedevilled by the closed political character of the North, becomes crucial. The choices are thus rather simple and limited. Either a free and fair electoral system can be maintained—and on this depends the possibility of recruiting the necessary leadership—or Nigeria must be prepared to face "a drastic alteration to the whole pattern" of her government, perhaps, through violent means.

NOTES

1. Max Weber, *Basic Concepts in Sociology*, translated by H. P. Secher, N. Y., Citadel Press, 1962, pp. 97–99. There is some similarity in K. Popper's notion of a 'closed society'—*The Open Society and its Enemies*, 3rd Edition, 1957, vol. I, pp. 173–74—with Weber's, especially the idea of society being conceived in organic terms and the lack of competitiveness. However, it would seem that Popper's contention that the concept of a 'closed system' or 'closed society' was first used, to his knowledge, by Henri Bergson—Ibid. p. 202 note to Introduction—is not strictly accurate as Weber antedated Bergson by almost two decades.

2. Weber, op. cit., p. 97.

3. Ibid., p. 99.

4. Loc. cit.

5. Except in the North where the election was a direct one between the NPC and the NPF, in the South, and particularly in the West, the election was in a number of constituencies a three or even five-cornered fight with members of the same alliance competing against one another. This was more the case with the UPGA than the NNA.

6. The NNDP (Nigerian National Democratic Party) was formed in early 1964 from the rump of the NCNC members of the Western House of Assembly and the AG parliamentarians who remained loyal to Premier Akintola during the 1962 crisis. The latter group, prior to the formation of the NNDP, existed as the United Progressive Party. The NNDP is thus essentially, a 'parliamentary party' in Duverger's terms. It does not exist outside the Western Region of Nigeria. The MDF (Mid-West Democratic Front) is the opposition party in the Mid-West. Like the NNDP, it is an amalgam of former AG members and the Mid-

West Democratic Peoples Party (MDPP), formed in 1963 by Apostle John Edokpolor in Benin under NPC patronage. The NDC, the last member of the NNA, is the Niger Delta Congress which contested the 1959 federal elections and is centred in the Rivers province of the Eastern Region. On this, see K. W. J. Post, op. cit., passim.

7. On the NPF, the Northern Progressive Front, see Chapter 5, p. 185 and Appendix.

8. The concession of ten seats was made to the NNDP in the West who before the elections adopted similar tactics to those of the North described in the text. Included in UPGA's electoral calculations was also the fact that in the reapportionment of seats following the 1963 Census, the North lost part of its initial advantage when its representation fell from 174 to 167; the West's (and Mid-West's) increased from 62 to 71, Lagos's from 3 to 4 while the East's fell from 73 to 70. For some details of the reapportionment, see *Sunday Express* (Lagos), 12th July 1964.

9. The NPF has as one of its candidates for Kano West, Mallam Shehu Mohammed Abbas (popularly known as Sarkin Shehu), a son of the late Emir Abbas of Kano and first cousin of Sir Mohammadu Sanusi who made him D. H. of Ungogo. Involved in the Kano situtaion were also the following factors on which the NPF banked. (i) Religion—the exploitation of Tijaniyya sentiment in Kano. Alhaji Aminu Kano, the NEPU leader, for example, visited Ibrahim Nyas of Kaolack in Senegal in September 1964. By the time of the elections, Aminu was circulating photographs of Ibrahim Nyas and himself in Kano. A calendar made from these pictures with Arabic inscriptions suggesting that Aminu Kano was an annointed of Ibrahim Nyas was being sold in Kano. At least two Tijaniyya *Mallams* were known to have given the NPF covert support— Alhajis Shehu Maihula and Tijani Yan' Awaki. On aspects of the Tijaniyya and Politics, see Record of Appeal from the High Court of Lagos to the Federal Supreme Court (Awolowo Treason Trial) vol. 2, pp. 170–72. (ii) Economic grievances arising from the supposed discrimination of the Northern government in not siting major industrial projects in Kano, the contrast being the cement works in Sokoto, brewing and textiles in Kaduna, cigarettes in Ilorin, etc. There was also rising unemployment caused in part by the movement of expatriate commercial firms from retail trade in the North.

10. This was also true of Western Nigeria.

11. The 'definitions' of what constituted 'illegal' meetings and 'insulting' language were so wide as to be all-inclusive. In a petition to nullify the election of the Prime Minister—returned unopposed—the petitioner gave instances of such arrests in his plea to the Court. See the text of his case in *Daily Times*, 13th March 1965 and *Daily Express*, 17th March 1965.

12. The meeting was held on the 22nd October 1964, The terms of the agreement can be found in the President's speech (which was not in fact given), *Sunday Times* (Lagos), 3rd January 1965.

13. The author with the aid of an interpreter interviewed M. Musa at Wudil.

14. Nominations closed on 18th December 1964. This was extended to the 19th. The Eastern representative on the FEC, however, announced from Enugu another extension to the 20th which the Chairman rejected from Lagos. *Sunday Express*, 20th December 1964 and *Daily Times*, 21st December 1964.

15. The figures for the East and West were fifteen and two 'unopposed'. The NNA made no objections to the East. In the West after the Returning Officer had declared the NNDP candidates for the two Ife Constituencies 'returned

unopposed' on the day of the elections, 30th December, the polling booths were opened to the electorate to cast their votes.

16. The East, Mid-West and Lagos representatives resigned, which left only the Chairman, and the representatives of the North and West. *Daily Times*, 30th December 1964 and 1st January 1965.

17. The boycott was announced over the wireless, mid-day 19th December, the day before the election. In Kano that evening, the writer observed NPC vans with loudspeakers announcing that the elections would be held, and UPGA vans stating the reverse. The boycott was only successful in the East where UPGA(NCNC) controlled the government, and Lagos—in three of its four constituencies. New elections were held in these areas on 19th March 1965.

18th. The crisis lasted for five days before agreement was finally reached, the main point of the agreement being the formation of a 'broad-based' government, which was generally interpreted to mean a national government.

19. With 163 seats, the North already had a majority to form a government by itself. That it did not seek to do this is largely due to its unwillingness to face a North-South confrontation.

20. These figures were not publicly released. It has been suggested that the 21·4m. figure for the north was in fact an inflation from 17·5m. which some claim is the accurate figure.

21. House of Representatives Debates, 5th December 1962, cols. 2734–36.

22. The Mid-West subsequently backed down and accepted the figures.

23. The NCNC finally accepted the figures for two reasons: (*a*) the refusal of its Federal Ministers to resign their offices, which would have been the case had they insisted on rejection once the Prime Minister had accepted the figures (see *Daily Express*, 16th March 1964) and (*b*) the fact that by this time, the NPC already had a majority in the Federal Parliament.

24. See, e.g., Report by the Conference on the Nigerian Constitution, Cmnd. 8934, London, 1953; Report by the Resumed Conference, Cmnd. 5059, London 1954; Report by the Nigerian Constitutional Conference, Cmnd. 207, London 1957; Report by the Ad-hoc Meeting on the Nigeria Constitutional Conference, Lagos, 1958. Report by the Resumed Nigeria Conference Cmnd. 569 London 1958.

25. Cmnd. 569, 1958.

26. L.N. No. 20 1963.

27. *Report by the Revenue Allocation Commission*—The Hicks-Phillipson Report—Lagos 1951; *Report of the Fiscal Commissioner*, Cmnd. 9026 London 1953; *Report of the Fiscal Commission*, Cmnd 481, London 1958. The Report of the fourth Commission (headed by an Australian, Mr. Binns), held in 1964, is still to be published.

28. The figures do not include reserves held by the Central Bank, but it is not expected that these alter the over-all picture.

29. Northern Nigeria Development Plan 1962–68: *First Progress Report*, Ministry of Economic Planning, Kaduna, 1964, p. 28.

30. For a critique of the Wheare 'model' see S. R. Davis, 'The Federal Principle Reconsidered', *Australian Journal of History and Politics*, vol. I, nos. 1 and 2, 1955/56; B. J. Dudley, 'The Concept of Federalism', *Nigerian Journal of Economics and Social Studies*, vol. 5, no. 1, March 1963.

31. M. Beloff, 'The Federal Solution and its Application to Europe, Africa and Asia', *Political Studies*, vol. 1, no. 2, 1953.

32. A regional government can of course raise a loan externally for a period

less than one year and have this renewed each time the loan lapses, without recourse to the Federal government, thereby blurring the restriction which thus becomes superficial and superfluous. It should also be noted that the restriction does not apply to such loans as contractor finance and suppliers credit. For the problems raised by the latter, see A. A. Ayida, 'Contractor Finance and Supplier Credit in Economic Growth', paper presènted at the Annual Conference of the Nigerian Economic Society, 5th–7th February 1965. Mr. Ayida is Permanent Secretary, Federal Ministry of Economic Development.

33. See J. P. Mackintosh, 'Federalism in Nigeria', *Political Studies*, vol. 10, no. 3, October 1962.

34. Ibid., p. 241–42.

35. The NPC leadership has often pronounced its determination to control the federal government for the next twenty-five years.

36. See e.g. Gerth and Mills, from Max Weber, *Essays in Sociology*, p. 294; Reinhard Bendix, *Max Weber—An Intellectual Portrait*, pp. 294–97.

37. An implicit assumption being made is that growth must necessarily depend on the Government. This is not unwarranted granted that private capital investment in *recent* years has not been very significant. For the country as a whole, the Development Plan envisages a cumulative balance of payments deficit of some £480m. made up of about £327m. from foreign official sources and not less than £157 from foreign private investment. The record of the latter so far is as follows, taking the period 1957–62.

Year	Volume £m	Year	Volume £m
1957	17·1	1960	19·0
1958	16·8	1961	30·0
1959	24·0	1962	20·0

SOURCE: United Africa Company, *Statistical and Economic Review,* April 1964, p. 42.

38. Northern Nigeria Development Plan: *First Progress Report*, p. 5. The second Progress Report shows slightly different sub sectoral headings which thus makes comparison with the First Progress Report difficult. However, the following provides a fairly good index of the performance of the economy. In sectoral and sub sectoral terms, 18·2% of estimated expenditure on the primary development sector was spent, representing an underspending of 1·9% of the Plan target; on transport, 13·9% (–8·0% of Plan target); Education, 10·4% (–9·5%); Health, 6·0% (+1·1%); Information, 0·6% (+0·5%); Social Welfare and Co-operatives, 4·5% (+2·0%). In terms of total, 97·5% of estimated expenditure was actually spent, an underspending of 2·5%. It should be pointed out that since figures for the achievement of physical targets are not shown, monetary measures provide only a poor guide to the performance of the economy.

39. Ibid., p. 6.

40. Ibid., p. 33.

41. See *Report of the Commission on the Review of wages . . . in Private Establishments*, (The Morgan Report), Lagos, 1964, and *Conclusion of the Federal Government on the Report of the Morgan Commission*, Lagos, 1964.

42. Investment in Education—*The Report of the Commission on Post-School Certificate and Higher Education in Nigeria*, Lagos, Federal Ministry of Education, 1960, p. 10.

43. Primary education is used here as an illustrative case. The situation in secondary school education is scarcely different. By 1964 there were under 12,000 pupils in place of the expected 12,750 in the North's secondary schools. The provincial distribution shows roughly comparable percentages to those for the primary schools.

44. *First Progress Report*, p. 32. Political factors influencing the efficiency of revenue collection is shown in the following table taken from Dr. Helleiner's 'A Wide-Ranging Development Institution: The Northern Nigeria Development Corporation 1949–62', *Nigerian Journal of Economic and Social Studies*, vol. 6, no. 2, July 1964, p. 251.

Outstanding Loans by NRDC to Persons, N.A.s and Co-ops. Year ends 1956–62

(£000's)

	March 31st 1956	1957	1958	1959	1960	1961	1962
Persons	28·0	47·3	205·2	428·2	701·9 (a)	731·9 (a)	1,348·3 (a)
N.A.s	213·9	212·4	334·8	507·0	538·0	491·2	479·1
Co-ops	1·5	—	—	1·5	2·3	1·1	1·4
TOTAL	243·4	259·7	540·0	937·3	1,241·2	1,224·2	1,828·8

(a) Includes reserves against default, 1960: 16.0m.; 1961: 16.0m.; and 1962: 12·5m.

45. *First Progress Report*, p. 32.

46. Once the decision to build a dam was taken, there can be little argument about its location. The question, however, is whether this is the best form of capital investment given the available resources and the over-all development needs. See, e.g., I. M. D. Little, *Aid to Africa*, Overseas Development Institute, 1964, "The Niger Dam is almost certainly going to be built too soon. Nigeria could get all the power it needs at one-fifth of the capital cost from natural gas." Ibid., p. 18. But then, natural gas is to be found only in the South.

47. Thus, e.g., between 1960 and 1962, the mileage of Trunk 'A' (federal roads) constructed and tarred by the federal government in each of the regions were as follows: North 149½ miles, West 19, East 85 and Lagos 3. House of Representatives Debates 8th April 1963, col. 694. *The Annual Report of the Works Division of the Federal Ministry of Works and Surveys 1960–61*, Lagos 1964, showed for the North, £3·3m. spent or scheduled to be spent on roads, West, £2·4m. and East £1·7m.; on aerodromes—cost of maintenance and buildings— the figures were, North £68,314, West £24,406 and East £26,542. Bridges planned in 1960 were as follows: North, one each of 40 feet, 160 feet and 240 feet span; East, two of 40 feet span and West, one of 40 feet span.

48. *Annual Report of the Federal Ministry of Labour for the year 1961–62*, Lagos 1964, paragraph 46, p. 12.

49. Ibid., paragraph 45, p. 12.

50. Balance of Payments 1958–62: Nigeria.

Year	Amount £m.	% of Total Payments
1958	—41	20·7
1959	—35	16·4
1960	—69	27·6
1961	—72	27·9
1962	—56	22·3

SOURCE: United Africa Company's *Statistical and Economic Review*, Issue 29, April 1964, p. 15.

51. M. S. Robinson, 'Nigerian Oil—Prospects and Perspectives', *Nigerian Journal of Economic and Social Studies*, vol. 6, no. 2, 1964, p. 227.

52. Dr. Nnamdi Azikiwe, in a public statement in the Press, pointed out that the agreement was a personal negotiation between himself and the Sardauna of Sokoto. There are only two extant copies of the 'agreement' he added, one in his keeping, the other with the Sardauna.

53. Economic difficulties arose, for instance, with the volume of spending on primary education and the relation of this to total spending. Note the fall of about 200,000 in primary school enrolment in the East between 1960 and 1961.

54. See the *Report of the Coker Commission of Enquiry into the Affairs of Certain statutory Corporations in Western Nigeria 1962*, 4 vols., Federal Ministry of Information, Lagos, 1962.

55. *Morning Post* (Lagos), 25th May 1962.

56. It is an interesting commentary on the NCNC as a whole that while in 1961 some of its leaders were negotiating an alliance with the AG, at about the same time a party Report by Mr. R. B. K. Okafor (then Parliamentary Secretary to the Minister of Justice) was suggesting moves to oust the AG from power. Okafor, op. cit., paragraph 13.

57. See *White Paper on the New Political Alignment in Western Nigeria* (Western Nigeria official Document no. 1 of 1964). This document was originally prepared by Messrs. T. O. S. Benson, Olu Akinfosile, R. A. Fani-Kayode, B. Olowofoyeku, A. Lamuye, and R. O. A. Akinjide—all of the NCNC. Also, *A Rejoinder to Dr. Ikejiani's statement on recent accusations of tribalism in the University of Ibadan*, NNDP Bureau of Information, Ibadan, 1964.

58. See the 'State House Diary', *Daily Times*, 13th January 1965. This 'diary' of events is alleged to be selective in its presentation. That the country was on the brink of collapse cannot be denied: the East threatened to secede; the armed forces, not clear as to whom it is responsible, had a cyclostyled letter distributed amongst its officers pointing out that the responsibility of the armed forces was to the Prime Minister; and an attempt was made to remove the Head of State.

59. Nnamdi Azikiwe, 'Essentials for Nigeria's Survival', *Foreign Affairs*, vol. 43, no. 2, April 1965, pp. 446–61.

60. J. S. Mill, *Representative Government*, Everyman 1948 edition, pp. 367–68.

61. Quotations are from Alhaji Ahmani Pategi's reply, in *Daily Express*, 24th March 1965, to Azikiwe's 'Essentials for Nigeria's Survival'.

62. Under the Constitution the Senate has only a six-months delaying power. L.N. No. 20 of 1963, Section 64 (2).

63. Section 42 (1) and (2) gives the composition of the Senate as (a) twelve Senators representing each region selected at a joint meeting of the legislative

Houses of the region from amongst persons nominated by the Governor; (*b*) four representing Lagos (the Oba of Lagos, a Chief chosen from amongst the White-Cap and War Chiefs of Lagos and two others) and (*c*) four others selected by the President acting on the advice of the Prime Minister.

64. Only once in its history has the Senate delayed legislation from the lower house. This was the Bill amending the Constitution of Northern Nigeria to provide for the President of the Sharia Court of Appeal to sit as of right in the Region's High Court.

65. With the possible exception of the West where the NNDP can hardly be said to be in control of the mass-electorate.

66. L.N. No. 20 of 1963 Section 35. Section 151 (1) states that Dr. Azikiwe shall be deemed elected President of the Republic on the date of the commencement of the Constitution. The removal of the President is provided for in Section 38.

67. Ibid., Sections 68 (4), 87 (2), (11) proviso to 92 (2) sets out the discretionary powers of the President.

68. Sections 93 (1), 101 (2) and (3).

69. The first incumbent of the Presidency publicly stated that he owed his office to the negotiation between himself and the Premier of the North. See note 1, p. 399 above.

70. The independence of the Audit and the Federal Electoral Commission, for instance, is guaranteed by Sections 134 (4), and 150 (3) and Section 50 (9).

71. On the Courts in general, see B. O. Nwabueze, *The Machinery of Justice in Nigeria*, Butterworths, 1963 and T. O. Elias, *The Nigerian Legal System*, Routledge and Kegan Paul, 1963 formerly published as *Groundwork of Nigeria Law*,

72. Under the Republican Constitution, the right of appeal from the Federal Supreme Court to the Privy Council was abolished.

73. On the conception of 'received law' see W. C. E. Daniels, *The Common Law in West Africa*, Butterworths, 1964; A. E. W. Park, *The Sources of Nigerian Law*, Butterworths, 1963. Under the Penal Code Amendment Law 1962, all people resident in Northern Nigeria automatically come under the Penal Code, which is based on Sharia Law. Prior to 1962 the non-Moslem could elect to be tried by the Magistrates Court. The Penal Code provides a codified Criminal Law for the whole of the North.

74. Dr. Azikiwe proposed that control over the Armed forces and Police should be vested in the President advised by the Privy Council composed of (*a*) past and present Heads of State, (*b*) Heads of Government, (*c*) Regional Premiers, (*d*) Presidents of the Senate and (*e*) Speakers of the House. Under the present constitution, control of the police lies with the Inspector General of Police assisted by Regional Commissioners responsible for day-to-day direction of police contingents in the Regions (Section 106). The Head of State is C-inC. of the Armed forces (Section 34), but over-all control rests in the Prime Minister.

75. See 22 (2).

76. But see the case made by S. S. Richardson in 'Opting Out: An Experiment with Jurisdiction in Northern Nigeria', *Journal of African Law*, vol. 8, no. 1, Spring 1964.

77. David La Van Grove, 'The "Sentinels" of Liberty? The Nigerian Judiciary and Fundamental Rights', *Journal of African Law*, vol. 7, no. 3, Autumn 1963.

78. The East and Mid-West regions do not keep local authority police forces.

79. On some of the problems by the Nigeria Police Force itself, see J. P. Mackintosh, op. cit., p. 246.

80. In Oshogbo in Oshun Division (Western Nigeria) for instance, the Nigeria

police spent part of its time removing party-political handbills from walls of houses while the L.A. police were busy replacing the same bills. The Superintendent of the Nigeria police in Oshogbo had in the interests of law and order earlier prohibited the sticking up of handbills. All the handbills were those of the NNDP, the government party in the Western Region.

81. It is not intended to suggest that the items enumerated exhaust what needs be 'reviewed' in the Constitution. Obviously there are other issues, for instance, Section 22 (1b) which precludes 'Chieftaincy questions' from the purview of the Courts jurisdiction in the determination of rights. This in effect forms chiefs or persons who were formerly chiefs into a separate class who can be removed or excluded from and to any part of a region by a regional government without any redress in law. See Section 75 (3d), (3e) of NNL no. 33 of 1963. Questions such as these, however, do not seem to have assumed a political character as those discussed in the text.

82. David B. Truman, 'Federalism and the Party System' in A. W. MacMahon (ed.), *Federalism: Mature and Emergent*, N.Y. Alfred Knopf, 1962 edition, pp. 115–16.

83. Compare, for instance, the Sardauna's Statement: ". . . a sudden grouping of the Eastern and Western parties (with a few members from the North opposed to our party) might take power and so endanger the North. This would be disastrous—it would therefore *force* us to take measures to meet this need." *My Life*, p. 229.

84. V. O. Key, *Southern Politics in State and Nation*, N.Y. Knopf, 1949, Chapter 14.

85. See B. J. Dudley, 'After the General Strike', *Financial Times* (London), 1st October 1964.

86. As an index to some of these, see Federal Government Development Programme 1962–68: *First Progress Report*, sessional paper No. 3 of 1964, Federal Ministry of Economic Development, March 1964, and National Development Plan—*Progress Report 1964*, Lagos, 1965.

Conclusion

Post second world war political developments backed by buoyant world prices for commodity export crops saw the emergence of extreme regionalism in Nigeria. The federalism to which this gave rise rested on what can properly be called 'the theory of regional security'. In effect this meant that the main political parties were to recognize their regional bases as their only and proper sphere of political action. The slogan of the times very accurately was "East for the Easterners, West for the Westerners, North for the Northerners and Nigeria for nobody".

In many respects, this arrangement worked well and proved reasonably satisfactory. 'Government' as the mass-electorate understood the term, began and ended with the regions. The AG controlled the West, the NCNC dominated the East, while the NPC reigned unchallenged in the North. The centre was a loose amalgam of all three. Representation was there divided equally between the North and the South, that is, the East and Western regions. At the level of the Executive, all three regions were equally represented by the same number of Ministers, which thus gave the edge to the South.

This 'nicely' balanced largely fragile arrangement was given a decisive jolt when in 1958 the decision was taken to alter the basis of representation at the federal level to one based on population. The initiative therefore tilted to the North, where political power in the interim period had shifted to the hands of the traditional Native Authority functionaries. They now dominated not only the Legislature but also, through the policy of Northernization, the bureaucracy. The NPC became the political expression of this class of functionaries who thereby provided the factor linking the party, the Executive and the bureaucracy together. The model for this is Carl Schmitt's doctrine of 'trialism'[1]—the unification of the Party, Government and the mass-electorate into a single whole.

This is not to suggest that pockets of dissidence, possible or actual, cease to exist. As this study has shown, these have not been totally eradicated: the Tivs and other minorities are yet to be conciliated;

possible opposition to the leadership could come from the lower ranks of the administrative class of the bureaucracy; the Emirs, though subdued are not subjugated and religion, specifically in the form of the Tijaniyya brotherhood of Islam, can still be exploited for political ends by opposing parties.[2] None the less, 'trialism' or the 'closed society' does imply that opposition, in whatever form, is barely tolerated and concretely, is regarded as attempts to subvert the 'state'.

With the change in the system of federal representation, the mono-lithic character of the North guaranteed it specific economic and political advantages. The change gave the North a veto on subsequent change. This in effect turns the largely rural and relatively under-developed North into the pace-setter for the rest of the federation—the more urbanized, more developed South. The resentment created by this socio-political imbalance, aggravated by a lagging economy, has grown into a serious threat to the stability of the federation. How the imbalance is to be resolved is uncertain. One possibility being advocated is a radical alteration of the structural base of the constitution. The rationale for structural change is the necessity to provide a framework which would enable the federal authority to take decisions which are not dictated by a regional government or combination of such governments. In other words, a federal autho-rity which is patently independent of the regions. This, as has been shown, the present structure does not allow for.

But such a change would be possible only if the bloc-voting in the existing regions were broken. The only effective way of doing this would be to create more states in the country. With the cultural and linguistic heterogeneity of Nigerian society, this could easily lead to the emergence of 'pocket-sized' regions if the creation of states is not based on some minimum acceptable criteria. If it is accepted that some such principles as geographical contiguity, rough com-parability in population size, economic viability relative to gover-mental functions, historico-linguistic affinity should guide the creation of new regions, then Nigeria could be broken into about ten states or regions: five in the North, two each in the East and West with the Mid-West remaining what it is.

The creation of states would lead to the emergence of new interests; a greater competition for federal benefits and therefore a more equitable distribution of federal aid. It would enforce the need for a wider consensus in decision-making. But primarily, the logic of more states would entail shifting the financial burden of development and welfare functions from the regional governments to the federal. (Already, expenditure on these items constitute a heavy strain on the recurrent budgets of the regions.) The corollary of this would be that the federal government takes control of the direction of, and responsibility for, the economy. Other things being equal, it should then be possible for resources to be allocated in a way which would maximize returns on them.

The qualification about other things being equal cannot be ignored as these relate to the necessity for playing the federal game according to its rules. But these are not issues which, in the last analysis, can be legislated for, though this is not to suggest that the existing legislation governing political recruitment, the conduct of census, the independence of the judiciary etc. are such that they cannot be improved upon. Legal rules and regulations serve only to prevent or check abuses. They can in no way guarantee that the enlightened leadership which a country needs would be forthcoming.

It should be obvious that the changes being suggested would have their greatest impact on the North. One consequence of which would be the social restructuring of the society thereby undermining the continued existence of the present leadership. For this reason the North might want to preserve the present political structure and to resist any attempts at the creation of new regions. But the alternatives to some such restructuring of the political system are either a one-party dominant state, which can scarcely be acceptable given the sociological realities of the federation, or, a forceful change of the whole system, not improbably through violence. The problem with violence, however, is that it breeds on itself. Once started, the result could easily be political and social chaos. In many respects, this then is the threat which faces the Nigerian federation.

NOTES

1. See Sir E. Barker, *Reflections on Government*, Oxford University Press, pp. 289–92.
2. For instance, the riot involving adherents of Tijaniyya and Kadiriyya brotherhoods which broke out on the 2nd April 1963 in the villages of Toranke, Jankuka and Jaja in Argungu Division of Sokoto province in which not less than fifteen people were killed (eleven NA policemen and four civilians) and a number seriously injured. *Daily Express*, 7th March 1965, *Morning Post* 8th March 1965 and 12th March 1965. See also Chapter 5, pp. 277–78.

Appendix I

A NOTE ON THE CLASSIFICATORY TERMINOLOGY OF
AFRICAN POLITICAL PARTIES

Recent attempts to provide a classificatory system for African political parties do not seem satisfactory. The first fairly consistent attempt was made by Thomas Hodgkin in his *Nationalism in Colonial Africa* where he distinguished 'proto-type parties' from 'political parties proper'. Within 'political parties proper', he then differentiates between 'mass' and 'patron' parties, the principle of differentiation being mainly that the former seeks to recruit individual members, whilst the latter is composed almost exclusively of the local 'notables'. Ruth Schacter-Morgenthau, in her 'Single Party Systems in West Africa,' The American Political Science Review, vol. 55, no. 2, June 1961, follows Hodgkin's precept in accepting the 'mass–patron' division. But in Hodgkin's later *African Political Parties*, this division is replaced by another, the distinction now being between 'mass' and 'élite' parties, with the implication that 'élite' and 'patron' denote the same type.

The expression 'mass parties' itself comes from Duverger's *Political Parties* where using the criterion of structural form, Duverger distinguishes between 'mass' and 'cadre' parties. In addition to the point about membership in relation to mass parties, Duverger added finance when he wrote that "the party is essentially based upon the subscriptions paid by its members . . . the mass party technique in effect replaces the capitalist financing of electioneering by democratic financing". Cadre parties for Duverger besides being made up of 'notabilities', are characterized by expertise in conducting a campaign and 'skill and technique' of organization, etc. Adherence to the party, he added, "is a completely personal act" (pp. 63–64). Presumably these additional characteristics of the cadre type parties made the term unsuitable to Hodgkin and thus explains his preference for 'patron' and 'élite'. He is thus in contrast to Mr. K. W. Post, who, in his *The Nigerian Federal Elections of 1959* endorsed Duverger's classificatory terminology.

Unlike Hodgkin, Ruth Schacter-Morgenthau and Post, R. L. Sklar, in his *Nigerian Political Parties* adopted a typology derived from Sigmund Neumann. In his chapter on 'Towards a Comparative Study of Political Parties' (in S. Neumann (ed.), *Modern Political Parties*), Neumann distinguishes between "parties of social integration" and "parties of individual representation", the criterion of differentiation here being one of 'function'. Neumann's classificatory system itself was based on the Tonnian dichotomy between 'community' and 'society' (*Gemeinschaft und Gesselschaft* translated in English as *Community and Society*). For purposes of completeness, it might be added that Neumann introduced other elements in making his distinctions. Thus, for instance, because he makes his 'parties of individual representation' almost identical with Hodgkin's 'Congress' or 'prototype' parties, he was induced to distinguish a sub-type, parties of total integration, from the general class of parties of social integration.

What is particularly relevant in all these classificatory systems is that Hodgkin, Schacter-Morgenthau and Post all accept the term 'mass-party', but separately use élite, patron, cadre, to denote essentially the same type thereby suggesting a disagreement on the descriptive content of these terms. While one need not dispute the prescriptive use of concepts the individual employs, the explanatory force of such concepts can be questioned, and an exercise of this type will reveal the operational inadequacy of terms such as patron, élite, cadre and expressions such as parties of social integration etc., at least when applied to the African experience. Thus, to take the Duverger–Post typology of mass-cadre parties: The criteria of differentiation are membership and finance. In terms of the latter, there could be hardly any difference, say, between the NPC, NCNC and AG of Nigeria. All of these now have to rely on government funds shovelled into the party through private contracts, loans, development projects, etc. In Duverger's term, party financing is now 'capitalist financing'. This was obvious, in the case of the AG in the Report of the Coker Commission of Enquiry. The NCNC now relies very largely on funds from the Eastern Nigeria Development Corporation, the Eastern Nigeria Marketing Board and the African Continental Bank—all of which are linked one to the other. The NPC, on the other hand, depends largely on funds from the Native Authorities. In terms of membership, these parties also share common characteristics. They are, in the main, dependent on the local 'notabilities', the difference being one merely of the class of notables. With the NPC and the AG in its early phase, these are the traditional notables; the NCNC and the AG (in its latter phase), on the 'professional' notables of lawyers, doctors, businessmen and University teachers and school masters.

Hodgkin's 'patron' and 'élite' terms fare no better. The term 'patron' connotes elements of being a figurehead, passivity in participation or moral support, etc. To view the leaders of the NPC in these terms would be grossly misleading. The term 'élite' on the other hand, is to borrow Professor Ryle's phrase systematically misleading, purporting both to name and to describe. In its 'naming' function, élite is a term of 'reference'. Hence when used, the question 'Élite in reference to what groups or class?' can still be asked, and the answer to this is by no means certain or clear. Descriptively, 'élite' covers a host of characteristics, not all of which are consistent one with the other.

In the same way, the Neumann–Sklar classificatory terminology can be shown to be inappropriate. In the first place, the dichotomy on which this is based may be said to suffer from the fault of reification or the fallacy of misplaced concreteness. It is difficult, for instance, to attach any meaning to Tonnies' statement that "the Community constitutes a spontaneous natural social group, older than the individual". And secondly, the distinction between parties of individual representation and those of social integration hardly makes sense since functionally, all parties claim *both* to represent and to integrate.

Now, to argue that these terms are inadequate as typological categories, is not to suggest that there are no differences between the parties they refer to. An examination of the mode of ascription of rights and obligations, within, say, the NPC and the NCNC, of the allocation of offices and the recruitment of leadership, of the type of politics characteristic of these two parties in their decision making process, would show how different they are. With the NCNC, its internal politics can be said to be that of 'mass societies' (cf. Kornhauser, *The Politics of Mass Society*), reflected equally in its decision-making and its recruitment of leadership; offices, rights and obligations are thus ascribed, based on individual achievement, not prescribed and dependent on birth and traditional status-rankings. The NPC, as this study shows, exhibits features dia-metrically opposed to that being predicated of the NCNC. It is therefore suggested that if parties like the NCNC, NEPU and UMBC can be conceptualized as 'mass parties' (in the sense advocated), parties such as the NPC, are best described as 'status parties' following here in the tradition of Max Weber (cf. Gerth and Mills, *From Max Weber—Essays in Sociology*). While it is not suggested that the terminology here advocated may not be open to objections, it is contended that as defined they are the least objectionable.

Appendix II

Commission was told on 9th August 1961 to examine and make recommendations for increasing the efficiency of the Zaria N.A., especially:

1. N.A. Council and central administrative organization.
2. Staff, redundancy, appointment and promotion.
3. Control and Management of the N.A. finances.

Commission saw the Emir, Waziri and all eighteen councillors. (AG and NEPU gave no aid or evidence.)

Zaria Emirate has four dynasties: Bornawa, Katsinawa, Mallawa and Sulebawa. For 73 years it has been held by the Bornu dynasty. "During the last 20 years of this period, a very strong character, the Emir Tafaru, exercised almost absolute personal control of the N.A." "Nepotism, inefficiency and dishonesty went unchecked. The Council was essentially a Monarch's Court, with heavy Yan Sarki representation, mostly from the Emir's dynasty . . ." The N.A. lost the confidence both of the public and of its staff. "The reforms of 1957 were sound, but there was never any real intention by the N.A. to make them work or to turn them to advantage." Capacity at all levels was very poor. The new Emir took over in September 1959; 1st November 1959, the Premier addressed the new Emir-in-Council and gave the N.A. a clear warning to put its house in order. An N.A. Committee was appointed to do this but "it shirked the main issues and proved ineffective". Later the Premier met the Council again and "exhorted it to preserve its unity and to work as a team for the progress of the Emirate"—no avail. So this Commission was set up.

The N.A. Council was:

(a) 6 (3) (b) Emir, Waziri, District Head of Zaria City and District Amiku Ciroma, Mallawa Dynasty.
(b) 6 (3) (a) M. Nuhu Bayero, Dan Iya (Bornu); M. Muhammadu Sain Alkalin Alkali; M. Yahaya Pate, Sarkin Yaki (half Bornu); M. Bawa Bambo, Sarkin Zanna; M. Mihammadu

Lawal, Barde (Katsina); M. Sulaimanu, Katuka (District
Head and Bornu); M. John Tafida, Dangaladima (District
Head and Bornu); M. Muhammadu Fagaci (District Head);
Alhaji Ahmadu, Sarkin Fada, MHA, (Parliamentary Secre-
tary Ministry of Finance) M.P.; I. Ibrahim, Sarkin Ruwa;
Alhaji Isma'ila Ahmed, Dallatu, MHA.

(c) 6 (3) (c) Alhaji Shehu, Madaki (District Head and Bornu);
Alhaji Unaru, Wali (District Head and Bornu); M. S'idu
Zango, Iyam Gari, MHR (District Head); M. Maude Gyani,
MHR; M. Dawa Jan Kassa; Alhaji Baba Ahmed. These
are 1 nominated by Outer Council for Norther Areas, 2
for Zaria area and 3 for Southern. (Only those from the
relevant area could vote.)

This seems a badly balanced Council. Seven of the 18 are 'Yan
Sarki', 5 of whom are Bornu. Also 7 District Heads holding half
of the Outer Council nomination of 6. It is the Yan Sarki of Bornu
"upon whose co-operation and loyalty the Emir has always been
uncertain". It sat silent but stopped the Emir pressing reforms.
"During this period, the Native Admin. lacked a decisive lead and
received neither encouragement nor supervision from the N.A.
Affairs continued much as in the last years of the reign of Emir
Ja'afaru." The Waziri should have done more. Sarkin Yaki, Secretary
to the Council and head of Central Administration, Police and Information has caused much resentment and should go to a District.
Nuhu Bayero has been a "failure in the dual role of Councillor and
Schools Manager and is a member of the Opposition 'Yan Sarki
group'. He had better remain but be moved from education. The
other four Bornu men must go. The Emir made his son Sarkin
Tsabta and father-in-law Wakilin Gona, both very bad appointments. But they also want a check on the Emir becoming as autocratic as Ja'afaru. Alkalin Alkalai and Sarkin Ruwa must go as too
old and mischievous. Alhaji Ahanadu, Sarkin Fada has been too
busy on Regional affairs and must go.

Recommendations:

As the Government proposed except for the retention of M. Nuhu
Bayero. They do not suggest Alhaji Ahmadu, Sarkin Fada.

The seven personal members will be responsible for the following
seven portfolios: Education, health, legal matters, natural resources,
police, prisons and works. These will last till the District Councils
that chose them are dissolved.

x

Three main points:

1. 'Yan Sarki representatives down from 7 to 3, and from each of the main dynasties. (No Sulebawa of sufficient experience and the Emir is not counted as a Katsina man.)

2. District Heads down 7 to 2, both ex-officio and not to hold portfolios—Zaria City and Sabon Gari.

3. Elect representatives direct from the District Councils and not, as before, by nomination from groupings of Outer Members". This reduces the total number of councillors by 2. They want 9 to leave and propose 4 new elected and 3 new personal members. They want an Assistant District Officer as Secretary to the Council for a year. "The Emir must lead and avoid retaliation against former councillors who are members of other dynasties." The Waziri must do better. The Commission must remain in being to review its handiwork later on. The Premier's representative must sign departmental reports before they go to the Council. Council meetings not attended by District Officer or Resident are void. Apart from the Waziri who is to go on running finance and administration, portfolios should be swapped round. Changes in the Council should not alter the representation of one member per dynasty. No more District Heads. The Emir must tour more often without a large retinue. There must be monthly reports by Heads of Departments. Promotions and appointments to be only by the Establishments Committee or by a full meeting of the Council and with written advice signed by the Government adviser. Establishments Committee has worked on a 'live and let live' basis, e.g. the appointment of the Wakilin Goma and the Sarkin Tsabta. (These are the Emir's father-in-law and son.) The Report outlines details for the reconstruction of the Establishments Committee, the Finance Committee and the Tenders Board.

N.A. agrees to delegate financial authority to all District Councils before 31st March 1963.

Commission to remain in being till the Minister of Local Government is satisfied with the action of the Council.

"We recommend the re-issue of the Government's 'Declaration in its Relations with N.A.'s' and the P.M.'s letter No. P. M. 138/98 of 22nd June, 1960 to all N.A. Councillors."

The Premier gave the N.A. two warnings. "In its findings the Committee reported that one of the major causes of the inability of the N.A. Council to function smoothly and efficiently was constant intrigue between the rival dynastic groups in the Council which prevented the Council from acting as one loyal and united corporate body."

The Follow Up

4th January 1962. Following on the letter of 23rd September 1961, the Executive Council has considered the Report and made the following decisions:

(a) N.A. Council and Councillors
(b) Committees and Tenders Board
(c) Establishments
(d) Finance

"Many points not covered by the decisions given and which are considered of importance should be referred to this Ministry for the Minister's direction."

Councillors removed from the Present Council are:

M. Nuhu Bayero, Dan Iya—(Bornawa)
M. Muhammudu Sani, Alkalin Alkalai
M. Yahaya Pate, Sarakin Yaki (Bornawa)
M. Suleimanu, Katurka—(Bornawa)
M. John Tafida, Dangaladima—(Bornawa)
M. P. I. Ibrahim, Sarakin Ruwa
Alhaji Umaru, Wali—(Bornawa)

The Emir's Court is to be reconstituted with the Waziri as Deputy President and with the Councillor for Legal Matters and M. Muntaka Comassie as members. Quorum 3 but always including the Councillor for legal matters. No new districts will be set up.

Reports are to be made:

1. In two months Councillors must say what they have done to improve their depts.
2. Recommend retirements of old, illiterate useless officials.
3. Keep up-to-date personal files on established staff.
   Must report progress by 15th April 1962.
   No leakage of secret council debates.
   Resident must enforce reforms, Emir must tour more often with a small retinue.
   Minister is to speak on 8th January 1962.

Government Recommendations

Annexe A

N.A. Council is to be:

A. Ex Officio   Emir of Zaria (Katsina Dynasty)
(6 (3)b of law)   Waziri of Zaria (N.A. Office)

District Head of Zaria City and Home District
(M. Aminu Ciroma, Mallawa Dynasty)
Dist. Head of Zaria Sabon Gari (M. Sa'idu Zango,
Iyan Gari) MHR.

B. Personal   Alhaji Shehu ,Madaki
(6 (3)a of law)   Hon. Alhaji Ahmadu, Sarakin Fada, M.H.A.
Mallam Muhammadu Buhari (on resignation as
Chief Alkali)
M. Muhammadu Lawal Barde (Katsina Dynasty)
M. Bawa Gambo, Sarkin Zanna

C. Elected   Alhaji Isma'ila Ahmed, Dallatu, MHA
Alhaji Abdu (on resignation from Ministry of
Education)
Alhaji Dikko (on resignation from District Head-
ship of Kachia)
M. Muhammadu, Fagaci
1 elected by District Council of Girra and Igabi
1   ,,   ,,   ,,   Kuban and Soba
1   ,,   ,,   ,,   Ikara and Zongon
Katab
1   ,,   ,,   ,,   Cikun, Kajura,
Kaciya and
Kagarko
1   ,,   ,,   ,,   Zaria Kewaye and
Zaria Sabon Gari
1   ,,   ,,   ,,   Kaura and Lere

"Further additions or alterations to Council membership, following respecification of the Council, should not increase the respecified dynastic representation of one Bornu representative, one Katsina representative (in addition to the present Emir who it is hoped will be impartial) and one Mallawa representative, though one representative of the Sulebawa dynasty could be added, should a suitable candidate appear."

Council meetings to be null and void if neither the Resident nor the D.O. is present.

Portfolios to be:

(a) Central and District Administration.
(b) Education (including Public Enlightenment and Information and Social Welfare)
(c) Health
(d) Legal Matters
(e) Natural Resources (Agricultural Forest, Veterinary)

(*f*) Police and Prisons
(*g*) Works
(*h*) Finance

The Waziri is to be responsible for District Admin. only. Councillors to prepare memoranda "which, before submission to the Council, must be initialled as having been seen by the respective Provincial Representative of the Ministry concerned, where this Rep. does not attend the meeting". (In the past proper memos have not been prepared and Council Papers consisted solely of Agendas and Minutes.)

D.O. to be Secretary to the N.A. Council only as long as it takes to train a Secretary.

Annexe B

The N.A should establish a Finance Committee, an Establishments Committee and a Tenders Board.

(*a*) Finance Committee	— Chairman, Deputy Chairman, 1 Councillor of Finance 1 Dist. Head Zaria Home Dist., 1 non-elected councillor 2 elected Councillors (in 3 monthly rotation)
(*b*) Established Committee	— Chairman, Deputy Chairman, 1 Councillor of Education 1 Dist. Head Zaria Sabon Gari, 2 elected councillors in 3 monthly rotation, Staff Officer.
(*c*) Tenders Board	— Chairman, 1 Waziri, 1 Councillor of Works, 1 non-elected councillor, 2 elected Councillors in rotation.

D.O. to attend all meetings, which are invalid without him. Resident can initiate proposals and on reference by the D.O. to him, veto.

Annexe C

Promotions to senior posts only to be considered by full council after councillor has received written advice from the Government Adviser. Secretary to the Emir to be appointed. M. Nuhu Bayero, Dan-Iya, to be transferred or retired. Wakilin Gona retired. Sarkin Tsabta to be trained for alternative work and replaced by M. Ya'u Lere MHA. Wakilin Yaki da Jahilici to be retired. M. John Tafida, Dangaladima, District Head, Zagon Katab to be retired.

Post of Wakilin Sarki is not approved.

Heads of Departments can be sacked if inefficient on recommendation by Resident and Premier's approval.

Provincial Adviser of Ministers can delay and have appointment of Dept. Heads reconsidered.

If an Audit query is not answered to the satisfaction of the Resident within a month, the Departmental Head gets a warning and if no answer in another month, the sack.

Finance

No capital work without Resident's permission if the matter is in the Estimates or Minister of Local Government if not.

(*b*) N.A. to "increase tax to the maximum amount economically possible and politically advisable; also make and apply adequate arrangements, to the satisfaction of the Resident, for the effective taxation of wealthy and salaried persons . . ."

(*c*) Reorganize Native Treasury as Senior Auditor and D.O. advise.

(*d*) N.A. to delegate financial authority to all District Councils before 31st March, 1963. "The N.A. should apportion to those Councils the major share of miscellaneous revenue originating from their Districts and all of any rate which they raise on their own initiative, otherwise they will fail for lack of funds."

(*e*) N.A. Treasury is downgraded to grade 'B' for 'Advance' and the D.O. is to take over control of Zaria N.A. finance for two years.

Note: The letters 6 (3) (a), 6 (3) (b) refer to the Native Authority Law, 1954, (LNN No. 4 of 1954), Section 6, sub-section 3 (a) etc. The whole of Section 6 relates to 'Appointment to Native Authorities' and specifies the class of persons to be appointed. Appointments of people under Section 6 (3) (a) require the approval of the Premier. Those under 6 (3) (b) and 6 (3) (c), the Minister of Local Government.

Appendix III

EXTRACTS FROM THE WHITE PAPER OF THE GOVERNMENT'S POLICY FOR THE REHABILITATION OF THE TIV NATIVE AUTHORITY AFTER CONSIDERATION OF THE REPORT OF THE COMMISSION OF INQUIRY IN AFFAIRS OF TIV.

". . . with the creation of a Chief-in-Council in 1960 the balance of power was transferred from the Council (sic Chief-and-Council) to the Tor Tiv. Those in authority did not behave with tact and party politics was brought into the sphere of administration.

"The District administration was confused. These were Tax Collectors, Kindred Heads and Clan Heads all of whom were responsible for the collection of tax while the latter two were responsible for Law and Order. None of them had any innate or traditional authority cutside their own compounds . . . But they realized that the power of their appointment and dismissal was in the hands of the Native Authority and not in those of the people . . . This allowed them to become autocratic and oppressive to their people."

A Proposed System of Local Government for the Tiv: Governing Factors

"Political parties are completely contrary to the Tiv political structure and one or the other must go. As it is impossible to prohibit party politics the political structure must be modified. Political parties in Tiv exploit local tensions, so it is necessary to instal safeguards. The Tiv resent authority and persons holding authority. So any party in power is liable to lose its support; when in opposition it is likely to gain support.

Emphasis must be placed on diffuseness of power and decentralization, and the system of local government should accord as far as possible with the indigenous social structure.

Abuse of Office: In 1948 an Administrative Officer wrote 'abuse of office in default of constant checking by seniors and age-mates is a vice to which the Tiv are specially prone'. This is true today, but the traditional checks have been greatly weakened or are non-existent.

Chiefs: In the Tiv context a chief tends to act as a focus for stresses and strains in the group over whom he exercises power. In the Tiv context therefore it is essential that executive functions, judicial functions and authority should not be exercised by the same man.

Use of Force: The Tiv will never respond to force but can be easily persuaded by the use of reason.

Education: Education has greatly affected the traditional way of life in Tiv. The traditional checks, being a supernatural nature, now exercise little if any control over the educated elements, Education has also given rise to unemployment which forms fertile ground for politicians.

The Constitution and Functions of the Native Authority

The Office of Tor Tiv: . . . There is little doubt that the majority of the people of whatever political party want the office to be retained.

Some Tiv consider that the Native Authority should be a Chief-in-Council, others favour a Chief-and-Council. But it is clear that there is no place for a chief with authority in the indigenous Tiv context.

The Native Authority Council: It is too late now to attempt to establish a Native Authority Council that does not adequately reflect the strength of the local political parties. . . . It is considered that the basis for representation on the N.A. Council should be by Districts and not clans. Elections . . . should be indirect by and from the elected members of the District Councils; one member per district . . . this will mean that there will be between 30–35 elected members on the N.A. Council. . . . There should be 14 ex-officio, traditional and nominated members. . . .

The previous system of an Executive Committee was quite unsuccessful. For the Tiv the Committee system is undoubtedly the most satisfactory system. It tends to diffuse powers and thereby prevent abuse of office.

. . . at least the following committees will be needed:

Finance and General Purposes Committee; Establishment; Committee; Social Services; Natural Resources; Local Government; Lands and Works Committee.

The composition of the Committees should reflect as far as possible the strength of the main political parties and there should be a minimum of one member from each party. Also as far as possible the Committees should reflect the main division of the Tiv tribe within the Tiv N.A. but their size should not exceed five to seven members.

District Organization: . . . the basic unit of local government should be the Kindred and, to a lesser extent, the Clans . . . As a convenient size for local government unit is 5–8,000 taxpayers the clans as they stand should be split or amalgamated along natural lines to form 30–35 Districts approximating to this size. By 'natural lines' it is implied that small clans will amalgamate to form a single district while a large clan will be dissolved to form two districts. No large clan will be split and then amalgamated with other clans to form two districts.

Maintenance of Law and Order—The Courts: It is considered that Grade B Civil and Criminal courts become discredited by some of their Presidents being involved in a greater or lesser degree in politics. These courts can provide a most useful valve for the relaxation of tension but only if they are impartial. The best solution therefore is that a very good Inspector of Native Courts should be posted to the Division.

Native Authority Police: The N.A. Police became discredited both in 1960 and again in the 1964 disturbances. . . . The Tiv N.A. Police . . . should remain under the operational control of the Nigeria Police until such time as they are completely reorganized.

Action to be taken by the Government: The Office of Tor Tiv: The office of a Chief, known as Tor Tiv, should remain and continue to be graded as First Class Chief.

The N.A. should be a Chief-and-Council.

The Office of Deputy Tor Tiv: should be abolished. In the absence of Tor Tiv the N.A. should elect a person to act for the Tor Tiv in accordance with their standing regulations.

The N.A. Council: . . . should adequately reflect the political party strengths. Elections . . . should be indirect by and from the elected members of each District and Town Council and each sub-N.A. Council; one member from each. . . . There should be ex-officio members: Tor Tiv, President of the Makurdi sub-N.A., Sarkin Abinsi, Sarkin Katsina Ala; (ii) the five senior clan heads should be nominated for the life of the N.A. They should not be members of a Native Court. (iii) maximum of five members recommended by the Council for nomination by the Government to represent the following special interests: (*a*) one Hausa representative from Gboko; (*b*) one Argo/Nupe representative from Makurdi; (*c*) one Jukun representative from Abinsi; (*d*) one Turu/Hausa representative from Katsina Ala and (*e*) one Cattle Fulani to represent Fulani interest.

(Other items follow on the N.A. Standing Committees, Central Administration, District Administration, Relationship between the Provincial Administration, Professional and Technical Officers and the Native Authority, etc. These however, are largely administrative and not strictly political issues.)

Appendix IV

Name

1. The Association shall be known as 'The Northern Peoples Congress' and shall have its headquarters at Kaduna.

Motto

2. The Motto of the Northern Peoples Congress shall be 'One North: One People Irrespective of Religion, Rank or Tribe'.

Objects

3. To adopt and cultivate means that would foster better understanding and co-operation between the members and the Association and the Northern community generally, so that by such co-operation we of the North may be able to attain to that unquestionable height so desirable especially at this time of our existence and thus enabling us to have one common ideal and objective.

4. To study and strive to preserve the traditions which bound culture to the past, while reforming these traditions to render them capable of meeting modern conditions.

5. To educate the Northerners of their civic and political responsibilities, to organize them to accept the leadership of the Northern Peoples Congress, and to support its candidates for elections to the Regional and Central Legislatures and to Local Councils.

6. To study the cultural, social, political and economic pastimes of the Northerners so that they can adjust themselves to the present changing world with a view to overcoming all the difficulties and barriers that are placed before them.

6a. To appeal to the members to submit themselves to party discipline and loyalty; and those of them elected into the Regional Legislature shall be requested to work assiduously towards the implementation of party programmes of work for all Departments of Government.

7. To inculcate in the minds of the Northerners a genuine love for the Northern Region and all that is northern, and a special reverence for Religion, Laws and Order and the preservation of good

customs and traditions, and the feeling that the sorrow of one northerner shall be the sorrow of all and that the happiness of one is also the happiness of all.

8. To make every possible effort in order to hasten the date of Self-Government for Nigeria and the consideration of introducing of a 'Permanent Federal Constitution'.

9. To seek for the assistance and co-operation of or to give aid to any organization or individual in or out of the Northern Region whose aims and aspirations coincide with those of the Party.

Membership

10. The membership of the Congress is open to all people of Northern Nigerian descent irrespective of creed, rank or tribe.

11. Every member shall on enrolment, pay an entrance fee of two shillings and such member shall be given the party's membership card costing 6d.

12. Every member shall on enrolment sign a 'Pledge of Loyalty' as set out in Appendix A of the Constitution.

Subscription

13. The members shall pay subscription of 3d a week or one shilling a month, or twelve shillings annually payable in advance (discretional).

Annual Convention of the Congress

14. The Supreme Authority of the Congress shall be vested in its Annual Convention which shall have absolute power to decide major policies of the party and to consider matters referred to it by the Executive Committee.

15. The Annual Convention shall have supreme power over the Congress and shall be attended by the officers and representatives of the branches observing the following conditions, that:

(*a*) All representatives shall be active members of the branches they represent.

(*b*) Fifty representatives shall form a quorum at the Convention.

(*c*) The Central Organization shall be responsible for the lodging of branch representatives.

16. The Convention shall be held during Xmas recess at such place as may be appointed by the Executive Committee or the President. At least two months' notice shall be given to the branches by the General Secretary, emergency meeting excepted.

17. The Annual Convention or a Special Convention of the Congress shall have the power to:

(*a*) Amend the Constitution;

(*b*) Remove from office any officer of the Congress;

(*c*) Elect any officer provided in the Constitution;

(*d*) Impose any levy on the branches;

(*e*) Make any negotiations or decree and initiate any policy in the interest of the Congress;

(*f*) Appoint any sub-committees as may be deemed necessary or advisable to carry out duties assigned to them;

(*g*) Govern the Executive Committee.

18. The matters on the Agenda of the Annual Convention must reach the General Secretary at least six weeks before the date of the meeting. The agenda shall be sent to the branches at least one month before the Convention meets.

19. Special Convention or Emergency Meeting of the Congress may be convened by the Executive Committee or the President, should it be considered necessary or if it is desired by one third of the branches of the Congress. Such special or Emergency Convention shall be held within one month from the date of application and at such time and place as shall be determined by the Executive Committee or the President.

20. All decisions taken at the Annual Convention and Special or Emergency Convention shall be final and conclusive, and shall be binding upon all the branches as the voice of the whole members of the Congress.

21. Travelling expenses of the officers of the central organization shall be paid from the central fund and those of the branch officers shall be paid for by their respective branches, but financial aid from the central fund of the Congress may be extended to any branch representative attending Annual or Emergency or Special Convention as it is found necessary to do so by the Executive Committee or the President.

22. The right of admission to the meeting of the Congress is strictly reserved and no person or group of persons shall be allowed to enter the meeting place of the Congress without the express permission of the President.

23. Each branch shall submit to the General Secretary the names of its representatives elected to attend the annual Convention not later than mid-November of each year, Emergency or Special Convention excepted.

Voting

24. Voting at the Annual Convention shall be conducted thus:

(*a*) Every officer of the Congress attending the Convention shall have a vote;

(*b*) Branch representatives of each branch shall jointly have one vote known as "Card Vote" or shall have a vote each individually.

Officers of the Congress

25. The officers of the Congress shall be the General President, Vice General President, General Secretary, Assistant General Secretary, Financial Secretary, Publicity Secretary, Two Auditors, Education Advisor, Economic and Welfare Officer, Legal Adviser, Treasurer and Assistant Treasurer.

26. The above officers shall be elected by the Annual Convention and any vacancy that may occur later in any of the offices shall be filled by the Executive Committee for the period unexpired.

27. At the end of the formal discussion of Congress all offices shall be declared vacant and the election of officers shall be by secret ballot or show of hands as the Presiding Chairman may direct. The retiring officers shall be eligible for re-election.

28. The President shall preside over all general or Committee Meetings and shall give suggestion and views on all matters affecting the Congress. The President shall have a casting vote. He shall in conjunction with the General Secretary sign all vouchers on the Congress Treasury Forms.

29. The General President shall together with the General Secretary and the Treasurer sign all withdrawals from the Bank unless he and the Executive Committee delegate others to do so.

30. In the absence of the President the Vice-President shall preside over meetings and perform such duties as shall be assigned by the President.

31. The General Secretary shall attend all meetings of the Executive Committee and of the Annual Convention; he shall see to the proper keeping of Congress books provided for that purpose and execute the general correspondence of the Congress. He shall notify officers of their appointment and prepare the order of agenda for each meeting of the Executive Committee. In the event of the General Secretary's dismissal or resignation he shall over hand to the President all records, files, and other properties of the Congress in his possession.

32. The Treasurer shall receive all monies for and/or on behalf of the Congress and pay within one week into any approved bank which the Executive Committee approves. He shall have with him for imprest an amount not exceeding £10 (Ten pounds). He shall not pay any bill except in a written order signed by both the President and the General Secretary. He shall keep true and proper income and expenditure account annually and prepare a Balance Sheet of the Assets and Liabilities of the Congress subject to auditing by the Congress Auditors.

33. The Financial Secretary shall assist the Treasurer in Secretariat work appertaining to finance of the Congress.

34. The Auditors shall from time to time audit the accounts of the Congress and finally submit reports to the General Annual Convention.

Executive Committee

35. The Executive Committee shall be responsible for general administration of the Congress in the intervals between Annual Conventions.

36. The members of the Executive Committee shall be all officers of the Congress and the President and Secretary of every branch.

37. Six members shall form a quorum of the Executive Committee.

38. The Executive Committee shall meet once a year during Easter at a place and time as the President shall appoint; due and sufficient notice shall have to be given to the members, special or emergency meeting excepted.

39. The Executive Committee shall administer the business and offices of the Congress. The Committee shall have power to deal with appeals from branches and individual members of the Congress. The Committee shall have power to appoint a delegation either inside or outside Nigeria to deal with matters in which the Congress is interested or asked to do so by authority.

40. Every decision or order of the Executive Committee shall be binding on all members and branches. No order or decision of the Executive Committee shall be questioned, reversed, controlled or suspended except by way of an appeal to the Annual Convention.

41. The President shall have power to permit an accredited representative or a branch member to attend an Executive Committee Meeting as an observer but shall not participate in debate unless authorized by the President.

42. The President shall have power to order the expulsion of any member or representative if the person's conduct is not conducive to the moral code of the Congress.

Branches of the Congress

43. Every branch of the Congress shall be bound by this constitution and all amendments hereof which may be made hereafter and shall give an undertaking that it shall be loyal to any decision of the Congress, Annual Convention and the Executive Committee, and shall co-operate with other branches of the Congress in their views on payment of 2s.; efforts and determination to achieve the aim and objects of the Congress.

44. The membership of any branch shall start from the day it is registered by the Congress on payments of 10s. 6d. amount known as registration fee. Each branch shall be given a free copy of the constitution but individual members can obtain their copies on payment of 2s.

45. A member who is not satisfied with the decision of his branch can appeal to the Executive Committee. Again if he is not satisfied with the decision of the Executive Committee, he can appeal to the General Annual Convention. A member desirous of appeal shall send notice of his appeal within a month to the General Secretary who shall take steps to place the appeal on the agenda of either the Executive Committee or the Annual Convention as the case may be. In case of an appeal the Executive Committee may suspend an execution on such a decision pending a hearing by the Annual Convention whose decision is final and conclusive.

46. Each branch shall appoint its own local officers, namely President, Vice-President, Secretary, Assistant Secretary, Treasurer, Financial Secretary, Publicity Secretary, Auditor and any other local officers that may be considered necessary. No person shall hold office in any branch who does not pay his fees regularly.

47. Each branch shall have for its management the local branch committee which shall consist of the local branch officers and members elected by the branch. The branch committee shall manage the affairs of the branch and be under the immediate authority of the branch.

48. The Executive Committee of the Congress may dissolve any branch which they may consider unnecessary or the further continuation thereof they consider to be detrimental to the interest of the Congress and the local branch officers shall cease to hold office as from the date of such dissolution and all the money and other properties held by the branch or its officers shall thereupon be vested in the Trustees to be held in trust for the Congress as the Executive Committee may direct.

49. A branch may be entitled to make byelaws to meet certain

desirable conditions subject to the approval of the Executive Committee.

50. Each branch shall forward to the General Secretary by 1st November a full report of its activities for the year through its provincial headquarters.

51. Each branch shall hold one general meeting every month and one executive meeting every month, emergencies excepted. Six members or a quarter of the members shall form a quorum of the Executive and General Meetings respectively.

52. All branch officers shall discharge their functions and local affairs in accordance with duties of their offices as assigned to them by the branch executive committee.

53. The branch Treasurer shall keep an imprest of amount not exceeding one pound. He shall make any payment authorised by the President and Secretary. He shall keep an accurate and correct account of monies he has received and paid out. He shall prepare an accurate statement to be submitted to the General Meeting. He shall together with the branch President and Secretary sign all withdrawals from the Bank or any other saving institutions, approved by the branch executive committee.

54. The report of branch auditors shall be placed before the Branch Annual meeting.

Provincial Committee

55. The Provincial Committee is set up in every province to deal with Congress matters of overall provincial interest.

56. The members of the Provincial Committee shall be the President and Secretary of every branch within a Province. The Chairman and Secretary of the Provincial Committee are to be elected by the branch delegates attending the meeting.

57. Any officer of the Central Organization shall be a member of the Provincial Committee of his province.

58. The duties of the Provincial Committee shall be to:

(a) Promote mutual understanding between all branches within a province.

(b) Deal with provincial matters in the best interest of the Congress.

(c) Canvas for membership of the Congress and establish new branch within the province.

(d) Perform all duties as may be assigned by the Regional or Central Secretariat.

(e) Pass all necessary information of provincial matters to the

Regional or Central Secretariat of the Congress without due delay.

(f) Act as co-ordinating body between the central or the regional body and the branches.

59. Every Provincial Committee is responsible for its arrangement of local meetings.

60. Copies of the minutes of the Provincial Committee meetings shall be forwarded by the Provincial Secretary to the Regional and Central Secretariat not later than two weeks after the meeting.

Central Working Committee

61. The Central Working Committee shall administer the business and affairs of the Congress subject to the decision of the Congress subject to the decision of the Executive Committee and of Annual Convention.

62. The Committee shall if so desired be given power to discharge all functions of the Congress on behalf of the Central Organization or the Executive Committee.

63. The Secretary of the Working Committee and one other member as may be appointed by the Executive Committee shall be empowered to sign all vouchers for the expenditure incurred by or on behalf of the Central Organization, the Executive Committee or the Working Committee in carrying out duties in the best interest of the Congress.

Parliamentary Committee

64. All the Congress members of the Regional and Central Legislatures shall be members of the Parliamentary Committee.

65. The members must submit themselves to party loyalty and discipline and have got to work assiduously towards the implementation of party policy.

65a. Since the Parliamentary Council is such a large body, it will be convenient to form a small committee, Parliamentary Council Committee which will discuss and decide what line the Party will take in connection with everything that will come before the House. The Committee will meet regularly before or after the meeting of the House.

65b. The Chief Whip or his Deputy will always preside over the meeting of either the Parliamentary Council or that of its Committee. A secretary has to be appointed to record the proccedings of both bodies.

Y

Party Policy

66. The ministers in consultation with the Parliamentary Committee and the Executive Committee of the Congress shall draw up their respective programmes of work of Department under their portfolios.

67. Amongst the ministers in the Executive Council a leader of the Government-Business shall be appointed to carry out the policy of the Congress.

68. The Congress ministers in the Executive Council must give their full support and co-operation to the leader of the Government Business and they must also consult him on all matters of major issue before such matters are brought before the Exco. for discussion or otherwise.

69. The policies of the Congress must be channelled to the proper lines whereby they may champion the requirements and needs of all the people of the North.

70. There shall be as many bodies of men as possible employed in making research work for the ministers in respect of the policy of the Congress.

71. Party whips shall be appointed among the members of the Regional Legislature to control the discipline of the party and to persuade members in the House to defend the policy of the Congress.

72. The Parliamentary Committee shall appoint amongst themselves the members of the following committees:

(*a*) Motions Selection and Preparation Committee.
(*b*) Bills Selection and Preparation Committee.
(*c*) Spokesmen Panels Committee.
(*d*) General Purposes Committee.

General Organization Funds

73. The funds of the Congress are derived from the following sources:

(*a*) Registration fees.

(*b*) Annual subscription from branches (33½%) of branch revenue.
(*c*) Levies.
(*d*) Donations.
(*e*) Public collections, concerts, etc.

The Congress members of the Regional and Central Legislatures shall be requested to pay a certain precentage of their membership salaries to the progress of the Congress.

Amendments to Constitution

74. It is only the Annual Convention or the Executive Committee that has any right to alter, vary, repeat, add or amend any of the clauses of the Constitution.

75. In the event of any question arising as to the interpretation of any of the clauses of the Constitution of the Congress, the question shall be referred to the Central Secretariat for determination and any explanation given shall be final and binding upon all members.

Dissolution

76. The Congress shall not dissolve itself except on an 80% majority vote taken at Annual Convention provided the debts and liabilities lawfully incurred on behalf of the Congress shall have been discharged and the remaining debts if any devoted to a purpose or purposes.

Passed at 1953

....

General President

....

General Secretary

APPENDIX A

PLEDGE OF LOYALTY

I, ...(name in block letters) on my word of honour hereby take the pledge that I shall submit myself to Party discipline and loyalty in that I must accept the leadership of the NPC and support its candidates for elections to the Regional and Central Legislature and to the Local Councils. So help me God.

....

Witness to signature   Signed by

Appendix V

Part 1. Preamble

1. This Instrument is for the meantime the rules and regulations governing the United Front formed by the progressive organizations in the Northern Region of Nigeria with a view to ensuring that all opposition parties and other bodies representing the interests of the oppressed peoples of the North work together and face the NPC and its allies—who are their common enemy—with a united view.

2. The organizations so far taking part in the Front are the following: the NEPU, the UMBC, the Northern Youth Movement, the Kano Peoples Party, the Zamfara Commoner Peoples Party,[1] (the Nigeria Tin Mines Workers' Union, the Middle-Belt Tin Mines Workers' Union, the Northern Federation of Labour).[2]

3. This decision was motivated by the fact that these parties and organizations taking part in the Front are all opposed to feudalism and Imperialism, the official representatives of which in the North is the NPC. The parties and organizations are convinced that as long as all those who are opposed to oppression, suppression and exploitation in this country are not united and wage a determined struggle against the forces of reaction and oppression represented by the NPC and its like, so long will the people of this country remain under feudal oppression and Imperialist domination.

4. Confident of the glorious future that lies ahead of their coming together and confident of the fact that by their coming together those forces in co-operation with other forces who believe in progress and unity of this country and the well-being of its people, the Front shall make an important contribution towards the final liberation of the toiling masses of the North in particular and all oppressed and exploited masses of the Federal Republic of Nigeria, the organizations mentioned above have agreed to and hereby formed this Front. They have also pledged themselves to work together and co-operate with all progressive forces for the realization of peace, democracy and social progress in Nigeria.

Part 2. Name

5. The name of the Front shall be The Northern Progressive Front and hereafter to be referred to as the 'Front'.

Part 3. Aims and Objectives

6. The aims and objectives of the Front shall be:

  i. To organize, unite, educate and lead the people of the North irrespective of their rank, religion or ethnic grouping to win political power and establish a truly democratic society in the North in particular and Nigeria generally.

  ii. To wage a relentless struggle against feudalism and Imperialism in all their forms and ensure full freedom, democracy and progress for the toiling masses of our people.

  iii. To work for a rapid development of our national economy so as to raise the living standards of our people by modernizing our agriculture, establishing more industries with particular emphasis on heavy industries and ensuring full participation and control by our own people of our commercial and industrial life.

  iv. To fight against all forms of social evils and unjustices, oppression and exploitation whether foreign or local and work for their complete eradication.

  v. To work for the creation of more states in Nigeria so as to guarantee lasting unity and stability of our country.

  vi. To fight for the full emancipation of our women folk and ensure that they are given the franchise.

  vii. On national and international levels the Front shall work and co-operate with other organization having similar objectives.

Part 4. Membership

7. Membership into the Front shall be by organization. Any organization wishing to join the Front shall apply to the governing body of the Front which shall decide on its membership. If the organization is accepted into the Front, it shall abide by the rules and regulations of the Front and shall work for the realisation of the programme and principles of the Front. Membership fee shall be five guineas. The fee once paid is not refundable.

Part 5. Central Organ

8. The Front shall have a central organ to be known as the Executive Committee, which shall comprise of representatives of all

the organizations taking part in the Front. Representation into this committee shall be determined by the numerical strength of the organizations taking part in the Front which shall be decided by joint consultation. The Committee shall be the governing body of the Front and shall have the following powers:

(a) To prepare and implement the programme and policies of the Front.

(b) To establish a central secretariat in Kaduna for the Front and sub-secretariats wherever necessary.

(c) To elect the officers of the Front and set out their functions and duties; direct and supervise.[3]

(d) To arrange field activities and lay down financial policies for the Front.

(e) To conduct negotiation for and on behalf of the Front.

9. The Committee shall elect the following as officers of the Front: (a) The Chairman, (b) Deputy Chairman, (c) Secretary, (d) Two deputy Secretaries, (e) Treasurer, (f) Financial Secretary, (g) Secretary for propaganda, publicity and information.

10. The officers of the Front shall hold office for one year and at the end of which new election for officers shall be held. Any member of the committee who loses the confidence of his organization shall automatically be removed from the Committee.

11. The Committee shall set up three committees: Organization, Political and Financial Committees. The committees are responsible to the Executive Committee.

12. The Committee shall meet at least once a month but it can hold emergency meetings to be summoned by the Chairman and Secretary of the Committee. The committee shall make its own standing orders.

Part 6. Central Working Committee

13. The officers mentioned in the third paragraph above shall be the Central Working Committee of the Front.

14. The CWC shall be responsible for the execution of the policies and programmes laid down by the Executive Committee and shall also be responsible for the day-to-day administration of the Front. It shall be guided by the Executive Committee for its work.

Part 7. Other Matters

15. All deliberations and decisions of the Front shall be conducted through democratic processes whereby agreement has to be reached

by unanimous or majority decision. Full right of expression shall be guaranteed to members of the Front at all levels.

16. This agreement and amendment hereto shall be subject to the approval of the Executive organ of the organizations taking part in the Front and shall come into operation at a date to be set out by the Committee after it shall have obtained the consent of the organs referred to in the beginning of the paragraph. Meanwhile the provisions of this Instrument shall provisionally be put into operation as are found necessary.

17. For the purposes of the forthcoming general elections and for any other election in the North, the Front shall enter into such an election as a single entity. Arrangements will however be made to eliminate any confusion as regards symbol and nomination of candidates.

Part 8. Amendment

18. Addition, commission and alteration to this Instrument may be made by the Committee after ascertaining the opinion of the individual organizations taking part in the Front and shall be done in accordance with section 15 of this Instrument.

NOTES

1. Have since crossed over to the NPC.
2. Expressions bracketed were removed from the final Instrument.
3. The present officers of the Front were not elected.

Appendix VI

Two NPC Political Songs:
Translated from the Hausa

The Song of Garba Kyakya

by

Abdullahi Bayero
Zargon Aya, Zaria, 8.4.1958

I

1. O God forgive, For the sake of Mohammad the Chosen,
   All the evil planned against us, May it be turned to our good,
   For we are all law abiding.

2. They held a convention at Ibadan, They gave lectures and
   preached sedition,
   Adegoke made accusations[1], But there was no organization,
   And the useless hypocrites were dismissed.

3. The cursed, the gross evil-doers, There is no hope for them to
   attain the good,
   Sardauna means no evil, His aim is for us to get on well,
   Disturb not yourself therefore with the worthless.

4. A gathering of hooligans is a profitless organization,
   And none amongst us wears the cloak of a hooligan,
   God grant to the shiftless ones, That they may end in destruc-
   tion,
   That we may see them no more, the worthless ones.

5. The NPC gave us birth, SALAMA[2] nurtured us,
   Sardauna do not desert us, Lest our land ceases to be ours,
   Ignore the worthless ones.

6. Everyone has witnessed your defecting[3], And of those who support you,

Today see your leader, Who has realized he no longer likes you,
And has gone repenting to the Sardauna.

7. You insult your elders, But you know your place in the after-life,
You'll be sent to hell, Because that is your place of return,
You will remain there without mercy.

8. The worthless are without honour, We do not want them in our
employ,
Make haste and seek the way, Walk properly in the right path,
So that you may obtain mercy.

9. Sardauna we greet you, We fully support Northernization
(Because we have education), So that our children will find
occupation,
And cease serving the infidels.

10. Kaduna worships you, The Ministers like you,
The youths adore you, All the women love you,
Because you freed them serving the infidels.

11. Because the NPC has got the lead, It has ambitious rivals,
Garba Kyakya has arisen, And with the power of the Mighty
God,
He will destroy the hypocrites.

12. In Kaduna we have one annointed, Who reaches out for the
welfare of all,
Because the NPC is now the government, Na kyakya Abubakar
the lionhearted,
Has stopped serving the infidels.

13. He's left NEPU and found peace, At last he's realized their
worthlessness,
And the deceitfulness of the members; Now he no longer supports it,
Now he's stopped serving the infidels.

14. The Ministers love you[4], Because they appreciate your worth,
Know then those hold dear your welfare, Respect your elders
and betters,
And you will be recompensed.

15. While the Sardauna loves you, None in Kaduna will hate you,
Show then your diligence, May God grant you a good life,
And may your offspring be blessed.

16. Aliyu Makama you are known,[5] For the good deeds you do,
     A fine and blessed elder, Greetings to you Makama,
     A thousand greetings, May we receive your blessing.

17. If God loves you, Men will also love you,
     You overcome those envious of you, What can they do to your
     light?
     So ignore then the worthless ones.

18. Whoever is hostile to us, Because of this simple song,
     Which we sing for your pleasure, Turn them into crows O God,
     That gather groundnuts from the ridge.

19. Garba na kyakya we know you, For your acts of good will,
     But there are men of ill will, Who come across your path,
     Be not deceived by their useless gossip.

20. All who display ill will towards you Garba, May their way be
     paved with innumerable hardships.
     Let them roam like one demented, Let them be taken into hell,
     O God,
     Let them be denied bliss.

CHORUS: Now all thuggery has stopped,
         Let there be no more bitterness.

NPC Song No. 17.

by

Shehara Sa'ad 14.12.57

II

1. O God protect us from the evil of the after-life, That is Jahan
    Nama or Hawiya,[6]
    By the grace of our Shaikh Usmanu, All our enemies will suffer.

2. By the grace of our Shaikh, By the grace of the *Sura* al-
    Rahman;[7]
    O Lord, O Lord, the Merciful, All our enemies will sink.

3. Good news to you all Northerners; I saw in my sleep,
    That the NPC will inherit Kaduna, May God grant it thus for
    the sake of the saints.

4. Our adversaries have been astonished, Because the true sons have
   appeared;
   They've no truck with misleading parties, They know the NPC is
   Truth.

5. We thank God who made the lightning, So that we can see the
   crooked ones;
   Who begun among themselves a strife, That they all fell into a
   well.

6. I took a stick to hit a dog, Then I saw the bastard turn around;
   The dog and the bastard are one, How are you king of filth?[8]

7. Whenever you set off on a journey, Turn back if you see the
   bastard;
   There is evil in store in the journey, If you just see the bastard in
   the morning.

8. On seeing the bastard turn back, Recite Ayat al-Kursiya or
   Qulya;[9]
   Recite Bismillah 101 times, And make Kabbara[10] 21 times.

9. If you see the bastard give him a bone, And leave him severely
   alone with it;
   The bone will separate you from him, Because he will be busy
   gnawing at it.

10. The bastard is tunku[11] cursed be him, An expert at pulling rela-
    tives apart;
    I'm certain he's no intention now, Of seeing the North in good
    welfare.

11. Cursed be the shameless child, He is a complete loss to the world;
    I'll love to see his encounter with God, Who will plunge him into
    hell.

12. There's their leader has gone round, And supported the naked
    Truth,
    And just left you in deep despair, Join the Salama and obtain
    peace of mind.

13. Bastard of Gombe I know you not, I have not come to Gombe
    for your sake,
    Because I see your parents you know not, Untruthful people I
    fear not.

14. Our elections are now by single ballot, In secret and in one day,
An adult at the age of twenty-one, Has questions to answer before
he votes.

15. At the registration he's asked, To show evidence of having paid
tax,
If none, push him aside, He is of no value in the world.

16. We do not support any nominations, We have educateds in
Nigeria,
If uneducateds are taken, They'll only cause chaos in Nigeria.

17. The recent convention in Zaria, NPC impressed the world,
300 cars toured the city, Tudun Wada and the immediate en-
virons.

18. Our rivals have turned around, They thanked Saraduna the man
of truth,
They met together in a body, They tore up the cards of falsehood.[12]

19. Any right thinking man will not despise farming, All the world's
wealth comes from agriculture,
The best harvest lies hereafter with farmers, Oh you people let's
be grateful for farming.

20. The NPC chosen the HOE, The HOE is the symbol of the NPC,
Let everyone be conscious of the hoe, For it unearths the world's
wealth.

21. Where are you farmers, come and hear, Increase your efforts and
tire not,
By God, Allah you do help, The beauty of the body lies in the
fullness of the bowels.

22. Millet and guinea corn do help, So do groundnuts and cassava,
All types of food assists well-being, And conviviality comes after
a full stomach,
Hunger breeds ill will.

23. Whenever you go to cast your vote, Our box is the one coloured
green,
On it is the picture of the hoe, That is the sign of peace and content,
Know you that the NPC is truth.

24. Alhaji Adam, road supervisor, That is the man with no guilt,
He is my hero of all workers, In the whole of Bauchi province.

25. Usman Kaltungu, O leader of the NPC, By God, but not for you,
    By God the NPC would not have progressed, In Bauchi province
        as a whole.
    May God grant that we finish well and successfully.

26. My friends you said you were the good ones, Why then do I find
        you on a horse,
    After the ninth day of the month, You hit the horse on the nose
        with a club,
    Certainly whoever looks down on the NPC will perish.

27. Worthy people of the NPC, All honest and truth loving,
    We ask people of Kaduna, of the honourable honest Rafih,
    Our party manager as a whole.

28. Abdullahi Raji our party organizer, Garba Abuja the men of
        yesterday,
    Where is the hardworking Abba Ansari, Amongst them there is
        no traitor,
    May God grant that you all end well.

29. Ahmada Kwambo and M. Wada, Honest Yesufu Dantsoho,
    Abubakar Tuga, the warrior, I love to live with honest people,
    You are the swords that need no sharpening to cut off the heads
        of the untruthful.

30. Maikano Dutse, glory of the North, Local Government Minister
        of the North,
    The object of pride of Kano people, He does not owe you any-
        thing,
    He is a jewel of silver and gold.

31. Ohikere, the star of Okene people, A complete man in all respects,
    He does not owe the Okene people, Northerners look and
        understand,
    He is a supporter of the naked truth.

32. Ibrahim Musa Gashash, Zealous in all he does,
    (Land however small) be it a grain of sand, he gives not to any
        Southerner.
    Only to the Northerner and justly too.

33. Alhaji Sardauna, our leader, The honourable Ahmadu Sokoto,
    The NPC is always on the march, And before three years to come,
    It will expand to the banks of the red sea.

34. Honest and righteous Tafawa, Rule over the country of Nigeria,
    God has entrusted to you wholly, Just keep your honesty and
        truthfulness,
    You will be triumphant over the untruthful.

35. Everybody takes pride in his hero, So I take pride in mine,
    The NPC is a water lily, Whoever steps on it will sink,
    My friend go and save your hero, Because there's someone's hero
        suffering.

CHORUS: The vulture, King of filth, Son of woman, a heartless ass.

NOTES

The Song of Garba Kyakya

1. The reference is to Adegoke Adelabu, the Yoruba NCNC leader from
Ibadan who died in a car accident in 1958.
2. Salama, the NPC slogan: lit. salvation, being made free.
3. I.e. Mallam Aminu Kano, the NEPU leader.
4. I.e. the Sardauna of Sokoto.
5. Aliyu Makaman Bida, Northern Minister of Finance and treasurer of the
NPC.

NPC Song No. 17

6. Jahan Nama and Hawiya are two of the seven hells mentioned in Quran.
7. A chapter of the Quran.
8. The Hausa word translated as 'bastard' is *dan wanche*, one who is illegitimate, the reference being to NEPU.
9. Sections of the Quran.
10. The prayer 'Allah Akbar'.
11. A common animal very much despised.
12. Membership cards of NEPU.

Select Bibliography

GENERAL WORKS

Almond, C. A., and Coleman, J. S., *The Politics of Developing Countries*, Princeton, 1960

Anderson, J. N. D., *Islamic Law in Africa*, H.M.S.O., 1954.

Asad, M., *The Principles of State and Government in Islam*, California U.P., 1961.

Austin, D., *Politics in Ghana 1946–60*, Oxford University Press, 1964.

Bendix, R., *Max Weber: An Intellectual Portrait*, Heinemann, 1960.

Catlin, G. E. G., *Systematic Politics*, Allen & Unwin, 1962.

Duverger, M., *Political Parties*, Heinemann, 1954.

Eisenstadt, S. N., *From Generation to Generation*, Routledge, 1961.

Encyclopedia of Islam, Luzac, 1913.

Evans-Pritchard, E. E., and Fortes, M. (eds.), *African Political Systems*, Oxford University Press, 1940.

Fage, J. D., An *Introduction to the History of West Africa*, Cambridge, 1955.

Fallers, L1. *Bantu Bureaucracy* (Oxford for EAISER, n.d.)

Gaudefroy-Demombynes, M., *Moslem Political Institutions*, Allen & Unwin, 1950.

Gibb, H. A. R., *Mohammedanism*, Oxford University Press, 1957.

Gouldner, A. W. (ed.), *Studies in Leadership*, Harper, 1950.

Hodgkin, T., *African Political Parties*, Penguin, 1961.

Key, V. O., *Politics, Parties and Pressure Groups*, Crowell, 1961.

Lasswell, H. A., and Kaplan, A., *Power and Society* Routledge, 1952.

Leiserson, A., *Parties and Politics*, Alfred Knopf, 1958.

Lipsett, S. M., *Political Man*, Heinemann, 1960.

Lugard, F. D., *The Dual Mandate in British Tropical Africa* (1929), new edition, Frank Cass 1965.

Middleton, J., and Tait, D., *Tribes without Rulers*, Routledge, 1958.

Michels, R., *Political Parties*, Collier, 1962.

Miller, J. D. B., *The Nature of Politics*, Duckworth, 1962.

Mosca, G., *The Ruling Class*, McGraw-Hill, 1939.

Nadel, S. F., *The Theory of Social Structure*, Cohen & West, 1957.

Neumann, S., *Modern Political Parties*, Chicago U.P., 1956.

Oakshott, M., *Rationalism in Politics*, Methuen, 1962.

Robinson, R. *et al.*, *Africa and the Victorians*, Macmillan, 1961.

Runciman, W. G., *Social Science and Political Theory*, Cambridge, 1963.

Ruxton, F. H., *Maliki Law*, Luzac, 1916.

De Smith, S. A., *The New Commonwealth and Its Constitutions*, Stevens, 1964.

Southall, A., *Alur Society*, Cambridge, n.d.

Southall, A., *Social Change in Modern Africa*, Oxford U. P., 1961.

Trimmingham, J. S., *A History of Islam in West Africa*, Oxford U.P. 1962.

Watt, M., *Islam and the Integration of Society*, Routledge, 1961.

Weber, M., *Essays in Sociology*, trans. by Girth & Mills, Routledge, 1948.

Weber, M., *The Theory of Social and Economic Organisation*, translated by Parsons & Henderson, Oxford U. P. 1947.

Weber, M., *Basic Concepts in Sociology*, Citadel Press, 1962.

Zolberg, A. R., *One Party Government in Ivory Coast*, Princeton, 1964.

NIGERIA

A Day in the Life of a Nigerian Emir, translated from an account by the Sultan of Sokoto, Commonwealth Leaflets, no.3, n.d.

Abraham, R. O., *The Tiv People*, Crown Agents, 1940.

Akiga, B., *Akiga's Story*, translated by R. M. East, I.I.A.L., 1939.

Backwell, H. F., *The Occupation of Hausaland* 1900–1904, Lagos, 1927.

Baker, T. M., The Social Organization of the Birom unpublished thesis of the University of London, 1954.

Barth, H., *Travels in North and Central Africa*, Minerva edition 1890; Centenary Edition, 3 volumes, Frank Cass, 1965.

Bello, Sultan Mohammed, *Infaku'l Maisuri*, translated by E. J. Arnett as *The Rise of the Sokoto Fulani*, Lagos, n.d.

Bello, Sir Ahmadu, *My Life*, Cambridge, 1962.

Bohannan, P., *Judgement and Justice among the Tiv*, I.A.I. 1957.

Bohannan, Paul and Laura, *The Tiv of Central Nigeria*, I.A.I., 1957.

Bovill, E. W., *Caravans of the Old Sahara*, Oxford U.P., 1933.

Burdon, J. A., *Northern Nigeria: Historical Notes on Certain Emirates and Tribes*, Waterlow & Sons, 1909.

Cameron, Sir D., *The Principles of Native Administration and their Application*, Lagos, 1934.

Campbell, M. J., *The Law and Practice of Local Government in Northern Nigeria*, Sweet and Maxwell, 1963.

Cohen, R., The Structure of Kanuri Society—unpublished thesis, University of Wisconsin, Microfilm, 1960.

Coleman, J. S., *Nigeria: Background to Nationalism*, Berkeley, 1958.

de St. Croix, F. W., *The Fulani of Northern Nigeria*, Lagos, 1944.

Daniel, F. de F., *A History of Katsina*, Colonial Office, no. 18177, n.d.

Daniels, W. C. E., *The Common Law in West Africa*, Sweet & Maxwell, 1964.

Downes, R. M., *The Tiv People*, Kaduna, 1933.

Ezera, K., *Constitutional Development in Nigeria*, Oxford U.P., 1960.

Elias, T. O., *The Nigerian Legal System*, Routledge & Kegan Paul, 1963.

Flint, J. E., *Sir George Goldie and the Making of Nigeria*, London, 1960.

Forde, D. et al., *Peoples of the Niger-Benue* Confluence, I.A.I. 1955.

Gunn, H., *The Pagan Peoples of the Central Area of Northern Nigeria*, I.A.I. 1956.

Gunn, H. and Connant, F. P., *Peoples of the middle Niger Region of Northern Nigeria*, I.A.I., 1960.

Hassan and Shua'ibu, *A Chronicle of Abuja*, Ibadan, 1952.

Hassan and Shua'ibu, *The Gwari Tribe in Abuja Emirate*, Lagos, n.d.

Hodgkin, T., *Nigerian Perspectives*, Oxford U.P. ,1960.

Hogben, S., *The Mohammedan Emirates of Nigeria*, Oxford U.P., 1933.

Hoppen, C. E., *The Pastoral Fulbe Family in Gwandu*, Oxford U.P., 1958.

Ibn Fartua, Imam Ahmed., *History of the First Twelve Years of the Reign of Mai Idris Alooma of Bornu*, translated by R. H. Palmer, Lagos, 1926.

Kirk-Greene, A. H. M., *Adamawa Past and Present*, I.A.I., 1958.

Kirk-Greene, *Principles of Native Administration in Nigeria—Select Documents 1900–47*, Oxford U.P., 1965.

Kirk-Greene, *Barth's Travels in Nigeria*, Oxford U.P., 1962.

Kirk-Greene, *A Redefinition of Provincial Administration or A Northern Nigerian Approach* n.d.

Kisch, M. S., *Letters and Sketches from Northern Nigeria*, Chatto, 1910.

Lugard, F. D., *Political Memoranda*, 1906, new edition in preparation by Frank Cass.

Meek, C. K., *The Northern Tribes of Nigeria* 2 vols., London, 1925.

Meek, C. K., *Tribal Studies in Northern Nigeria* 2 vols., Kegan Paul, 1931.

Meek, C. K., *A Sudanese Kingdom*, Kegan Paul, 1931.

Mockler-Ferryman, A. F., *British Nigeria*, Cassell, 1920.

Mockler-Ferryman, A. F., *Up the Niger*, London, 1892.

Morell, E. D., *Nigeria, Its Peoples and Its Problems*, 1915; new edition Frank Cass, 1967.

Nadel, S. F., *A Black Byzantium*, Oxford., 1942.

Nadel, S. F., *Nupe Religion*, Routledge, 1954.

Northern Nigeria Annual Reports, 1900–11.

Northern Nigeria Provincial Gazetteers (various) 1920/21

Nwabueze, B. O., *The Machinery of Justice in Nigeria*, Butterworth, 1963.

Nwabueze, B. O., *The Constitutional Law of the Nigerian Republic*, Butterworth 1964.

Orr, C. W. J., *The Making of Northern Nigeria*, 1911, new edition, Frank Cass, 1965.

Odumosu, O., *The Nigerian Constitution*, Sweet & Maxwell, 1963.

Palmer, H. R., *Sudanese Memoirs* 3 vols., Lagos, 1928. Reprinted by Frank Cass, 1967.

Palmer, H. R., *The Bornu Sahara and Sudan*, Murray, 1936.

Park, A. W. W., *The Sources of Nigerian Law*, Butterworth, 1963.

Perham, M., *Native Administration in Nigeria*, Oxford U.P., 1937.

Post, K. W. J., *The Nigerian Federal Election of 1959*, Oxford for NISER, 1963.

Robinson, C. H., *Hausaland*, London, 1896.

Z

Shaw, F. (Lady Lugard), *A Tropical Dependency*, 1905, reprinted by Frank Cass 1964.

Shultze, A., *The Sultanate of Bornu*, 1913, reprinted by Frank Cass, 1967.

Sklar, R. L., *Nigerian Political Parties*, Princeton, 1963.

Smith, M. G., *Government in Zazzau*, I.A.I. 1960.

Smith, M. G., *The Economy of the Hausa Communities of Zaria*, H.M.S.O., 1955.

Smith, Mary, *Baba of Karo*, Faber, 1954.

Schon, J. F., *Mangana Hausa*, London, 1885.

Sciortino, J. S., *Notes on Nassarawa Province*, Waterlow & Sons, 1920.

Stenning, D. J., *Savannah Nomads*, Oxford U.P., 1959.

Tilman, R. O. and Cole, T. (eds.), *The Nigerian Political Scene*, Duke, 1962.

Temple, C. L., *Native Races and their Rulers*, 1918, new edition, by Frank Cass, 1967.

Temple, O., *Notes on the Tribes, Provinces, Emirates and States of the Northern Provinces of Northern Nigeria*, 1919, reprinted by Frank Cass, 1965.

Tomlinson, G. J. F. and Lethem, G. J., *A History of Islamic Political Propaganda in Nigeria* 2 vols., Waterlow & Sons, 1927.

Wellesley, D., *Sir George Goldie*, Macmillan, 1934.

Wheare, J., *The Nigerian Legislative Council*, Faber, 1950.

Wilson-Haffenden, C. J., *The Redmen of Nigeria*, 1930, reprinted by Frank Cass, 1967.

ARTICLES

Anton, T. J., 'Power, Pluralism and Local Politics', *Administrative Science Quarterly* vol. 7, 1963.

Apter, D., 'The Role of Tribalism in the modernisation of Ghana and Uganda', *World Politics*, vol. 10, no. 2, 1960.

Apthorpe, R. J., 'The Introduction of Bureaucracy into African Politics,' *Journal of African Administration*, vol. 12, no.3, 1960.

Apthorpe, R. J., 'Political Change, Centralisation and Role Differentiation', *Civilizations*, vol. 10, no. 2, 1960.

Arnett, E. J., 'A Hausa Chronicle', *Journal of the Royal African Society*, vol. 9, 1910.

Azikiwe, N., 'Essentials for Nigeria's Survival', *Foreign Affairs*, vol. 43, no. 2, 1965.

Baker, T. M., Political Control among the Birom, Proceedings of the 5th Annual Conference, WAISER, Ibadan, 1956.

Bascom, W., 'Urbanism as a Traditional African Patter', *The Sociological Review*, vol. 7, no. 1, 1959.

Bohannan, P., 'The Migration and Expansion of the Tivs', *Africa*, vol. 24, 1954.

Bohannan, P., 'A Tiv Religious and Political Idea', *South-Western Journal of Anthropology*, vol. 11, no. 2, 1955.

Bohannan, Laura, 'A Genealogical Charter', *Africa*, vol. 22, 1952.

Brown, P., 'Patterns of Authority in West Africa', *Africa*, vol. 21, 1951.

Buchanan, K., 'The Northern Nigeria—The Geographical Background to its Political Duality', *Geographical Review*, vol. 43, no. 4, 1953.

Burdon, A., 'The Fulani Emirates of Northern Nigeria', *Geographical Journal*, vol. 24, 1904.

Clifford, M., 'A Nigerian Chiefdom', *Journal of the Royal Anthropologica Institute*, vol. 66, 1936.

Cohen, R., 'The Analysis of Conflict in Hierarchical Systems', *Anthropologica*, vol. 4, no. 1, 1960.

Coupland, R., 'Northern Nigeria—South of Lake Chad', *The Times* (London) 15.2.34.

Dahl, R. A., 'A Critique of the Ruling Elite Model', *The American Political Science Review*, vol. 25, 1958.

Daniel, F. de F., 'Shedu dan Fodio', *Journal of the Royal African Society*, vol. 25, 1926.

Davis, S. R., 'The "Federal Principle" Reconsidered', *Australian Journal of History and Politics*, vol. 1, nos. 1 and 2, 1955/56.

Deutsch, K. W., 'Social Mobilization and Political Development', *The American Political Science Review*, vol. 55, 1961.

Dion, L., 'Political Ideology as a Tool of Functional Analaysis in Socio-Political Dynamics: An Hypothesis', *Canadian Journal of Economics & Political Science*, vol. 25, no. 1, 1959.

Dry, D. P. L., The Hausa Attitude to Authority, Proceedings of the First Annual Conference WAISER, Ibadan, 1952.

Dudley, B. J., 'The Nomination of Parliamentary Candidates in Northern Nigeria', *Journal of Commonwealth Political Studies*, vol. 2, no. 1, 1963.

Dudley, B. J., 'The Concept of Federalism', *Nigerian Journal of Economic and Social Studies*, vol. 5, no. 1, 1963.

Dudley, B. J., 'After the Strike', *The (London) Financial Times*, 1.10.64.

East, R. M., 'Recent Activities of the Literature Bureau, Zaria', *Africa*, vol. 14, 1943/44.

Eisenstadt, S. N., 'African Age Groups', *Africa*, vol. 24, 1954.

Ember, M., 'Political Authority and the Structure of Kinship in Aboriginal Samoa', *American Anthropologist*, vol. 64, no. 5, 1962.

Fegan, E. S., 'Some Notes on the Bachama Tribe', *Journal of the African Society*, vol. 29, 1930/32.

Freemantle, J. M., 'A History of the Katagum Region', *Journal of the Royal African Society*, vol. 10, 1911.

Greer, S. and Orleans, P., 'Mass Society and Parapolitical Structure', *American Sociological Review*, vol. 27, no. 5, 1962.

Grove, D. La Van., 'The "Sentinels" of Liberty? The Nigerian Judiciary and Fundamental Rights', *Journal of African Law*, vol. 7, no. 3, 1963.

Goody, J., 'Feudalism in Africa', *Journal of African History* vol. 4, no. 1, 1963.

Greenberg, J. H., 'The Influence of Islam on a Sudanese Religion'. *Monograph of the American Ethnological Society*, no. 10, 1946.

Greenberg, J. H., 'Islam and Clan Organization among the Hausa', *South-Western Journal of Anthropology*, vol. 3, 1947.

Greenberg, J. H., 'Linguistic Evidence for the Influence of the Kanuri on the Hausa', *Journal of African History*, vol. 1, no. 2, 1960.

Howeidy, M., 'Northern Nigeria's Parties', *West Africa*, 2nd January, 1952.

Harris, P. G., 'Notes on the Yauri of Nigeria', *Journal of the Royal Anthropoligical Institute*, vol. 40, 1910.

Helleiner, C. K., 'A Wide Ranging Development Institution—the Northern Region Development Corporation', *Nigerian Journal of Economic and Social Studies*, vol. 6, no. 2, 1964.

Imam, A., 'The Nigerian Constitutional Proposals', *African Affairs*, vol. 45, 1946.

Kaberry, P., 'Primitive States', *British Journal of Sociology*, vol. 8, 1957.

Kirk-Greene, A. M., Traditional Authority and New Leadership Cadres (mimeographed, n.d.)

Kilson, M., 'Authoritarianism and Single Party Tendencies in African Politics', *World Politics*, vol. 15, 1963.

Lewis, I. M., 'Classification of African Political Systems', *Rhodes-Livingstone Journal*, vol. 25, 1959.

Leiserson, A., 'The Place of Parties in the Study of Politics', *The American Political Science Review*, vol. 49, 1955.

Mackintosh, J. P., 'Electoral Trends and the Tendency Towards a One Party', *Journal of Commonwealth Political Studies*, vol. 1, no. 3, 1963.

Mackintosh, J. P., 'Politics in Nigeria: The Action Group Crisis,' *Political Studies*, vol. 11, no. 2, 1963.

Mackintosh, J. P., 'The Nigerian Federal Parliament', *Public Law*, Autumn, 1963.

Mackintosh, J. P., 'Federalism in Nigeria', *Political Studies*, vol. 10, no. 3, 1962.

McDill, E. L., and Ridley, C., 'Status, Anomia, Political Alienation and Political Participation', *American Journal of Sociology*, vol. 68, no. 2, 1962.

Meek, C. K., 'The Katab and their Neighbours', *Journal of the African Society*, vol. 28, 1929.

Meek, C. K., 'The Kulus of Northern Nigeria', *Africa*, vol. 7, 1934.

Meek, C. K., 'The Religions of Nigeria', *Africa*, vol. 14, 1943/44.

Mohr, R., 'Social Organization of the Angas', *Anthropos*, vol. 35, 1958.

Michels, R., 'Some Reflections on the Sociological Character of Political Parties', *The American Political Science Review*, vol. 21, 1927.

Nadel, S. F., 'Nupe State and Community', *Africa*, vol. 8, 1935.

Niven, C. R., 'The Kabba Province of the Northern Provinces of Nigeria', *Geographical Journal*, vol. 68, 1926.

Orr, C. W. J., 'The Hausa Race', *Journal of the Royal African Society*, vol. 7, 1908.

Palmer, R. H., 'The Bornu Girgham', *Journal of the Royal African Society*, vol. 11, 1912.

Palmer, R. H., 'The Kano Chronicle', *Journal of the Royal Anthropological Institute*, vol. 38, 1908.

Palmer, R. H., 'History of Katsina', *Journal of the Royal African Society*, vol. 26, 1927.

Palmer, R. H., 'The Central Sahara and Sudan in the 12th Cent. A.D.', *Journal of the African Society*, vol. 26, 1927.

Palmer, R. H., 'The Future of the N.A's', *W. A. Review*, Aug. 1939.

Pedraza, H., 'A Feudal Survival in Nigeria', *The Listener*, 6th February 1947.

Perham, M., 'Nigeria Today (ii)', *The (London) Times*, 12th December 1932.

Pollock, J. K., 'The British Party Conference', *The American Political Science Review*, vol. 32, 1938.

Rattray, R. S., 'The Founder of Nigeria', *The Fortnightly*, April 1935.

Redfisch, F., 'The Dynamics of Multilineality on the Mambila Plateau', *Africa*, vol. 30, 1960.

Reed, L. N., 'Notes on Some Fulani Tribes and Customs', *Africa*, vol. 5, 1932.

Richardson, S. S., "Opting Out": An Experiment with Jurisdiction in Northern Nigeria', *Journal of African Law*, vol. 8, no. 1, 1964.

Robinson, M. S., 'Nigerian Oil-Prospects and Perspectives, *Nigerian Journal of Economic & Social Studies*, vol. 6, no. 2, 1964.

Rosman, A., 'Social Structure and Acculturation Among the Kanuri of Bornu', *Transactions of the NY Academy of Sciences*, Series 2, vol. 27.

Schacter, R., 'Single Party Systems in West Africa', *The American Political Science Review*, vol. 55, 1961.

Schact, J., 'Islam in Northern Nigeria', *Studies Islamica*, vol. 8, 1957.

Seligman, R. S., 'Political Recruitment and Party Structure', *The American Political Science Review*, vol. 55, 1961.

Seligman, R. S., 'The Study of Political Leadership', *The American Political Science Review*, vol. 44, 1950.

Seton, R. S., 'The Igala Tribe of Northern Nigeria', *Journal of the African Society*, vol. 29, 1929/30.

de Smith, S. A., 'Westminster's Export Models', *Journal of Commonwealth Political Studies*, vol. 1, no. 1, 1961.

Smith, M. G., 'Kagoro Political Development', *Human Organisation*, vol. 10, no. 3, 1960.

Smith, M. G., 'The Hausa System of Social Status', *Africa*, vol. 29, 1958.

Smith, M. G., 'Kebbi and Hausa Stratification', *British Journal of Sociology*, vol. 12, 1961.

Smith, M. G., 'On Segmentary Lineage Systems', *Journal of the Royal Anthropological Institute*, vol. 86, 1956.

Smith, M. G., Social Organisation and Economy of the Kagoro, Colonial Office, MS. GN 653–39109F., 1952.

Smith, M. G., The Social Structure of the Northern Kadara, Colonial Office MS. GN 653–39110, 1952.

Smith, M. G., Political Organisation in Hausaland, Institute of Commonwealth Studies, Seminar paper P1/59/4 session 1959/60 MS.

Temple, C. L., 'The Government of Native Races', *Quarterly Review*, Oct. 1918.

Tremearne, A. J. N., 'Notes on the Kagoro', *Journal of the Royal Anthropological Institute*, vol. 42, 1912.

Wallace, T. W. 'The Tiv System of Elections', *Journal of African Administration*, vol. 10, 1958.

Whitlesley, D., 'Kano: A Sudanese Metropolis', *Geographical Review*, vol. 27, 1957.

Wright, C. F., ' "Indirect Rule"—As an Afro-American Sees It,' *West African Review*, Dec. 1943.

Yeld, S. R., 'Islam and Social Stratification in Northern Nigeria', *British Journal of Sociology*, vol. 11, 1960.

GOVERNMENT PUBLICATIONS: FEDERAL

Report of the Native Courts (Northern Provinces) Commission of Enquiry Sessional Paper no. 1, Lagos, 1952.

A Note on Muslim Religious, Social and Political Movements in Nigeria, Nigerian Secretariat, Lagos, 15th December, 1953 (unpublished ms.)

Report on the Kano Disturbances 16th–19th May 1953, Lagos, 1953.

Report of the Coker Commission of Inquiry into the Affairs of Certain Statutory Corporations in Western Nigeria 1962, Lagos, 1962.

Report of the Commission on the Review of Wages, etc. (*The Morgan Commission Report*), Lagos, 1964.

Conclusion of the Federal Government on the Report of the Morgan Commission, Lagos, 1964.

Annual Report of the Mines Division of the Ministry of Mines and Power, Lagos, 1964.

Investment in Education, Lagos, 1960.

Annual Report of the Works Division of the Ministry of Works and Transport, Lagos, 1964.

Statistics of Education in Nigeria in 1963, series no. 1. vol. 3, 1965.

The Digest of Statistics.

The National Development Plan: *First Progress Report 1962–63*, Lagos, 1964.

National Development Plan: *Progress Report 1964*, Lagos, 1965.

NORTHERN NIGERIA

Report on the Meetings of the Advisory Council of Emirs 1930.

Northern Provinces Advisory Council, Summary of Proceedings, 1932.

Conference of Residents—Northern Provinces, Nov. 1937, Summary of Proceedings.

Conference of Chiefs of the Northern Provinces—Summary of Proceedings, 1938, 1939, 1941, 1942 and 1943.

Report on Land Tenure, Niger Province by C. W. Cole, Kaduna, 1949.

Report on Land Tenure, Zaria Province by C. W. Cole, Kaduna, 1949.

Report on Land Tenure, Kano Province, by C. W. Rowling, Kaduna, 1949.

Report on Land Tenure, Plateau Province, by C. W. Rowling, Kaduna, 1949.

Report on Local Government in the Northern Provinces of Northern Nigeria, by K. P. Maddocks, and D. A. Pott, Kaduna, 1951.

Progress Report on Local Government in the Northern Region of Nigeria, by D. A. Pott, Kaduna, 1953.

Population Census of Northern Nigeria 1952/53.

Native Courts Commissions of Enquiry 1949–52, Gaskiya Corporation 1953.

Report on the Exchange of Customary Presents, Kaduna, 1954.

Provincial Authorities, Report by the Commissioner Mr. R. S. Hudson, Kaduna 1957.

Preliminary Statement of the Government of Northern Region of Nigeria on the Report of the Commissioner Appointed to advise the Government on Devolution of Powers to Provinces, Kaduna, 1957.

Statement of the Government of the Northern Region of Nigeria on the Report of the Committee of Inquiry Appointed to Investigate Allegations about Ilorin Native Authority, Kaduna, 1958.

Report on the Public Service Commission 1954–57, Kaduna, 1958.

Report on the Public Service Commission for the period ended 31st Dec. 1962, Kaduna, 1963.

Report on the Public Service Commission for the period ended 31st Dec. 1963, Kaduna, 1964.

How Northern Nigeria Trains its Own Administrative Officers, Institute of Administration, Zaria, 1960.

Standing Orders of the Northern House of Chiefs, Kaduna, 1959.

Annual Reports of the Northern Region Development and Production Board.

Annual Reports of the Northern Region Development Corporation.

Annual Reports of the Northern Region Marketing Board.

Staffing and Development of the Public Services of Northern Nigeria, Report by Dr. D. Kingsley and Sir Arthur N. Rucker (mimeographed 1961).

Speech by the Premier of Northern Nigeria . . . to Zaria Native Authority Council, 3rd August 1961, Kaduna, n.d.

Administrative Instructions to Provincial Commissioners and Provincial Secretaries, Kaduna n.d.

White Paper on Government's Policy for Rehabilitation of the Tiv N.A., Kaduna, 1965.

Local Government in Northern Nigeria, Kaduna, 1962.

Local Government Year Book 1963, Institute of Administration, Zaria, 1964.

Taron Kwamitin Bada Shawara Kan Al'Amuran Muslulunci, Kano, NA Press 1963.

A Guide to the Penal Code, Kaduna n.d.

Notes on the Penal Code, Annotated by S. S. Richardson, Kaduna n.d.

Provincial Annual Reports of Northern Nigeria 1951–62.

Report on the Director of Audit on the Accounts of the Government of Northern Nigeria for the year ended 31st March 1963, Kaduna, 1964.

Report of the Accountant General of the Government of Northern Nigeria, Kaduna 1964.

Public Accounts Joint Committee-Session 1962/64, Minutes of Evidence, Kaduna, n.d.

Report of the Special Meeting of the Northern Legislature held on the occasion of the Self-Government celebrations on Friday, 15th May 1959, Kaduna, 1959.

Development Plan 1962–68, Ministry of Economic Planning Kaduna, n.d.

Northern Nigeria Development Plan 1962–68: First Progress Report, Kaduna n.d.

The Industrial Potentialities of Northern Nigeria, Kaduna, 1963.

Northern Nigeria Gazettes.

Who's Who in the Northern Legislature.

HANSARDS

Debates of the Federal House of Representatives 1952–64.
Debates of the Northern House of Assembly 1950–64.
Debates of the Northen House of Chiefs 1952–64.

PARTY PUBLICATIONS

Northern Peoples' Congress: Reports, Documents and Manifestos (various) NPC Headquarters Secretariat, Kaduna.

Nigerian Elements Progressive Union: Reports, Documents and Manifestos (various) NEPU Headquarters Secretariat, Kano.

United Middle Belt Congress: Reports, Documents and Manifestos (various), UMBC Headquarters Secretariat, Jos.

NEWSPAPERS

West Africa (London); *Daily Times* (Lagos); *Sunday Times* (Lagos); *Daily Express* (Lagos); *Sunday Express* (Lagos); *Morning Post* (Lagos); *Sunday Post* (Lagos); *Nigerian Citizen* (Zaria); *Gaskiya Tafi Kwabo* (Zaria); *Daily Mail* 1961–63 (Kano); *Northern Star* (Kano); *The Comet* (Kano); *The Middle-Belt Herald* (Jos).

MISCELLANEOUS

Nigeria Year Books 1960–65 (Lagos).

United Africa Company: *Statistical and Economic Review*, Issue 29, April 1964.

Record of Appeal from The High Court of Lagos to the Federal Supreme Court (Awolowa *et al.* treason trial), 11 vols.

Index

345

DATE DUE
